9781258398873

Book Three · YOUR COMMAND OF WRITTEN ENGLISH

YOUR MASTERY OF ENGLISH is a complete course in English, written by a distinguished educator, with special sections prepared by other authorities. It carries the reader from the very fundamentals of grammar and rhetoric to the advanced study of the language in all its phases. Every person who is eager to perfect his individual command of thought and expression can find in this modern, comprehensive treatment the means and the methods whereby the desired skill may be acquired. The journey toward this goal is illuminated and diversified by self-examining and self-correcting exercises and stimulating practices—all based upon those laws of learning that grant a sure attainment of a disciplined art.

This course tells how to write all kinds of letters, with many examples, for friendly and social correspondence, and contains a complete exposition of the preparation of all principal types of business letters. It presents constructive ideas on voice training and on public speaking, furnishes information about the preparation of radio scripts and their delivery, and demonstrates the value of good English in business, professional, and social life.

YOUR MASTERY OF ENGLISH affords a fine evaluation of great literature, with copious excerpts from prose and poetry which will be an inspiration to the student. Finally, he who has pride in his proficiency in English will return to this superb authority for guidance on every phase of English that arises in daily life.

YOUR MASTERY
OF
ENGLISH

By Charles Swain Thomas, Litt. D.
HARVARD UNIVERSITY

BOOK THREE

Your Command of Written English

P. F. Collier & Son Corporation
PUBLISHERS · NEW YORK

YOUR MASTERY OF ENGLISH

Copyright, 1941, by

P. F. COLLIER & SON CORPORATION

CP

Sample letters selected by Mr. Ward from outside sources are reproduced by permission: sales letter, p. 277, C. G. Conn, Ltd. (*Printers' Ink*, Dec. 12, 1935); trapshooting letters, pp. 281-284, Remington Arms Company, Inc. (*Printers' Ink*, Dec. 1, 1939); charge account acknowledgment, p. 285, Gimbel Bros., Inc.; collection letters, pp. 288-289, Geo. G. McKiernan & Co. (*Printers' Ink*, Oct. 20, 1939); account revival letters, p. 295, *Printers' Ink*, Sept. 13, 1940, p. 296, Leon Godchaux Clothing Company, Ltd. (*Printers' Ink*, Feb. 2, 1940).

PRINTED IN THE UNITED STATES OF AMERICA

CONTENTS OF BOOK THREE

	Page
Chapter I. EXAMINING YOUR TOOL MASTERY—YOUR COMMAND OF AUTOMATISMS	1
Application of the Twofold Division to Written Expression	3
Acquired Automatisms	3
Penmanship	3
Typing	3
Spelling Automatisms	5
Capitalization Automatisms	7
Punctuation Automatisms	8
Grammar Automatisms	9
Word Meanings and Automatisms	11
Inglis Test of English Vocabulary	12
Automatisms in Sentence Patterns	14
The Paragraph-Indentation Automatism	14
Signs and Symbols—Abbreviation Automatisms	15
Automatisms in Syllabication	16
Automatisms in Italicizing Words	17
The Need for Unsparing Effort	19

PRACTICES

1. Spelling—Words Pronounced Alike but Spelled Differently	23
2. Spelling—Frequently Misspelled Words	24
3. A Test in Spelling	24
4. Spelling—Supplying Missing Letters	25
5, 6. Capitalization	26
7. Pluralization	27
8, 9. Possessives—Possessive Pronouns	28
10. Adverbs—Position in Sentence	29
11. Grammar—Pronouns	30
12. Italicizing	30
13. Punctuation	31
14. Multiple-Choice Vocabulary Test	32
15. Lapsed-Letter Test	33
KEYS TO PRACTICES	34

CONTENTS OF BOOK THREE

Page

Chapter II. THE CREATIVE PHASE OF WRITING . . . 39

Creative Expression and Automatisms 39
Preparatory Work in Creative Writing—Importance of Clear
    Ideas 41
    Making the Outline 41
Getting a Firm Grasp of Ideas 43
    Assertions of the Ill-informed 44
    How Do We Get and Test Ideas? 44
    Emerging Ideas 45
    Attempting Expression Before the Thought Is Clear . . 45
    A Personal Experience in Clarifying a Thought . . 45
Concrete Listing of Items 47
A Discussion of an Industrial Problem 52
Outlines and Outlining 57
    Definition of an Outline 57
    The Topical Outline 58
    The Sentence Outline 59
    Writing Without the Outline 61
    The Outline a Safe and Serviceable Guide . . . 61
Specific Suggestions 62
    Main and Subordinate Ideas 62
    The Finished Essay 67

PRACTICES

1. Errors in English 68
2. Homonyms 69
3. A Homonym Test 69
4. Punctuation of Sentences 71
5. Punctuation of Sentences 72
6. Restrictive and Non-Restrictive Clauses 72
7. Sentence Structure 73
8. Punctuation of Paragraphs 73

KEYS TO PRACTICES 74

Chapter III. PRACTICES ON CREATIVE WRITING . . . 77

Introduction 77

PRACTICES

1. Making the Outline—The Writing of the Theme . . 78
2. Developing the Completed Essay From the Outline . 81
3. Creative Reading 82
4. Objective and Subjective Methods 84
5. Re-creating Odors by Words 89

CONTENTS OF BOOK THREE

	Page
6. Writing to Express Personal Convictions	90
7. Incidental Writing	91
8. The Personal or Informal Essay	92
9. The Empathy Theme	94
10. The Empathy Theme—Identifying Oneself with an Inanimate Object	101
11. The Empathy Theme—Imagining an Experience	103

Chapter IV. THE WRITTEN COMPOSITION AS A WHOLE . 107

Introduction . 107
Postulates for the Written Work . 108
    The Main Topic . 108
    The Subtopics . 109
    Comparison of Planned and Unplanned Writing . 110
    Rapid Writing of First Draft . 114
    The Research Paper . 115
    Revision . 120

PRACTICES

1. Revision . 129
2. Clarity . 130
3. Multiple-Choice Vocabulary Test . 131
4. Position of Words and Phrases . 133
5. Parallelograms . 133
6. Unnecessary Repetition . 134

    KEYS TO PRACTICES . 135

Chapter V. PARAGRAPH STRUCTURE . 137

Introduction . 137
The Isolated Paragraph . 138
Unity . 139
    The Topic Sentence . 139
    Paragraph Development . 145
Coherence . 146
    Order . 146
    Parallel Construction . 150
    Connectives . 152
Emphasis
    Proportion
    Climax
Related Paragraphs
    The Introductory Paragraph
    The Amplifying Paragraph

CONTENTS OF BOOK THREE

	Page
The Transitional Paragraph	158
The Concluding Paragraph	159

PRACTICES

1. Paragraphing When Revising Manuscript	160
2. Paragraphs of Definite Purpose	162
3. Descriptive Paragraphs	162
4. Topic Sentences	163
5. Development by Definition	163
6. Sound and Movement in Paragraphs	164
7. Emphasis by Contrast	165
8. Specific Detail in the Paragraph	166

Chapter VI. SENTENCE STRUCTURE 167

Introduction	167
The Value of the Simple Sentence	168
The Compound Sentence and Coordinate Ideas	169
Punctuation of the Compound Sentence	170
The Complex Sentence and Subordinate Ideas	171
The Use of the Participial Phrase	172
The Relationship of the Parts of Sentences Must Be Unmistakable	173
Good Sentence Structure Demands Proper Tense Sequence	174
The Mingling of Loose and Periodic Sentences Helps to Secure Variety in Sentence Structure	175
Your Sentences Should Be Euphonious	176
Good Sentences Must Possess Unity	178
Good Sentences Must Possess Coherence	180
Good Sentences Must Possess Emphasis	181

PRACTICES

1. Sentence Structure	183
2. Sentence Structure	183
3. Sentence Structure	184
4. Sentence Structure	185
5. Original Sentence Structure	185
6. The Sliced Paragraph Device	186
7. Correct Placing of Words, Phrases, and Clauses	187
8. Split Infinitives	188
9. He, She, It, They	189
10. A Paragraph Expressing Opinion and Criticism	189
11. The Point of View	190
KEYS TO PRACTICES	193

CONTENTS OF BOOK THREE

	Page
Chapter VII. WORDS	197
Introduction	197
Vocabulary Tests and Vocabulary Mastery	198
Denotation and Connotation of Words	203
The Derivation and History of Words	204
Anglo-Saxon and Latin Words	209
Specific and General Words	210
Words That Appeal to the Senses	212
Individuality in Phrasing	215
Malapropisms	218

PRACTICES

1. Malapropisms Corrected 219
2. Malapropisms—Lapsed-Letter Test 219
3. Choice of Words to Avoid Malapropisms . . . 220
4. Malapropisms Corrected 221
5. Malapropisms Corrected 222
6. Choice of Words in Narration 222
7. Choice of Words in Narration 223

KEYS TO PRACTICES 225

Chapter VIII. THE FRIENDLY LETTER 227

Introduction	227
Letters of Famous People	228
Sharing a Friend's Grief	231
A Letter of Condolence	232
A Letter to a Sick Friend	232
The Letter Acknowledging a Gift	233
The Congratulatory Letter	234
The Letter of Invitation	239
The Letter of Acceptance	241
The "Bread and Butter" Letter	241
The Semiformal Invitation—Acceptance—Regrets	244
A Letter of Advice	245
A Letter to Help a Young Friend Secure a Position	246
A Letter of Apology	247
Summary	247

PRACTICES

1. The Informal Letter 248
2. The Letter With a Purpose 253
3. Creative Writing Skill and Letter Writing . . . 254

CONTENTS OF BOOK THREE

	Page
Chapter IX. THE BUSINESS LETTER, *By Peter T. Ward*	257
The Receiver of the Letter	258
The Writer	260
The Letter	261
Accuracy of Diction	262
Simplicity of Diction	263
Vigor of Statement	263
Arrangement of Detail	265
The Fault of Wordiness	266
The Form and Appearance of the Letter	267
The Sales Letter	272
Follow-up Letters	279
Credit and Collection Letters	284
Claim and Adjustment Letters	289
Letters of Inquiry	296
Answers to Inquiries	297
Purchasing Letters	300
Response to Purchasing Letters	301
Chapter X. TELEGRAMS, CABLEGRAMS, AND RADIOGRAMS	303
Wide Use of Telegraph and Cable	303
Rules for Preparing Telegrams	303
How to Save in Wording Telegrams	308
How to "File" Telegrams	310
Major Uses of the Telegram in Business	311
Classes of Telegraph Service: Full-Rate Telegrams—Day Letters—Night Letters	314
Other Telegraph Services: Telegraphic Money Orders—Gift Orders—Telegraphic Shopping Orders—Messenger Errand and Distribution Service—Air Reservations—Express Packages	318
Time Differences for International Communications	319
Classes of Cable Service: Ordinary or Full-Rate Cablegrams—CDE or Code Cablegrams—Urgents—CDE Urgents—Deferreds—Cable Night Letters	322
Preparation of Cablegrams	323
Plain-Language Messages—Code Words and Messages	323
Marks and Terms Identifying Merchandise	324

CONTENTS OF BOOK THREE

	Page
Marks Connected with Figures	324
Addresses—Registered Code Addresses	324
Acknowledgments of Receipt	324
Prepaid Replies	325
The Radiogram in Communication	325
Types of Radiograms: Ordinary Radiograms (Full-Rate and CDE)—Urgent Radiograms—Deferred Radiograms—Radioletters—Prepaid Replies—Radiograms to Follow Addressee—Radiograms to Ships at Sea	325
Other Services: The Telautograph—Wireless Photographs	330

PRACTICES

1. Interpretations of Telegraphic Symbols	331
2. Composing Telegraphic Messages Within the Ten-Word Charge	331
KEYS TO PRACTICES	332
Supplement. CONVENTIONS IN SOCIAL AND POLITICAL CORRESPONDENCE	333
PARLIAMENTARY PRACTICE	357

YOUR MASTERY OF ENGLISH

BOOK THREE
YOUR COMMAND OF WRITTEN ENGLISH

CHAPTER 1
EXAMINING YOUR TOOL MASTERY—YOUR COMMAND OF AUTOMATISMS

AS A BOY I was fascinated by the skill of the telegraph operator. I used to stand outside the single railway station of my native town and watch Lon Ireland deftly handling the key that clicked whatever message the moment demanded—routine information concerning the coming and departure of trains, a reservation for a Pullman ticket, press dispatches, or the private telegrams which the townspeople wished to send. It was easily and dexterously done. And I never knew of his making a mistake. He had, it seemed to me, perfectly mastered his technique—the Morse code and the way it could be rapidly applied. To me it seemed little short of the miraculous.

Even as I view it now in retrospect, some of that wonder still persists, but as I have gradually acquired more knowledge of the laws of learning and as I apply them now to the analysis of particular demands of the telegraph operator of that older era, I realize how long and persistent practice had developed the hand that so rapidly clicked out those varied sequent dispatches. Most of us, had we set our mind to the task could, by systematic discipline, have learned to send all those messages over the wires.

This operator had so thoroughly learned the Morse code and its technical application that the movements of the key were easily and automatically performed. Each correct response was an automatism. He need give no thought to the mere routine working of the instrument; he could concentrate upon the import of the message.

In support of the great value of these automatic responses, let me quote this paragraph written by William James. It is taken from the chapter "Habit" in *Psychology*.

The great thing in all education is to *make our nervous system our ally instead of our enemy*. It is to fund and capitalize our acquisitions and live at ease upon the interest of the fund. *For this we must make automatic and habitual, as early as possible, as many useful actions as we can*, and guard against the growing into ways that are likely to be disadvantageous to us, as we should guard against the plague. The more of the details of our daily life we can hand over to the effortless custody of automatism, the more our higher powers of mind will be set free for their own proper work. There is no more miserable human being than one in whom nothing is habitual but indecision, and for whom the lighting of every cigar, the drinking of every cup, the time of rising and going to bed every day, and the beginning of every bit of work, are subjects of express volitional deliberation. Full half the time of such a man goes to the deciding, or regretting, of matters which ought to be so ingrained in him as practically not to exist for his consciousness at all. If there be such daily duties not yet ingrained in any one of my readers, let him begin this very hour to set the matter right.*

But the acquiring of these automatic habits is only one division in the sphere of learning. Mastery of any subject depends upon two different processes:

1. The first is mechanical and usually implies a certain mastery of the tool. Practice and routine gradually bring the normal learner to a point where the separate manipulations of this tool are performed unconsciously, automatically. Each correct response is an *automatism*.
2. The second is a type of activity that always demands the alert and thoughtful attention of the performer; the task is done with a purpose; it has as its objective a completed product—or a portion of a completed product. Behind it, always, is the creative motive—the intention to produce something.

These two processes, while subject to these analytical differences, are seldom seen separately. They are closely interwoven, closely interlaced, mutually operative. The tool activities possess in themselves little value; they take on values when they are applied to a special creative task. The mere mastery of the Morse code was of no special value to the telegraph operator; the intelligent direction and application of that mastery to the instrument could impregnate the message with special value—sometimes rather slight, at other times very great.

---

*Copyright, 1892, Henry Holt & Company, New York.

Application of the Twofold Division to Written Expression.

When you apply this twofold concept to the topic of written expression, you become conscious of the countless writing activities that all normal adults now unconsciously perform; you make your responses automatically; each correct reaction is an automatism. Notice how this matter of acquired automatisms works out in special areas.

Acquired Automatisms

Penmanship.

You no longer pause when you wish to write the letter *a* or the word *and*. You can copy them on paper; you can write them in the dark; you can trace them in the air. It doesn't require any thought; it can all be done as automatically as you perform your separate steps in walking or take your separate breaths in breathing. Your penmanship is automatic. It is not so nearly perfect as you would wish, perhaps, but still it doubtless reveals a rather high level of legibility and correctness.

The most important consideration in handwriting is legibility. Form your letters carefully; distinguish between your *n*'s and *u*'s; dot your *i*'s, and cross your *t*'s. One point seldom receives adequate emphasis—leave ample space between the lines. Concrete evidence of the value of liberal spacing is seen by contrasting the writing in the examples on page 4, taken from Woolley's *New Handbook of Composition*.*

Typing.

Or perhaps most of your written work is done on a typewriter. You have learned to type by the touch method, and now with your acquired skill you don't even have to look at the keyboard. You know what letters or words or sentences you want to type and your fingers just fall swiftly and automatically upon the proper keys. The idea—already formed subjectively—soon finds its objective expression in the clearly and perfectly typed record in the regularly spaced lines on the clean-cut paper before you.

It may not be quite so finished and faultless and artistic as that. Only the expert attains this automatic mastery in typing—or in any other realm of technique. But in its rarer strata you do see these rarer manifestations of speed and skill. Most performances, unfortunately, reveal deficiencies in automatic control. Perfection remains an ideal.

---

*Copyright, 1907, D. C. Heath & Company, Boston, Mass.

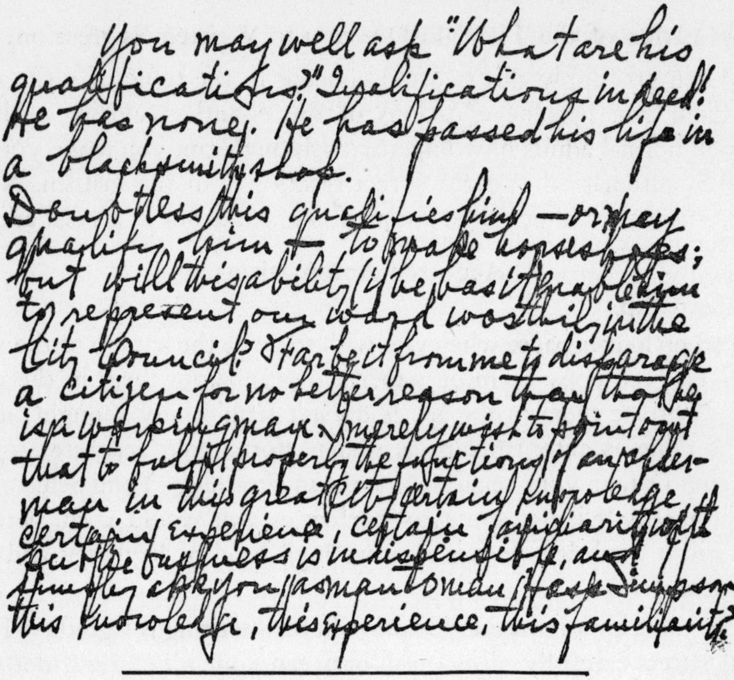
You may well ask "What are his qualifications?" Qualifications indeed! He has none. He has passed his life in a blacksmith shop.
Doubtless this qualifies him — or may qualify him — to make horseshoes; but will this ability (if he has it) enable him to represent our ward worthily in the City Council? Far be it from me to disparage a citizen for no better reason than that he is a workingman. I merely wish to point out that to fulfill properly the functions of an alderman in this great city certain knowledge, certain experience, certain familiarity with public business is indispensable, and I simply ask you as man to man: Has he any of this knowledge, this experience, this familiarity?"

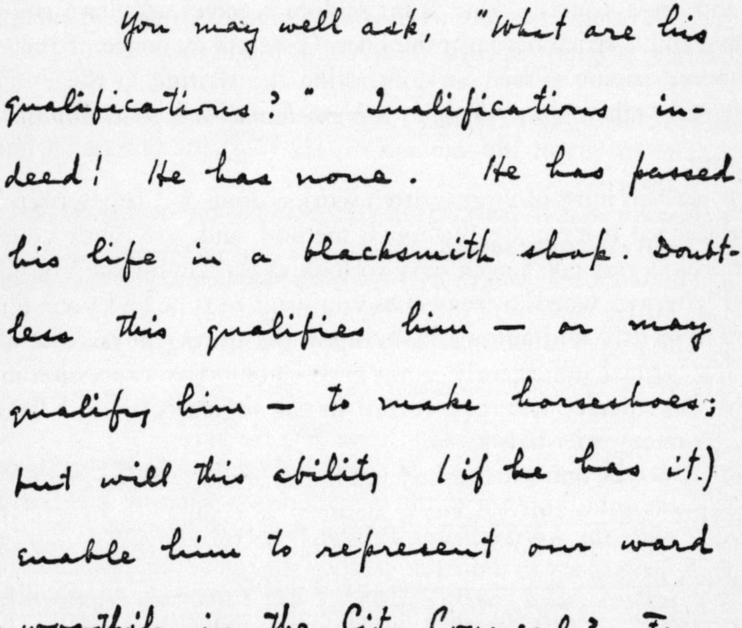
You may well ask, "What are his qualifications?" Qualifications indeed! He has none. He has passed his life in a blacksmith shop. Doubtless this qualifies him — or may qualify him — to make horseshoes; but will this ability (if he has it.) enable him to represent our ward worthily in the City Council? Far

LEGIBILITY IN HANDWRITING

In penmanship and typing there are certain mechanical matters that you have discovered to be important. There is, for instance, the matter of margins. Ordinarily we establish a frame for each sheet. On the larger sheets a full inch border is approximately correct for top and bottom and for the left-hand and right-hand sides. On smaller sheets the borders are proportionately narrowed. Keep your left-hand margin perfectly straight. Guard against a scraggly right-hand margin. Don't crowd your bottom lines.

Spelling Automatisms.

The number of correct spellings that have become automatic would probably prove surprising could we list them all. There are so many words that are short and simple and easily mastered. You have been familiar with them since early childhood. You meet them every day in your reading and you meet them frequently in your writing. You could scarcely escape learning them by the score—by the hundreds, even. But still you make mistakes. You haven't enough automatisms. Confronted by alternate forms you perhaps hesitate. Try it and see. Here are twenty-five common words. In some cases only one form is correct; in other cases both forms are correct. Underline each word that is here properly spelled. The Key is found on p. 20.

1. His chief *offense* (*offence*) was inaccuracy in expression.
2. The officers of the senior class *lead* (*led*) the procession into the chapel.
3. It was a *truely* (*truly*) great performance—the staging was excellent and the acting superb.
4. His *judgment* (*judgement*) is always based on a careful and discriminating analysis of the facts.
5. The proper *alignment* (*alinement*) and spacing of material always adds to the appearance of a typewritten page.
6. One of the most impressive scenes in the picture shows the ceremony where they *anoint* (*annoint*) the king.
7. Although it is generally considered *alright* (*all right*) to abbreviate the title *Professor* in the salutation of a letter, it is preferable to write the word in full—*My dear Professor Walker*.
8. A masterpiece in the art of creating the right atmosphere for a story is Poe's *weird* (*wierd*) setting of *The Fall of the House of Usher*.
9. Without looking to see if any cars were approaching, the boy darted *across* (*accross*) the street to get his ball.

10. The *siege (seige)* of the city lasted several days.
11. After she had finished the poster she deftly *eraced (erased)* all the preliminary pencil marks.
12. Perhaps we had better wait another half hour so that if Mary *tries (trys)* to reach us she will not be disappointed.
13. He *plys (plies)* his trade diligently.
14. On what dates is the Metropolitan Opera *coming (comming)* to our city this winter?
15. It is a small camp that can accommodate only about *forty (fourty)* boys.
16. Before a decision is made, each *separate (seperate)* factor should be considered carefully.
17. The coach asked everybody in the cast to return at seven o'clock *tonite (tonight)* for the dress rehearsal.
18. I think that you had better make *sure (shure)* whether that schedule runs according to standard or daylight saving time.
19. The price of *shugar (sugar)* is extremely high.
20. As he is a much better player than I, I fear that I shall *loose (lose)* this game.
21. He *smooths (smoothes)* the surface carefully before he begins his work.
22. Mary took the part of the *Angle (Angel)* of Peace in the play that her class gave at school last night. Her wings and her white costume were most impressive.
23. The *dining room (dinning room)* was beautifully decorated for the birthday party.
24. She had not made up her mind *whether (weather)* she would make the trip at Thanksgiving or Christmas.
25. They have a wonderful view from their *poarch (porch)* on the second floor.

There are twenty-eight correct spellings in the foregoing list. If you scored *twenty* you did *fairly well;* if you scored *twenty-five* you are a *very good* speller; if your score was *twenty-six* or more, let's call it *excellent.* The mastery of twenty-six or more indicates an unusually large number of acquired automatisms in the field of spelling. There are still many words to master and many possibilities for the process of writing to be interrupted by your doubts, but your past efforts have brought you large rewards. In spelling no one attains absolute perfection.

Capitalization Automatisms.

You perhaps have a fairly good knowledge of capitalization. Automatically you commence every sentence with a capital. You know the difference between a common noun like *grease* and the name of the country *Greece;* you differentiate between a common adjective such as *able* and a proper adjective such as *Albanian.* You know that you never make a mistake in writing the pronoun *I* as a capital letter; you write the *O* with a capital in such exclamatory phrases as *O Caesar! O Time! O Spirit of Ancient Greece;* and you are equally careful to spell the names of divinities such as *God, Christ,* and *Zeus* with capital letters. There are scores upon scores of other such practices that have for you become automatic. You employ capital letters in such instances just as naturally and just as surely as you spell short, simple words correctly. You have been so seriously concerned in perfecting these practices that you now have a very large number of acquired automatisms in this field.

But again, just how complete is your mastery of capitalization? How many situations cause you to hesitate? Let's test it out in the italicized words of the twenty-five sentences that follow. Some of the capitals are correctly used; others are incorrectly used. Mark with a check the sentences that are right. (See Key on p. 21.)

1. The vote of the *South* can be closely estimated.
2. We have been traveling *West* most of the afternoon.
3. I shall see you at *easter.*
4. This should be printed in *roman* type.
5. We ought to visit *Niagara Falls.*
6. The bard sang of *jehovah* and *his* commands.
7. Can you recite the *Ten Commandments?*
8. One correct complimentary close for a friendly letter is *Sincerely Yours.*
9. *Brown university* is in Providence.
10. He took *French leave* last Wednesday.
11. Let us dine at the *Century Club.*
12. Here is the motto he quoted: "*honesty* is the best policy."
13. A *King* should remember his obligation to his people.
14. He was elected *president* of his society.
15. If a class in *geometry* could be organized, I should like to join.
16. She is now employed at the *congressional library.*
17. We ought to start a campaign for a *town library.*

18. The *bible* has many examples of rhythmic prose.
19. Mark Twain has written about the *Mississippi River*.
20. Did you hear that *negress* sing last Sunday?
21. I live on *Forest street*.
22. We have been motoring on the new *Macadamized* road.
23. These flowers will bloom next *spring*.
24. He quoted Tennyson's line:
    "In the *spring* a young man's fancy lightly turns
    to thoughts of love."
25. How are you planning to spend the *Fourth* (of July)?

Punctuation Automatisms.

You may have been surprised when some friend has informed you that he never punctuates as he writes; when he finishes a letter or any piece of writing he goes back over each sentence and puts in his punctuation marks. Well, at least he does better than the youth who, after omitting all signs of punctuation from his letter, set down at the bottom of the last page a liberal supply of periods, commas, semicolons, colons, and interrogation marks and graciously granted his correspondent the privilege of properly placing them.

Good habits in writing naturally assume the process of punctuating as you write. The marks fall into place with the same automatic precision that proves your skill in capitalizing proper nouns, crossing your *t*'s, and dotting your *i*'s. Convention long ago set its demands and steadily you have tried to conform.

But the demands that a previous convention has set are not always rigid. Changes may gradually take place and individuality may boldly assert itself. However, since custom holds strong sway, we must hearken to its major mandates. How literally you obey, you may discover as you fill the places in the following frame. (See Key to Punctuation Test, p. 21.)

Punctuation Test

	Correct	Incorrect or Undesirable	Changes
EXAMPLE: I saw Robert, Henry and Helen at the station.	......	√	Comma after Henry.
1. He lost a week's wages.	......	......	......
2. I shall always remember the school and it's influence.	......	......	......

TOOL MASTERY—COMMAND OF AUTOMATISMS

3. I must call John who is to go in our car.
4. There is Roger Taylor; he is our best ball player.
5. Crazed by pain he finally went to the dentist.
6. May I go with you to the picnic.
7. Robert shouted to Sidney, "Throw the ball to third base!"
8. I told him "that our daughter is very ill."
9. Address the letter to Philip Jones, Jr.
10. When writing, punctuation should be automatic.

You will recall that the subject of punctuation is fully treated in Book One (Chapter VIII) of this series. Always, detailed questions are likely to arise. Determination to find the right answer to each punctuation problem will finally enable you to acquire such a command of automatisms that the actual process of composition will be seldom slowed down for lack of knowledge concerning the proper mark to use. You will, however, be conscious of various practices among writers of repute. There is, moreover, a modern tendency toward fewer punctuation marks. Formerly addresses on envelopes were freely sprinkled with commas. Now we use very few—more frequently, indeed, we use none. The whole theory behind the practice is clarity of expression. Many misunderstandings, many lawsuits, arise because of the presence or the omission of punctuation marks. A good craftsman will always be seriously concerned to make such use of his punctuation marks as will prove of most help to the reader in comprehending the writer's thoughts.

Grammar Automatisms.

Do you still pause sometimes in writing a sentence and wonder whether you should use *who* or *whom*, *he* or *him*, *dive* or *dove*, *they* or *them*? And I am wondering if you would ever fall into such an error as this, which a well-educated man recently made in a letter he was writing:

"The novel was of great interest to all three of us—my wife, my daughter, and *I**."

Perhaps the best way for you to answer inquiries concerning your acquired competence is to take a brief and simple test. Here are twenty sentences that demand definite decisions upon certain grammatical points. Check in the left-hand column of the frame the sentences that are *correct*—those that contain no grammatical errors. And also check in the right-hand column the sentences that are wrong. Following this, correct the error. (See Key to Grammar Test, p. 21.)

Test in Grammar

	Correct	Incorrect	Changes
EXAMPLE: He invited John and I to the picnic.		✓	Change *I* to *me*—object of the verb *invited*.
1. I could of won that game.			
2. Everybody but him had read the news.			
3. He was caught by the rope and drug around the block.			
4. That man don't deserve our pity.			
5. I came near being drowned.			
6. Each man must bring their own car.			
7. Sell your corn to whoever will buy.			
8. We couldn't scarcely see the path.			
9. Let's stroll a little ways down the street.			
10. Do you like these kind of peaches?			
11. A knowledge of these first-aid facts always help a person who is injured.			
12. I never dreamed of it's poisoning you.			
13. I feared the culprits to be them.			
14. I never dreamed of its being they.			
15. I did not think of Robert's accepting our invitation.			

---

*Here the nouns *wife* and *daughter*, and the pronoun that follows are in the objective case—in apposition with *us*. Since nouns and pronouns used in apposition are in the same case as the noun or pronoun with which they are appositively used, the writer of the letter should not have used the nominative form *I*; he should have used the objective form *me*.

16. Measles have broken out in our neighborhood.   ....
17. He needs more clothing.   ....
18. He need not expect our help.   ....
19. He dare not go.   ....
20. Each of them has his own copy of the book.   ....

Few persons ever attain such a command of grammar that they never make a mistake. Such mistakes are naturally more excusable in rapid speech; they are not to be excused in written English—especially in situations where the writer has an opportunity for revising his sentences. Failure to make these revisions is due either to carelessness or to ignorance of correct usage. A perfect craftsman will never be satisfied until he has gained not merely the necessary knowledge of grammatical theory but such a mastery of expression as will automatically summon the correct form. Errors in this game of English may be as costly and as reprehensible as errors in professional baseball. In most business establishments and in most social circles demands for grammatical accuracy are particularly exacting. What can you say of your own proficiency in the knowledge and use of acquired automatisms? Study your test scores.

Word Meanings and Automatisms.

You already know a surprising number of words. You read your newspapers every day; you have some time for books and magazines. Some of your friends have excellent vocabularies and you have learned many words from their conversations and letters. But you are nevertheless constantly coming across terms and phrases that are novel, and strange, and unrevealing. Your dictionary is in constant requisition—but there remain so many vocabulary sectors unexplored—so many individual words still uncaptured!

But mere pursuit usually carries with it the mood of animated pleasure and spirited acquisitiveness. Some persons even go as far as to say that they are less interested in the victory than in the race; they care little for the quarry but they care a great deal for the chase. Personally when it comes to the matter of vocabulary, I confess a keener interest in the captured quarry of words. The search may richly provide its moments of quickened curiosity and transitory fascination, but the newly acquired word is available for future practical service. We really never know just how valuable the later uses of this new word may prove to be, but we are grateful that it is now really ours.

No one ever knows just how many words he has at his command. The number runs, in most instances, far into the thousands. But whatever the total may be on each today, it should for all of us be larger on each tomorrow.

Here, again, is an opportunity for a brief, immediate test on twenty-five words in current use. How many do you know?

Inglis Test of English Vocabulary*

Select from among the five possibilities for each numbered item the one word that is the nearest synonym to the italicized word in the left-hand column.

EXAMPLE. An *astute* answer—*shrewd*, hasty, discourteous, loud, ambiguous.

1. Do not *abandon* me.	persecute	desert	mock	irritate	
	restrain				
2. He was granted *absolution*.	permission	forgiveness		power	
	recognition	authority			
3. He was *accorded* privileges.	rendered	refused	assured	promised	
	deprived-of				
4. An *acrimonious* answer.	discouraging	friendly	bitter	slangy	
	haughty				
5. An *admirable* person.	excellent	tragic	vain	naval	
	shrewd				
6. He *affronted* me.	amused	faced	addressed	went-before	
	insulted				
7. You *allay* my fears.	justify	calm	arouse	increase	
	confirm				
8. He *ameliorated* conditions.	concealed	approved	stated	improved	
	studied				
9. An *ancillary* committee.	executive	standing		temporary	
	newly-appointed		subordinate		
10. A marked *antithesis*.	development	copy	dislike	contrast	
	symptom				

---

*The complete Inglis Tests are published by Ginn and Company and are copyrighted by the President and Fellows of Harvard University. This portion from Form A (copyright 1924) is reprinted here through the courtesy of the publishers and with the approval of the Graduate School of Education, Harvard University [where the tests were originally made by Professor Alexander Inglis].

The Key for this test is printed on page 22. Do not consult it until you have made a record of your decisions upon each item.

TOOL MASTERY—COMMAND OF AUTOMATISMS

11. He *appraised* the estate. — set-a-value-on, mortgaged, bought, sold, developed
12. He is noted for *arrogance*. — ignorance, wickedness, pride, indifference, foolishness
13. His *associates* fear him. — enemies, employees, colleagues, pets, relatives-by-marriage
14. An *atypical* Scotchman. — witty, literary, canny, unrepresentative, genuine
15. An *autonomous* people. — rebellious, self-governing, mechanical, oppressed, art-loving
16. They *baffled* our plans. — approved-of, encouraged, heard, ridiculed, foiled
17. A *basic* truth. — obvious, unknown, powerful, fundamental, unpleasant
18. He *beseeches* aid. — entreats, grants, spurns, offers, obtains
19. The shore looks *bleak*. — inviting, habitable, desolate, rocky, precipitous
20. He escaped with his *booty*. — life, companion, bargain, plunder, foot-covering
21. He *braved* the storm. — escaped, described, dared, prophesied, expected
22. The *buccal* cavity. — lime-kiln, false-heel, mouth, tooth, yawning
23. A *buxom* widow. — flirtatious, forlorn, rustic, thrifty, plump
24. He was a victim of *calumny*. — chance, slander, disease, drugs, prejudice
25. These are *capillary* tubes. — boiler, inner, elastic, hair-like, strong

Your Percentage Score.

You will probably wish to compute your percentage score on this Vocabulary Test. Count the number of words that you marked correctly. Multiply this number by 4. The product will give you your mark computed on a scale of 100.

> A score of 92% or more is excellent.
> A score of 80%—92% is good.
> A score of 68%—80% is fair.
> A score below 68% is below the average.

Whatever your score proves to be, you will naturally wish that a similar test taken a few weeks later will indicate a higher degree of accomplishment. Here, age, experience, interest, and concentration yield very positive results. You can get other forms from the publishers and thus provide yourself with a reasonably accurate instrument for measuring your later vocabulary achievements.*

Automatisms in Sentence Patterns.

While it is evident that opportunities for acquiring automatisms in sentence patterns are scant—contrasted with the opportunities in other sectors of English mastery—it is nevertheless apparent that we can develop our habit so that we more naturally fall into the custom of beginning some of our sentences with a subordinate rather than with a principal clause.

In seeking for concrete evidence of this my eye wandered back to the opening sentence of the preceding paragraph. Almost automatically—not *wholly* so, perhaps—I wrote the subordinate clause *While it is evident*—and the rest of this clause. And, again, I discover that this second paragraph is a further illustration of an automatically patterned sentence.

That these are practices that we acquire is evident when we read what our young children write. We pick up Junior's recent letter—a series of four simple sentences such as these: *We reached camp at six. We had supper. We sat around the fire after supper. We went to bed at nine o'clock.* The style is not exactly illiterate; rather it is immature—just as Junior's mind is immature. Later, as he develops, he will discard this single pattern and learn by practice the advantages of variety and the flexibility of sentence forms. His automatisms are just now severely limited to a few capital letters, the period at the end of the sentence, and the correct spelling of very simple words. But he is only nine years old; the major portion of the world is before him. Somewhere in the unexplored areas of style he will discover, among other valuable accessories, the enriching possibilities of the subordinate clause.

The Paragraph-Indentation Automatism.

The paragraph has practically but one automatism—and the name for that is *indentation* (or *indention*). This is a purely mechanical matter. Those who have mastered it simply start the first sentence of a paragraph—a unit of thought—approximately a half inch to the right of the established left-hand margin. Since on paper 8 x 11 this left-hand mar-

---

*Consult the vocabulary tests that are printed elsewhere in *Your Mastery of English.*

ginal line is usually an inch from the outer vertical edge of the paper, the first word of the paragraph would ordinarily start approximately an inch and a half from the left-hand vertical edge of the sheet. Of course writers and typists do not hold themselves rigidly to these distances, but one who accepts these suggestions will not stray far from conventional practices.

There are many other ideas that the word *paragraph* suggests, but they belong more properly to the other hemisphere of the learning process—the creative hemisphere. The one major enumeration on the automatic side is indentation. Every good writer of longhand, every good typist, knows its purpose and value.

Signs and Symbols.

In the field of arbitrary signs and symbols we may possibly have acquired a considerable number of automatisms that we use in our writing. Perhaps in the commercial field the most common of these are the ampersand—&; the sign for the dollar—$; the cent—¢; the pound sterling—£; the percentage symbol—%; the account sign—a/c; and the sign for at—@, used in bills or orders. Bookkeepers in certain lines of business may frequently use these: B/E—Bill of Exchange; B/L—Bill of Lading; B/S—Bill of Sale.

All who have studied arithmetic are familiar with these four: + plus; — minus; × the multiplication sign; and ÷ the sign for division. The signs used in higher mathematics are of infinite variety and are employed for the most part only by specialists.

Every trade, every science, every art, every profession has invented certain signs or symbols to meet certain special, certain technical demands. Most of these the average person does not use; it is only those of wide, general application that we should include in our list of necessary automatisms.

Abbreviation Automatisms.

Even as children in the earlier grades of school you began making your acquaintance with the more frequently used abbreviations. The two letters and period *Mr.* standing before a name you probably learned so many years ago that you do not remember the time when this abbreviation seemed unfamiliar. And doubtless the abbreviation *Mrs.* was also quickly mastered in those early years. First you recognized each of these when you read them in your primary books. A little later you were probably writing them in your own original sentences. You now use them so freely that you scarcely think of them as items that you once had to learn. With greater or lesser effort on your part—the particular degree being now long forgotten—they came to take their part in your list of acquired automatisms.

Naturally your mastery is still severely limited. As a general rule you have learned only those that you have been forced to learn.

As a test of your present acquirements you may find it enlightening to go through this short list of rather commonly used abbreviations and check those that you cannot immediately explain. When you have finished your checking, compute your score. The Key to the test is printed on p. 22.

Test of Commonly Used Abbreviations

1. ad lib.	7. Cor. I	13. loc. cit.	19. q. e. d.
2. A 1	8. Dec.	14. Messrs.	20. recd.
3. a. m.	9. E. S. T.	15. op. cit.	21. supt.
4. amt.	10. et al.	16. p. m.	22. Ye Olde Town
5. bbl.	11. etc.	17. p. o.	23. Y. M. C. A.
6. colloq.	12. i. e.	18. P. S. T.	24. Y. W. C. A.

In examining the record that you make on this test, you may be curious to discover why your score is high or low. Perhaps in your own practices you have had occasion to use very few abbreviations. You may have formed the habit of writing out in full words that others abbreviate. You have noticed that some persons in writing *Professor Daniel T. Root*, for example, abbreviate the title and write *Prof.* This abbreviation is in growing disfavor. The title of *Doctor*, however, is regularly abbreviated—*Dr.*

What abbreviations you ultimately decide to master for your own daily writing will depend largely upon your particular vocation and your particular taste. The real value of knowing the abbreviations is often more definitely related to your reading than to your writing.

Automatisms in Syllabication.

How automatic is your division of words at the right-hand margin of your writing sheet? The law against dividing syllables you must, as your own constable, rigidly enforce. If you do not know the correct division, consult some dictionary of established authority. Here is a general hint that you may find valuable: The separate parts of a divided word must be pronounceable. This will prevent your dividing such a word as *too, where,* or *through.*

You might test your own present knowledge of proper syllabication by dividing the following twenty words. Write down each word into separate syllables before you consult the Key, which is printed on p. 23.

Test of Syllabication

1. bachelor	6. balbriggan	11. banister	16. baroness
2. bacteria	7. balustrade	12. banqueter	17. barricade
3. badminton	8. banal	13. barbaric	18. basilisk
4. bafflement	9. bandanna	14. barefaced	19. battalion
5. bailiwick	10. bandoleer	15. barometer	20. beatitude

These few simple rules may prove helpful in practice:

1. Never divide the one-syllable words.
2. Never allow one letter of a word to stand alone. Wrong: *e nough; cit y.*
3. Never split a syllable. Wrong: *univ ersity; susp ect.*
4. Never fail to put the hyphen at the end of a line that ends with a divided word. Do not put the hyphen at the beginning of a line.
5. When in doubt about proper syllabication, consult the dictionary.

Automatisms in Italicizing Words.

Every practiced writer learns to underscore words which in printed form would be italicized. Convention, while not absolutely rigid, generally favors the use of italics in cases here enumerated:

1. Italicize titles of books, magazines, pamphlets, monographs, newspapers, musical compositions, and works of art.
    a. I am reading Dickens's *Hard Times.*
    b. Here is last Sunday's issue of *The* New York Times.*
    c. Have you a late copy of *Collier's?*
    d. The best number on the program was Beethoven's *Ninth Symphony.*

---

*The word *the* in the titles of newspapers and periodicals is not always capitalized. It is capitalized in titles of books and works of art—*The Return of the Native; The Last Supper.*

e. There is a reproduction of Rodin's *The Thinker*.
   f. Here is the copy of *Harper's* containing the article of which I spoke—"Storm Center of Brookline."*
2. Italicize the names of ships.
   He went down with the *Titanic*.
3. Italicize foreign phrases that have not been fully absorbed into English. Since it is not always easy to know what words have been naturalized, we need, in special cases, to consult the dictionary. Special designating marks are used to indicate the unnaturalized words.
   He prides himself on being one of the *élite*.
4. Italicize words, letters, signs, and figures when they are definitely referred to in such sentences as these:
   a. Do you always make a distinction between the words *infer* and *imply?*
   b. You may have noted the letter *e* in the older spelling of the word *judgement*. Modern usage favors *judgment*.
   c. He is careless in his penmanship; he makes no distinction between his *u's* and his *n's*.
   d. Don't use the ampersand, &, for the word *and* in the body of your writing. You may use it when copying the names of firms that have established for themselves the form: Funk & Wagnalls Company.
5. Don't fall into the habit of freely underlining words that you wish a reader to emphasize. Rely strongly upon the structure of your sentence and the intelligence of the reader. In rare cases underscoring for emphasis may be justified. Many persons in reading aloud from the King James Version of the Bible mistake the italicized words; these words are not used for emphasis; they indicate the use of an English word that does not appear in the original language but is employed to bring out more clearly the meaning in translation. In the second verse of Genesis, for example, we have this sentence: "And the earth was without form and void; and darkness *was* upon the face of the deep." The italicized word *was* does not occur in the original; it is supplied by the translators.

We have called attention to the fact that laws for underscoring or italicizing words are not absolutely rigid. Book titles are sometimes

---

*Some writers prefer to use quotation marks around all titles. The practice has full authoritative support. The current tendency to reserve the quotation marks for titles of chapters or separate articles is here illustrated.

printed without either italics or quotation marks. The names of ships are often printed in roman type. And the same is true of the titles of musical compositions, famous paintings, and famous statues. Knowledge of these varying practices will aid you in stressing the importance of making your individual choice among the accepted practices and adhering closely to what your own independent judgment favors. The choices indicated in this section may be your preference. Establish a judgment and use it habitually, for though there are various usages, a writer must, in a unit of work, be unfalteringly consistent.

The Need for Unsparing Effort.

A reading of this chapter, with its emphasis upon automatisms in written English, may have impressed you with the progress which the years have brought to you personally. Study and practice and recognition of the daily occupational demands for correct written expression have developed perhaps a certain consciousness of acquired proficiency. If it were not so, your associates—or the members of your own family—would have told you. But even though your test scores and other proofs of achievement may be responsible for a reasonable degree of gratification, you would be insensitive indeed, if they had not at the same time swept into your vision large and scattered areas of English still unwon, that invite your diligent cultivation.

The spelling of certain words checks the course of your speeding pen—or stills the clicking of your clattering typewriter. Does *embarrass* have two *r*'s, and is this spelling of *m a c a r o o n* correct? Will these pestering orthographical problems finally be overcome?

And what about grammar? Will it ever cease to bother us? "Shall I," you wonder, "ever learn when a relative clause inevitably demands a comma? And should *dining room* be written with or without a hyphen? Do *spring* and *autumn* sometimes demand capitals and sometimes not? And if so, when? And yesterday in my reading I noticed *South* with a big *S*, and here it is with a small *s*—*south*. Just as I think I have my teeth set in an item the thing eludes me—it's like that fluffy pink candy you buy at circuses and fairs. Or perhaps you'll understand the elusion better when you try to pick up a drop of mercury with your thumb and finger! *Elusion!* Is that right? It looks queer! Perhaps it should be *illusion?*"

And countless other questions concerning words will constantly arise. No single person ever attains command of more than a fraction of the total number of words that the dictionaries list. It would be odd indeed if new words did not confront you—especially if you choose the type of companion or the level of literature that alert intelligence covets. You should not be so much troubled by your lack of knowledge of recurring words as by the lethargy that allows you to be complaisant in the midst of a discovered mediocrity. Whatever be your present level, there are lexicon ladders that reach to the higher floors.

And there are instruments and apparatus available for the bridging of most of your English gaps. Not all the engineering problems—be they mechanical or linguistic—are easy to solve, but in the midst of the labor of solving them you may be encouraged by an aphorism that Browning phrased for us in *The Statue and the Bust*.

> And the sin I impute to each frustrate ghost
> Is—the unlit lamp and the ungirt loin.

There is the text for a sermon that has never been written. You may preach it extempore to your listening self. The continued practice of the preachment may give you a command of more automatisms than were ever dreamed of in the philosophy of Hamlet or Yorick—or anyone else.

KEYS TO TESTS

Key to Correct and Incorrect Spellings

1. offense, offence
2. led
3. truly
4. judgment, judgement (*judgement* is an older spelling of the word. Although it is still considered correct it is not preferred and should be avoided.)
5. alignment, alinement
6. anoint
7. all right
8. weird
9. across
10. siege
11. erased
12. tries
13. plies
14. coming
15. forty
16. separate
17. tonight (to-night)
18. sure
19. sugar
20. lose
21. smooths
22. Angel
23. dining room (use the hyphen for the adjective: "He opened the dining-room window.")
24. whether
25. porch

Key to Capitalization Test

1. ✓
2. west
3. Easter
4. ✓ (The small letter is currently preferred.)
5. ✓
6. Jehovah, His
7. ✓
8. Sincerely yours,
9. Brown University
10. ✓
11. ✓
12. Honesty
13. king
14. ✓
15. ✓ (Usually capitalized by the British.)
16. Congressional Library
17. ✓
18. Bible
19. ✓
20. Negress (The capital letter is preferred.)
21. Forest Street
22. macadamized
23. ✓
24. Spring (Tennyson capitalizes the word. The small letter should not be counted wrong.)
25. ✓

Key to Punctuation Test

	Correct	Incorrect or Undesirable	Changes
1.	✓		
2.		✓	Omit the apostrophe.
3.		✓	Insert a comma after *John*.
4.	✓		
5.		✓	Insert a comma after *pain*.
6.		✓	Change the period to an interrogation point.
7.	✓		
8.		✓	An indirect quotation is not enclosed in quotation marks.
9.	✓		
10.	✓		

Key to Grammar Test

	Correct	Incorrect	Changes
1.		✓	Change *of* to *have*.
2.	✓		
3.		✓	Change *drug* to *dragged*.
4.		✓	Change *don't* to *doesn't*.
5.	✓		
6.		✓	Change *their* to *his*.
7.	✓		

8. ✓ Change *couldn't* to *could*. *Scarcely* expresses the negative idea. We don't want two negatives.
9. ✓ Change *ways*, a plural to *way*, a singular.
10. ✓ Change *these* to *this*.
11. ✓ Change *help* to *helps*. The subject *knowledge*, which is singular, here demands the singular form *helps*.
12. ✓ Change *it's* to *its*—the possessive form.
13. ✓
14. ✓
15. ✓*
16. ✓ Change *have* to *has*.
17. ✓
18. ✓
19. ✓ *Dares* is also correct.
20. ✓

Key to the Inglis Vocabulary Test

1. desert
2. forgiveness
3. rendered
4. bitter
5. excellent
6. insulted
7. calm
8. improved
9. subordinate
10. contrast
11. set-a-value-on
12. pride
13. colleagues
14. unrepresentative
15. self-governing
16. foiled
17. fundamental
18. entreats
19. desolate
20. plunder
21. dared
22. mouth
23. plump
24. slander
25. hair-like

Key to Test of Commonly Used Abbreviations

1. at pleasure
2. first class
3. *ante meridiem*—before noon
4. amount
5. barrel
6. colloquial
7. Corinthians I
8. December
9. Eastern Standard Time
10. *et alii . . . aliae*—and others
11. *et cetera*—and others
12. *id est*—that is, namely
13. *loco citato*—in the place cited
14. Gentlemen
15. *opere citato*—in the article or book cited
16. post master
    post meridiem—afternoon

---

*Do not use "'s" if you wish to bring out the idea of surprise that *Robert* accepted. You then emphasize the fact that it was natural for others to accept, but surprising that *Robert* should.

17. post office
    postal order
18. Pacific Standard Time
19. *quod erat demonstrandum*—
    which was to be proved
20. received
21. superintendent
22. the—as in Ye* Olde Towne
23. Young Men's Christian Association
24. Young Women's Christian Association

Key to Test of Syllabication

1. bach' e lor
2. bac te' ri a
3. bad' min ton
4. baf' fle ment
5. bail' i wick
6. bal brig' gan
7. bal us trade'
8. ban' al
9. ban dan' na
10. ban' do leer
11. ban' is ter
12. ban' quet er
13. bar bar' ic
14. bare' faced
15. ba rom' e ter
16. bar' on ess
17. bar ri cade'
18. bas' i lisk
19. bat tal' ion
20. be at' i tude

PRACTICES

Your constant need in mastering English is not merely to have ideas to express, but to be ready and accurate in your power to express them. As a means of perfecting your readiness and your accuracy, this series of Practices is here provided.

PRACTICE 1

Spelling—Words Pronounced Alike but Spelled Differently

In each of the following sentences you will find in parentheses two words that are pronounced in exactly the same way, but that have different spellings and different meanings. In the blank provided at the right of each sentence write the word that is appropriately suited to the context of the sentence.

1. The (ascent, assent) up the mountain was so steep that several in the party wanted to turn back. ....
2. The bride looked very beautiful as she walked down the (aisle, isle). ....
3. It was impossible to (altar, alter) the plans at such a late moment although we were convinced that the new plans were more expeditious. ....

---

*The Y used in expressions of this type is a survival of an Anglo-Saxon letter known as thorn—*þ*. Its modern equivalent is *th*. The form *þe*, used to express an archaic note, is often incorrectly read *ye;* it should be read *the.*

4. Since the business venture they wish to start demands a large amount of (capital, capitol), they may have to give up their plan. ....
5. She wore a beautiful (pendant, pendent) which set off her black dress most effectively. ....
6. Although we were all convinced of his (gilt, guilt), we did not have enough evidence to convict him. ....
7. I must remember to order some new (stationary, stationery) when I am in town today. ....
8. This is the (forth, fourth) consecutive year that he has won the tennis championship. ....
9. In O'Neill's *Days without End* we have the effective portrayal of the (dual, duel) aspects of an individual's personality. ....
10. His (complement, compliment) was not insincere; it was genuine. ....

PRACTICE 2

Spelling—Frequently Misspelled Words

Here is a list of frequently misspelled words. Have someone read you each word followed by the sentence in which it is used. How many of the words can you spell correctly?

1. *irreconcilable* — The two were *irreconcilable* after their quarrel.
2. *retrieve* — He is doing everything he can to *retrieve* the loan.
3. *parallel* — Washington Street runs *parallel* to Houghton Street.
4. *aggravate* — Walking will *aggravate* the pain in his foot.
5. *adjourn* — Congress will probably *adjourn* at the end of June.
6. *accommodate* — The new hotel can *accommodate* two hundred and fifty persons.
7. *picnicking* — They plan to go *picnicking* next Sunday.
8. *illustrate* — They will *illustrate* the paper with several cuts.
9. *crystallize* — If the solution is properly saturated it will *crystallize*.
10. *congeal* — The wound is not very deep and so the blood will soon *congeal*.

PRACTICE 3

A Test in Spelling

Some of the italicized words in the following sentences are incorrectly spelled. In the blanks provided at the right of the sentences spell the words correctly. Place a check mark in the blank if you think that the word is spelled correctly as it now stands. Compare yours answers with the key and compute your score.

1. We had not seen the old homestead for many years and we were disappointed that it looked so *delapidated*.   ....
2. He is just an *acquaintence* of mine; I do not know him very well.   ....
3. The new system proved to be more of a *nuisance* than a help.   ....
4. He declined in *deference* to a more experienced person who had also been nominated for the position of secretary.   ....
5. They are *planning* to take an eighteen-day bicycle tour of the White Mountain region of New Hampshire.   ....
6. Although he studies hard and acquires a great deal of knowledge he does not have the capacity to *descriminate* and judge for himself the comparative importance of what he has learned.   ....
7. They have *omitted* the important footnotes that I asked them to include.   ....
8. We have purchased some expensive *apparratus* for the *labratory*.   ....
9. The questions of the *prosecuting* attorney completely bewildered the witness.   ....
10. They went over the terms very carefully before they made the *agreement*.   ....

PRACTICE 4

Spelling—Supplying Missing Letters

Fill in the missing letters of the words that are incompletely spelled.

1. It was impossible to p......rsue him, for we had no clues as to the direction he had taken.
2. After the s......ge was over, the soldiers s......zed as much plunder as they could.
3. His ......llusion to Falstaff's soliloquy on honor was extremely à propos.
4. A month ago he was transfe......ed to the advertising department.
5. The same princip...... applies to the solution of all these problems.
6. He was di......atisfied with the plans that had been made.
7. He succeeded in getting an extremely remunerative position and is therefore no longer depend......nt on his family.
8. The judge found the defend......nt not guilty.

9. He considered the whole affair outrag......ous and inexcus......ble.
10. Be sure that the cashier rec......s your bill.
11. He inte......upted my train of thought and now I have forgotten what I started to say.
12. Marion finally succeeded in making them stop their arg......ment.
13. I shall send you the pictures as soon as they have been develo......ed.
14. I was extremely di......a......ointed to find that he had accomplished so little.

PRACTICE 5

Capitalization

Make the necessary capitalizations in the following sentences.
1. almost every story in this book deals with biblical heroes.
2. this is dr. howard stone; you know his brother, milton, who is also a doctor.
3. john and bill attend the same high school—fielding high school.
4. i am wondering if my mother will be able to leave early enough to make the fast train, the trail blazer.
5. this I beheld, or dreamed it in a dream:—
   there spread a cloud of dust along a plain;
   and underneath the cloud, or in it, raged
   a furious battle, and men yelled, and swords
   shocked upon swords and shields.
   —edward rowland sill, *opportunity*.
6. john said, "please come here, jim, and help me with this work."
7. when we were in england we visited oxford, westminster abbey, and stratford on avon.
8. to bring out her point effectively she quoted the new testament.
9. the meeting of the friends association will take place this coming sunday evening.
10. will you please give this book of poems to miss timmins?

PRACTICE 6

Capitalization

Capitalize whatever words you think ought to be capitalized.
1. we expect tom and thelma and the baby to spend new year's day with us.
2. we went to the theatre to see *our town* last night, and a week from tonight we are going to see *the pirates of penzance*.
3. emily and i are going to the world's fair on our vacation.
4. he asked me to lend him the book when i finished reading it.

5. my mother and my aunt sally went to the baseball game yesterday afternoon.
6. mr. stevenson is a professor of latin at the university.
7. please, father, take us to the football game saturday.
8. he said that he would bring *the new york times* home tonight.
9. the king and queen of england were guests of the united states a short time ago.
10. new york is farther south than boston.
11. last summer we spent two weeks at the browns' camp in maine.
12. james and his wife are going to spend the holiday season with us.
13. we are going to have a big party at our home on new year's eve.
14. the speaker centered his address around the frequently quoted lines from robert burns's poem *to a mouse,*
>   the best-laid schemes o' mice an' men
>   gang aft a-gley,
> an' lea'e us nought but grief and pain
>   for promis'd joy.
15. shall i begin the letter my dear sir, or just dear sir?

PRACTICE 7
Pluralization

In each of the following sentences you will find a word in parentheses. Pluralize this word and write the plural form in the blank space that is provided immediately following the word.

1. Several of them have given (analysis) .... of the situation, but no definite steps have been taken.
2. I glanced over the (write-up) .... in several of the papers and they all spoke very favorably of the play.
3. There are three or four (cemetery) .... in that vicinity.
4. It is a great challenge to all of the (democracy) ....
5. Of all the (dormitory) .... on the campus I think I should prefer to live in Clayton.
6. I am not sure which of the (academy) .... she prefers to attend.
7. I am expecting one of my (sister-in-law) .... to visit me over the coming holidays.
8. The Christmas (wreath) .... in the windows made the homes look very warm and festive.
9. The teacher wrote two (motto) .... on the blackboard.
10. The recipe calls for two (teaspoonful) .... of sugar.
11. Sir Walter Scott's poem, *The Lady of the Lake,* is presented in (canto) ....

12. The device I have just shown you is operated by the use of (pulley) ....
13. They are (alumnus) .... of the school I graduated from.
14. We liked to listen to the singing of the (thrush) ....
15. He has never stated just what his (belief) .... are in the matter.

PRACTICE 8

Possessives

Many of the words in parentheses in the sentences that follow should be in the possessive case. In the blanks provided in the margin, write the correct possessive form for these words.

1. (Frank and Jean) Aunt Marion is coming to visit them for a week.
2. Why don't you take (Mr. Sears) course? I think you will find it extremely interesting.
3. We have at least three (week) work to do on the project.
4. We greatly enjoyed (Doris) dancing and (Janet) playing.
5: These books of (Uncle John) make excellent reading.
6. My sister (Alice) new home is only about a fifteen (minute) walk from here.
7. My (mother-in-law) garden is one of the loveliest I have ever seen.
8. (Evelyn and Marion) mothers were in the same class at college.
9. The (Secretary of State) duties are very onerous and complex.
10. The (faculty) decision will be printed in the *School News* that comes out next Friday.

PRACTICE 9

Possessive Pronouns

1. Make five sentences illustrative of the use of a possessive pronoun used before a noun.
2. Make five sentences illustrative of the use of a possessive pronoun used in the predicate.
3. Make five sentences illustrative of the possessive pronouns, *yours, mine, theirs, his, ours* not in the predicate.

PRACTICE 10
Adverbs—Position in Sentence

Unless we are watchful of the position of adverbs in the sentence, we shall sometimes fail to say exactly what we mean. The adverbs that we should watch with special care are: *almost, barely ever, fully, hardly, just, merely, never, only, nearly, quite, scarcely*. In general, adverbs should be placed next to the words they modify. Note the improvement made by the changed position indicated in the right-hand column.

COLLOQUIAL	IMPROVED
I *only* talked to him once.	I talked to him *only* once.
I *nearly* told everyone at the office.	I told *nearly* everyone at the office.
I *scarcely* drank any water.	I drank *scarcely* any water.
I have *hardly* eaten a dozen waffles in my whole life.	I have eaten *hardly* a dozen waffles in my whole life.
That is the tallest tree I have *almost* ever seen.	That is *almost* the tallest tree I have ever seen.

Form sentences of your own in which each of these ten adverbs is properly placed.

1. ever
2. fully
3. just
4. merely
5. never
6. quite
7. truly
8. kindly
9. specially
10. naturally

In your use of *hardly* be particularly careful that you do not use a double negative in such sentences as these:

> I can *not hardly* climb that hill.
> He *can't hardly* make a living.

Since *hardly* is itself a negative it is wrong to introduce the extra negative *not*. We should say:

> I can *hardly* climb that hill.
> He can *hardly* make a living.

The adverbs *never* and *scarcely* occasion similar difficulties.

DO NOT SAY:	SAY INSTEAD:
He *won't never* succeed in business.	He *will never* succeed in business.
I *can't scarcely* take another step.	I *can* take *scarcely* another step.

PRACTICE 11

Grammar—Pronouns

Correct any pronouns you consider wrongly used in the following sentences.
1. Either Sally or Betty left their jacket here last night.
2. John and myself have been invited to the formal dinner party that is to be held at the Freemont Hotel Wednesday evening.
3. If you have room in your car, will you take Bill and I with you?
4. I have invited Marilyn rather than she.
5. I have played tennis longer than her.
6. If there is anyone here who has objections to this plan let them speak up now.
7. When the examination was over, everyone said that they had found it very hard.
8. I like those kind of chocolate cookies best.
9. When you have them developed, won't you send me some of them pictures you took?
10. Each of them has expressed their own opinion in this matter.

PRACTICE 12

Italicizing

Underscore the words that you think should be italicized in the following sentences.
1. I have just finished reading a very interesting article which appeared in the December issue of the Atlantic Monthly.
2. They played Beethoven's Eroica, which is one of my favorite symphonies.
3. When we went to Europe we sailed on the Leviathan.
4. I always hesitate over the spelling of the word embarrass.
5. Her pronunciation is very indistinct; she always slurs final g's, t's, and similar sounds.
6. Do you think he understands clearly now the distinction between ingenious and ingenuous?
7. I think that it might be well to include Debussy's Clair de Lune on our program.
8. Remember to pronounce the first n in the word government.
9. That is the case as it now stands, n'est-ce pas?
10. Be sure to impress every one with the fact that the material must be in by 3 o'clock on Tuesday afternoon.

PRACTICE 13

Punctuation

1. The following poem, when punctuated correctly, makes several specific, sensible statements. Can you punctuate it correctly?

> A funny old man told this to me
> I fell in a snowdrift in June said he
> I went to a ball game out in the sea
> I saw a jellyfish float up in a tree
> I found some gum in a cup of tea
> I stirred my milk with a brass key
> I opened my door on my bended knee
> I beg your pardon for this said he
> But 'tis true when told as it ought to be
> 'Tis a puzzle in punctuation you see

2. Punctuate each of these two sentences in two different ways, thereby giving each of the sentences two different meanings.

> Woman without her man is helpless.
>
> Mrs. Fiske says Miss Anglin is America's greatest actress.

3. Punctuate the following telegram in two different ways and you will get two diametrically opposite statements.

> No price too high

4. By adding a comma to the following sentence you can correct the misstatement that now exists.

> The Damson estate near Mt. Kisco was sold to Mr. Sidney Howard, a playwright as a result of an advertisement in the Westchester County News.

5. By adding a comma to the following sentence you can correct the misstatement that now exists.

> Walking sedately before the bride, came her small nephew, George Slaughter, carrying the ring and two little nieces of the groom.

George Green, a boy in the tenth grade was asked, on an examination, to correct the expression, "Leave me go." Naturally, the teacher expected the word "Let" instead of "Leave." But George knew how to punctuate, and wrote, "Leave me. Go!"

PRACTICE 14
Multiple-Choice Vocabulary Test

In each of the following sentences one word is italicized. Each sentence is followed by five words or groups of words, one of which corresponds more closely to the meaning of the underlined word in the sentence than the other four. Place in the parentheses at the end of the line the number of the word, or group of words, which corresponds most closely to the italicized word.

1. Patience is his *dominant* characteristic.
    1. only 2. endearing 3. peculiar 4. good 5. chief ( )
2. After much argument, he finally *acquiesced*.
    1. understood 2. demurred 3. refused 4. yielded
    5. departed ( )
3. The *conservation* of certain wild animals is an important study.
    1. extinction 2. history 3. distribution 4. habitat
    5. saving ( )
4. The *ebullition* of the mob increased.
    1. anger 2. disapproval 3. excitement 4. rejoicing 5. size ( )
5. He had become *inured* to city life.
    1. antagonistic 2. wedded 3. indifferent 4. accustomed
    5. averse ( )
6. They watched his *agile* motions.
    1. indolent 2. slow 3. nimble 4. pantomimic
    5. spasmodic ( )
7. The individuals are *emancipated* by the law.
    1. educated 2. governed 3. freed 4. protected
    5. restrained ( )
8. He was the *fiscal* secretary.
    1. fifth 2. private 3. foreign 4. state 5. financial ( )
9. It was an *abortive* attempt.
    1. fruitful 2. unsuccessful 3. ingenious 4. painful
    5. unwise ( )
10. The *benign* old gentleman sat alone.
    1. queer 2. emaciated 3. florid 4. insane 5. kindly ( )
11. His property was *confiscated* after the war.
    1. returned 2. renovated 3. seized 4. sold 5. unclaimed ( )
12. The *delinquency* of the children was evident.
    1. evident 2. enthusiasm 3. backwardness 4. intelligence
    5. misconduct ( )

13. These relief measures were *expedient*.
    1. suitable 2. heinous 3. politic 4. expected 5. delayed (   )
14. The *iconoclast* was imprisoned.
    1. thief 2. watchman 3. pyromaniac 4. radical 5. debtor (   )
15. The workmen tried to get some *indemnity*.
    1. increase 2. revenge 3. rating 4. compensation
    5. recognition (   )
16. The river *meanders* through the land.
    1. cuts 2. surges 3. rushes 4. flows 5. winds (   )
17. His *sardonic* expression was disturbing.
    1. satanic 2. cruel 3. scornful 4. insulting 5. passionate (   )
18. His *bucolic* manners seemed out of place.
    1. pedantic 2. irritable 3. humorous 4. countrified
    5. sentimental (   )
19. The young man is very *voluble*.
    1. versatile 2. amusing 3. enthusiastic 4. critical
    5. talkative (   )
20. He made an *egregious* error.
    1. slight 2. financial 3. gross 4. deliberate
    5. unnecessary (   )
21. The shop was filled with a *promiscuous* array of goods.
    1. confused 2. delightful 3. lavish 4. orderly
    5. attractive (   )
22. That is a *virulent* liquid.
    1. delicious 2. poisonous 3. viscous 4. spicy 5. sour (   )
23. The *accrued* interest amounted to very little.
    1. compounded 2. doubled 3. annual 4. accumulated
    5. diminished (   )
24. The *audacity* of the speech took them by surprise.
    1. vigor 2. boldness 3. bitterness 4. frankness
    5. ruthlessness (   )
25. The city was built at the *confluence* of the rivers.
    1. bend 2. source 3. junction 4. mouth 5. outlet (   )

PRACTICE 15

Lapsed-Letter Test (1)

For each of the italicized words in the right-hand column find the synonym that, fully spelled, properly supplies the blanks in the skeletonized words of the sentences.

EXAMPLE. We sat down to a s--p----s feast.   *magnificent*
(sumptuous)

1. He was presented with an award in recognition of his m--i--r--u- services.   *deserving reward*
2. He was c-g--z--t of the unfavorable factors in the proposed change.   *aware*
3. The court ruling set a p--c-d--t for similar cases.   *pattern, example*
4. Although he could not find the weakness in the argument, he was sure that the reasoning was f--l-c--u-.   *mistaken*
5. His analysis of the situation was very s--e-f--i-l.   *lacking depth*
6. Before this article is sent to the printer you should strike out the i--e--v--t paragraphs.   *unrelated.*
7. Many words were d--e--d when the water fell on the paper.   *blotted out*
8. Although the matter was not of outstanding importance, it was, on the other hand, not a matter for l--i-y.   *frivolity*
9. He uses a very c--p--h--s-v- outline as a guide for his lectures.   *inclusive*
10. The article l--d-d the charitable work the institution had done.   *praised*

KEYS TO PRACTICES

Key to Practice 1: Spelling

1. ascent
2. aisle
3. alter
4. capital
5. pendant
6. guilt
7. stationery
8. fourth
9. dual
10. compliment

Key to Practice 3: A Test in Spelling

1. dilapidated
2. acquaintance
3. √
4. √
5. planning
6. discriminate
7. √
8. apparatus, laboratory
9. √
10. √

TOOL MASTERY—COMMAND OF AUTOMATISMS

Key to Practice 4: Spelling—Supplying Missing Letters

1. pursue
2. siege, seize
3. allusion
4. transferred
5. principle
6. dissatisfied
7. dependent
8. defendant
9. outrageous, inexcusable
10. receipts
11. interrupted
12. argument
13. developed
14. disappointed

Key to Practice 5: Capitalization

1. Almost every story in this book deals with Biblical heroes.
2. This is Dr. Howard Stone; you know his brother, Milton, who is also a doctor.
3. John and Bill attend the same high school—Fielding High School.
4. I am wondering if my mother will be able to leave early enough to make the fast train, the Trail Blazer.
5. This I beheld, or dreamed it in a dream:—
   There spread a cloud of dust along a plain;
   And underneath the cloud, or in it, raged
   A furious battle, and men yelled, and swords
   Shocked upon swords and shields.
   —Edward Rowland Sill, *Opportunity**
6. John said, "Please come here, Jim, and help me with this work."
7. When we were in England we visited Oxford, Westminster Abbey, and Stratford on Avon.
8. To bring out her point effectively she quoted the New Testament.
9. The meeting of the Friends Association will take place this coming Sunday Evening.
10. Will you please give this book of poems to Miss Timmins?

Key to Practice 6: Capitalization

1. We, Tom, Thelma, New Year's Day
2. We, *Our Town, The Pirates, Penzance*
3. Emily, I, World's Fair
4. He, I
5. My, Aunt Sally
6. Mr. Stevenson, Latin, University
7. Please, Father, Saturday
8. He, *The New York Times*
9. The, King, Queen, England, United States
10. New York, Boston
11. Last, Browns', Maine
12. James
13. We, New Year's Eve
14. The, Robert Burns's, *To Mouse*, The, Gang, An', For
15. Shall, I, My dear Sir, Dear Sir

*Courtesy of Houghton Mifflin Company, Boston, Mass.

Key to Practice 7: Pluralization

1. analyses
2. write-ups
3. cemeteries
4. democracies
5. dormitories
6. academies
7. sisters-in-law
8. wreaths
9. mottoes, mottos
10. teaspoonfuls
11. cantos
12. pulleys
13. alumni
14. thrushes
15. beliefs

Key to Practice 8: Possessives

1. Jean's
2. Mr. Sears's
3. weeks'
4. Doris's, Janet's
5. Uncle John's
6. Alice's, fifteen-minute or fifteen minutes'
7. mother-in-law's
8. Evelyn's, Marion's
9. of the Secretary of State
10. faculty's, of the faculty

Key to Practice 9: Possessive Pronouns

These are examples. Your own sentences may differ.

1. a. Here are *his* skates.
   b. Do you see *their* car?
   c. *Your* sentences are excellent.
   d. *Her* understanding of the use of a restrictive clause is perfect.
   e. I saw the man and the woman in *your* car.
2. a. That mistake was *yours*.
   b. This one is *mine*.
   c. That farm is *hers*.
   d. This house is *theirs*.
   e. This trick is *ours*.
3. a. That error of *yours* was bad.
   b. Oh, that bad habit of *mine* will crop out.
   c. A child of *theirs* died.
   d. *His* diction is excellent.
   e. This tennis court of *ours* is in bad shape.

Key to Practice 11: Grammar—Pronouns

The italicized words represent the corrections.

1. Either Sally or Betty left *her* jacket here last night. (*Their* would be correct only if the jacket was jointly owned by Sally and Betty.)
2. John and *I* have been invited to the formal dinner party that is to be held at the Freemont Hotel Wednesday evening.
3. If you have room in your car, will you take Bill and *me* with you?
4. I have invited Marilyn rather than *her*.
5. I have played tennis longer than *she*.

TOOL MASTERY—COMMAND OF AUTOMATISMS

6. If there is anyone here who has objections to this plan let *him* speak up now.
7. When the examination was over, everyone said that *he* had found it very hard.
8. I like *that* kind of chocolate cookies best.
9. When you have them developed, won't you send me some of *those* pictures you took?
10. Each of them has expressed *his* own opinion in this matter.

Key to Practice 12: Italicizing

1. *Atlantic Monthly*
2. *Eroica*
3. *Leviathan*
4. *embarrass*
5. *g*'s, *t*'s
6. *ingenious, ingenuous*
7. *Clair de Lune*
8. *n, government*
9. *n'est-ce pas*
10. No italics. (Should there be some special reason for strongly emphasizing either *3 o'clock* or *Tuesday*—or both of these items, italics would be correct.)

Key to Practice 13: Punctuation

1. A funny old man told this to me.
   "I fell in a snowdrift. In June," said he,
   "I went to a ball game. Out in the sea
   I saw a jellyfish float up. In a tree
   I found some gum. In a cup of tea
   I stirred my milk. With a brass key
   I opened my door. On my bended knee
   I beg your pardon for this," said he,
   "But 'tis true when told as it ought to be.
   'Tis a puzzle in punctuation, you see."
2. Woman, without her man, is helpless.
   Woman! Without her, man is helpless.
   Mrs. Fiske says Miss Anglin is America's greatest actress.
   "Mrs. Fiske," says Miss Anglin, "is America's greatest actress."
3. No price too high.
   No! Price too high.
4. The Damson estate near Mt. Kisco was sold to Mr. Sidney Howard, a playwright, as a result of an advertisement in the *Westchester County News*.
5. Walking sedately before the bride, came her small nephew, George Slaughter, carrying the ring, and two little nieces of the groom.

Key to Practice 14: Multiple-Choice Vocabulary Test

1. chief (5)
2. yielded (4)
3. saving (5)
4. excitement (3)
5. accustomed (4)
6. nimble (3)
7. freed (3)
8. financial (5)
9. unsuccessful (2)
10. kindly (5)
11. seized (3)
12. misconduct (5)
13. suitable (1)
14. radical (4)
15. compensation (4)
16. winds (5)
17. scornful (3)
18. countrified (4)
19. talkative (5)
20. gross (3)
21. confused (1)
22. poisonous (2)
23. accumulated (4)
24. boldness (2)
25. junction (3)

Key to Practice 15: Lapsed-Letter Test (1)

1. meritorious
2. cognizant
3. precedent
4. fallacious
5. superficial
6. irrelevant
7. deleted
8. levity
9. comprehensive
10. lauded

CHAPTER II

THE CREATIVE PHASE OF WRITING

IF YOU think the phrase *creative writing* is new, I should like to have you recall the fact that the term *creative writing*, along with the term *creative reading*, was used by Ralph Waldo Emerson in his essay *The American Scholar* more than a hundred years ago. The more frequent use of the two phrases in recent times reflects the emphasis we are now placing on creative work and upon the recognition, in all kinds of learning, of the importance of initiative and independence and all purposeful designs. The word *automatism*, so frequently employed in these volumes, when divorced from creative activity has, as you are well aware, a merely mechanical or technical connotation. Used in connection with the creative process, the term automatism refers to each of those necessary tools that are directly helpful in the shaping of any product, whether that product be a statue, a picture, a cartoon, a macadamized highway, a bridge, a building, an essay, a poem, a short story, a novel, a drama, an editorial, a sermon, or indeed any form of activity that demands for its effective outcome the twofold process which we have so strongly emphasized in various sections of *Your Mastery of English*.

Creative Expression and Automatisms.

Since emphasis in the preceding chapter has fallen upon the theory and practice of the mechanical or technical achievements—the acquiring of *automatisms* necessary in written expression—emphasis in this chapter will correspondingly fall upon the thoughtful, the purposeful, the *creative* side of writing.

Such a division of emphasis, I must repeat, has no hard and fast boundaries. The mechanical and the creative do not run in parallel grooves, separate and insulated; they are cooperating agencies. The creative is the dominant factor. The automatisms, if fully mastered, stand ready at all times to lend their aid in the execution of the particular written work at hand—a business or friendly letter, an essay, a committee report, a memorandum, an outline, an agenda, the minutes of a meeting, a story, a novel, a poem, a drama, a biography, a character sketch, a radio script, advertising copy, an editorial, a feature article, a sermon—any product, indeed, in which a person is using written words and conventionalized symbols for the outward expression and recording of his thinking.

Any one engaged in the actual process of writing down his thoughts is necessarily making constant use of the many automatisms he has mastered. Every once in a while, however, his writing pace is halted. In a business report he is preparing, he starts, for instance, to use the word *principal* in this sentence: "The interest will grow less as you make each monthly payment on the *principal*." But the writer is not sure of the spelling of this last word. Should it be *p-r-i-n-c-i-p-l-e* or *p-r-i-n-c-i-p-a-l*? Let him recall this helpful device: When the meaning of the word is *rule*, end the word *principle* as *rule* ends—

ru *le*
princip *le*

In every other meaning, end the word, whether adjective or noun, with *al* — *p-r-i-n-c-i-p-a-l*.

The spelling of such a word is only one instance of the thousands where a writer with a sense of craftsmanship is sure to be interrupted during his written expression. He learns to accept such interruptions as normal, trusting that the process of gradual but constant achievement will make them less frequent. The man who stopped to master the spelling of *principal*, should never have to stop again for that particular item. Indeed, the mastery of each such item as it occurs is the way in which anyone gains control of any art.

The writer will, of course, have to stop for other decisions—items of punctuation, capitalization, compounding, abbreviations, contractions, italicizing, grammatical forms, indentions, and choice of the correct word. This last problem—not a purely mechanical one—offers a continual and a peculiarly stimulating challenge of selection and order of placement.

Interruptions must be accepted as a part of the writer's task, just as they must be accepted by every artist and by every artisan in any line of activity. Constant practice will not eliminate interruptions; it will, however, greatly reduce their number. The great compensation resides in this fact: in the very process of creative writing we are all the while achieving control over many varied kinds of automatisms. It is this creative phase of the problem which will now engage our more special attention.

Preparatory Work in Creative Writing—The Basic Importance of Clear Ideas

In all written work the matter of chief concern is a firm and familiar grasp of the idea. And you must have not merely the grasp of the general idea which you wish to express, but you must have also a clear conception of many of the separate divisions and phases of that idea. If you are to express yourself fully, clearly, and effectively in your letter, your report, or your essay—or whatever be the form of your message—you will have done some very careful prevising. You will not merely have thought *about* it; you will have thought *through* it. You will have charted your course; you will have made your blueprint. The major message will stand out in unmistakable major fashion; it will, at the same time, be effectively enforced by both a methodical division and a complete integration of its separate parts. It will, in all important instances, clearly be analyzed and fully synthesized. The analysis will properly phrase itself in outline form.

Making the Outline.

As a concrete illustration of what this general theory of major and minor divisions means when translated into the narrowed performance of a specific task, let us take a single example. You are preparing to write an explanation of a primary defect which you have discovered in your own composition practice; you are to give to your brief explanation this simple title—*My Major Difficulty in Writing*.

Here in a very condensed form is an outline that may serve to guide you in establishing the main idea and to aid you in thinking through some of the different subordinate points that will serve as supports in your analysis of the problem which confronts you in your early attempts at creative writing:

I. Major difficulty—creating and re-creating sense images
    A. Confusion in color and form concepts
    B. Confusion in sounds
    C. Limitations in identifying sensations of taste
    D. Limitations in identifying sensations of odors
    E. Lack of sensitiveness in touch responses
II. Possibility of correcting the defect

Let us now see how this outline may be worked out in a completed essay, with all ideas synthesized. Here is the first draft.

MY MAJOR DIFFICULTY IN WRITING

As I attempt to analyze my difficulties in writing, I naturally discover many personal limitations. I feel myself hampered by my lack of acquired automatisms. When I start the actual task of composition of an essay or story—or whatever I chance to attempt—I have a multitude of sensations I should like to interject at suitable places; but the actual concepts of these sensory impressions are curiously blurred and intermingled. They are too much like the appearance of objects seen through a diffusing fog; or like a general sensation of complex and mingled noises—no single one of them identified, or identifiable.

Perhaps my actual sense of sight or acuteness of vision is below the normal. When I try to visualize the unseen or the imagined, I may lack the sure perception of color and form which the accurate observer possesses. Often as I view with companions a sunset or a rainbow or the aurora, I am astonished as they name shades and tones and contours that my unpracticed eye cannot perceive.

The sounds which others are able to identify and name are equally beyond my powers. When I note the capacity of certain persons with the gift of absolute pitch, their sense of differentiation and identification seems little short of the miraculous. And yet I am not wholly deaf or wholly powerless as I walk through these areas of sound. I do get some delightful echoes when my imagination listens, for example, to "the horns of Elfland faintly blowing."

In the sector of taste perhaps my achievements are more nearly normal, but even here I am reminded of the story told of a trained wine tester. He was testing the flavor of a hogshead of Chianti. Even though he pronounced it excellent he detected, he thought, an alien flavor—very slight—of leather and iron. Later when the huge cask was emptied, the owners found at the bottom a tiny key attached to a miniature strap of leather. Surely my own sense of taste, in contrast to that of this expert, is very dull indeed.

Smells are not so difficult for me to identify. As I wander among the flowers of my garden—perhaps after an afternoon shower has cleared the atmosphere and granted the blossoms their special moment of a fuller diffusion of fragrance—many of these varied distillations I am easily able to detect and name. But again, as I contrast my powers with those of other members of my family, I am conscious of my limitations—conscious, too, of the lack of a vocabulary that would adequately convey to others the sensations that I am eager to share.

And touch—I fear that my fingers are a bit callous and my perception of heat and cold, hunger and thirst, the statuesque and the slowly moving—I fear that all these sensations are less acute in me than in those writers who have made their readers shiver with the terrible cold that overtook Tolstoi's *Master and Man*, or suffer with the blasting heat and drought of that August afternoon which Thomas Hardy describes in *The Return of the Native*—a heat that was partially responsible for Mrs. Yeobright's death:

> The sun had branded the whole earth with his mark, even the purple heath-flowers having put on a brownness during the dry blazes of the few preceding days.*

I do not propose to surrender to what is an obvious defect. There are, I think, opportunities to develop a keener receptivity to all these fine sensory impressions. Deliberate pause upon the separate sense experiences that each hour allows should serve as a distinct aid. In thinking of these various responses, I shall attempt to label them with words and phrases which will not merely be an aid to me in noting individual peculiarities but will offer specific help in conveying impressions to others. Furthermore, as I read I shall watch the methods which other writers employ and will make an earnest endeavor to share their sensations and their emotions. I shall be equally alert as I listen to the conversations of my friends. By such discipline and practice I shall hope to cure what seems now to be my chief difficulty in writing, for I realize the need for the sharp focus and the clear-cut impression. A failure to experience means a failure to express.

Getting a Firm Grasp of Ideas

The preceding essay embodies the confessions of a writer who feels that her failure in written expression is due principally to a personal lack of clearly perceived sensory impressions—a failure to experience what the well-trained or the naturally acute senses of other persons may normally experience. Because these sense impressions lack sharpness and precision of outline, the written expression lacks this coveted manifestation of sharpness and precision. If a sense impression be vague and ill-defined, it is obvious that the expression or the communication of that impression will be vague and ill-defined. Let us again be specific. Could you who have had, we shall assume, no real or imagined experience in tasting or seeing pepper-pot soup—could you possibly give to another a clear concept of the taste, color, or texture of pepper-pot? Experience, actual or imagined, must be yours before you can write vividly about it.

And what is true about such a strongly individualized article as pepper-pot is true of other ideas within the area of sensation. You must get a firm hold of what seems to you to be a fact, or truth, or concept or

---
*Courtesy of Harper & Brothers, New York.

impression before you can effectively communicate the idea to others—be that idea concrete or abstract. You may be wrong about some conception, but it does not seem wrong to you; it is perfectly clear; you can communicate it to others.

Assertions of the Ill-informed.

You have heard ignorant or ill-informed persons assert convictions that you knew were based upon a false premise or incompletely perceived factors; but because these persons had full faith in their judgments and saw things very clearly, they could—even in their ignorance—speak effectively about them. To an observer on the desert a mirage may be as real as the object itself. His description of what is a mere fancy may be as convincing as if it were an unmistakable fact. His way of expressing an untruth may possess all the stylistic qualities we desire in the expression of a truth. It is often the writer's sense of sureness that provides impelling power for his utterance.

From the standpoint of mere expression it is better for you to be confidently ignorant and carefully catch an untruth than to be confused in your thinking and carelessly muff a whole truth.

This fact, however, does not, of course, minimize the value of truth. The eventual strength and validity of utterance must have this absolute support, for others, seeing this lack will lose confidence in what you are asserting.

The greatest among the possible Samaritans to the ailing writer on the wayside is an intellectual clarity.

How Do We Get and Test Ideas?

Where do we get ideas? Most of them come from our family, our school, our associates, our experiences. As credulous children we believe what we are told or what we later read. We do not in our earlier years do much reasoning about things. We gather our concepts from those in whom we have confidence. It is our age of easy belief and acceptance. We are told that the earth is round, and though it may seem flat we repeat confidently the words—*The world is round.*

As reason develops we grow more skeptical and we begin to demand proof of certain postulates that we are asked to accept. We sometimes find the offered proofs unsatisfactory. We feel perplexed. What is told us seems contrary to our own experience and we try the difficult task of sifting truths from the maze of errors and prejudices that so often surrounds them.

THE CREATIVE PHASE OF WRITING

Oftentimes these truths do not come to us clearly. We read books, we attend lectures, we listen to conversations; but these may merely add to our confusion and perplexity. Finally, as a result of quiet and prolonged thinking, a fact, an idea, a concept, or a principle emerges; and we find our sense of logic gratified—as an inventor, after repeated trials, succeeds in making an ingenious device that really works.

Emerging Ideas.

Those of you who have stood by a photographer in a dark room and watched the development of a properly exposed film will understand the dramatic significance of an idea coming from obscurity into light. The film at first is a mere unrevealing spread of black surface. But, after the right chemicals are poured on it, this black surface begins to change; soon lights and shadows emerge. Finally the details stand out in clear, fully disclosed reality. In a similar manner, when you can perceive a stark truth, you can make it stand forth in your writing—provided, of course, you are technically proficient in handling words, sentences, paragraphs, and the necessary paraphernalia of style. Get the idea clearly in mind and then the idea will itself serve you in communicating it to others. But getting the idea clearly in mind may be a slow process.

Attempting Expression before the Thought Is Clear.

From what I have written about the help a writer secures from a clearly conceived idea, I hope no one will get the notion that he should not attempt to write or talk about a topic before the topic is clearly understood. Talk and discussion may dissolve the doubts. The mere attention that we give to our written statement of a problem may be the means of solving it.

There is some relationship, but vaguely understood, between thought and expression. Some persons—perhaps all of us—can do some thinking without words, but we often find that the complete thought is partly shrouded until it is clarified by phrasing. By setting down words or combinations of words we may be providing a method for the clearer perception of true relationships.

A Personal Experience in Clarifying a Thought.

I had, of course, long known that there is an intimate connection between the mechanical side of language and creative expression—

both oral and written. I had of course known, too, of the similar connection between the mechanical side of reading and the process that allows us to understand and appreciate certain selections that we read. But the varied relationships were general, vague, and ill-defined. They became clearer when I one day set down in my notebook, in contrasting positions, these paired items:

Mechanics . . . . . . *The creative process*

Then I experimented with other similar contrasts:

Tools. . . . . *Products which the tools produce*
Techniques. . . . . . . *What techniques accomplish*
Skills. . . . . *What applied skills produce*
Automatic acts (automatisms) *Creative or purposeful activity*

The word *automatisms*, when somewhat arbitrarily limited to *correct responses*, includes all those reactions that we make unconsciously. You will recall the paragraph on "Habit" which I quoted from William James's *Psychology*. He tells, you remember, how very important it is for us to train our minds so that they will perform a multitude of functions unconsciously, spontaneously, *automatically*. It is by this means that our mental powers are freed for their higher activities—activities that are purposeful, productive, *creative*. The more numerous our acquired mental automatisms are—other things being equal—the more effective our mental activities.

All these contrasts—the twofold aspects of behavior—are, you will note, general in character. Naturally I wished to apply them to the narrowed sphere in which my more special interests lie—the field of English. I set down, first, these contrasted items:

Automatisms . . . . *Creative English expression*

But as there are two kinds of creative expression—oral and written—I sought a separate division for each.

Automatisms in oral expression . . *Creative oral English expression*
Automatisms in written expression . *Creative written English expression*

I next made a similar division for reading:

Automatisms in reading English . . *Creative reading in English*

A Corrective Note.

Although I had set these out as a series of contrasts, I realized the need for strict accuracy demanded explanatory comment. Each two pairs of processes—the one on the right and the other on the left— have indeed this twofold aspect; the processes contrast because they are different, but not because they oppose each other; the processes are, on the contrary, genuinely cooperative. Moreover, we do not learn a whole elaborate set of automatisms and then use them all in a later series of creative tasks; in the midst of our creative work we are daily acquiring new automatisms. The two processes, as we have repeatedly discovered, are closely interlinked, closely interwoven, closely interleaved. Those on the left are the *means;* those on the right the *ends* to be accomplished; those on the left are *tools* to be used in fashioning the *products.*

Concrete Listing of Items

We all realize that one great test of our mastery of a major idea is our ability to list minor items comprehended by the major. You make some such general statement as this: "Most of our larger American cities are near some great body of water." "For instance?" New York; Boston; Philadelphia; Chicago; Cleveland; Detroit; San Francisco; Baltimore; New Orleans; Buffalo. So, with the general statement, "To speak efficiently we must have many automatisms at our fingertips."

Use the same type of test. Prepare a selected list of *automatisms necessary for oral expression;* and a second list of *types of oral expression.*

SELECTED LIST OF AUTOMATISMS NECESSARY FOR EFFECTIVE ORAL EXPRESSION

I. WORDS
   Meaning
   Pronunciation
   Enunciation
   Emphasis
   Correct grammatical form of nouns, pronouns, verbs, adjectives, and adverbs.

II. PHRASES
   Distinction between the idioms and phrases that are and are not acceptable.

III. SENTENCES
>   Recognition of sentence patterns
>   Inflection of tone

IV. VOICE
>   Pitch
>   Pace
>   Modulation
>   Inflection
>   Emphasis

Automatisms function orally in purposeful and creative ways in these forms:

A SELECTED LIST OF TYPES OF CREATIVE ORAL EXPRESSION

Narration—stories, personal experiences, incidents, adventures, dreams, fables
Conversation
Telegraph and telephone messages
Group discussions and individual talks
Explanations, directions, reports
Radio talks
After-dinner speeches
Producing plays
Oral book reviews
Oral précis making
Solving puzzles or problems
Making decisions and explaining them

None of these various types of creative oral expression can be effectively presented by a speaker who has not acquired a certain degree of control of the four different kinds of automatisms in the preceding list. Continued practice in conversation and public speaking will of course result in an ascendingly higher degree of mastery.

I applied the same method of testing to the second kind of expression—written language expression. At first I made a list of certain items that I labeled *automatisms in written expression;* I followed this with a list of various kinds of *creative expression in written English.* Here are the two lists:

THE CREATIVE PHASE OF WRITING

I. Selected List of Automatisms in Written Expression

A. THE WHOLE COMPOSITION
1. Place and capitalization of title
2. Spacing between title and beginning line of the theme
3. Spacing between letters, lines, and words
4. Margins—top, bottom, and sides
5. Numbering the pages of the theme
6. The forms of business and social letters

B. PARAGRAPH
1. Indentation
2. Length

C. SENTENCES
1. Capitalization of beginning words
2. End punctuation marks
3. Inner punctuation marks
4. Form or pattern

D. PHRASES
1. Distinction between idioms and phrases that are and are not sanctioned by good usage

E. WORDS
1. Meaning
2. Spelling
3. Capitalization
4. Italicizing
5. Abbreviations
6. Special symbols
7. Contractions
8. Compoundings
9. Syllabication—hyphen at end of line
10. Correct forms of nouns, pronouns, verbs, and other parts of speech—*any correct language response, in short, which through drill or through habitual repetition becomes automatic*

II. Selected List of Items Which Illustrate Creative Expression in Written English

A. Narration-stories, personal experiences, incidents, adventures, dreams, fables

B. Conversation as set down in written form
C. Telegraph and telephone messages
D. The substance of a letter, business or social
E. Reports on group discussions and individual talks
F. Explanations, directions, recipes, reports
G. Radio scripts
H. Outline of talk, report, or theme
I. Writing plays
J. Writing verses
K. Producing plays
L. Criticism of books
M. Précis making
N. Expansion of topic sentence
O. Solving puzzles or problems
P. Making decisions and explaining them in written form

After I had finished this dual topic of English expression, I ventured upon the problem of reading. Again I separated the process into the *automatic* and *creative*, remembering as I did so what William James had said about automatisms and what Emerson had said about creative reading.*

The two lists follow:

I. SELECTED LIST OF AUTOMATISMS NECESSARY FOR EFFECTIVE READING

A. THE PRINTED PAGE AS A WHOLE—GENERAL APPEARANCE
Margins—top, bottom, and sides
Division into sections or chapters
Running title at top of page
Title of particular selections
Line spacing
Word spacing
Graphs
Pagination
Variations in kinds of type

---

*I remembered, too, what Ruskin had written in *Sesame and Lilies*. Ruskin takes a passage from Milton's *Lycidas* and analyzes it with such minute care that one who habitually reads poetry or prose hastily and perfunctorily is amazed to discover what he has missed. The essayist not only helps us to read Milton's poem *creatively;* he employs a method that will aid us to read any selection, poetry or prose, creatively. This matter of *creative reading* and its relation to *creative writing* is emphasized repeatedly in the course on *Your Mastery of English.*

THE CREATIVE PHASE OF WRITING

B. PARAGRAPHS

Indentation of paragraphs
Varied length of paragraphs
Conventional capitalization of letters and words
Conventional use of italic type, and other type forms
Abbreviations
Contractions
Punctuation marks
Compounding of words

C. SENTENCES

Appearance of sentence patterns
Conventional capitalization
End punctuation marks
Inner punctuation marks

D. WORDS

Meaning
Spelling
Capitalization
Italicizing
Abbreviations
Special symbols
Contractions
Compoundings
Syllabication—hyphen at end of line

II. SELECTED LIST OF ITEMS THAT CREATIVE READING DEMANDS

A. Understanding the exact meaning of the author's words, sentences, and paragraphs
B. Getting the writer's main ideas, mood, and general design of the entire selection
C. Sharing the writer's emotion, humor, and sense impressions
D. Appreciating the author's style
E. Subjecting the writer's thoughts and opinions to challenge and judgment

All these various subtopics can be merged into this single assertion: Creative reading means that one first enters as fully as possible into coincident thinking, sensing, and feeling with the writer and then subjects the whole to personal challenge and judgment.

I have analyzed in the preceding paragraphs the steps which I followed in the clarifying of a major concept. They are not the exact steps that anyone else would follow, but they undoubtedly are analogous to certain processes which each of you may have individually experienced as a significant idea, once hazy in your mind, has cleared itself from the curtaining murk to stand at length fully disclosed. In its clear revealed outline it is now like that fully developed film that the hypo bath in the dark room has fixed with its unmistakable configuration in lights and shades.

The process of thinking through a hazy topic is not an easy one. It offers, however, the reward of seeing in clear vision and proper perspective a view that was previously vague, hazy, or distorted—or, to change the figure, to accord with the title of this section, you learn the satisfaction that comes with an acquired ability *to grasp an idea firmly.*

We gain from our analysis of our topic a higher respect for creative work in English. With a greater acquired skill in routine performance we see what futile creatures we would be if we should not apply our tools to the effective fashioning of a worthy product. "In God's name," says Carlyle, "create something!" Ideas are all about us. Take them and fashion them into a worthy product—a letter, a report, a set of minutes, a conversation, a contribution at a conference, a radio talk, a magazine article, an essay, a short story, a debate, a panel discussion, a critical comment on a political principle—any written or oral expression that provides an outlet for your creative exuberance.

Study carefully your own creative writing, even though your attempts be limited to the informal letters that you send to your friends or to members of your own family. Read them over before you mail them. If a particular one is stupid or trite or hazy—or faulty in some unnamable way—slip it into the grate and write another for the mailbox.

You will get valuable suggestions from the study of the creative writings of others. Nor am I now thinking principally of the methods of our professional writers; I am thinking also of the help we can derive from an examination of the writings of business men intent upon the clear presentation of their ideas—ideas that have an important bearing upon their practices and policies.

A Discussion of an Industrial Problem

Here is a report prepared by Alfred P. Sloan, Jr., the Chairman of the Board of General Motors Corporation—a report that summarizes certain significant facts concerning the automobile industry. It is reprinted with a few inconsequential deletions. Analyze its structure and apply your discoveries to this problem of creative writing.

THE AUTOMOBILE INDUSTRY—ITS FUTURE GROWTH*

It is traditional that the automobile industry has grown and prospered as it has been able to provide better value for the customer—as it has made its products available for the use and enjoyment of an increasing number through improving quality and lowering real prices. This has been a continuous and evolutionary process and one that has resulted in the ownership within the United States of approximately 70% of all the world's motor cars. Furthermore, the development through research of better means and methods for utilizing the products of forest, mine and farm —all of which participate in the industry's increasing productivity —has, through increased values and lower prices, in turn meant new job opportunities, larger payrolls and added contributions to the economy as a whole.

These long term factors have had, and should continue to have, an important favorable effect on the development of the automobile industry. Economically, however, the volume of automotive sales, and more particularly year to year fluctuations, must necessarily vary as national income goes up and down. The most outstanding characteristics of this relationship are two: (a) as the trend of the national income changes from year to year, the volume of automobile sales falls below the average relationship when business declines and rises above when business improves, and (b) the volume of the industry increases in general at an accelerated rate as the level of the national income rises.

The reason for the first relationship is that in periods of lowering national income prospective purchasers become conservative in their outlook. They are inclined to continue to use cars already in their possession. Under such circumstances there results a reduction in the total car mile inventory, as represented by the condition of the cars in use. Conversely, when business is improving customers become more liberal in their purchases as their confidence in the future increases, hence the number of new cars sold increases more rapidly. This is reflected in an increase in the inventory of car miles in the hands of users through the accelerating purchase of new cars. Such changes in buyers' psychology, together with the fluctuation in national income, make the automobile industry subject to sudden and wide ups and downs in volume.

As to the second relationship, there is economic justification for

---

*Reprinted by courtesy of The General Motors Corporation.

the fact that the volume of the automotive industry increases at an accelerated rate with rising national income. As that income rises, there is a widening spread between income and the normal outlay for the essentials of food, shelter and clothing—the necessities of life, let us say. This margin of income over and above what is needed for such bare necessities, permits the purchase of comforts, conveniences and luxuries, thereby adding to the enjoyment of life, improving the standard of living and accelerating our economic and social progress.

The higher the national income rises the more this spread is reflected down through the lower income groups, thus accelerating new car sales and superimposing upon such sales still additional sales due to the stimulation of the used car market—an important limiting factor in the sale of new cars. Thus a greater portion of the community enjoy new cars. More families become two or three car owners. And a far greater number are able to afford better used cars, or to become used car owners.

It is important here to call attention to the distinction between the number of cars and trucks that may be sold in any one year and the total number registered, or in use, during that year. This is shown on the chart on the right of the center page spread. Actual sales of motor cars during the past twenty years have been subject to wide variations, as already explained, and as indicated on the chart. On the other hand, ownership as measured by the number of vehicles registered shows a persistent upward trend until 1929. Even since 1929—a period generally characterized by uncertain business conditions—the registration of passenger cars and trucks in the United States has increased more than 10%, indicating the extent to which the motor car has become a permanent and an essential part of the daily life of the community and the importance placed upon it as a means of individual and commercial transportation.

Since 1929 the rate of increase in total registrations, or motor vehicles in use, has materially lessened, being to an important degree the result of sharply lowered levels of national income characteristic of the past ten-year period. This has an adverse effect upon the productivity of the automotive industry in that fewer sales are made to new users of cars. In addition, the average age of cars in use has become greater, which means fewer replacement sales. At the same time the inventory of available car miles in the hands of owners has been substantially lowered, even taking into consideration the greater mileage being built into the recent products.

These facts seem to be perfectly clear. When the economic barriers that have been erected during the past few years against the expansion of enterprise are removed and business can go forward with confidence as to its future opportunities, there will be assured to the automotive industry a reservoir of demand represented by the shortage in inventory of car miles now existing. And as the national income increases there are possibilities for expansion in the number of car users through the broader spread between this increased income and the cost of the necessities of life. Thus, there does not seem to be any justification for believing that the automotive industry has reached the maximum of its growth. While its development cannot be expected to continue at the rapid rate that characterized the earlier years, there is every reason to believe that as soon as our national policies permit the resumption of a normal upward trend in the national income, the automotive industry will enjoy, and at an accelerated rate, a degree of that prosperity.

—Alfred P. Sloan, Jr., *Chairman*

Perhaps for the foregoing report, *The Automobile Industry—Its Future Growth*, the author constructed—actually or mentally—some such outline as this.

Outline of the Automobile Industry— Its Future Growth

I. INTRODUCTION
Automobile industry has systematically provided America with better products at lower prices. At the same time it has provided employment for a large number of workers.

II. BODY
A. Volume of national products varies with national income.
1. As business declines sales decrease
a. Customers grow conservative and hesitate to spend
2. As business improves, sales increase
a. Customers develop confidence in their power to earn and purchase
b. Volume of sales grows at an accelerated rate, because margin of cash savings increases
B. Rate of registration likely to continue through depression years, even though the volume of sales may be less. Business demands cars and trucks.

III. CONCLUSION
When barriers are removed against business, the automobile industry will expand; it will supply the accumulated shortage of the depression years.

This outline is, as indicated, only a surmise. The report may possibly have been prepared with no actual, objective listing of topics. They may have existed merely in the writer's mind and found their ordering and their phrasing only in the process of the composition. Of this, however, we may be sure: items similar to those set down in the outline were in the author's mind, and they finally found expression in the closely organized material that appears in the printed paragraphs.

By this emphasis upon the written outline I do not mean to imply that every excursion into the writing field demands the sort of definite blueprint which I have described. Certainly most of us do not bother with these preliminaries when we start to write a friendly letter. And the very informal essay may, I suppose, properly trace its uncertain pattern as it saunters along its irresponsible way. Some short stories and novels, their authors have later confessed, were written without any methodical prevising. Some of the long serial narratives of Dickens and other famous novelists, for example, developed only as the editor's demands for each succeeding issue grew insistent.

Plays, too, have occasionally been written with loose structure and unprevised denouements. And, once the play has been tried out before an audience, changes are often made. Some plays, indeed, are provided with gaps for "*ad libbing.*"

We are, however, clearly conscious of the painstaking efforts that go into the outlining of all writers who have a serious task to perform and wish to do it in a craftsmanlike manner. The outline, analogous to the architect's blueprint or the traveler's sketched itinerary, is designed as an economy measure—to ensure a consistent course, to provide a proper allotment of space for various topics, to avoid omissions, to secure coherence and unity—to carry out the intent in the most efficient way.

Each day you are likely to be doing something significant in the field of creative writing. Your telegrams, your business correspondence, your reports, your friendly and your family letters, your office memoranda, the varied units of work that your pen or pencil or typewriter records—all these are to be classified as examples of creative writing. The term, in short, includes any form of written expression which creatively sets forth in words your thoughts, fancies, facts, opinions, comments, criticisms, dreams, feelings, convictions, doubts, meditations, experiences, plans, or desires. It is power to put such expressions

THE CREATIVE PHASE OF WRITING

into recorded form. This power, among other achievements, helps to distinguish man from the other creatures of this earth.

Out of this discussion of creative writing there emerges then, the salient fact that the best preparation for writing is a perfectly clear understanding of the things you are going to say. If you are to tell a story, know that story perfectly; if you are to describe a scene, know that scene as thoroughly as you know your own living room or office; if you are to write an explanation—of a new machine, a game, a change in business procedure, a process in manufacture, a new method of farming, or the application of a federal law to your own business—be sure you know the necessary facts; if you are to present an argument, gather all the material necessary to sustain your own reasons and overthrow the defense of your opponents. Thorough preparation, thorough organization, thorough prevising, perfect clarity of conception—these supply you with your best support for the written presentation of your ideas. One of the devices that will prove of great practical help is a carefully prepared outline; it is to a writer what a chart is to a navigator or what a blueprint is to an architect.

Outlines and Outlining

Later we have an outline of a short bit of composition work entitled *Our Conversation Club*.* This outline represents the attempt to previse the topic. It is primarily concerned with the major idea which the words of the title express—*Our Conversation Club*. But the mind is at the same time almost equally concerned with the subordinate ideas—the officers, the members, the proposed place of meeting, the time of meeting, and with plans for the evening program. These articulating parts provide the substance of the theme and serve as the supports. You will note, as you examine it, just how the entire outline is formed and how its plan is ordinarily determined by silent hearkening to the voice of simple logic and systematic arrangement.

Definition of an Outline.

An outline, we may therefore affirm, is an orderly arrangement of the various important ideas that are to be included in an oral or a written unit of expression. It is particularly applicable to an exposition or an argument.

---
*See Book Three, Chapter III.

The symbols and forms ordinarily used to indicate the relationship of the different ideas that compose an outline are indicated by the following arrangement, which reveals a system of coordination and subordination.

```
I. _____
   A. _____
   B. _____
      1. _____
      2. _____
         a. _____
         b. _____
         c. _____
         d. _____
            (1)* _____
            (2)* _____
               (a)* _____
               (b)* _____
II. _____
```

The Topical Outline.

Let us apply this system of outlining to a general topic in which we are all interested—the way that we do our writing. We can give our special topic the title, *Steps in Writing an Essay*. After concentration upon this particular idea, we may reduce the results of our thinking to this form—a form that discloses four main steps with sub-points under each.

A Sample Outline in Topical Form for a Short Composition Entitled "Steps in Writing an Essay"

I. PRELIMINARY THINKING
    A. Narrowing the topic
    B. Phrasing of title to express the dominant notion
    C. Forecasting the general mood and trend

---

*Only in rare instances will the degree of subordination be carried as far as the divisions indicated by the symbols (1), (2); (a), (b). Indeed, most outlines will be very simple—only two or three steps in subordination. Even in a rather detailed brief only four degrees may be employed.

II. MAKING THE DETAILED OUTLINE
   A. Choosing between the topical and the sentence forms
   B. Arranging the coordinating and subordinating ideas
III. WRITING THE FIRST DRAFT
   A. Submitting to the outline as guide
   B. Rapid writing of first draft, with only slight attention to the nicer points of phrasing
IV. REVISING AND REWRITING
   A. Testing unity, coherence, and emphasis in the whole
   B. Testing unity, coherence, and emphasis in the paragraph
   C. Testing unity, coherence, and emphasis in the sentence
   D. Correct mechanical errors, as, wrong spelling, capitalization, grammar, punctuation, indentation, diction, abbreviations, and division of words at end of line

The type of outline illustrated here is known as a *topical outline*. In a topical outline the divisions and the subdivisions name ideas that are expressed by phrases or by single words.

The Sentence Outline.

The contrasting type of outline expresses its separate ideas in complete sentences. This second type, which we may call the *sentence outline*, is illustrated by the following skeletonized concept of a theme in a different field, but one in which all of us are individually concerned.

BASIC PRINCIPLES IN A PERSONAL SAVINGS AND
INVESTMENT PROGRAM

THEME: Every person who desires to be financially independent should be guided by certain investment principles which the experiences of the years have established. There are seven which are of general application.

I. As soon as your earning period begins, plan to put aside a certain portion of your monthly wage.
   A. A good savings bank will provide safety.
   B. A good cooperative bank may provide safety and incentive for more regular saving.
   C. Some form of insurance policy should be purchased.

II. When five hundred dollars or more are available it may be advisable to invest in a home, a small farm, or in stocks or bonds.
   A. A home offers a satisfying sense of permanency and security.
   B. A small farm is desirable for those in special situation or of special tastes.
   C. Stocks and bonds when fortunately chosen offer income and reasonable security.

III. As the investment fund grows, it should be reasonably diversified.
   A. Since economic conditions change so rapidly, concentration in a single security or a single type of security involves too great a risk.
   B. There should be a proper allotment of funds among bonds, common stocks, preferred stocks, and other sorts of investments, such as real estate or partnerships.
   C. Those with limited capital may secure diversity by purchasing stocks of well-managed investment trusts.

IV. Only persons who have reasonably high incomes should buy speculative stocks; but speculative stocks may at times offer special opportunities and may be purchased by those who can afford to take risks.
   A. Mining stocks, though highly speculative, may prove profitable.
   B. Money placed in new inventions, though speculative, may bring high returns.

V. Funds, however conservatively placed, must be vigilantly watched.
   A. Changes in the neighborhood may impair real-estate values.
   B. New inventions may render valueless certain industries in which your funds are invested.
   C. Changes in fashion increase values in one direction and decrease them in another direction.
   D. The business cycle may endanger or enhance values.

VI. Investment problems can be satisfactorily solved only by considering the individual needs and situation.
   A. Annuities may be desirable for those who have no dependents, but persons buying these annuities should hedge against inflation.
   B. Where liberal incomes are secure, reasonable risks can be taken, but a widow, or anyone with small capital, should guard against speculation.

  C. Likelihood of continued invalidism makes strong special demands.
  D. Investment returns must always be measured by the tax situation.

VII. It may be admitted that there are no investments which are absolutely safe, for war and world economics are unpredictable. Experience, however, does beget confidence in United States Government bonds, insurance companies, and savings banks. Even though returns are meagre, funds are reasonably secure. Indeed one of the truths to remember in considering the investment problem is this: Safety and security are reasonably possible only in areas where the income return is slight.

Whether you use this form or the topical-outline form is a matter of personal preference.

Writing Without the Outline.

A person may have formed the habit of writing or dictating reports —or other documents—without first preparing an outline. This procedure, it may be freely admitted, is possible for one who has a logical mind and a retentive memory. Such a person has prevised the main topic, made its subdivisions, and arranged a plan of attack. The entire scheme exists only in the mind; but it has been so clearly prevised, that the development into a complete whole reveals the logic that governed the process.

There are other persons who never form an outline of any sort. They take a topic, think about it carefully, become impressed with one point which they deem important, reduce to written form their ideas upon that particular point, and lay those written paragraphs to one side and trust the future to fit them into place. As other sections are written, they, too, are set aside. The distributions are a bit haphazard; but there is a faith in the writer's mind that final revision, a due attention to transitional sentences, and a liberal use of the rhetorical chisel and mortar will result in a creditable mosaic.

The Outline a Safe and Serviceable Guide.

A method like the preceding can seldom be wholly satisfactory structurally; the sutures are likely to be too obvious and the neighboring bits rigid and sundered. We can, accordingly, rather definitely assert the value of a plan. The habit of careful prevising that finds its visible and finished results in the prepared outline—perhaps revised and re-revised—is, for most writers, the safer and the more satisfactory method. It is an economy measure. It saves your time; it saves you from the extra effort of revision; it develops your power of logical sequence and relationships—both coordinate and subordinate. The completed outline is the first tangible award for each particular creative task. The second award comes when the finished piece of writing lies before you—clearly phrased, neatly typed, correctly paged—a complete artistic unit.

Specific Suggestions

Following out any method that you wish, set forth a complete outline of some topic on which your thoughts have recently focused. The topic may be directly related to your daily work, or it may be one on which you have done some casual reading but no systematic study. The list that follows is merely suggestive:

1. Why Nations Engage in War
2. The Possibilities of an Enduring Peace
3. The Salient Points in the Presidential Campaign
4. The Faults and Virtues in My Education
5. How Luck Has Played Her Game With Me
6. The Three Factors That Have Most Influenced My Life (or Opinions)
7. An Objective Analysis of My Own Personality
8. Laying Out My Plans for Adult Learning
9. A Current Book Worth Recommending
10. Further Mastery of My English

Main and Subordinate Ideas.

Let us take another illustration and see how this plan of developing a major idea is helpfully furthered by discovering and naming the subordinate ideas. The major concept with which you are now toying, concerns the sorts of writing you prefer to read—not the sorts that can be identified by naming the forms of discourse, such as letters, poetry, biography, narration, description, exposition, or argument; and not such sorts as are definitely divisible into newspapers, periodicals, and books. You are not thinking of these objective categories. What you would like to discuss in your essay centers upon matters less tangible;

they are points of style. Choosing from all the various forms of discourse and from writings that may be found in newspapers, periodicals, and books, what are some of the characteristics that, you discover, have for you a very strong personal appeal?

In your endeavor to phrase a title that effectively conveys this concept, you hit upon the word *flavor*. In choosing ice cream, you are guided by your flavor preferences. In reading, you prefer certain bits of writing because they have a certain flavor. Can you embody that idea in your title? Try this: *Flavors in the Writings I Enjoy*. But there are so many flavors you enjoy. You cannot mention all of them, but you can mention certain ones that appeal to you personally.

Now do a bit of *prevising*. Force the results of prevising into the matrix of an outline.

OUTLINE—CERTAIN FLAVORS IN THE WRITINGS I ENJOY

I. FREE ACKNOWLEDGMENT OF PREFERENCES
   A. Humor
   B. Picturesqueness
   C. Rhythm
   D. Sincerity

II. DANGERS IN NARROW LIMITINGS

Now that you have this little chart to serve as your guide and compass, go out into the wide open spaces and see what sort of quarry you can capture. Here, perhaps, is the net result of the chase.

CERTAIN FLAVORS IN WRITINGS I ENJOY

Is there any reason, I wonder, why we should not freely confess our major reasons for reading. I am not referring to our morning and evening indulgences that the press supplies. Of course we want to be informed about the daily happenings — depressing though the news may be. Nor am I thinking of the sort of reading that our particular occupation may suggest—the farm journal, the trade paper, the shopping news. I am focusing comment upon the sort of literary provender that is untouched by the ravages of time and is concerned with the function of delighting and nourishing the inner spirit of human beings. I am thinking of those passages or stanzas or generous selections that carry with them the more enduring and the more endearing flavors within the substance of words. There are many, many of these flavors, but I am selecting for illustration and comment only four. They will serve to give you a hint of what I had in mind when I phrased the central idea of this short essay on certain flavors that literature distills.

The first of these four is *Humor* ... It may be the type of humor that produces the explosive laugh, but more likely it is the pleasant turn or the skillful probing that finds its outlet in the inner chuckle or the scarcely discernible smile. You will better understand one phase of what I mean when I recall for you W. S. Gilbert's apostrophe *To the Terrestrial Globe*,*

> Roll on, thou ball, roll on!
> Through pathless realms of Space
> Roll on!
> What, though I'm in a sorry case?
> What, though I cannot meet my bills?
> What, though I suffer toothache's ills?
> What, though I swallow countless pills?
> Never *you* mind!
> Roll on!
>
> Roll on, thou ball, roll on!
> Through seas of inky air
> Roll on!
> It's true I've got no shirts to wear;
> It's true my butcher's bill is due
> It's true my prospects all look blue—
> But don't let that unsettle you!
> Never *you* mind!
> Roll on!
>
> [*It rolls on.*]

The second flavor I have chosen is labeled *Picturesqueness*. It is the sort of quality that veers away from the ordinary grooves and allows originality to carve its cameos in its own inventive ways. The first person who used the word *skyscraper* was, you see, not following the crowd who were content with calling it a *tall building*. I am thinking too of Anne Lindbergh's remark in *Listen, the Wind* when, after a series of fatiguing vexations and embarrassing delays which she and her famous husband experienced, finally one night they were able to crawl into a restful bed and *pull the comforting dark over their heads*.

And the third flavor I have listed is *Rhythm*. I am not thinking merely of the rhythms in poetry, though as I write, many of them are repeating their echoes in my innermost ear. I am thinking as well of the rhythm of prose. As a matter of fact I have never been able to draw a satisfactory boundary line between the two.

As a revealing example of this difficulty of drawing a clean-cut boundary line between prose and poetry, I am quoting here a sentence written by a physicist who was deeply intent upon his reso-

---
*Courtesy of The Macmillan Company, New York.

lution to express as clearly as possible the simple idea that there is no force that can stretch a strand of thread or string into a perfectly straight horizontal position. He phrased this idea in these words:

> There is no force, however great, can stretch a cord however fine, into a horizontal line that shall be absolutely straight.

Some anonymous person later pointed out that this sentence, written as prose, is a perfect example, perfect in its meter and rhyme, of what we have come to designate as the *In Memoriam Stanza*—though, as a matter of fact, Tennyson was not the first poet to employ it.

Printing the sentence in verse form, we have this:

> There is no force, however great,
> Can stretch a cord, however fine,
> Into a horizontal line
> That shall be absolutely straight.

The rhythmic echo from poetry that for some reason which I cannot fathom is now silently beating out its measured tones is set in the musical blank verse of John Milton. You will find the lines at the very close of *Paradise Lost*. For to Adam and Eve paradise is now indeed lost; they are saddened exiles yielding with reluctance, yet with resignation, their forfeited garden to others.

> Some natural tears they dropped, but wiped them soon;
> The world was all before them, where to choose
> Their place of rest, and Providence their guide.
> They, hand in hand, with wandering steps and slow,
> Through Eden took their solitary way.

As an illustration of the beauty of rhythmic prose I could choose—as any lover of literature could—scores upon scores of examples. Several possibilities come to me at this moment, but I discover the unseen oscillating needle that is to dictate my selection is resting now upon a passage that you yourselves, after reading *The Forsyte Saga*, might perhaps have selected. I am thinking of old Jolyon's last hours on that burning Indian summer afternoon as he sat with his dog Balthasar under the oak tree by the swing waiting for the beautiful well-groomed Irene in her gown of violet-grey—the beautiful Irene to whom the Fates were to deny him the privilege of holding out his hand in a joyously cordial welcome.

> It was quite shady under the tree; the sun could not get at him, only make the rest of the world bright so that he could see the Grand Stand at Epsom away out there, very far, and the cows cropping the clover in the field and swishing at the flies with their tails. He smelled the scent of limes, and lavender. Ah! that was why there was such a racket of bees. They were excited—

busy, as his heart was busy and excited. Drowsy, too, drowsy and drugged on honey and happiness; as his heart was drugged and drowsy. Summer—summer—they seemed saying; great bees and little bees, and the flies too!

The stable clock struck four; in half an hour she would be here. He would have just one tiny nap, because he had so little sleep of late; and then he would be fresh for her, fresh for youth and beauty, coming towards him across the sunlit lawn—lady in grey! And settling back in his chair he closed his eyes. Some thistledown came on what little air there was, and pitched on his moustache more white than itself. He did not know; but his breathing stirred it, caught there. A ray of sunlight struck through and lodged on his boot. A bumble-bee alighted and strolled on the crown of his Panama hat. And the delicious surge of slumber reached the brain beneath the hat, and the head swayed forward and rested on his breast. Summer—summer! So went the hum.

The stable clock struck the quarter past. The dog Balthasar stretched and looked up at his master. The thistledown no longer moved. The dog placed his chin over the sunlit foot. It did not stir. The dog withdrew his chin quickly, rose and leaped on old Jolyon's lap, looked in his face, whined; then leaping down, sat on his haunches, gazing up. And suddenly he uttered a long, long howl.

But the thistledown was still as death, and the face of his old master.

Summer — summer — summer! The soundless footsteps on the grass!*

The fourth flavor on my list is more difficult to identify by a brief citation. *Sincerity* in writing somehow impregnates the passages of a selection just as it does the life of a good man or woman. Often you cannot tell how you get from your talk and associations with a person this conviction of absolute honesty and forthrightness of being. The sentence of one who is strikingly insincere may be identical with the sentence uttered by the one who is strikingly sincere, yet the one somehow betrays his fault and the other his virtue. Perhaps it is in the mode of utterance, a revealing posture, a glance of the eye, or a character-labeling gesture. There are comparable items in style.

Dorothy Canfield Fisher, reviewing *These Are Our Lives*, a book which relates actual experiences of many wage-earning men and women of North Carolina, closes her comment with a paragraph which touches directly this important topic of sincerity in writing.

> Authentic first:—the first impression, the final impression made on the reader by these life stories is that they are true, that they have not been doctored to make them prove anything, either by the person who took them down in their rambling, deliciously folksy lingo, or by any editor in the WPA office. I have never

---

*Copyright, 1920, Charles Scribner's Sons, New York.

set foot in the deep South myself, I know nothing about the life of the working people there. I do not need such special knowledge, only experience of life itself to feel that this volume is authentic. It has that unmistakable accent of natural, unforced truth-telling which speaks out from an honest voice, a clear and honest eye. And how racy with the rich diversity of humanness are these tales! With what easy power they tear down out of the mind the cheap and foolish idea that "poor people" are different from other people! Here are we, ourselves, as we would be if we had been born Southern wage-earners, white or black—as we are. Those commentators who have exclaimed that this book contained "invaluable" and "vivid" and "pungent" stuff are right. But first of all these should have told us that it is the very stuff of living.*

This enumeration of flavors is incomplete. There are others that I enjoy—many others that the majority of readers enjoy.

The Finished Essay.

The foregoing comment on the satisfying flavors in style is your captured quarry. But let us be very honest in our account of its origin, its development, and its final form.

As you view this little essay in its printed dress, you will not assume that these brief paragraphs slipped from under a rapidly coursing pen —or perhaps from underneath the roller of the typewriter—in the precise form they have here. Writing is difficult. To think of it as easy is to think of it ignorantly. An examination of the manuscripts of famous authors reveals their fallibility. Their revisions and deletions and their testimonies concerning the pages they have rewritten and destroyed—all these reinforce the story of the false startings and false steppings common to the beginner not yet expert in his craft.

Only with study and practice may improvement come. Common mistakes will become less frequent; tangled thoughts and phrasings will be more easily unsnarled; the minutiae of the mechanical side of writing will prove less bothersome. But only with practice.

PRACTICES

The various practices that follow are offered as a means for your further perfection in the mechanics of English, since you must, for the fashioning of your product, keep your tools well sharpened. You must be more and more proficient in spelling, punctuation, capitalization, vocabulary, grammatical forms, derivatives,—indeed in all the processes that add to your store of automatisms.

---

*Copyright, 1939, *The Key Reporter*.

PRACTICE 1
Errors in English

1. Mrs. Edmund L. Trobridge, the former Miss Nettie Lemon, was recently married in the Second Church of Emmoryville; *they* will live on Chestnut Street.
2. I *can't hardly* see in this dark closet.
3. The sound of the many voices *were* confusing to the speaker.
4. If I had thought of this happening I would never have *went* on that picnic.
5. Here is one of the pencils which *sells* for seven dollars a gross.
6. I never thought of *it's* effect on the crowd.
7. Look! *There's* John and Robert at the upstairs window.
8. She was asked to write a sonnet. *Which* was something she could not do.
9. John said to George that *he* could not go.
10. The cast has finished *its* practice and *have* gone to their separate homes.

Comments and Corrections.

1. The pronoun *they* has no antecedent. Instead of *they*, say, *Mr. and Mrs.* Trobridge.
2. Here is an example of the double negative; instead of *can't hardly*, say *can hardly*.
3. Since the subject of the sentence is *sound*, a singular noun, we must have a singular verb in the predicate. Change *were* to *was*.
4. We should never say *have went*; say *have gone*.
5. Change *sells*, a singular verb, to *sell*, a plural verb. The antecedent of the relative pronoun *which* is *pencils*. As *pencils* is plural, *which* is plural—and demands a plural predicate.
6. The possessive form of the personal pronoun *it* is *its*. The apostrophe is used for the contraction *it is*.
7. Change *there's*—a contraction of *there is*—to *there are*. The subject of the sentence is *John and Robert*—a compound that requires the plural predicate *are*.
8. Do not allow your relative clause to stand alone; make it a part of the sentence. Change the sentence to read, "She was asked to write a sonnet—a task, which, she said, she could not do."
9. This sentence is ambiguous; you can make the meaning clear by one of two possibilities:
    - (*a*) John said to George, "You cannot go."
    - (*b*) John said to George, "I cannot go."

10. The collective word *cast* may, as subject of a sentence, take either a singular or plural verb in the predicate. The choice depends upon the desired implication: if you wish to imply that the cast is a single unit the verb should be singular—*has finished*. Here, however, because the *members have gone to their separate homes*, you should use the plural verb—*have finished*. The revised sentence would then read, "The cast *have* finished *their* practice and *have gone* to *their* separate homes." An altered form, with a slightly different implication, is possible; "The cast has finished its practice; each member has gone home."

PRACTICE 2

Homonyms

In each of the following sentences you will find a pair of homonyms in parentheses. In the blanks provided in the margin write the one that satisfies the meaning the sentence is trying to convey.

1. It will be impossible to (affect, effect) this change without the permission of the director.
2. Our old homestead has been torn down and a new building is now being erected on the (site, cite).
3. The terms of the (peace, piece) treaty were rejected.
4. The dress was made of a very delicate and (shear, sheer) material.
5. There is a lovely picture of Janet on the (mantle, mantel) above the fireplace.
6. Jim is still a (miner, minor) and so he cannot vote in this election.
7. In her haste she pulled up the (root, route) of the flower too.
8. It would be better if the chairs in the classroom could be made (stationary, stationery).
9. Many important issues are at (stake, steak) in this campaign.
10. I am going to (brows, browse) around the library this afternoon.

PRACTICE 3

A Homonym Test

In each of the following sentences are two or more blanks in which the dashes represent the number of letters in the words to be inserted.

All of the omitted words in any one sentence are spelled and pronounced alike, but each has a different meaning.

                  lay   lay

EXAMPLE: The --- member --- in the hammock and whistled an ancient ---.
                                                                                                               lay.

1. The ------ bay, the creditor ------ his debtors, the ------ of the wagon are broken.
2. The ----- pursued "the even ----- of his way," but I did not grasp the ----- of his remarks.
3. In spite of my ------- orders, they failed to ------- the package by -------.
4. As the queen mounted the steps of the -----, two members of her ----- held up her -----.
5. It was a frail -----, but the boatman was clever at his -----.
6. The posse started to ----- the thief, but lost him halfway along the -----, although he had left behind him a ----- of lost articles.
7. In the ------ of the day, he had purchased a suit of clothes, and had matriculated at the university for a ------ of study.
8. The hen must ----- her -----, but she need not ----- over her troubles.
9. As the cock ----, the boat ---- took to the oars.
10. Connect the two words with a -----. Practice down to the first -----. ----- yourself for an onslaught.
11. The ------ squeaked as we came to a sudden stop beside a bank covered with rusty-brown ------.
12. You may ---- a bell, you may ---- a person, you may pay, or collect, a ----.
13. It required a ----- man to ----- a ----- in war-paint and feathers.
14. I met a ----- girl in a ----- blue dress, walking up the hill. When she spoke it was ----- that she was also a ----- speaker, though not in what the Friends call "the ----- language." Probably, too, she frequently had a ----- hand in cards.
15. As the ------ of the boat went adrift, John's ------ heart prompted him to ------ his assistance.
16. Take a definite -----, then ----- by your decision, and sit down at that ----- and write the letter.

17. We had a picnic on the - - -, and rowing homeward across the bay, we sang (somewhat out of - - -) until suddenly John interrupted in a plaintive - - - exclaiming, "I forgot my - - -." And that was the - - - to the situation in the story which follows.
18. As they sat on the - - - - - - -, he said, "I must - - - - - - - my house," and she said, "I must go to the hair-dresser's and have her - - - - - - - my hair."
19. As the - - - - - - - prepared to start the picture, the - - - - - - - broke and the little boat drifted away.
20. As they stood beside the - - - - -, Bill told Frank that he would - - - - - no more of his insolence.
21. The - - - - - - - came alongside and after we had put into it some of the load and the girl with the - - - - - - - hair, the boat was - - - - - - -.
22. He was - - - - - - than King Lear. He wove - - - - - - blossoms into his hair and colored his face with - - - - - -.
23. Said the - - - - -, "It is of - - - - - importance that you understand the - - - - - premise.
24. As the - - - - - - - -, in his - - - - - - - - robe, walked in the garden, he paused a few moments to listen to the singing of a - - - - - - - -.
25. I saw a knight with a - - - - - - on his head stoop and pick up a piece of - - - - - -.

PRACTICE 4

Punctuation of Sentences

Punctuate the following sentences.
1. What you don't really mean that he asked excitedly
2. There are several interesting ideas presented in this article ideas that are provocative and challenging
3. One thing is certain they will not arrive before Friday
4. Two understudies were asked to fill in at the last moment consequently the performance was a bit disappointing
5. He suffered from a weak heart this limited his activity a great deal
6. He came on time last night something he rarely does
7. In spite of his many failures he did not give up but continued to pursue the course he had set for himself
8. He is the only man who actually witnessed the accident
9. Mr. Ingles entered upon his shoulder he carried his little niece
10. They put on Shakespeare's *Merchant of Venice* which was a great favorite with the group

PRACTICE 5
Punctuation of Sentences

Punctuate the following sentences.

1. This is my cousin Marion who has come to stay with me for our Christmas vacation
2. John said that he would join us as soon as his work was finished
3. Yes I'll be glad to lend you the book for a week
4. There were oranges pears bananas grapes and peaches in the bowl
5. While we were eating a stranger knocked on the door
6. The first few chapters were very dull but important for they gave the necessary introductory information
7. You may turn on the radio very softly and I shall go into the next room where I can read
8. It is possible however that the picture will meet with such popularity that it will be held over a second week
9. The house is very small all the rooms are on one floor
10. There were two alternatives the first was to take a chance and call on the telephone the second was to send a special delivery letter

PRACTICE 6
Restrictive and Non-Restrictive Clauses

Punctuate the following sentences.

1. The two boys who had gone to the World's Fair were asked to give short talks about what they had seen
2. Students who wish to register for part time work must fill out their applications before 5 o'clock on Friday
3. Shelley's *Adonais* which was written in honor of John Keats is one of my favorite poems
4. I hope that I shall be able to answer all the questions that appear on our final examination
5. William Howard who has been assistant buyer of the men's clothing department has just been appointed buyer in Mr. Munroe's place
6. All of the portraits which are on display in this exhibit were done by the same artist
7. When the fog lifts you will be able to see the island which is just across the bay
8. The young man who took the lead in the amateur performance we saw last night shows a great deal of promise
9. Here is the book that I have been looking for
10. The boy who is walking toward us has just been elected president.

PRACTICE 7
Sentence Structure

Arrange each of the following groups of four simple sentences into a complex or a compound complex sentence.

1. We opened the door.
   We found an old man standing there.
   He was stooped and bent over.
   He leaned heavily on his cane.
2. The sky grew very dark.
   A thunder storm seemed threatening.
   We gathered our picnic things together.
   We hurried back to the car.
3. The players came on the field.
   The crowd cheered.
   The whistle blew.
   The game started.
4. This is an interesting book.
   It is a collection of adventure stories.
   The stories are well written.
   Children like the book.

PRACTICE 8
Punctuation of Paragraphs

Punctuate and capitalize the following paragraphs.

1. i would not change my way of life for yours said she we may live roughly but at least we are free from anxiety you live in better style than we do but though you often earn more than you need you are very likely to lose all you have you know the proverb loss and gain are brothers twain it often happens that people who are wealthy one day are begging their bread the next our way is safer though a peasant's life is not a fat one it is a long one we shall never grow rich but we shall have always enough to eat

   —Leo Tolstoy, *How Much Land Does a Man Need?*
   translated by Aylmer Maude

2. no race indulges more lavishly in hospitality and entertainment to close the door against any human being is a crime every one according to his property receives at a well-spread board should it fail he who had been your host points out your place of entertainment and goes with you you go next door without an invitation but it makes no difference you are received with the same courtesy

stranger or acquaintance no one distinguishes them where the right of hospitality is concerned it is customary to speed the parting guest with anything he fancies there is the same readiness in turn to ask of him gifts are their delight but they neither count upon what they have given nor are bound by what they have received
—Tacitus, *Germania*, translated by Maurice Hutton

KEYS TO PRACTICES
Key to Practice 2: Homonyms

1. effect
2. site
3. peace
4. sheer
5. mantel
6. minor
7. root
8. stationary
9. stake
10. browse

Key to Practice 3: A Homonym Test

1. hounds
2. tenor
3. express
4. train
5. craft
6. trail
7. course
8. brood
9. crew
10. brace
11. brakes
12. toll
13. brave
14. plain
15. tender
16. stand
17. key
18. shingle
19. painter
20. brook
21. lighter
22. madder
23. major
24. cardinal
25. morion

Key to Practice 4: Punctuation of Sentences

1. "What! You don't really mean that?" he asked excitedly.
2. There are several interesting ideas presented in this article—ideas that are provocative and challenging.
3. One thing is certain—they will not arrive before Friday.
4. Two understudies were asked to fill in at the last moment; consequently the performance was a bit disappointing.
5. He suffered from a weak heart; this limited his activity a great deal.
6. He came on time last night—something he rarely does.
7. In spite of his many failures he did not give up, but continued to pursue the course he had set for himself.
8. He is the only man who actually witnessed the accident.
9. Mr. Ingles entered; upon his shoulder he carried his little niece.
10. They put on Shakespeare's *Merchant of Venice*, which was a great favorite with the group.

Key to Practice 5: Punctuation of Sentences

1. This is my cousin Marion, who has come to stay with me for our Christmas vacation.

THE CREATIVE PHASE OF WRITING

2. John said that he would join us as soon as his work was finished.
3. Yes, I'll be glad to lend you the book for a week.
4. There were oranges, pears, bananas, grapes, and peaches in the bowl.
5. While we were eating, a stranger knocked on the door.
6. The first few chapters were very dull, but important, for they gave the necessary introductory information.
7. You may turn on the radio very softly, and I shall go into the next room, where I can read.
8. It is possible, however, that the picture will meet with such popularity that it will be held over a second week.
9. The house is very small; all the rooms are on one floor.
10. There were two alternatives: the first was to take a chance and call on the telephone; the second was to send a special delivery letter.

Key to Practice 6: Restrictive and Non-Restrictive Clauses

1. The two boys who had gone to the World's Fair were asked to give short talks about what they had seen.
2. Students who wish to register for part time work must fill out their applications before 5 o'clock on Friday.
3. Shelley's *Adonais*, which was written in honor of John Keats, is one of my favorite poems.
4. I hope that I shall be able to answer all the questions that appear on our final examination.
5. William Howard, who has been assistant buyer of the men's clothing department, has just been appointed buyer in Mr. Munroe's place.
6. All of the portraits which are on display in this exhibit were done by the same artist.
7. When the fog lifts, you will be able to see the island* which is just across the bay.
8. The young man who took the lead in the amateur performance we saw last night shows a great deal of promise.
9. Here is the book that I have been looking for.
10. The boy who is walking toward us has just been elected president.

Key to Practice 7: Sentence Structure

1. When we opened the door we found a stooped old man standing there, leaning heavily on his cane.
2. When the sky grew very dark we realized that a thunderstorm was

---

*With no comma after *island* the intention is to restrict the meaning to the *one island which is across the bay;* with a comma after *island,* the intention is to describe the place of the island. *You will be able to see the island*—and *it is just across the bay.*

threatening, so we gathered our picnic things together and hurried back to the car.
3. When the players came on the field the crowd cheered; then the whistle blew and the game started.
4. This collection of well-written adventure stories is an interesting book, and children like it.

Key to Practice 8: Punctuation of Paragraphs

1. "I would not change my way of life for yours," said she. "We may live roughly, but at least we are free from anxiety. You live in better style than we do, but though you often earn more than you need, you are very likely to lose all you have. You know the proverb, 'Loss and gain are brothers twain.' It often happens that people who are wealthy one day are begging their bread the next. Our way is safer. Though a peasant's life is not a fat one, it is a long one. We shall never grow rich, but we shall always have enough to eat."*

—Leo Tolstoy, *How Much Land Does a Man Need?* translated by Aylmer Maude

2. No race indulges more lavishly in hospitality and entertainment; to close the door against any human being is a crime. Every one according to his property receives at a well-spread board; should it fail, he who had been your host points out your place of entertainment and goes with you. You go next door, without an invitation, but it makes no difference; you are received with the same courtesy. Stranger or acquaintance, no one distinguishes them where the right of hospitality is concerned. It is customary to speed the parting guest with anything he fancies. There is the same readiness in turn to ask of him. Gifts are their delight, but they neither count upon what they have given, nor are bound by what they have received.†

—Tacitus, *Germania*, translated by Maurice Hutton

---

*Courtesy of the Oxford University Press, London, England.
†From the *Loeb Classical Library*, courtesy of the President and Fellows of Harvard College.

CHAPTER III

PRACTICES ON CREATIVE WRITING

PERHAPS you have read a good many books that told you how to write. Telling another person how to write is a good deal like telling someone how to swim, or skate, or play tennis. There are, to be sure, hints that may be given, but naturally the real test comes in the actual doing. In your case, you realize, as you think of getting your thoughts down on paper, that you are not a novice. You have done a great deal of writing—done it along with your daily routine of living and earning your living. But now you are a little more serious about the way you are going to do the task. Let's make an assumption.

You are interested in writing something and you are determined to do the work just as well as you can. Is it a letter to a friend? Is it a suggestion to your partner or employer? Is it a report that you as head of a department are making to your firm? Is it a contribution to the mailbag of your morning paper? Is it an essay for your club? Is it an incident that you would like to get down in written form? Is it a proposal for some civic improvement in your community? Is it an announcement of your candidacy for some office? Is it a character sketch? Is it a biography? Is it a simple description of a bit of landscape that caught your eye as you were yesterday riding along the Dover Road? Is it a comment on a book or magazine article that you have recently read? Is it an account of your own method of writing?

Unless the matter be very slight, very transitory, very informal, the first act is one of prevision—the careful anticipation of the finished written product and the orderly steps necessary in the process.

PRACTICES

You will note that the Practices here provided place little emphasis upon the acquirement of automatisms; they deal, instead, with theme and organization. They encourage original prevising and original writing. They are prepared with the conviction that we learn to do by doing. The experiments that we make in our written expression tend, at the same time, to develop both the mastery of mechanics and facility in creative production.

PRACTICE 1

Making the Outline

For illustrative purposes, let us assume that you have in mind a new club that you would like to see formed—a club that you have tentatively named *Our Conversation Club*. Concentrating your thought upon this idea, you decide to set forth the plans in systematic form. When the main idea and the subordinate ideas are in clear perspective, you finally draw up a brief outline.

PLAN FOR OUR CONVERSATION CLUB

I. OFFICERS
    A. President
    B. Secretary

II. MEMBERS
    A. Men and women
    B. Representatives of varied tastes, interests, and occupations

III. PLACES OF MEETING
    A. Homes of members
    B. Annual banquet at hotel or clubhouse

IV. TIME OF MEETING
    A. First and third Wednesday of each month at 8 p.m.
    B. From November through May

V. PROGRAM FOR EACH MEETING
    A. Conversation centered on definite topic
        1. Leader's introduction
        2. Members' informal discussion
    B. Simple refreshments
    C. Informal social meeting

The Writing of the Theme.

With the outline as your guide, you now proceed with its development into a finished piece of writing. Here you should proceed as speedily as possible. Commence at the beginning and develop your paragraphs and sentences as fully and as freely as a first draft permits. Do not bother too much with mechanical details. Select your words with reasonable care but do not be too fussy. You will naturally have a fair control of your sentence patterns, your paragraph structure, and the powers that enable your written document to reveal your intended meaning.

When the actual task of writing or typing this first draft is complete, you will, of course, feel the need for carefully revising it, because no matter how carefully you drew up your outline or how clearly you prevised the whole, errors will have crept in. You will not be satisfied with certain words you have chosen, certain sentence patterns you have formed, certain paragraphs you have constructed. Possibly there will be misspellings, mistakes in grammar, faults in unity, coherence, or emphasis. Painstaking revision is always a part of the craftsmanship of good writing.

The outline for *Our Conversation Club* may be developed into the short essay. After you have read this first draft, consider carefully the various ways in which revision would improve it.

Before you read the finished theme try writing one of your own, following carefully the outline. Compare your essay with the one below.

OUR CONVERSATION CLUB

Most of us would probably agree with a recent writer who asserted that among the most vital forces in education—forces that exert influences both good and bad—are the immediate companions whom we meet in our informal relations. These companions may be the members of our family, our associates in business, the guests who visit us in our homes, the hosts who entertain us at dinner parties, the men and women and young people with whom we come in contact at school, at church, at community gatherings, or in the routine transactions of our daily occupational experiences. Ordinarily we too severely limit our concept of education; we think of it as a formal process—the process of the schools. Of course the schools are important; but may it not be true, as a matter of fact, that the most vital, the most lasting, the most direct educational drives spring from our informal contacts?

A small group, convinced of the force of this doctrine, is deeply interested in forming a conversation club, where simple, friendly procedures will grant us an opportunity of sharing in this sort of mutual, informal, intensely personal education.

The officers would be few in number—perhaps a president, who would conduct the meetings and have general directing powers, and a secretary, who would keep whatever records are necessary and assume responsibility for such duties as commonly rest with such a functionary. The routine work would be extremely

28. Organized Religion in the Modern World.
29. Systematic Enlargement of My Vocabulary.
30. Budgeting My Time.
31. My Daily Hour in Creative Writing.
32. Planning My Next Tour.
33. Preaching a Sermon to My Listening Self.
34. Reviewing My More Serious Mistakes.
35. Disciplining Children.
36. Disciplining Parents.
37. Disciplining Myself.
38. Lost Alignments.
39. Experimenting With Paragraphs.
40. Reorganizing My Office.
41. Leakage in Profits.
42. Re-embarking in Business.
43. The Moral Responsibility of Being Well Dressed.
44. Establishing Credit.
45. Mirrored Imperfections.
46. Conflicting Desires.
47. Acquiring New Automatisms.
48. An Objective View of My Family.
49. An Objective View of My Business Associates.
50. Our Neighboring Hospitals.

Do not feel under any special obligation to use any of the suggested titles. Change the wording in any way you please—or choose a topic in which you have a vital personal interest—one that will stimulate you to your most vigorous expression.

Perhaps you have noticed that none of these are especially *timely*—they probably do not touch directly upon the events that our daily press is now headlining. Such references have indeed been purposely avoided. We are in these volumes dealing with ideas that have a permanent rather than a transitory interest. But in your choice of a topic for outlining and development into a finished form, you may prefer to select one of strong current appeal.

PRACTICE 3

Creative Reading

Ralph Waldo Emerson in his essay *The American Scholar* discusses the good and bad uses of books. If the reading of books makes you passive and dependent, you had better avoid them; if the reading stimulates you to do your own active thinking, you should cherish them. They help to give you a look toward the future; they perform a creative function. Read this short extract and get Emerson's enthusiasm for the creative powers of man—powers that have in them something of the divine.

But genius always looks forward. The eyes of man are set in his forehead, not in his hindhead. Man hopes. Genius creates. To create,—to create,—is the proof of a divine presence. Whatever talents may be, if the man create not, the pure efflux of the Deity is not his;—cinders and smoke there may be, but not yet flame. There are creative manners, there are creative actions, and creative words; manners, actions, words, that is, indicative of no custom or authority, but springing spontaneous from the mind's own sense of good and fair.

A little further on in *The American Scholar* you find the paragraph which contains the two phrases of which I have spoken—*creative reading* and *creative writing*.

One must be an inventor to read well. As the proverb says, "He that would bring home the wealth of the Indies must carry out the wealth of the Indies." There is then creative reading as well as creative writing. When the mind is braced by labor and invention, the page of whatever book we read becomes luminous with manifold allusion. Every sentence is doubly significant, and the sense of our author is as broad as the world. We then see, what is always true, that as the seer's hour of vision is short and rare among heavy days and months, so is its record, perchance, the least part of his volume.

You will do well to reread this extract many times. You must indeed be an inventor to read—really read. In real reading you think what the author thinks; you sense what the author senses; you feel what the author feels. Of course you do not necessarily accept these thoughts, these sensations, these emotions as your own. Your thinking and sensing and feeling are your initial efforts to understand what he is saying; you will later subject this to impartial challenge. You will weigh it on your experience scales. Should you write out the results of this challenging and this weighing—expressing in what you write your honest personal judgments—you would, in the wake of this creative reading, be doing a bit of creative writing.

Try it immediately after rereading the two extracts from *The American Scholar*. Concretely you could do this. Read a paragraph or two—more, if you like—from Jack London's *To Build a Fire*, or from a story of your own selection, and then tell how completely— or how incompletely—you have entered into the author's thought, sense, feeling, or emotion.

PRACTICE 4
Objective and Subjective Methods

In order that readers of *Your Mastery of English* may have at hand a story that makes constant appeals to the sensation of cold, we are reprinting here Jack London's story *To Build a Fire*.

Note that we catch the first cold breath in the first sentence: "Day had broken exceedingly cold and gray." A few lines later: "There was no sun nor hint of sun." And in the next paragraph: "The Yukon lay a mile wide hidden under six feet of ice."

As you follow the lines, carefully list in sequence the words and phrases that indicate objectively the severity of the cold.

Later you will find another method used—the *subjective*. The method is known as *description by effect*. The author first, you see, gives us the objective facts—the temperature is 50 below zero! Yes, colder than that; it was 75° below zero—107° of frost. But these bare facts are not so impressive as the facts that come later. Soon the cold becomes ominous: the traveler's spittle crackled explosively in the air; his red beard became frosted solidly. Later he became frightened. Even the dog, the big native husky that trotted by his side "experienced a vague, menacing apprehension that made it slink along at the man's heels."

As you continue your study, you will discover the importance of the later objective facts that are mentioned, but they are of deeper importance because of the effect upon the unnamed traveler who gradually senses more and more clearly the menacing effect that finally brings the closing catastrophe.

Here is an illustration of what the psychologist calls empathy. You feel yourself growing cold, you are suffering with the traveler; you are chilled with his chill; numbed with his numbness; frozen with his freezing. Read carefully to see how these effects are produced.

TO BUILD A FIRE[*]
As Condensed by the "Reader's Digest"

Day had broken exceedingly cold and gray when the man turned aside from the main Yukon trail and started up a little-traveled trail which led through the fat spruce timberland. It was nine o'clock. There was no sun nor hint of sun. Though the day

---

[*]From *Lost Face*, by Jack London, copyright, 1910, The Macmillan Company. Courtesy of Mrs. Charmian London.

was clear, there was a gloomy pall over the face of things. This did not worry the man. It had been days since he had seen the sun.

He flung a look back along the way he had come. The Yukon lay a mile wide and hidden under six feet of ice and snow. North and south, as far as his eye could see, was unbroken white. But the absence of sun, the tremendous cold, the strangeness and weirdness, made no impression on the man. It was not because he was long used to it. This was his first winter here. The trouble with him was that he was without imagination. He was quick and alert in the things of life, but only in the things, not in the significances. Fifty degrees below zero impressed him as being cold and uncomfortable, and that was all. It did not lead him to meditate upon his frailty as a creature of temperature, able to live only within certain narrow limits of heat and cold.

As he turned to go on, he spat speculatively. There was a sharp, explosive crackle that startled him. He spat again. And again, before it could fall to the snow, the spittle crackled. He knew that at 50 below, spittle crackled on the snow; but this had crackled in the air. Undoubtedly it was colder than 50 below. But the temperature did not matter. He was bound for the old claim on Henderson Creek. He would be in camp by six o'clock: the boys would have a fire going, and a hot supper ready.

He plunged in among the big spruce trees. The trail was faint; in a month no man had come up or down. At his heels trotted a dog, a big native husky. The animal was depressed by the tremendous cold. It knew this was no time for traveling. Its instinct told it a truer tale than was told the man by his judgment. In reality, it was not merely colder than 50 below zero; it was 75 below zero. That meant 107° of frost! The dog experienced a vague, menacing apprehension that made it slink along at the man's heels, questioning eagerly every unwonted movement as if expecting him to go into camp and build a fire. The dog had learned fire, and it wanted fire.

The man's red beard was frosted solidly, the ice deposit increasing with every breath he exhaled. If he fell down, this crystalline beard would shatter itself, like glass, into brittle fragments. As he walked along he rubbed his cheek-bones and nose with the back of his mittened hand. The instant he stopped they went numb. He was sure to frost his cheeks, he knew, but frozen cheeks were never serious.

He was keenly observant of where he placed his feet. Once, coming around a bend, he shied abruptly. The creek, he knew, was frozen to the bottom, but there were springs that bubbled out from the hillsides and ran along under the snow. They were traps, hiding pools of water that might be three inches deep, or three feet. That was why he had shied in panic. He had felt the give under his feet and heard the crackle of a snow-hidden ice-skin. And to get his feet wet in such a temperature meant danger.

At 12 o'clock the day was at its brightest, yet the man cast no shadow. The sun was too far south to clear the horizon. The man unbuttoned his jacket and drew forth his lunch—carried against his naked skin to keep the biscuits from freezing. The action consumed but a quarter of a minute, yet in those seconds the numbness laid hold of the exposed fingers. He struck the fingers against his leg and returned them to the mitten. He tried to take a mouthful of biscuit, but the ice-muzzle of his beard prevented. He had forgotten to build a fire and thaw out. He chuckled at his foolishness, and as he chuckled he noted that the stinging which had first come to his toes when he sat down was already passing away. He wondered whether the toes were warm or numb, and decided they were numb.

He was a bit frightened. That man from Sulphur Creek had spoken the truth when telling how cold it sometimes got. And he had laughed at him! That showed one must not be too sure of things. He got out matches and proceeded to make a fire. From the undergrowth he took firewood. Working carefully from a small beginning, he soon had a roaring fire, over which he thawed the ice from his face and ate his biscuits. For the moment the cold was outwitted. The dog took satisfaction in the fire, stretching out close. When the man pulled on his mittens, settled the ear-flaps of his cap, and took the creek trail, it yearned back toward the fire. This man did not know cold.

Then it happened. At a place where the soft, unbroken snow seemed to advertise solidity beneath, the man broke through. He wet himself halfway to the knees before he floundered out to the firm crust.

He cursed aloud. This would delay him an hour, for he would have to build a fire and dry out his footgear. He climbed the bank. On top, tangled in the underbrush about the trunks of several small spruce trees, was a high-water deposit of dry firewood. He threw down several large pieces for a foundation. The flame he got by touching a match to a small shred of birch bark that he took from his pocket.

He worked slowly and carefully, keenly aware of his danger. He squatted in the snow, pulling the twigs out from their entanglement in the brush and feeding directly to the flame. He knew there must be no failure. When it is 75 below zero, a man must not fail in his first attempt to build a fire—that is, if his feet are wet. If his feet are dry he can run along the trail and restore circulation. But the circulation of wet and freezing feet cannot be restored by running when it is 75 below.

The cold of space smote the unprotected tip of the planet, and he received the full force of the blow. But now he was safe, for the fire was beginning to burn with strength. He remembered the advice of the old-timer on Sulphur Creek, and smiled. The old-timer had been very serious in laying down the law that no man must travel alone in the Klondike after 50 below. Well, here he was; he had had the accident; he was alone; and he had saved himself. Yet he had not thought his fingers could go lifeless in so short a time. Lifeless they were, for he could scarcely make them grip a twig, and they seemed remote from his body. When he touched a twig, he had to look and see whether he had hold of it. The wires were down between him and his finger-ends.

Before he could cut the strings of his moccasins, it happened. It was his fault—or, rather, his mistake. He should not have built the fire under the spruce tree. The tree carried a weight of snow, and each time he had pulled a twig he had agitated the tree. One bough capsized its load of snow, which grew like an avalanche as it descended without warning upon the man and the fire; and the fire was out!

The man was shocked. It was as though he had just heard his death sentence. Then he grew very calm. It was up to him to build the fire again. Even if he succeeded, he would likely lose some toes. He gathered dry grasses and tiny twigs. He could not bring his numbed fingers together to pull them out, and in this way he got many bits of green moss that were undesirable, but it was the best he could do.

When all was ready he reached in his pocket for a second piece of birch bark. He could hear its crisp rustling, but try as he would, he could not clutch it. He threshed his arms back and forth, beating his hands against his sides. After a time the first far away signals of sensation in his fingers grew stronger till they evolved into a stinging ache that was excruciating, but which the man hailed with satisfaction. He stripped the mitten from his right hand and fetched forth the birch bark, then his bunch of sulphur matches. But the cold had already driven the life out of his fingers. In his effort to separate one match from the others the whole bunch fell in the snow, and his dead fingers could not clutch them. He drove the thought of his freezing feet out of his mind, devoting his whole soul to the matches. He watched, using the sense of vision instead of touch, and when he saw his fingers on each side of the bunch, he willed to close them; but the wires were down.

After some manipulation he managed to get the bunch between the heels of his mittened hands and carried it to his mouth. The ice crackled and snapped when by a violent effort he opened his mouth and picked a match with his teeth. Twenty times he scratched it against his leg before he succeeded in lighting it. But the burning brimstone went up his nostrils, causing him to cough spasmodically. The match fell into the snow and went out.

The old-timer was right, he thought in a moment of controlled despair: after 50 below, a man should travel with a partner. Suddenly he bared both hands, caught the whole bunch between the heels of his hands, and scratched the matches along his leg. They flared into flame, 70 sulphur matches at once! As he held the blaze to the birch bark, he became aware that his flesh was burning. He could smell it. He jerked his hands apart. The birch bark was alight. He began laying twigs on the flame.

He could not pick and choose, for he had to lift the fuel between the heels of his hands, but he cherished the flame carefully and awkwardly. It meant life. The cold made him shiver, and he grew more awkward. A large piece of green moss fell squarely on the little fire, his shivering made him poke too far, and the twigs were hopelessly scattered and went out.

A poignant and oppressive fear came to him as he realized that it was no longer a matter of merely losing hands and feet. It threw him into a panic, and he ran up the creek bed, along the old, dim trail. The running made him feel better. Maybe, if he ran on, his feet would thaw out; and anyway, if he ran far enough, he would reach camp and the boys.

It struck him as curious that he could run at all on feet so frozen that he could not feel them when they struck the earth. He seemed to skim along above the surface, but several times he stumbled, and finally he fell. When he tried to rise, he failed. He must sit and rest, he decided, and next time he would merely walk and keep on going. He noted that he was feeling quite warm and comfortable. And yet when he touched his nose or cheeks there was no sensation. Then the thought came to him that the frozen portions of his body must be extending. He tried to keep this thought down, for he was afraid of the panic it caused. He started another wild run.

And all the time the dog ran with him. When the man fell down a second time, it curled its tail over its forefeet and sat in front of him, facing him, curiously eager and intent. This time the shivering came more quickly upon the man. The frost was creeping into his body from all sides. The thought drove him on, but again he staggered and pitched headlong.

It was his last panic. When he had recovered his breath, he sat up and entertained in his mind the conception of meeting death with dignity. He was bound to freeze, and he might as well take it decently. With this new-found peace of mind came the first glimmerings of drowsiness. A good idea, he thought, to sleep off to death. There were worse ways.

"You were right, old hoss; you were right," the man mumbled to the old-timer of Sulphur Creek. Then he drowsed off into the most comfortable sleep he had ever known.

The dog sat facing him and waiting. The brief day drew to a close in a long, slow twilight. There were no signs of a fire, and never in the dog's experience had it known a man to sit like that in the snow. As dusk drew on, its eager yearning for the fire mastered it, and it whined. But the man remained silent.

The dog crept close to the man and caught the scent of death. This made the animal bristle and back away. A little longer it delayed, howling under the cold stars.

Then it turned and trotted up the trail in the direction of the camp where, it knew, were the other food-providers and fire-providers.
—Jack London

PRACTICE 5
Re-creating Odors by Words

The article that follows is typical of many that appear on the woman's page of many a daily paper. Since this particular article is evidently written by a woman who is keenly sensitive to fragrant odors, it is reprinted here, with the suggestion that you test your own powers of re-creating in words the odors you hold in pleasant memory. Here are only a few of the odors you are to imagine: *lavender, marigold, mallow, green moss.* Reproduce these—and all the rest that the Well-Groomed Lady must have very keenly experienced as she wrote these aromatic paragraphs.

WELL-GROOMED LADY
*Finds Complete Line of Herbal Cosmetics
And Is Happy with Memories They Arouse*

The Well-Groomed Lady nourishes a positive passion for herbs. She had a very lovely great-aunt whose bureau drawers were always scented with delicate herbs, done up in satin cases. And this same gentle elderly lady always seemed to have a fragrance all her own, so that even now, as the Well-Groomed Lady walks down the street, past a lavender vendor, she can see in her mind's eye, very clearly, her great-aunt.

And then when it became almost a fashion to start a herb garden in your backyard, or even your window box, she followed right along, inspired by her pleasant memories. She has since discovered a whole line of cosmetics which are made with herbs, different and satisfying.

Of course, they make the Well-Groomed Lady think of English countrysides, but more than that of familiar scenes round and about New England. And as women of an earlier generation used "potions" made from the oils of herbs and flowers so now do women use creams and lotions made from the same secret formulas.

The cleansing creams are so aromatic as to smell clean, if you know what the Well-Groomed Lady means. They are soothing, too, and whisked on and off several times a day will almost make you forget that you live in a grimy city. One is called Marigold, the other Rose Mallow, the former for normal or oily skins, the latter for dry. There's a smoothing cream, a lubrication treatment, which comes in Marigold and Rose Mallow and the foundation cream of the series is also compounded of herbs. Calendula is contained in the Marigold series, known for its soothing effect and mild astringency. The Rose Mallow, true to its name, has rose mallow oils which have always proved beneficial to dry skins.

There are astringents and lotions with such enticing names as these: elder flower, milk of peaches, rose petal. There is a motorist's balm, and the Well-Groomed Lady, remembering the effects of brisk weather on her face, made a mental note of that. The Floral Cleansing Milk is a grand thing for career girls to have, to clean up before that date.

The bath essences range from carnation, a spicy, but delicate scent, to green moss, lemon verbena, wild thyme and many others. Relaxing they are, too. Bath bags, to be hung in the tub, like a tea ball is in tea, herbal hand jelly, eye pads, soap, dusting powder, talcum, and pot-pourri.... A Pomander Ball which used to keep away evil spirits is now used to keep mustiness out of linen and other closets.

The Well-Groomed Lady thought the whole collection more fun than a picnic, and each single item perfect for a small distinctive gift.*

PRACTICE 6
Writing to Express Personal Convictions

In the extract that follows the writer has strongly felt and vigorously expressed an opinion. Your own views are (1) practically identical, (2) in partial accord, (3) decidedly different. Express your personal convictions on the topic as clearly and as cogently as the writer of this editorial has expressed his.

RELIGION IN POLITICS

About the last thing that people fancy go together are religion and politics. Take the Lewiston municipal elections, for instance. It isn't a matter of creeds or sects or dogmas. But, to any right-minded person, it should be a matter of principle.

---

*Copyright, 1939, the *Boston Evening Transcript*.

The understanding of this simple truth makes politics and religion one; for principle is not something which can be left behind in the church pew on Sunday night or confined to the prayer meeting or vesper service. It follows a person right into his home, his social affairs, his private business, and into public affairs, also.

An election, then, can best be understood as a choice of the best possible means of bringing into municipal service the largest demonstration of principle. Candidates should stand or fall on this issue. Voters should cast their ballots with as clear a conception of it as possible.

But principle eliminates graft; it substitutes efficiency for favoritism; it means the largest progress consistent with due economy; it means honesty and service through and through—and that is real religion.

We may miss it again and again, in choices of candidates or in election results; but the fact remains as unalterable as God Himself. Who can doubt or gainsay this? Neither Jew nor Gentile, Catholic nor Protestant.*

PRACTICE 7

Incidental Writing

There may be nothing in this sort of incidental writing that serves a definite purpose in the practical routine tasks of the everyday world. It is just a bit of mental byplay in the world of ideas—as figure skating, or tap dancing, or hoop-rolling are physical diversions in the world of sport. Many of you who may not have previously tried this informal and personal sort of verbal indulgence may be induced to let your pens venture freely forth. Perhaps one of these titles may entice you.

1. Cleaning Out the Attic of Your Mind
2. Hoop-rolling My Pet Ideas
3. The Miser Fingers His Paper Profits
4. Roping Them in—Steers or Suitors
5. Our Country Cousins Come to Town
6. Our City Cousins Invade Our Country Home
7. Cashing In on Idle Thinking
8. Reaching for the Stars—and Slipping
9. The Follies of Thrift
10. Major Losses and Minor Profits
11. Restraining My Thoughts Toward the Obtrusive Salesman at the Other End of the Line
12. The Ideas That Wouldn't "Jell"
13. "Parents! Obey Your Children"

*Editorial by Arthur G. Staples, copyright, *Lewiston* (Maine) *Evening Journal.*

14. My Daughters Become My Educators
15. Nightmares in the Daytime
16. Buying Thoughts for a Penny —and Getting Cheated!
17. Undictated Letters
18. The Interior Decorator Submits His Estimates
19. My Antipathy for Certain Words—and People
20. The Friends Who Shrivel Your Cockles

PRACTICE 8
The Personal or Informal Essay

Closely akin to the type of essay we have been considering is one which is ordinarily called the personal or informal essay. It is not designed so much for presenting a systematic body of information as for casual comment, light amusement, fanciful adventure, whimsical indulgences, or humorous entertainment. Of such are many of the contributions of Charles Lamb in *Essays of Elia*, Gilbert Chesterton in *Varied Types*, Jerome K. Jerome in *Idle Talks of an Idle Fellow*, Frances Lester Warner in *Endicott and I*, and those extremely popular syndicated articles of the late O. O. McIntyre which ran under the heading *Man about Town*.

You can take any one of a score of ideas that flit in and out of your mind, and you can write very personally, very informally about it. You have, as we previously assumed, developed a hobby—*words*, perhaps. Something starts you off and you cast your ideas into some such care-free style as this:

WORDS AS A HOBBY

Words are my hobby. They are always offering some new facet of interest. Not long ago a bit of my own writing fell under the critical eye of a careful typist. She paused on a sentence which I had with unquestioning confidence written—"The boy hollowed loudly to his father." When the typist hesitatingly brought my manuscript to me, her challenging brow was wrinkling over the word "hollow." "You didn't mean *hollow*, did you? I never saw the word. I always said *holler*."

"Oh no, surely not!" I was trying in my carefully modulated, extemporized tone to imply that I was conscious of the fact that she holds a college degree and is really a very intelligent and highly trained secretary, that she was, in fact, merely suffering some temporary aberration. The word "holler" was, to be sure, a form that I had heard in my boyhood, but heard only from the vulgar folk in the neighborhood. On occasion Jim Gross, one of these vulgar folk, would unblushingly say, "I hain't got no pencil," or "I hadn't ort to have went." And Jim was an expert in "hollering"!

More recently I have been solemnly saddened to see the word "holler" in print—not as obvious dialect, but in paragraphs that are supposed to be of reasonably decent diction. However, Webster's *New International Dictionary*, Second Edition, offers me this solace: "*holler*—illit. var. of *hollo, hollow.*" My secretary has read this evidence, now knows that "holler" is an illiterate variant of "hollow"; she also knows that "hollow" is a perfectly respectable word.

My present most active hobby seems to be centering in the various activities that may effectively disseminate these significant items of information. I'm enjoying this new form of the old game of logomachy; it has a certain relationship to the newer spirit of *semantics*.

"Semantics," closely allied as it is to the hobby I am now cultivating, is a word which most readers doubtless know. Perhaps they will therefore be all the more receptive to its analyzed implications discussed in Stuart Chase's illuminating book, *The Tyranny of Words*.

Mr. Chase uses the word in considering the inherent difficulties of communicating ideas. "The term which is coming into use for such studies," he writes, "is *semantics*, matters having to do with signification or meaning. You had best get used to this term, for I think we are going to hear it with increasing frequency in the years before us."

A simple-hearted man blithely—or grimly—says, "I always mean what I say and I always say what I mean." But *does* he? And even if he does say what he means, do his hearers completely grasp the meaning of what he has said? If every speaker or writer could fulfill the boast of this simple-hearted Gascon, and if every listener could come into exact coincident understanding with this confident mood of clarity and precision—if such nice agreement were habitually possible, we should then have little occasion for a discussion of semantics. But such, unfortunately, is not the case. Language is so much the product of environment and prejudice that semantics inevitably plays an important role.

In my own boyhood days I frequently heard the word "clever." It was colloquially employed to designate a good-natured person anxious to be accommodating and willing to go out of his way in neighborly acts of kindness. A stranger who moved into that community had always thought of "clever" as identical with "talented," "skillful," and "intellectually alert"—aptly applied in the expression "a clever trick." He was accordingly a bit baffled when, on inquiring where he should regularly buy his foodstuff, he was advised to patronize old Ezra Brown—"He is a very *clever* grocer." Here is another justification for the hobby of semantics.

My interest in semantics has recently received another stimulus. It was invoked by my reading of the November Letter of the Institute for Propaganda Analysis—which, by the way, Mr. Hearst, who doesn't like Hadley Cantril's activities in behalf of truthful analysis, has adroitly shifted to "Propaganda Institute." In this November Letter we are told how the skillful propagandist works with words. He takes advantage of the acquired emotions which center in terms of glittering generalities—words or phrases such as *truth, freedom, honor, liberty, social justice, public service, the right to work, loyalty, progress, democracy, the American way, Constitution defender*. An unprincipled propagandist can easily maneuver these emotional catch words so as to further the particular cause which he is just then endeavoring to promote. He doesn't want his hearers or readers to cogitate and slowly prove; he wants them to palpitate and swiftly approve.

While I was being tempted to this discussion of hobbies and semantics a bit further, the dinner chimes suddenly sounded. Under their echoes and under the savor of their unworded invitation, I found that my interest in verbals was being mysteriously diverted toward an interest in viands.

PRACTICE 9
The Empathy Theme

Some time ago in a seminar group who were anxious to learn more about the writing process, I hit upon the suggestion of what I called *The Empathy Theme*. I carefully explained the significance of this psychological term *empathy*. As most of you probably know, it is a name that we give to the process of entering imaginatively into the feelings or experiences of another person. When you are watching a horse race, you find yourself going around with the jockey who is riding the horse which you have picked as the winner. When you are watching a football game where your favorite team has pushed its opponents down to the goal line, you feel yourself unconsciously crowding and pushing them toward the goal posts. That feeling is *empathy*. You are imaginatively sharing the thoughts and feelings and energies of others.

If you could assemble a small group of congenial associates, you might carry out an experiment in creative writing similar to the one which proved so stimulating to this seminar group. The account, written by one of the members,* is changed in only minor items.

---
*Jessie A. Southard, *The English Leaflet*, No. 261, Cambridge, Massachusetts.

AN EXPERIMENT IN WRITING BY EMPATHY

Each member of the group was asked to write in class suggestions for imaginary situations, such as *I find myself a successful novelist, a newspaper editor, a stoker*. In the four or five minutes allowed, a remarkably large range was covered:

> I find myself a skilled hypnotic operator.
> I find myself a successful opera singer.
> I find myself on a dog-sled in Alaska.
> I find myself a member of Byrd's party.
> I find myself seeing my first book in print.
> I find myself alive after death.
> I find myself a murderess.
> I find myself an ignorant peasant woman in Italy.
> I find myself an extrovert.
> I find myself a successful business man.
> I find myself absolutely penniless.
> I find myself a woman of wealth.
> I find myself kidnapped by bandits.
> I find myself a portrait painter.
> I find myself a queen.
> I am attacked by a wildcat.
> I find myself an innocent victim of a murder accusation.
> I find myself the composer of a great symphony.
> I find myself at sea in a rudderless, oarless boat.
> I find myself the wife of the President of the United States.
> I find myself the author of a really fine book of travel.
> I find myself in a kindergarten.
> I find myself in a Hudson Bay trading post.
> I find myself a missionary in China.

After exchange of the papers on which the subjects were written, each of the group was given between twenty and twenty-five minutes in which to place himself imaginatively in one of the situations suggested by the list which he had received and write whatever might result from his attempt at transfer of personality. No restriction was placed on the form that this might take. The following subjects were chosen:

> I find myself absolutely penniless.
> I find myself a successful opera singer.
> I find myself in a rudderless, oarless boat.
> I find myself the composer of a great symphony.
> I find myself in a kindergarten.
> I find myself a successful business man.
> I find myself a portrait painter.
> I find myself a missionary in China.

It is hardly necessary to say that the papers were written hurriedly, yet in almost every instance the result was a unified, balanced piece of work. In one or two cases, there was an uncertainty of treatment easily explained by the lack of time in which to plan the outcome of the situation, or by a somewhat narrow subject in which information as well as imagination was necessary for a plausible treatment.

The papers varied in length from 202 to 439 words, with an average length of 341.* Had all of the allotted time been used for writing, this would mean about sixteen words a minute; but most of the group used from a sixth to a quarter of the time deciding which of the subjects suggested they would choose and sketching mentally its possibilities, so that the actual average was much higher.

Although the experiment was not in any sense intended as a vocabulary test, it is interesting to note that the number of different words used on the individual papers varied from 100 to 242; that is, from 42% to 59% of the total number of words were used only once. Comparing these papers with others of approximately the same length which were written outside class, and presumably composed at leisure, in one case the percentage dropped from 53% to 36%; in a second, it rose from 54% to 61%; in a third, from 51% to 56%; and in a fourth, from 55% to 60%. While this proves nothing, it would seem to indicate that we have less command of our vocabulary when working under stress, although several found that they wrote more easily and with less revision.

The form in which the papers were written varied, of course, according to the subject chosen and the taste of the writer, although the limitations of the subject were such that all the papers were in the first person. Those who wrote as a composer of a symphony and as one alone at sea, gave, quite definitely, narratives of past experiences, colored by their emotional settings. The account of the business man combined a very compact narrative of past events with a brief analysis of their effect upon him. The portrait painter depicted vigorously his attitude toward painting, indirectly revealing his own character and that of his wife, as well as their attitude toward one another. One writer, who chose the presentation of a missionary in China, was prevented by her intense dislike of the imaginary situation from putting herself into a created personality, and instead she tried to discover how she could, by any possibility, find herself so placed. The one who found himself penniless indulged in a somewhat confused reminiscence, such as might follow a nervous shock or a period of unconsciousness. The remaining papers were in the form of monologues, running comments on the situations in which the writers imagined they

---

*In this connection it is interesting to note that in the WPA organization the entire daily schedule was established, after long experimentations, at 300 words for the writers. Of course, this standard met with criticism.

found themselves. These various forms into which the papers fell suggest that even though similar subjects be chosen by or assigned to a class, a tiresomely similar set of papers need not result. There was no allowance made in this assignment of subjects for individual tastes or experience. Exercise of imagination was, however, demanded of all, the exercise of a faculty which develops and strengthens through use. By means of it, the individual may travel at will, may relieve the monotony of his own life by participation in many lives.

The papers which seemed most plausible were those which made most use of detail, or which made a strong sensory or emotional appeal. These demanded a creative effort from the reader as well as the writer. The following quotation exemplifies this:

> I stepped, without too noticeably stumbling, onto the platform, raised my baton, and, obediently, something happened. Through the rushing in my ears, a single clear cadence found its way, I had no idea from where, for my eyes were filmed. Certainly I had never written that heavenly melody, I, the boy who had struggled through my half hour of music lesson each Monday after school with my eye on the clock and my uninspired fingers pounding out exercises. In fact, I seemed never to have heard it, when—there—was that strain slightly familiar? The volume was increasing; more instruments joining—a rhythmic tattoo—or was that my throbbing temples? What could I do about the climax that I felt was irrevocably nearing? It was pouring in on me from every side, mounting higher and higher. If once my ears became submerged, I could never keep on moving that stick. Then suddenly the climax swept over me and both my arms were raised to meet it.
>
> Silence for a moment before it was broken by a different sound, this time from behind me, a crackling, exciting volley of applause, a stamping and a shouting with staccato calls and cheers.
>
> The little boy with one eye on the clock and stubborn, pounding fingers, turned, dazed and doubting, to face his audience.

It is easy for the reader to identify himself with the writer and forget that the position is wholly imaginary. *Clear cadence* is contreated with *the rushing in my ears. Uninspired fingers pounding out exercises, rhythmic tattoo,* and most vivid of all, *a crackling, exciting volley of applause, a stamping and a shouting with staccato calls and cheers,* all help create the illusion. It was necessary to have some knowledge of orchestral effects with which the imagination might work, but on this foundation the writer built an actual participation in the sounds of a concert. For some of those who heard the paper, there was an immediate reaction that the rising flood of sound was like a rush of water, though the effect had been gained unconsciously. It was developed by such words and phrases as *rushing, volume, mounting higher and higher, became submerged, swept over me.* Their unconscious consistency shows how thoroughly the writer had been immersed in the imagined flood of cess, as well as in the struggles with her lessons, the biting words of criticism, the difficulties with the maestro.

Emotional appeal is dominant also in the portrayal of the business man, particularly in the account of his entrance into commercial life.

> Suddenly, in 1892 the death of my father and mother, and the panic of the following year that swept away the accumulated security of those preceding years. I'll not dwell upon the story of that shock, the sense of loneliness, the long look down that dark avenue of crowding fears, that terrible period of harassed adjustment.

Here the restraint which merely suggests the reactions of the reader is more effective than a detailed portrayal of the emotions would be.

In all of these papers, there is a certain vividness and compactness of phrasing which resulted from the stress under which the papers were written. Most of the group admitted that they wrote best at the eleventh hour, when the writing—letter, article, whatever it might be—*had* to be finished. Such a demand upon the writer results in a concentration which seems to increase the ease with which ideas present themselves in adequate phrasing. There is a sureness of touch, a finality of expression, which are not evident in more leisurely writing. Most of the group found unusual ease in the writing of the papers, because the limited time and field demanded complete concentration.

The assignment was concluded by a discussion of the reasons for individual choice of subject and its development. In some cases the working out of the idea could be traced to some experience of the writer; in others the development was colored by reading, plays, or moving pictures. Experience, real or vicarious, furnished the material with which imagination could work.

This experiment, for obvious reasons, is given in detail. The method of group cooperation is often a source of keen stimulation, for it offers whatever help may reside in a common task impregnated with a competitive element. The array of titles called forth by the emphasis upon empathy is suggestive of the breadth of the areas here displayed and also of the immense territories beyond the present boundaries. Anyone reading this list can readily make up one that is equally varied, equally invigorating. Moreover, anyone reading the material actually produced is able to see what can be accomplished by earnest writers who are allotted twenty-five minutes to complete a given task—select a subject, plan it, write it, revise it. To reveal the potentialities of such an experiment required the full explanation and the concrete evidence. It should offer the stimulus for similar experimentation by many groups interested in the possibility of developing their powers in creative writing.

PRACTICE 10
The Empathy Theme—Identifying Oneself With an Inanimate Object

The method of identifying yourself with an inanimate object often serves to quicken your imagination. As a pupil in the elementary school you may have been given this title, *The Autobiography of a Penny*. Perhaps your imagination was immediately stirred and you followed this disk of copper from the bright and shiny time it was minted, down through the circling years to the dull verdigrised time when it fell from a tramp's soiled pocket into the open sewer of some far away city. Later, in your maturer years, that method perhaps seemed to you a bit childish or time-worn. But read the following from the *Chicago Tribune*, and decide whether or not Dr. Irving S. Cutter has found the device effective.

INTIMATE CONFESSIONS OF A MEAL

I am a meal of many factors and consist of a generous slice of roast lamb, a helping of cauliflower, a baked potato, a vegetable salad, coffee with sugar and cream, and pumpkin pie. For some time a white uniformed cook was busy in my preparation. Placed upon an assortment of dishes I am transported from the kitchen and find myself spread before the gentleman whom I am to nurture.

He looks at me appraisingly and I gaze at him with equal steadfastness. His smile of satisfaction is contagious and I grin back. He is of such a genial appearance that I feel content to work out my destiny through him. I know that he is intrigued and that his saliva and gastric juices are beginning to flow. He has good teeth and the first thing I know I am masticated thoroughly and have started on my trip down the esophagus.

When I arrive in the stomach I am greeted cordially. But how I have changed. My ingredients are all intermingled and I am sure that any one would have difficulty in identifying the pumpkin pie. Already I have a desire to dissolve—to blend more intimately with my host. Soon I experience a definite sense of compression. I am conscious that I am being pushed forward. After a while I am dumped out of the stomach into the first portion of the intestine which I understand is called the duodenum.

Even before this I should have told you that I seem to be floating in a new kind of liquid—the gastric juice. It tastes sour at first, but I like it. Furthermore, I realize that many of my elements were undergoing some sort of solution, becoming smaller and smaller as we traveled onward.

In this new corridor I was met with a reception committee of several new substances—chiefly bile from the liver and the output of the pancreas. They cavorted about with great joy because apparently it had been some hours since they had been provided with entertainment. They took my supply of protein and split it into simpler and more soluble materials. They helped themselves to my fat and, by molding and patting, they converted my carbohydrates into sugar. I could almost hear them cheer as they watched me dissolve.

I am no longer acid—that is, strongly so, and every little fat globule is broken up into thousands of smaller ones. I had a chance to chat with the Bile King for a minute, and he told me they liked to have plenty of fat, as it is a help in preventing the stomach from shoving too much into the intestine at once.

By this time I was ready to resume my passage to the small intestine. I found that most of my roast lamb had been transformed into amino acids, ready for rebuilding into tissues of my consumer. My fats had become fatty acids, so that I could scarcely recognize their faces. Soon I found that some of my best and most valuable constituents were being absorbed. The pancreas told me that the smooth, velvety projections—called villi—which line the intestinal tube were grabbing some of my essentials and carting them away.

From then on I dwindled away until about all that remained was a lot of coarse fiber that nobody in my neighborhood seemed to want. At every turn of the road I encountered pixies and gnomes, called hormones and enzymes, that had the power of seizing the best parts of me and toting them off. One little elf whispered that he was "fed up"—ready to depart for the liver.

At this stage apparently I fell asleep because the next thing I knew I was drifting along the portal circulation en route to the liver. But I was not allowed to rest there long. After washing and cleansing I was thrust into the outgoing current which I found was the bloodstream, where I was reunited with millions of particles of my former self. For several days thereafter I had a grand time meeting my many fragments, formerly proteins, fats and starches. These components are now blood cells or forms of nutriment, all floating along at high tide, rejoicing in the fact that they have done a good turn in nourishing the kindly chap who looked upon them with so much favor.*

And now that you have found Dr. Cutter's article on nutriment interesting, don't you want to try out this method on a topic of your

---

*Copyright, 1939, the *Chicago Tribune*.

own choosing? Phrase your own title if you wish—but, if you prefer, choose one of these.

1. The Jallopy Broadcasts His Story From the Wreckage Lot
2. Jack Frost Outlines His Plans for the Night
3. The Old Locomotive Discovers That His Nose Is Broken
4. The God of War Outlines His Campaign
5. The Star Discovers the Earth
6. The Electric Eye Does a Bit of Meditating
7. The God of Propaganda Laughs a Vicious Laugh
8. Husband for a Day (by the Wife)
9. Wife for a Day (by the Husband)
10. The Sofa Tells a Romantic Tale
11. The Newly Invented Machine Indulges in Prophecy
12. The Granite Block in Soliloquy
13. Shakespeare's Brain Awakes and Remembers and Understands
14. One Dead Author to Another
15. One Dead General to Another

PRACTICE 11

The Empathy Theme—Imagining an Experience

Let me suggest this for students stimulated by the Empathy theme.

In a book of essays entitled *Ebony and Ivory** by Llewelyn Powys, there is a narrative essay, "A Leopard by Lake Elmenteita," which describes a personal experience of the author. The incident occurred in British East Africa, where Mr. Powys was then the manager of a large stock farm. A leopard had killed a calf, and the herd of cattle were in danger.

Before you read the account here reprinted let your imagination create a situation in which your problem of shooting the leopard is in some respects similar to the problems that confronted Mr. Powys. Since he has used the fifth stanza of William Blake's poem, *The Tiger*, as the epigraph to his story, I am here quoting the lyric entire. After reading it, phrase your experience. Then compare it with Mr. Powys's adroit narrative.

---

*Copyright, 1923, Harcourt, Brace and Company, Inc., New York.

THE TIGER

Tiger, tiger, burning bright
In the forest of the night,
What immortal hand or eye
Could frame thy fearful symmetry?

In what distant deeps or skies
Burnt the fire of thine eyes?
On what wings dare he aspire?
What the hand dare seize the fire?

And what shoulder, and what art,
Could twist the sinews of thy heart?
And when the heart began to beat,
What dread hand and what dread feet?

What the hammer? What the chain?
In what furnace was thy brain?
What the anvil? What dead grasp
Dare its deadly terrors clasp?

When the stars threw down their spears,
And water'd heaven with their tears,
Did He smile His work to see?
Did He who made the lamb make thee?

Tiger, tiger, burning bright
In the forest of the night,
What immortal hand or eye
Dare frame thy fearful symmetry?

A LEOPARD BY LAKE ELMENTEITA

Is there any animal more astounding, more amazing than a leopard? With what terrible precision his gilded limbs have been designed to deal out death, and in what a wonderful way his furtive and treacherous beauty symbolizes the soul of the strange continent which he inhabits.

"Bwana, bwana, chui n'kwesha pigga m'toto gombi!" "Master, master, a leopard has killed a calf!" Well do I remember how those words came to me from the cattle yards as early one morning I emerged from my hut in the highlands of British East Africa. I had been in the country only a few weeks and it was the first time an open attack had been made on the homestead by a leopard. I had heard leopards about often enough. The house I lived in was situated on the edge of a great forest and almost every night I would lie awake listening with awestruck intentness to the sound of their barking as it went echoing between the white pillar-like tree trunks. Until the sound was over, all else would be silent, the very tree hyraxes remaining mute as with small blinking eyes they waited for its menace to die down into the circumambient darkness. With padded footfall to and fro these great cats would steal over the maiden-hair ferns and moonlit mossgrown stones of the forest floor, but until this particular night none of them had approached the farm buildings which were built out upon the open veldt. I went to the shed and was shown the place between two rough cedar logs through which the leopard had crept. There had been rain in the night and with the help of some natives I tracked it by its spoor for a considerable distance until the grass grew so thick that we could no longer find any trace of it. I concluded that it had got away for good, and returned to my house. At noon, however, a Masai herder came in to say that he had discovered the half-eaten body of a calf near the shore of Lake Elmenteita.

He conducted me to the place and there under the shadow of a high cliff which jutted out over the water I found the mangled animal. Very little of it had been devoured, so that there seemed every prospect of the leopard's returning to the kill as soon as darkness fell. I therefore made up my mind to wait for it.

The late afternoon found me clambering about the rocks of the escarpment looking for a good position in which to pass the night. I found what I wanted at last, a flat, inaccessible ledge some forty yards above where the calf lay. The moon I knew was almost full, so that if the sky remained clear it seemed that there was a good chance of taking my revenge. I stuck a tiny piece of white paper on the sight of my rifle so as to render it visible even in a dim light.

It was a weird and isolated place, that escarpment, and as I sat watching the sun slowly sink toward the rim of the mountain range beyond the Rift Valley, I became aware of a strange thing. It was as though all Africa at that enchanted hour was under some curious influence, as if it waited expectantly with indrawn breath for this half of the earth's globe to turn itself once again toward the spangled darkness of ultimate space. Unfamiliar noises rose from the water before me, and it was not till several minutes had passed that I realized their origin. Slowly, surely, from every quarter of the lake the monstrous amphibia were drawing in toward the shore. Presently I could see their colossal hippopotamus-heads rising to the surface, now here, now there, as they lolled and yawned together in fabulous droves waiting impatiently for the fall of darkness when they would be able to come up out of the water and graze upon the cold dew-drenched grass of their midnight pasturage. The sun went down at last and from where I crouched I watched their huge unforgettable forms slipping and floundering through the rushes which bordered upon the edge of the lake where the silver froth lapped against the strand.

With the coming of the night the whole air became vibrant, quivering, palpitating. From innumerable scaly throats a song of praise rose to the Creater of the world. In shrill and high tones that fantastical chorus throbbed and hummed against my ear drum. Now and again far above my head would sound the romantic alien call of some wild fowl winging its solitary way through the night. I waited and waited. A damp air, chilling and invisible, rose from the lake. It had about it the smell of thousands of unrecorded years that had passed in quiet procession over these remote waters, while century after century trees grew to their prime and rotted to water-logged decay, while century after century the bones of fabulous equatorial animals accumulated upon the slimy mud of the lake's bottom. It had about it the smell of water-pythons, of incredible crustacea, of the fecund spawn of insects.

Then suddenly, loud and clear, breaking in upon the stillness of that wide moonlit stretch of water while every flag and every reed seemed to tremble, sounded the harsh note of a hungry leopard. And not only the reeds trembled, for scarcely had the first echo subsided than, like a city slum waked suddenly from sleep, a deafening clamor rose to the stars. The baboons which roosted in the rocks amongst which I sat had heard it. Turning my head I could see them clambering higher and ever higher in the dim light, clinging with their muscular black hands to the stony shelves or huddling one against another, hairy limb against hairy limb, in the deeper recesses of the cliff. It was then for the first time that I realized how nightly the barbarous imaginations of these hideous monkeys are haunted with panic fear of their crafty and subtle enemy, which leaps suddenly upon them out of the darkness and tears out their eyes! Gradually the barking of the leopard grew nearer. I got my rifle ready. I surmised that the animal was coming along a narrow game-path which threaded its way between the boulders at the foot of the escarpment. All now was once more silent. Not a rustle, not the cracking of a twig to tell of the animal's approach, or to disturb the spell-bound stillness of that amazing midnight landscape which under the liquid light of the moon lay extended in agonized suspense.

Like some wide plain of abandoned polar ice, the tropical lake lay silent and immutable, and from the depths of the dark forest away on the left no sound rose. What had come over the baboons? I wondered. Were their superficial brains once more clouded in a nervous sleep? Or were they, with narrow wide-open antique eyes, peering over their grotesque snouts in abject alertness for their enemy?

Suddenly the leopard, elongated and serpentine, was crossing an open space below. There was something horrible and uncanny about the absolute silence of its movements. For a few moments I watched it. Delicately, daintily, it nibbled at the carcass, stepping round the mutilated body with fastidious tread. I pulled the trigger at last. Undoubtedly I had missed, for look as I might through the uncertain light I could see nothing. It was just as though at the report of my rifle a ghost-leopard had vanished into the air.

Slowly the time dragged by as I waited for the dawn. In the small hours of the morning I fell asleep. When I awoke it was already past six and the first rays of the great equatorial sun were glancing down upon Africa. Cold and stiff I stood up and looked about. Shafts of fine golden light were slanting down upon the basalt rocks, upon the flamingos in the shallows—and upon the miraculous spotted body of a dead leopard which, outstretched in all its bizarre beauty, lay by the edge of those far-off mysterious waters which are called by the natives Elmenteita.

CHAPTER IV

THE WRITTEN COMPOSITION AS A WHOLE

THIS particular volume, *Your Command of Written English*, is designed for those who recognize that the actual experiences of everyday life demand, for each ambitious person, a growing proficiency in the language expression of ideas—a growing proficiency in oral expression, a growing proficiency in written expression. All of you who gain your promotions in life recognize the fact that your daily occupational and social needs call more and more insistently for the exercise of your communicating skill. You become conscious of the specific responsibilities which the pen or the typewriter imposes. When you set down your ideas in written form, you are presumably preparing a record that is going to meet the eye of an intelligent reader, or a group of readers, who will view this product of yours in a critical attitude—not, perhaps, in an unfriendly or a coldly censorious attitude, but certainly in a challenging attitude. Here before them are your words, your sentences, your paragraphs all in ordered crystallized form—exposed line upon line in black and white. The evidence of your skill—or lack of skill—is unmistakable. What will be the judgment of this intelligent reader or this group of readers?

A few days ago a committee report in mimeographed form came to my desk for inspection. It represented a prodigious amount of painstaking investigation by a reputable workman. Much of the document was excellent. It had been organized with care; it displayed revealing bits of genuine craftsmanship. Some of the paragraphs were phrased with far more than ordinary cleverness, force, and precision; it displayed in places unusual understanding and penetration. As I read the earlier portions of the long manuscript, I began to think I was going to be able to commend it as a whole. But soon one error after another appeared; some of these errors were purely mechanical—errors in spelling, errors in punctuation, errors in grammar and diction. And in occasional passages I discovered errors in fact—misstatements and unwarranted conclusions. As I continued my reading, I grew more and more skeptical of the validity of the whole report. Before it could be finally presented, it would, I decided, have to be carefully revised.

You have all had experiences similar to this. You have been reading, let us say, a friendly letter, a business letter, an office memorandum, a detailed analysis of a proposed change in business policy, a page of advertising copy, a quarterly report, a set of minutes, a summary of an address you yourself may have given—or any one of the many types of written composition that the day's routine supplies. You were judging it as a complete whole, and you were thinking again of the principles that underlie effective composition. You wondered why these principles had been so grievously ignored.

Involuntarily, perhaps, you may be thinking now of an important business letter or report or copy for a circular that you yourself are soon to prepare. What are some of the principles that are to guide you in getting your ideas arranged in well-organized form and phrased in appropriate diction? How are you going to avoid adverse judgments concerning your written work? Let us see if we cannot prepare a set of helpful postulates, together with comments upon each, that will assemble for you all the more important suggestions for the written composition as a whole.

Postulates for the Written Work

The Main Topic.

Have clearly in mind the main idea that the entire written unit is to express. Ordinarily the main idea can be appropriately indicated in the title. Dale Carnegie had a very definite concept when he phrased the long but explicit title for his book—*How to Win Friends and Influence People*. The various items within his volume bear directly upon this specific query: "How are you going to win friends and influence people?" The title for the set of books which you are now reading, *Your Mastery of English*, is the condensed expression of a major intention—the intention to assemble in series an organized body of material on personal achievement in English. It was written with the design of providing help for each reader who desired practical suggestions for such a mastery. The appeal is direct. It is not *a* mastery of English; it is not *the* mastery of English; it is *your* mastery of English—such a mastery as will enable you to express more effectively your thoughts, your sensations, your feelings.

It is apparent that the title of any piece of written work provides

THE WRITTEN COMPOSITION AS A WHOLE

a natural and effective means for the initial accenting and clear-cutting of the topic. This very fact suggests its immediate corollary: since the title is important, punctilious care should be expended in its wording. Rather than a fanciful or far-fetched phrasing, select the words that simply and fully and exactly focus attention upon the main idea. Here are examples of well-known titles that illustrate this concept:

The Decline and Fall of the Roman Empire	Abraham Lincoln Walks at Midnight
How We Think	The Outcasts of Poker Flat
The Lady or the Tiger	How Santa Claus Came to Simpson Bay
The Man With the Hoe	
General William Booth Enters Into Heaven	I Have a Rendezvous With Death
	Love's Minor Frictions
Mending Wall	The Wonder of Words

The phrasing of the title is not the only point. Your focus upon this main idea will naturally assemble in the narrowed circle the more important subpoints. This fact is so important that it deserves a separate postulate.

The Subtopics.

The focus of your attention upon the main point of your writing project will summon several supporting subpoints, which you can arrange in the form of an outline. You are, we shall assume, proposing to write of your plan to buy a small farm. You may know very little about farm life, but at least your interest just now centers upon this proposed purchase. You have decided upon your title—*The Farm I Should Like to Buy*. As you ponder your topic, four subtopics suggest themselves and these you arrange in appropriate sequence. It is not difficult to make a simple outline to serve you as a guide.

THE SORT OF FARM I SHOULD LIKE TO BUY

I. Size—twenty or thirty acres
II. Location—near a college
III. Buildings—barn; house; garage
IV. Soil—suitable for fruits and vegetables for home consumption and marketing—a means of livelihood and security

But perhaps you are not personally interested in farms. You would prefer to concentrate upon some title in an entirely different field.

Why not concentrate upon one of the following and see what subtopics suggest themselves for inclusion in a short but complete outline?

1. My Latest Hobby
2. A Proposed Change in Routing Our Shipments
3. Arranging a Family Budget
4. Points to Consider in Buying a Car
5. Plans for Granting Vacation Periods to Employees
6. A Plan for a Local Library
7. A Wife's Allowance
8. Plans for a Wedding
9. Life-insurance Problems
10. My Investment Program
11. A Talk at the Scout Meeting
12. My Choice of a Nursery School
13. Problems of a Charge Account
14. Reasons for Going to an Old Folks Home
15. Spending Money
16. Plans for Remodeling Our House
17. Our Neighborhood Problems
18. Reasons for My Church Activities
19. My Reasons for Not Joining a Church
20. A Reading Program
21. Our Moving-Picture Perplexities
22. Shall My Son Be a Pacifist?
23. Analyzing the Stock Market
24. My Greatest Household Problem
25. Odd Jobs About the House
26. Care of a Lawn
27. The Best Kind of Refrigerator (or Heating Unit)
28. Shall I Insulate My House?
29. Linoleum or Rugs?
30. Thoughts About Oriental Rugs
31. A Letter to a Student Entering College
32. A Letter to a Student Seeking a Job
33. A Letter to Be Filed With My Will
34. Comments on a Book or Magazine Article That Deeply Impressed Me
35. Security for My Later Years
36. My Quarrel With Education
37. My Quarrel With Politicians
38. My Quarrel With the Newspapers
39. My Quarrel With Modern Business

Comparison of Planned and Unplanned Writing.

Compare the values of the writing that is planned and the writing that is unplanned. Whatever be the type of writing you are to attempt, there are two general methods to consider. One is to begin writing something or other in some form or other, in some mood or other, and expect a miracle, a series of chance happenings—or, perhaps, hours of arduous revision—to whip the whole into shape. The other method assumes that time and effort are saved by careful, detailed planning before any writing is done at all.

Now the first method—the unplanned—is not to be curtly dismissed or branded as worthless. Many writers have testified to the values they derive from just forcing themselves to sit down at a desk, with a batch of paper and starting to write—anything! With the paraphernalia for the expression of ideas before them, the ideas gradually emerge from hidden places and somehow get themselves harnessed into words—as they do, for example, when we sit down to write a letter to an intimate friend.

Just how the processes of the mind effect the final product is all a bit of a mystery; the writers themselves can seldom explain the tracing and the retracing of faltering steps in the seemingly aimless excursion. Asked how it is done, and why they maunder along in this frivolous fashion, they might perhaps respond, "Well, how can I know what I'm going to write about until I somehow scribble some fragments down on paper?" The answer, to be sure, doesn't sound very convincing; but some good writing has evolved from those who—without any specific ideas at command—deliberately trick themselves into expression by the bait of the displayed apparatus—paper, ink, pen—and an idling mind.

The contrasting method to this informal philandering with ideas is the method that demands a clear prevising and rigid organization of the entire project—with the main idea clearly conceived and with the separate subordinating ideas assembled to support the whole.

By referring to the discussion of the short outline of *The Sort of Farm I Should Like to Buy*, you will see the working of the mind systematically evolving a simple theme. In the writer's mind the idea did not exist merely as a single unit isolated from every other unit in the universe. It had definite relationships that expressed themselves as you see them arranged in the outline. It was not merely a vague, indefinite *sort of farm*; it was a farm clearly seen in relationship with the four listed subtopics—*Size; Location; Buildings; Soil*. Each of these naturally carries its unlisted load of minor items that might in turn have a *sub-*subordinate arrangement. But such an enumeration in a short essay is unnecessary.

For a long exposition or for an extended argument, the outline would, of course, be greatly enlarged and elaborated. The degree of enlargement and elaboration would naturally depend upon the nature of the subject and the character of the readers or audience to be addressed. The first essential demand would be the clear and exact concept of the idea to be discussed; the second essential demand would be three or four or five subordinate ideas which would serve as your main supports. And these supporting ideas would probably have their separate and supporting subtopics.

As a practical method of approach to and preparation of a proposed exposition, may I suggest this? Supply yourself with a pack of blank cards—library cards 3 x 5—which can be bought at any stationer's store or at a ten-cent counter. Equipped with these, you have a means of recording in convenient form any idea that you think worth the capture. The specific item for each specific listing does not need to be of major importance; to you it seems just then of some value and worth salvaging. Let us see how the plan works out in an individual case.

You have discovered a new delight in words and think you would like to set down in simple essay form some of your interests and discoveries. You choose as your title *Wayfaring With Words*. You are not going to be hurried in this task of essay writing; you are planning to assemble the ideas gradually. As you already have your topic well in hand, you will not have to do any long and detailed research work in the library. Equipped with your blank cards, you are hoping to use them in your capture of chance ideas—one card for each idea. You will be diligent in recording items as they occur, each probably in its singular unrelated form, but capable of later inclusion and integration in your essay. Here, for example, are three separate entries that illustrate the type of note that you have jotted down.

Some words, originally regarded as slang, have gradually won a dignified place in our language. Examples: *mob; van; wig.*

What will be the fate of such words as *exam, frat, prof, dorm, dude?*

The word *nickname* is derived from the Middle English *ekename*, literally an *also* word. It is easy to see how the casual pronunciation of *an ekename* would naturally change to *a nickname*.

Our word, *gawky*, comes from an English dialect word which means *left-handed*. Because a left-handed action often appears to be an awkward action, a gawky person is one who is awkward or clumsy or clownish.

Assuming that during two weeks you have as many as twenty or twenty-five entries, each on a separate card, you will then, as a preparation for the final organization of your material, sit down at your desk with your assembled deck, prepared for a game of solitaire wherein the object is to get your material logically organized. Perhaps you will find duplicate entries. Some, moreover, too trivial to go into the essay, you will discard. You discover at length that you can arrange the items under four distinct heads, as follows:

WAYFARING WITH WORDS
  I. Words of Anglo-Saxon origin
  II. Enrichments from the French, owing to the Norman Conquest
  III. Technical words and how they are formed
  IV. Individual achievements in vocabulary building

This method of carefully prevising your written work is in harmony with the modern demands for practical efficiency. In business we dislike the policy that is casual, furtive, and haphazard. We like to see a project that is thought out even to its minuter details. There will, in the actual operation of any plan, be many opportunities of trying out both the general principles that govern the project and the minuter items that have been previsioned. That is why automobile manufacturers establish their testing grounds. Of course, it is freely admitted that *the best laid schemes o' mice and men gang aft a-gley*, but that fact does not forestall the engineer in his plans for constructing a bridge nor persuade an architect that a hazy notion for building a home should not be resolved into a clearly developed blueprint. An outline for an essay may need to be changed. It probably will be changed. But the fact that a plan may need to be fully *revised* does not alter the fact that it should first be fully *prevised*.

Rapid Writing of First Draft.

The actual task of writing a composition may be done at a rather rapid pace. After the outline is complete the actual work of developing it—writing it in longhand or typing it as you compose—may be done rather hurriedly. You need not at this stage of the operation be too particular about the words that you select or the sentence patterns that you form. Get into the very center of your task and let its spirit and substance support you. Here is an outline to follow. Follow it. Here is a general theme to express. Express it. Here are important subpoints to explain. Explain them. Here are examples and illustrations to include. Include them. Here is a mood to impart. Impart it. And if there be a preachment to be preached, preach it!

Not many, when they sit down at their desks, know in advance what words they will use or what sentences they will form. In rapid writing these words and sentences seem to flow out of the nowhere into the here. We assume for the moment that they are freighted with cargoes that were listed on their bill of lading—but that for the moment is the unsubstantial substance of things hoped for, the unsupported evidence of things not seen. The final result is subject to checking and double checking when revisions are being made.

In saying that this actual process of composing may be done at a rather rapid pace, I deliberately insist upon the word *may*. I should never think of writing *must*. People differ widely in their ways of writing, and such differences should be respected—should be encouraged. Some write so slowly and so critically that their finished manuscripts need no revision. Some make the revisions as they go along and for a finished draft trust to a later recopying—or to a typing by a secretary who has learned the technique of deciphering pages filled with deletions, alterations, and interlinings. All these various ways are but proofs of the infinite varieties of human behavior, for styles of behavior manifest themselves in differences in writing—as they manifest themselves in every other area of activity.

The deduction to be drawn from this is obvious. Adopt the method which for you accomplishes the best results. It is a fact perhaps worth re-emphasizing, however, that rapid writing is more likely to carry with it the freshness and the zeal and the verve that every craftsman covets. But if we hurry the task of composing we must not hurry the task of revising.

The Research Paper.

The research paper demands a special method. The sort of essay we have thus far been assuming is one that does not demand any extended research in a library; it demands, rather, a searching of your own mind to discover those thoughts and fancies and remembered experiences that can be assembled into a satisfactory unit of written expression. It may of course require, for certain items, verification; you want to be perfectly sure about a certain fact and you may have to consult a certain reference book that explains that fact; you want to be perfectly sure of a certain quotation, and you may have to consult the book in which it appears. These, however, are matters of casual and comparatively slight moment.

A very different sort of essay is one that involves careful and painstaking research in a library, or detailed consultation of reference books, particularly encyclopedias, general guides, indexes, and special docu-

ments. For this type of work the following will be found useful:
The United States Catalog, 1902, 1912, 1928.

This reference work lists by title, author, and topic all books in English in print in the United States at the time of its publication. It is supplemented by the:
Cumulative Book Index, issued periodically.
Poole's Index to Periodical Literature, 1891-1908.

This index lists by title and author all articles published in the leading periodicals.
Readers' Guide to Periodical Literature, 1901-

This guide lists by title and author the material published in the leading periodicals.
International Index to Periodicals, 1913-

This reference book, emphasizing science and the humanities, lists by author and subject all the articles in a selected list of magazines.
The New York Times Index, 1913-

Since 1913 the *Times* has annually issued an index to its own more important material.
The World Almanac, 1886-

Published annually since 1886, *The World Almanac* assembles a mass of information on topics of interest to the public.

Other reference works which will be found helpful are:
Webster's New International Dictionary.
Funk and Wagnalls New Standard Dictionary of the English Language.
The New Century Dictionary.
The Winston Dictionary, College Edition.
The National Dictionary.
Encyclopædia Britannica.
The National Encyclopedia.
Lincoln Library of Essential Information.
Dictionary of American Biography.
The National Year Book.
The New International Year Book.
The Statesman's Year-Book.
Who's Who (English).
Who's Who in America.
Style Manual of the Government Printing Office.
Bartlett's Familiar Quotations.

THE WRITTEN COMPOSITION AS A WHOLE

Roget's Thesaurus of English Words and Phrases.
Bulfinch's Mythology.
Rand McNally Commercial Atlas and Marketing Guide.
Collier's World Atlas and Gazetteer.
Reader's Digest of Books.
Statistical Abstract of the United States.

When you have definitely made up your mind on the subject you are to discuss in your paper, be assured first that you are not attempting a topic too broad in scope for treatment in the length of essay that you have in mind. A common error is to attempt too much. A student whom I know started to write on the attitude of Wordsworth and Coleridge toward the political affairs of their own Georgian period. He soon found that topic too broad; he finally wrote on the attitude of these two poets toward Napoleon. He had not anticipated—as indeed few writers do—how quickly a subject expands once you begin your research. Be careful, therefore, to limit your theme. Any library attendant will be able to advise you.

The library attendant, moreover, has at her finger tips the books—or at least the titles of books in her card catalogue—that will likely grant you the readiest and most authoritative aid. She will probably direct you first to some good encyclopedia. At the end of the particular article on your subject, you will usually find a short but highly significant bibliography. When you have this list of books as a source of information, you will wish perhaps to secure something more recent—something that may have appeared in a magazine. Here the *Reader's Guide to Periodical Literature* is likely to be of great service. If you do not know how to use this *Guide*, have no hesitation in asking the librarian to give you the necessary help.

Make your notes on library cards 3 x 5, a separate card for each separate entry. At the end of the transcribed note always list the source of the information, author, title, page reference, and publisher. In most instances you will find it helpful to record also the date of publication of the book or periodical. And if your note contains the exact words of an author, be sure to put quotation marks around each quotation. You will employ this method in order to keep properly differentiated the three types of material you later admit into your finished papers: (a) the quoted material; (b) the paraphrased material; (c) your own original writing. Proper credit for the first two types will, of course, be given.

Should you in an essay on some present problems wish to comment briefly upon what an author has written, you could record the main idea on a card in some such fashion as this:

> *Escape from Present Fears*
>
> Mr. Avis D. Carlson in "Courage for To-Morrow" (*Harper's Magazine*, April 1939), after discussing the present atmosphere of turmoil and insecurity, reminds us that history gives us many examples of recurring periods in which the human race is seen blundering along in troublous, uncertain ways. Out of these periods it has always emerged. Moreover, it has emerged with added strength and firmer faith.

During the periods that you are making notes similar to these, you will not fail to jot down independent ideas of your own—ideas that seem at the time they occur to have elements of value and bear directly upon the topic that your paper is to discuss. You have chosen, let us

> Lord Dundreary produces laughter in his audience by his absurd confusions of proverbs. He is evidently very fond of quoting proverbs, but he never quotes them correctly. He doesn't say, as all the rest of us would, "Birds of a feather flock together." He says instead, "Birds of a feather—gather no moss." We laugh, I suppose, because of the unexpected incongruity that his strange shiftings create.

say, to write upon some topic relating to our sense of humor. You have just recalled an old play—Tom Taylor's *Our American Cousin*—that you saw in a recent revival. You were particularly amused by the character of Lord Dundreary. Thinking you may later make some pertinent use of Lord Dundreary in your analysis of the sense of humor, you jot down this memorandum and place it in its proper place in your files.

When in your period of preparation for your essay you think you may have assembled enough material, you get your cards together and study the possibility of a satisfactory organization. As you study them you see that the points you wish to include may be systematically arranged under four subheads. These subheads you accordingly set down under an appropriate title—a title that presumably concentrates within its phrasing the exact theme that you wish to discuss. You at least accept it as tentatively expressing your main idea.

And now with this main idea dominant, and with the four—possibly five or six—subheads definitely in mind as supports, you write your introduction and thus lead the readers to the discussion of the first important subhead in your outline.

Your writing pace and your writing manner will, of course, be your own. Personally, as I have already said, it does not seem to me of prime importance at this stage to pause too long upon particular choices of particular words or particular patterns of sentence structure. Your interest in your theme should hurry you forward by its own impetus. This and the momentum that your ideas now possess should reflect themselves in the force and thrust of your own style.

As you move from one subtopic to another you will, of course, remember that you are not merely getting your ideas down on paper, but you are trying to act as the personal guide of the party. You will therefore not simply project the group suddenly and blindly into new territory. You will keep them informed as to the direction you are taking them in and thus make by transition a comfortable mental journey. Will it help you any to say that you are the cicerone on this safari? But you are really more than a guide on this sight-seeing tour; you are yourself creating some of the objects which you are extemporaneously teaching them to see. And you are having a good time doing it.

Again, when your paper is complete there remains the serious work of revision. That is a task, however, that need not be performed immediately. Indeed, it is usually far better to put your sheets aside for the present. Go out and play a game of tennis, or go to your garden and hoe your beans, or take a spin in your car, or slip into the kitchen and bake a cherry pie. Later in the day—or preferably on the morrow—reassemble your sheets and be very cruel with them—particularly with your sentences. Slash them here, slash them there, transpose and re-transpose, add a phrase at the beginning, delete another near the end. Whip them into shape; question your organization; question your paragraphs and sentences; question your choice of words; recheck mechanical items; be your own severest critic. And don't listen too closely to hear what Mrs. Grundy is going to say.

Revision.

For most writers, revision is a necessary and a painstaking task. Mr. Gamaliel Bradford once spoke to me of a book review he had just handed to the editor for whom we were both working. As we talked of methods of writing, he surprised me by saying, "I revise very little. After I have thought out carefully what I have to say, I sit down and type the material on my own machine. I may change a word here, a phrase there. I seldom make a second copy."

That seemed to me then—as it seems to me now—a remarkable achievement. Mr. Bradford, to be sure, had attained that proficiency only after long, long years of practice; but to have attained it at all is truly significant—particularly significant when we realize the excellence of his prose style.

Experienced newspaper reporters do, of course, frequently hand in their first-draft stories. They have to do their work rapidly and meet the strict time schedules of the various editions. Their work, excellent as it is considering the haste in which it must be prepared, is often revised by the copy-desk editor—to say nothing of the revision which the reporter often makes before he has finished his script.

Mr. H. Robinson Shipherd has gathered some bits of testimony concerning the practices of other writers—testimony in sharp contrast with the habits of Mr. Bradford and the highly skilled newspaper man.

> Nothing in our fine art of writing seems more certain than this: all writers, expert professionals as well as plodding amateurs, regularly have to do a great deal of reworking. Even our facile Irvin Cobb protests that he has to polish his work and swear and perspire over it, "frequently almost expiring over it"; and he recalls

Thackeray's working three weeks over a single paragraph—and then throwing it away and beginning afresh! Mrs. Dorothy Canfield Fisher vividly describes the kind of reworking she does, in her account of "How 'Flint and Fire' Started and Grew," in *Americans All*. Joseph Conrad speaks of his "endless rewriting"; and says that he wrote *The Rover* "at least eleven times." In making *A Tramp Abroad*, Mark Twain threw away more than half of what he had written; he began and rewrote his magazine articles again and again; and he declares that his shortest story took him twelve years to write. Tennyson worked over some of his poems for years, before he published them. Stevenson insists that "no one ever had such pains to learn a trade as I had; but I slogged at it, day in, day out," with "dire industry"; and he confesses that "whole chapters of *Otto* were written as often as five or six times, and one chapter, that of the Countess and the Princess, eight times by me and once by my wife." We now know that Lincoln revised the *Gettysburg Address* repeatedly; we know that De Quincey spent six months of unremitting day-labor rewriting *Confessions of an Opium-Eater;* we have the sad-hearted confessions of Rousseau and of Newman about their endless labors in revision; we have Ariosto's sixteen versions of one stanza before he got it to suit him.*

The revisions that most of us make may be of six different types:

a. Mechanical faults, such as spelling, grammar, punctuation, compounding, and conventional forms
b. Material included
c. Organization
d. Paragraphing
e. Sentences
f. Words
g. Checking references

Mechanical Faults. Almost no one can prepare a manuscript of any considerable length and keep it free from mechanical errors—such as errors in spelling, punctuation, compounding, grammar, and conventional forms. Some latitude is allowable in these matters, but ordinarily it is a matter of strict correctness or strict consistency.

Everyone is liable to make a mistake in spelling. A writer who prides himself on his spelling ability recently doubled the *r* in *iridescent;* another inadvertently left one of the *l*'s out of *belligerent.* Another equally proficient in his general practice wrote *crystallize* with a single *l;* the *t* in the past tense of the verb *benefit* is so many times wrongly doubled that this redoubled form may sometime be

---
*H. Robinson Shipherd, *Manual and Models for College Composition*, Ginn and Company, Boston, copyright, 1928.

admitted as an alternative spelling of *benefited*. Any careful craftsman will always zealously try to keep his spelling consistent; the verb *practice*, for example, has two accepted spellings—p-r-a-c-t-i-c-e, or p-r-a-c-t-i-s-e. If it occurs more than once in your manuscript, see that the form first chosen is consistently chosen. A good current rule is to spell both noun and verb with the *c*.

Grammar is occasionally violated even by the most punctilious. Especially in rapid writing wrong forms intrude, and only the most rigid attention to details will keep the manuscript grammatically immaculate. Recently, while reading proof, I came upon this sentence: "A whole gamut of thoughts, sensations, and emotions are here displayed." The writer, feeling a sense of plurals in *thoughts*, *sensations*, and *emotions*, had carelessly used *are* instead of *is* as the predicate with the singular subject *gamut*. Similar slips in punctuating the sentence, in the compounding of words, and in irregular margins or other departures from conventional usage need to be carefully corrected. The process is often an arduous one, but when perfectly completed it carries with it the sort of accolade which any true and knightly craftsman may earnestly covet.

Material Included. In revising a manuscript you may once more question the material which you have included. Have there been careless omissions? Have topics or items been admitted which are in fact so irrelevant or so alien that final judgment urges either their discard or more condensed treatment? Seen now in the perspective of the finished product, they seem distorted. Something is necessary to secure the right proportion. How are you going to correct the fault?

Organization. A reading of a manuscript that you thought was finished may arouse disturbing queries concerning the entire outline that you so carefully constructed. The major topic and the supporting subtopics do not seem to assemble themselves into the satisfying whole that your imagination had forecast. You are especially disturbed because the parts do not closely articulate. There are gaps here, protuberances there, a lack of balance everywhere. You may be especially displeased because the subtopics which previously seemed to be placed in an order that led to a proper climax, seem now to produce no such cumulative effect. Subtopic C, which you had placed at the end, now seems weaker than the one which you had labeled in your outline as A. If further critical and impartial judgment supports your impression, there is nothing for an honest workman to do but tear the structure apart and proceed to entire remodeling. It may be a painful process; but you are a craftsman and you very properly spurn the jerry-built unit.

Paragraphing. When you examine your finished manuscript in the light of your own critical judgment and in the light of the principles emphasized in the chapter on Paragraph Structure, you may be confronted with further queries. You are not quite sure whether the material which is now marked by three separate indentations should not more properly be telescoped into one. Perhaps so. But I have frequently been solaced by remembering a device I first saw many years ago when I read Scott and Denny's *Paragraph Writing*. The authors use the brace system, which I am here reproducing from memory.

$$\left\{ \begin{array}{l} \{1.\} \\ \{2.\} \\ \{3.\} \end{array} \right.$$

Now there are two options. You may, in certain instances, properly cast your material either into *three* paragraphs or into *one;* it is a matter merely of personal preference. Naturally you must allow your logic and your common sense free play; they may in certain other instances demand two paragraphs and a change in phrasing that would insure a closer connection in thought. Allow the detailed instructions in Chapter V to be your personal guide.

Sentences. Barrett Wendell was only partially right when he said that paragraphs and whole compositions are matters for *prevision;* sentences are matters for *revision*. We have in the preceding sections seen that paragraphs and whole compositions must in some cases be changed. Of course, if our prevision could be trained to perfection no such changes would have to be made. Granted that your prevising has given you a good working outline, it is true that a critical attitude toward your writing will dictate changes in your sentences more frequently than in your paragraphs or in the theme as a whole. In my own experience I find that I make comparatively few revisions in general structure; I make many in sentence structure.

The types of changes necessary in sentence structure are so numerous and varied that only a few faulty examples are printed here. For other violations consult the chapter on Sentence Structure.*

---

*Chapter VI of this volume.

A phrase may be out of place, as you see in this:

Incorrect: "I saw the man when I went to the city at the corner drug store."

Revised: "When I went to the city I saw the man at the corner drug store."

A relative clause may be too far from its antecedent:

Incorrect: "I have been reading a book, *The Wonder of Words*, which was written by Isaac Goldberg that should be in every public library."

Revised: "I have been reading Isaac Goldberg's *The Wonder of Words*—a book that should be in every public library."

A subordinate clause which does not make a full and complete statement is sometimes set apart and wrongly forced into a sentence form.

Incorrect: "She was summoned to appear in court. Which she immediately did."

Revised: "When she was summoned to appear in court, she immediately obeyed."

Too frequently an unpracticed writer uses the passive voice when the active would effect a better balance and express the idea more strongly.

Ineffective: "The candidate hurried to the City Auditorium where a final address was given."

Revised: "The candidate hurried to the City Auditorium, where he made his final address."

Words. Revision of words is an exhilarating and never-ending sport. I suppose few writers finish a manuscript without some lingering questions concerning particular nouns, or verbs, or adjectives, adverbs, or some other parts of speech. Here is the type of question that almost anyone, having just finished some piece of writing, might appropriately ask: How really effective have I been in choosing the words that will carry to my readers the message that I have tried to convey?

While I was writing this section my telephone bell rang. A very competent secretary had called to ask me about the spelling of a word that she was trying to transcribe from the dictaphone. The word, she said, sounded as if it might be spelled f-i-n-e-a-g-l-i-n-g; it appeared in a sentence that spoke of some administrator's f-i-n-e-a-g-l-i-n-g. The word she had been unable to find in the dictionary. I explained that she could probably find it under its proper spelling—*finagling*. She was reassured. I am assuming, too, that she learned the correct pronunciation—*fi nā′ gling*.

Your immediate question might be: "Shall I use the word *finagling* in my own writing?" Perhaps. If it fits into your slightly jocular mood and properly reflects the idea of adroit and underhand methods, why not use it? It is of dialect origin and has never quite made its way into the upper stratified areas. Personally I have never used it. But I should use it if, addressing a certain group and urged by a particular instinct, I should feel that it would most effectively convey the meaning I am most eager to express.

Here is another specific inquiry. In revising your manuscript you came upon this sentence: "He was excessively fond of his work." Since you did not mean to imply that he was *entirely too* fond of his work, you see the necessity of changing *excessively* to *exceedingly*, which simply means that he was *very fond* of his work.

In a letter that you are rereading you note that you have written this: "May I kindly ask you to hurry the shipment so that the goods will arrive in ample time for the Christmas trade?" That word *kindly*, you discover, is misplaced; you are not wishing to express your own kindly tone of making a request; you are, instead, asking your wholesaler if he will not *kindly hurry the shipment*. You can change your statement to read: "May I ask if you will kindly hurry the shipment so that the goods will arrive in ample time for the Christmas trade?"

Your critical eye falls upon another word you have used—the word *opine*: "I opine that we can rely upon these data." Looking the word up in your dictionary, you discover that it is now chiefly used in humorous expressions. Certainly you have no such mood here. Instead of saying *I opine*, you can more appropriately say, "*I am convinced* that we can rely upon these data."

These are but scattered examples from among many types of queries that continually confront you in your writing. All of you have in specific instances asked yourselves such questions as these: Should I repeat a word that I used in a sentence that immediately precedes? Has the word the full support of authority? Will it convey to others what it conveys to me? Is the expression too trite? Is it too technical? Is it too learned? Is it too bizarre? Is it too precious? Is it sufficiently specific? Sufficiently exact? Does it fit into the prose rhythm of the sentence? Does it border too closely upon slang? Does it have the proper flavor? Does it harmonize with the prevailing mood? Does it carry the right connotation? Does it seem to accord with my own personality?

Oftentimes in revising our writing we grow dissatisfied with certain phrases or words; they do not fit into the rhythm of the sentence; or they occasion bad repetitions; or they do not accurately express our ideas. We detect the fault and yet we find it very difficult to think of a suitable substitute. We realize that something is wrong in our choice of a word, but we do not know what change to make. Probably we have come to regard the dictionary as an agent ready to supply us immediately with a synonym. Very likely, indeed, the dictionary will solve most of our perplexities; but if that medium should in any instance fail us, we may advantageously consult such books as Crabb's *English Synonymes* (Harper), Fernald's *English Synonyms and Antonyms* (Funk and Wagnalls), or Soule's *Dictionary of English Synonyms*, revised and enlarged by Alfred D. Sheffield (Little, Brown and Company). Another volume that I very frequently consult is Roget's *International Thesaurus of English Words and Phrases*, revised by C. O. S. Mawson (T. Y. Crowell).

As an illustration of the sort of help offered by this thesaurus, I open the Roget at random and read the list of adjectives printed as synonyms for the word *certain:*

sure	assured	well-founded	ascertained
absolute	solid	unqualified	positive
determinate	definite	clear	unequivocal
categorical	unmistakable	decisive	decided

And now turning to Professor Sheffield's list in Soule's *Dictionary of English Synonyms* under this same word *certain,* I discover the following:

indubitable	unquestionable	indisputable	undeniable
incontestable	incontrovertible	unquestioned	undisputed
undoubted	absolute	positive	plain
sure	past dispute	beyond all question	clear as day

Now for some reason you do not, in a particular context, like to use the word *certain*—it might conceivably rhyme awkwardly with *curtain*, which you regard as an important word in your sentence. You could surely find among these rich offerings from Dr. Mawson or Professor Sheffield a suitable substitute.

Some texts of this sort supply, moreover, a long list of antonyms (words of opposite meaning to the one in question). Frequently a change of word or a shift in the structure of your sentence will allow you to use an antonym that will even more crisply express your precise meaning, as the following will illustrate:

> *Original:* Even after he had established all his facts, he could not be certain of his deductions.
>
> *Revised:* Even after he had established all his facts, he was still *uncertain* of his deductions.

If all this searching in dictionaries and thesauri seems to imply a great deal of labor and delay, you must remember that in the final capture of the very word which gives the coveted force, piquancy, and precision to your style, you have received an award that grants real but intangible compensation for the expended effort. A growing skill in habitually choosing the right and timely phrase may prompt some one to say of you what Lowell in *A Fable for Critics* said of Emerson:

> Here comes Emerson first, whose rich words, every one,
> Are like gold nails in temples to hang trophies on.

One point for every writer to watch centers upon the question of provincial speech. As you critically reread your manuscripts, ask yourself this question: Have I used here any words or expressions that would be classed as provincialisms? Since we are, each of us, the victims—or the beneficiaries—of our own particular environments, we are not always able to differentiate between usage that may be national and usage that may be local. A day or two ago, for instance, in reading a manuscript that had been handed to me for criticism, I noticed the writer's use of the word *unbeknownst*—seriously used in a serious paragraph. Since *unbeknownst* is a dialect form, it was wholly out of place in that essay. It should be used only in a narrative writing that reports the provincial speech of a provincial character. Since the writer had presumably heard the word all his life, he did not realize his own improper use of it.

In your study you should, therefore, learn to make such distinctions. Here are a few illustrative examples of provincial words: *arroyo* for *gulley*; *homely* for *ugly*; *allow, calculate,* and *reckon* for *think*; *smart,* (in such a phrase as *a smart distance*); *clever* for *good-natured*; *boughten* (as distinguished from *homemade*); *disremember* for *forget*; *right* for *very* (he studies *right* hard); *favor* for *resembles* (he *favors* his mother). You can easily extend the list.

Another point to watch centers on what we term *improprieties*—words quite correct in themselves but used with meanings or in grammatical forms not sanctioned by good use. In the left-hand column are a few examples of improprieties:

Incorrect	*Correct*
a. I *suspicioned* him all along.	a. I *suspected* him all along.
b. His work will not be *effected* by the change.	b. His work will not be *affected* by the change.
c. He is *some* better this morning.	c. He is *somewhat* better this morning.
d. She is *anxious* to enter the contest now.	d. She is *eager* to enter the contest now.
e. I hope to *contact* him tomorrow.	e. I hope to *confer with* him tomorrow.
f. I feel *real* curious about the outcome.	f. I feel *really* curious about the outcome.
g. His penmanship has improved *considerable*.	g. His penmanship has improved *considerably*.
h. I greatly admired his clear, *trite* style.	h. I greatly admired his clear, *terse* style.

In order that our choice of words may be most effective we must keep continually on the watch for the older words in their current uses, for new words that express new ideas, and for ways of expression that will prove most effective for the specific message that we are at the moment most eager to express.

A third type of error to watch in revision is the *barbarism*. A barbarism is an unaccepted word obviously coined from another word. Several barbarisms are listed in the left-hand column (next page).

	Incorrect	*Correct*
a.	I fear this glass is not going to *jell*.	I fear this glass is not going to *jelly*.
b.	I shall go, *irregardless* of the expense.	I shall go, *regardless* of the expense.
c.	This lounge looks extremely *comfy*.	This lounge looks extremely *comfortable*.
d.	Don't forget your *hanky*, Louise.	Don't forget your *handkerchief*, Louise.
e.	These room decorations are very *tasty*.	These room decorations are *in excellent taste*.
f.	In our advertising campaign, we must make our customers *shirt-conscious*.	In our advertising campaign, we must make our customers *more alert to shirt values*.

Checking References. It is very easy to make mistakes in giving references to books or periodicals. We should be most punctilious in titles, names of authors, and in page numbering. And we must always carefully verify quotations. We can seldom rely upon our memories, and even if we are correct in copying the words, we are likely to make mistakes in the punctuation. The most rigid checking is here necessary.

PRACTICES

The exercises that follow are intended to aid in the study, criticism, and revision needed to make your composition effective.

PRACTICE 1

Revision

Here are several pairs of articles.* Which do you think is the final draft of each article? What are your reasons for your decision? In what ways do you feel the revised copy is superior to the original?

    1. I close. We are not, we must not be, aliens or enemies, but fellow countrymen. Although passion has strained our bonds of affection too hardly they must not, I am sure they will not be broken. The mystic chords which, proceeding from so many battlefields and so many patriotic graves, pass through all the hearts and all the hearths in this broad continent of ours, will yet again

---

*1. First Inaugural Address, March 4, 1861, Abraham Lincoln; 2. *On First Looking Into Chapman's Homer*, John Keats; 3. *The Influence of the Athenaeum on Literature in America*, Barrett Wendell, copyright, 1907, the Boston Athenaeum.

harmonize in their ancient music when breathed upon by the guardian angel of the nation.

I am loath to close. We are not enemies, but friends. We must not be enemies. Though passion may have strained, it must not break our bonds of affection. The mystic chords of memory, stretching from every battlefield and patriot grave to every living heart and hearth-stone all over this broad land, will yet swell the chorus of the Union when again touched, as surely they will be, by the better angels of our nature.

2. Oft of one wide expanse had I been told,
That low-brow'd Homer rul'd as his demesne;
Yet could I never judge what men could mean,
Till I heard Chapman speak out, loud and bold.

Oft of one wide expanse had I been told
That deep-brow'd Homer rul'd as his demesne;
Yet did I never breathe its pure serene
Till I heard Chapman speak out loud and bold.

3. Bronson Alcott used the library frequently. So did William Ellery Channing, whose range of serious reading seems to have been exceptionally wide. James Freeman Clarke read omnivorously here. So did Emerson, whose record of books drawn is unusually large. And George Ripley seems to have found here a great part of that fervid intellectual stimulus which made him, in his younger days, so powerful a force in the philosophic renaissance which they once fancied was to remake creation on the Boston plan.

Bronson Alcott used the library frequently. So did William Ellery Channing, whose range of serious reading seems to have been exceptionally wide. James Freeman Clarke read here omnivorously. The record of books drawn by Emerson is unusually large and heterogeneous. And George Ripley seems to have found here no small part of that fervid intellectual stimulus which made him, in his younger days, so powerful a force in the philosophic renaissance once expected to remake creation on the Boston plan.

PRACTICE 2

Clarity

Examine each of the following sentences carefully. Is the meaning the sentences should convey absolutely clear to you? Is there any ambiguity in the sentences? Make whatever changes you think are necessary for absolute clarity.

THE WRITTEN COMPOSITION AS A WHOLE

1. The rain came in the window which spoiled the cover of the book that was on the window sill.
2. Listening from the balcony the actors' words could not always be distinctly heard.
3. Looking out of the dining-room window, the ocean can be seen.
4. After ringing the bell several times the butler finally let us in.
5. Walking along down below we saw the people from the top of the Empire State Building and they looked very small.
6. I looked up at the sky; seeing a lot of clouds I wondered if it would rain.
7. Just as he went down the second time the lifeguard reached the man and saved him.
8. Going down Main Street from here, Milk Street is the fourth street on the left.
9. Wearing a handsome new fur coat I saw Mary walking down the street.
10. The window display was very pretty which had the patriotic decorations for Washington's Birthday.

PRACTICE 3
Multiple-Choice Vocabulary Test

Check the nearest synonym of each italicized word.

1. An *amenable* student.   industrious   dull   tractable   clever
2. His work was *appraised*.   flattered   condemned   complimented   evaluated
3. *Badinage* often helps a difficult situation.   knowledge-of-etiquette   tact   playful-raillery   common-sense
4. They object to *bathos*.   ablutions   anticlimax   display-of-feeling   quackery
5. A *captious* attitude.   censorious   sporting   broad-minded   indifferent
6. Such *cerebration* is unusual.   merrymaking   brain-action   tolerance   weather
7. *Delete* this material.   finish   condense   expand   strike-out

8. A curious *fetish*. — charm   habit   gesture   notion
9. The affair was a *fiasco*. — lawn-fête   failure   hoax   secret
10. A *flagrant* offense. — criminal   unimportant   monstrous   typical
11. Done *inadvertently*. — carefully   skillfully   brilliantly   through-negligence
12. An *ignominious* position. — humiliating   important   executive   strategic
13. The metaphor was *inept*. — vivid   unsuitable   unexpected   ingenious
14. A *laconic* remark. — loquacious   fastidious   terse   conservative
15. The *martinet* approaches. — strict-disciplinarian   small-bird   band-leader   dandy
16. A *modicum* of goodness. — dearth   small-quantity   special-kind   abundance
17. His ideas were *nebulous*. — individual   ordinary   striking   hazy
18. The evidence was *obliterated*. — spread-about   unexpected   erased   kept-back
19. Looking for a *panacea*. — bakery   cure-all   hospital   pleasure-resort
20. A *platitudinous* statement. — eloquent   concise   prolix   commonplace
21. The horse was *recalcitrant*. — refractory   intelligent   decrepit   well-broken-in
22. His point of view was *specious*. — expansive   deceptively-correct   continental   specialized
23. A *soporific* effect. — cleansing   refreshing   horrible   stupefying
24. This passage is *tautological*. — characteristic   repetitious   reasonable   admirable
25. A *venal* transaction. — mercenary   irregular   underhand   easily-pardoned

PRACTICE 4
Position of Words and Phrases

In each of the following sentences a change in the position of a word or phrase will bring out more clearly the intended thought. What changes in position would you suggest? Be able to give your reason for making the change. Remember that your purpose is primarily the clarification of thought, not merely the improvement of the sound of the sentence. The example provided below will give you the correct procedure.

Given: Absolute clarity in expressing his thoughts *at all times dominated* his written work.

Improved: (In their present position the words *at all times* may modify either *expressing his thoughts* or *dominated*.) To remove the ambiguity, you must express the sentence in one of the two following ways:
Absolute clarity in expressing his thoughts dominated at all times his written work.

or

Absolute clarity in expressing his thoughts dominated his written work at all times.

1. What I am about to say not only applies as a whole to the composition but also to the paragraph as a whole.
2. He was too tired often to do more than a little weeding after supper in his garden.
3. He told John as soon as he could that he would do his work faithfully. (This sentence may have two possible meanings as it now stands. Make it mean definitely that he told John *as soon as he was able to tell him*.)
4. I have not learned somehow to distinguish between him and his brother and between even his two sisters. (Make the first part of this sentence mean: *For some reason or other I have not learned to distinguish between him and his brother.*)
5. I think about going at nine o'clock usually. (The writer intended to say here that he customarily does his thinking at nine o'clock; he does not mean that he goes at nine o'clock.

PRACTICE 5
Parallelograms

Parallel construction has been violated in each of the following sentences. Unequal sentence particles have been joined by conjunctions.

Make the unequal sentence particles equal—two clauses, two phrases, or two words. The example below will reveal the procedure.

EXAMPLE

Not parallel: I was impressed by Henry's gentleness, and he was very competent.

Parallel: I was impressed by Henry's gentleness and his competence.

1. Being somewhat superstitious by nature and since he lacked red-blooded courage it is easy to understand why he retreated so quickly and his state of nervousness afterwards.
2. Watchfulness and to be cautious are attributes which distinguish the Scouts.
3. He told us to be careful about what we ate and our drinking water.
4. He believed earnestly that all was right with the world and we ought to be happy.
5. He explained to us the meaning of the passage and why the author used it.
6. I am sending you a book on how to get energy through vitamins and Dr. Philips's speech.

PRACTICE 6

Unnecessary Repetition

Some of these sentences contain words which merely repeat an idea which has already been clearly expressed. Such superfluous repetition weakens the sentence and occasionally confuses the reader. Rewrite the faulty sentences correctly. A few of them are correct as they stand.

EXAMPLE: I bought an untried automobile that had never been tested. *That had never been tested* is superfluous repetition of the same idea as in *untried*. It should be omitted. The correct form would be: I bought an untried automobile.

1. The searching party, although unsuccessful, finally decided to return back to the main camp.
2. Colonel Macdonald, I tell you, he was a fine old gentleman.
3. The stagecoach very slowly ascended up the steep, slippery hill.
4. Senator Blake is now very busy writing an autobiography of his life.
5. My father, who likes Italian opera very much, will enjoy the *Il Trovatore* broadcast.

THE WRITTEN COMPOSITION AS A WHOLE

6. The automobile company is sure that, if this winter is severe, that few people will buy cars next February.
7. The parade marched continuously all the morning without stopping.
8. Both errors alike come from the same source.

KEYS TO PRACTICES

Key to Practice 2: Clarity

1. When the rain came in the window it spoiled the cover of the book that was on the window sill.
2. The actors' words could not always be distinctly heard by those who were listening from the balcony.
3. The ocean can be seen from the dining-room window.
4. After we had rung the bell several times the butler finally let us in.
5. As we looked down from the top of the Empire State Building we noticed that the people we saw walking down below looked very small.
6. Seeing a lot of clouds when I looked up at the sky, I wondered if it would rain.
7. The lifeguard reached the man just as he went down the second time.
8. If you go down Main Street from here, you will find that Milk Street is the fourth street on the left.
9. When I saw Mary walking down the street, she was wearing a handsome new fur coat.
10. The window display which had the patriotic decorations for Washington's Birthday was very pretty.

Key to Practice 3: Multiple-Choice Vocabulary Test

1. tractable
2. evaluated
3. playful-raillery
4. anticlimax
5. censorious
6. brain-action
7. strike-out
8. charm
9. failure
10. monstrous
11. through-negligence
12. humiliating
13. unsuitable
14. terse
15. strict-disciplinarian
16. small-quantity
17. hazy
18. erased
19. cure-all
20. commonplace
21. refractory
22. deceptively-correct
23. stupefying
24. repetitious
25. mercenary

Key to Practice 4: Position of Words and Phrases

1. What I am about to say applies not only to the composition as a whole but also to the paragraph as a whole.

or

What I am about to say applies as a whole not only to the composition but also to the paragraph.

2. After supper he was often too tired to do more than a little weeding in his garden.
3. As soon as he could speak, he told John that he would faithfully do the work.
4. Somehow I have not learned to distinguish between him and his brother, nor even between his two sisters.
5. At nine o'clock I usually think about going.

Key to Practice 5: Parallelograms

1. Since by nature he was somewhat superstitious and cowardly it is easy to understand why he retreated so quickly and why he was so nervous afterwards.
2. Watchfulness and caution are attributes which distinguish the Scouts.
3. He told us to be careful about what we ate and drank.
4. He believed earnestly that all was right with the world and that we ought to be happy.
5. He explained to us the meaning of the passage and the reason why the author used it.
6. I am sending you a book on how to get energy through vitamins and I am also sending you a copy of Dr. Philips's speech on the same subject.

Key to Practice 6: Unnecessary Repetition

1. Omit *back*.
2. Omit *he*.
3. Omit *up*.
4. Omit *of his life*.
5. Correct.
6. Omit the second *that*.
7. Omit either *without stopping* or *continuously*.
8. Omit *alike*.

CHAPTER V

PARAGRAPH STRUCTURE

LONG AGO someone gave us the proverb, "Take care of the pennies and the dollars will take care of themselves." Years later, Professor Alexander Bain of the University of Aberdeen applied the basic idea of this maxim to a different situation. He said, "Look to the paragraphs and the discourse will look to itself, for although a discourse as a whole has a method or plan suited to its nature, yet the confining of each paragraph to a distinct topic avoids some of the worst faults of composition; besides which, he that fully comprehends the method of a paragraph will also comprehend the method of an entire work." To put it more succinctly, if you desire to learn to write well, first master the principles of paragraph structure. For a paragraph is only a composition in miniature, and the same principles apply to it as to a more extended discourse. As an essay is made up of paragraphs, so is a paragraph made up of sentences. To define it more fully, we may say:

A paragraph is a unit, or subdivision, of composition, and is made up of a series of closely related sentences, developing a single topic, or a phase of a given topic. It may be one of a group of connected paragraphs forming a composition of length, or it may be in itself a complete, though brief, discourse. Paragraphs of the first class are called *related paragraphs;* those of the second class are called *isolated paragraphs.*

There is no law governing the length of a paragraph, either isolated or related. It may vary greatly according to the purpose of the composition. In dialogue, usually, each separate speech forms a new paragraph, and in that case the paragraph may consist of only one sentence —perhaps not more than one line. In writing for publication, one thing that should not be overlooked is the appearance of the printed page. Variety in length of paragraphs is desirable in order to avoid monotony of form. Generally, the first line of each paragraph is indented, thus breaking the monotony of the page. Since, in narration, there is likely to be a good deal of conversation, it follows that these divisions occur more often there than in more serious kinds of work such as criticism, argument, and exposition, where longer paragraphs are used. The shorter paragraphs give the page a more broken, or open, appearance and therefore suggest a lighter type of subject matter. Very long paragraphs, especially those which cover an entire page or as much as two thirds of a page, present a solid, massive effect, suggesting to some persons what they call "dull" or "heavy" reading. Children soon learn to choose for their own enjoyment, as being easier and more interesting, books with the broken type of pages; and even many grownups, particularly the tired or mentally lazy, reject those with the more solidly printed pages as being unfitted to their mood. It has been roughly stated that a paragraph of more than three hundred words is long, and a paragraph of less than one hundred words is short. I give you this merely as a helpful suggestion, *not a rule.* Common sense, a feeling for proportion in values, and perhaps most of all, the nature of the subject must be your guide.

The Isolated Paragraph

Of the two classes of paragraphs, *isolated* and *related,* we shall first study the former. An isolated paragraph may discuss any subject which is simple enough to be so treated adequately though briefly. As an interesting example let us take the following selection:

> Lowell's legacy as a poet is great, but not greater than his legacy as a patriot. The true patriot does not love his country, labor, and suffer for it, simply because he happened to be born in it—that would be the infatuation of the egotist; but because, *being* born in it, his duty and pleasure are to help on all human progress by helping on first the progress of the land to which he belongs. This is Lowell's legacy as a patriot—not the sentiment "My country, right or wrong," but "My country—it shall never be wrong if I can help it!" The true patriot is not the one who says it is *my* country, and *its* institutions, that are sacred; but who says with Lowell, "It is Man who is sacred." The citizen who holds to this sacredness of humanity will be the most useful in securing institutions and a country whose services to humanity will make *them* also sacred in his own heart, and in the hearts of all good men.*

---

*Copyright, 1891, *Century Magazine.*

Unity

However, whether long or short, isolated or related, a paragraph must conform to certain very definite principles, the same principles which apply to the formation of sentences and to whole compositions —*Unity, Coherence,* and *Emphasis.* A paragraph is said to possess Unity when the idea expressed can be summarized in a single sentence. Therefore, it is clear that the shorter the paragraph the more easily is its Unity maintained; the longer the paragraph the more danger of a confusion of ideas. Especial care, then, must be taken in writing a long paragraph, to keep each sentence bearing upon the central thought. Let no extraneous ideas creep in. The following paragraph is an excellent example of Unity.

THE SATISFYING WHOLE

There is something in each of us that demands completeness. An unfinished building, a partially drawn design, an interrupted game, a broken pattern in a woven fabric, a theme cut short in the middle—each of these produces an unsatisfied feeling. There are, to be sure, fragments of rare beauty and significance, but always, as we look upon them, we feel that there is something lacking. We feel this lack very keenly—and sometimes very sorrowfully—when a delicate bit of china or glassware is shattered by some carelessness of ours. What was the perfect whole now lies broken on the floor. We pick up the three or four pieces and pathetically fit them to their former shape—vainly imagining a restored completeness. And then, growing more practical, we begin to wonder how the treasured article can be repaired. We are searching for the satisfying whole.

You see this paragraph passes the test of Unity—*the idea may be condensed into a single sentence.* It is not necessary to phrase this summary word for word as it may appear in the paragraph, but in this case, the first and last sentences may be combined: *There is something in each of us that demands completeness; we are searching for the satisfying whole.*

The Topic Sentence.

One of the surest means of attaining Unity is through the skillful use of the *Topic Sentence.* Plan the paragraph beforehand, building a foundation, as it were, before proceeding to erect the main structure. First, know definitely what you wish to say, then phrase a topic sentence for use in an outline (if not a written one, at least a mental one). In your outline, let the topic sentence be the main heading, then subdivide it into two or more minor headings.

The topic sentence, as its name implies, is one which indicates the topic to be discussed. Therefore, it should present clearly, unmistakably, and as briefly as possible, the main idea of the discourse. It need not be a complete sentence, but may be only a phrase. It may be placed at either the beginning or the end, or in the body of the paragraph; indeed, it need not appear at all, in so many words, but the idea must be there in some form, frequently merely implied, and must be kept clearly and steadfastly in the foreground of the writer's thinking. This is called the *implied method*. Every sentence must bear distinctly and definitely upon this central thought.

Argument and exposition usually demand a very definite statement of the subject. In such cases, it is generally best to place the topic sentence at, or near, the beginning of the paragraph, as illustrated in the following:

> We know now that *the most disastrous effects of the war were suffered after the war was over*, and especially after 1929 when the shortages caused by the war had been made good and the inflation of that time had run its course. The problems of agriculture to this day trace back to the war prices and the abnormal and temporary stimulus to cultivation and new developments. Moreover, prices and wages did not come down together after the wartime inflation. Farm prices dropped more than industrial prices, and hourly wage rates least of all, and the disorder in price and cost relationships which then originated has persisted. This disruption of prices and trade relations has ruined tens of thousands of business men, including farmers, and thrown millions of wage-workers out of employment.*

Especially is this method good in argument when a postulate is presented which must be proved by examples.

Sometimes in order to emphasize the argument or explanation, the topic sentence is placed at the end as well as the beginning. This method is especially valuable in spoken discourse; it rounds out the idea and gives a sense of completeness and unity. An excellent example of this is the following:

---

*Monthly Letter from the National City Bank of New York, October, 1939.

PARAGRAPH STRUCTURE

I begin with the postulate that *it is the law of nature to desire happiness.* This law is not local, but universal; not temporary, but eternal. It is not a law to be proved by exceptions, for it knows no exception. The savage and the martyr welcome fierce pains, not because they love pain; but because they love some expected remuneration of happiness so well that they are willing to purchase it at the price of pain—at the price of imprisonment, torture, or death. The young desire happiness more keenly than others. This desire is innate, spontaneous, exuberant; and nothing but repeated and repeated overflows of the lava of disappointment can burn or bury it in the human breast. On this law of our nature, then, we may stand as on an immovable foundation of truth. Whatever fortune may befall our argument, our premises are secure. *The conscious desire of happiness is active in all men.*
—Horace Mann, *Thoughts for a Young Man*

In some cases the proof is presented first, leading up to the topic sentence at the close. This plan is especially desirable where the postulate, if presented first, might antagonize the reader or listener. Whereas, if his interest is aroused by the presentation of the argument or explanation, he may become convinced by the time the end is reached. The following is a good example:

First, we shall do well to keep unbroken our worldwide Christian fellowship. War's hatreds must not sever the bonds by which Christians everywhere are bound to one another and to God. It is a cheering fact that in these recent years, when nations have been hostile and sundered, the Christian churches have held world conferences (which nations have not held) and that there Christians from all lands have met in instant mutual trust. We must keep these bonds: they are the true girding of mankind. If *Christ is Truth*, as we firmly believe, He cannot be merely parochial or national Truth: *He is Truth for the world, and all men are truly one in Him.**

We have seen the importance of the topic sentence in producing Unity in argumentative and expository paragraphs. In narrative and descriptive paragraphs it is less essential, and at the same time often more difficult, to state the central thought so succinctly, though in many cases it is quite possible. For example, in the following short story, you will notice that the first sentence, "As a child I was very

---

*Rev. George A. Buttrick, radio address over NBC, September 8, 1939. Published in *Federal Council Bulletin*, October, 1939.

much afraid of the dark," definitely gives the idea and suggests the dominant note which persists throughout the narrative.

> *As a child I was very much afraid of the dark.* When going through a dark room, I imagined all kinds of hideous creatures were around me and after me. I had an experience of that sort one night, which I shall never forget. As punishment for some misdemeanor, I had been told to go to my room. I went rather unwillingly, for I dreaded passing through the dark hall and up the long, dark stairway. After I had entered the hall and closed the door of the lighted living-room, shutting myself out in the darkness, I felt as if I were miles away from anyone, except the frightful creatures that live in the dark. The great mirror on the wall seemed to reflect all those mysterious horrors. When I reached the landing the big grandfather's clock just beside me called out in thunderous tones the hour of seven, making me jump about three steps which landed me at the top of the stairs. There I stood stock still, my hair on end, my eyes bulging from their sockets, for at the other end of the hall, appeared two small balls of fire! They kept creeping closer and closer. All the stories I had ever heard about bears and tigers popped into my head. Gathering around me now were all the hideous beings, pointing their fingers at me, and clutching at my dress and hair. Just then, Mary opened the nursery door, letting a flood of light into the hall. I sprang over the threshold to safety, and from the direction in which I had seen the two little balls of fire, my pet cat came walking in after me.*

In the following descriptive paragraph, too, you will see that the topic sentence is very definite. It tells us that "the dunes are in another world," and throughout the paragraph, the idea of distance is impressed upon us. "They are the horizon," "a pallid phantom of land" which "might wreathe and vanish at any moment," they are "far," in "an unapproachable place." And the last sentence, "They look like no coast that could be reached," completes the Unity of the picture. This is another example of repetition of the topic sentence at the last.

> *The dunes are in another world.* They are two miles across the uncertain and hazardous tide races of the estuary. The folk of the village never go there. The dunes are nothing. They are the horizon. They are only seen in idleness, or when the weather is scanned, or an incoming ship is marked. The dunes are but a pal-

---

*Adapted from "An Incident" published in *Composition and Rhetoric,* Thomas and Howe, copyright, 1908, Longmans, Green and Co., New York.

lid phantom of land so delicately golden that it is surprising to find it constant. The faint glow of that dilated shore quavering just above the sea, the sea intensely blue and positive, might wreathe and vanish at any moment in the pour of wind from the Atlantic, whose endless strength easily bears in and over us vast involuted continents of white cloud. The dunes tremble in the broad flood of wind, light, and sea, diaphanous and fading, always on the limit of vision, the point of disappearing, but are established. They are soundless, immaterial, and far, like a pleasing and personal illusion, a luminous dream of lasting tranquility in a better but an unapproachable place, and the thought of crossing to them never suggests anything so obvious as a boat. *They look like no coast that could be reached.**

—H. M. Tomlinson, *Old Junk*

When the topic sentence is only *implied*, as is generally the case in narration and description, the writer must with special care keep the central thought constantly and clearly in mind. As in every well-constructed paragraph, he must see that each sentence bears distinctly and unmistakably upon the theme, and he must allow no irrelevant ideas to intrude. When skillfully done, the result will give the desired effect and the paragraph will stand the test of Unity—the sense of it will be clear to the reader, and he will be able to summarize it in a single sentence, thus forming, for himself, the topic sentence.

In this descriptive paragraph from Maxim Gorky's *Malva*, the reader may easily supply the unphrased topic sentence:

> At intervals along the beach, scattered with shells and sea weed, were stakes of wood driven into the sand and on which hung fishing nets, drying and casting shadows as fine as cobwebs. A few large boats and a small one were drawn up beyond high-water mark, and the waves as they ran up towards them seemed as if they were calling on them. Gaffs, oars, coiled ropes, baskets and barrels lay about in disorder and amidst it all was a cabin built of yellow branches, bark and matting. Above the general chaos floated a red rag at the extremity of a tall mast.

Plainly, the implied topic sentence is *The fishing-ground was deserted*. It might be phrased differently, but the thought is clear.

Another illustration of the method is shown in the following narrative paragraph from Gorky's *Tchelkache*:

> Gavrilo rowed in silence; breathing heavily, he cast sidelong glances at the spot where still rose and fell the sword of fire. He

---
*Copyright, 1920, Alfred A. Knopf, Inc., New York.

could not believe that it was only, as Tchelkache said, a lantern with a reflector. The cold, blue light, cutting the darkness, awoke silver reflections upon the sea; there seemed something mysterious about it, and Gavrilo again felt his faculties benumbed with fear. The presentiment of some misfortune oppressed him a second time. He rowed like a machine, bent his shoulders as though expecting a blow to descend and felt himself void of every desire, and without soul. The emotions of that night had consumed all that was human in him.

Here the topic sentence may be expressed in these words: *Gavrilo was terrified.*

In certain cases an exception is made to the usual methods of securing Unity. Sometimes Unity is best secured by the lack of it. In narration, where we have the simplest, and, therefore, the most unified type of paragraph, the single speech, this exception may be made: If the writer wishes to give the impression of confusion in the mind of a character, he may, instead of beginning a new paragraph for each separate speech, place in one paragraph the remarks or exclamations of several persons all speaking at once. The central idea is that of confusion, and the paragraph will express the mental confusion of the character. The impression on the reader will be unified; whereas, if such a passage were written in separate paragraphs the result would be the opposite.

Similarly a narrative paragraph may contain an account of many and varying acts without violating the principle of Unity, if each of these diverse acts contributes to the development of the story and if they all lead up to one definite result, thus giving a unified effect. We see this illustrated in the following paragraph:

Lancelot sat and tried to catch perch ... *He tried to think, but the river would not let him.* It thundered and spouted out behind him from the hatches and leapt madly past him, and caught his eyes in spite of him, and swept them away down its dancing waves, and let them go again only to sweep them down again and again, till his brain felt a delicious dizziness from the everlasting roar. And then below, how it spread, and writhed, and whirled into transparent fans, hissing and turning snakes, polished glass-wreaths, huge crystal bells, which boiled up from the bottom, and dived again beneath long threads of creamy foam, and swung around posts and roots and rushed blackening under dark weed-fringed boughs, and gnawed at the marley banks, and shook the everlasting bulrushes, till it was swept away and down over the white pebbles and olive weeds, in one broad rippling sheet of molten silver, towards the distant sea. Downwards it fleeted ever, and bore his thoughts floating on its oily stream; and the great trout, with their yellow sides and peacock backs, lounged among the eddies, and the silver grayling dimpled and wandered upon the shallows, and the May-flies flickered and rustled round him like water-fairies, with their green gauzy wings; the coot clanked musically among the reeds; the frogs hummed their ceaseless vesper-monotone, the kingfisher darted from his hole in the bank like a blue spark of electric light; the swallows' bills snapped as they turned and hawked above the pool; the swifts' wings whirred like musket-balls, as they rushed screaming past his head; and ever the river fleeted by, bearing his eyes away down the current, till its wild eddies began to glow with crimson beneath the setting sun. *The complex harmony of sights and sounds slid softly over his soul, and he sank away into a still daydream, too passive for imagination, too deep for meditation.*

—Charles Kingsley, *Yeast*

In Lancelot's mind was confusion, but the impression left on the reader is one of Unity, secured partially by the first and last sentences and partly by the repetition of the references to Lancelot, himself, his eyes, and his head. The reader never loses sight of the fact that Lancelot is the center of all this turmoil of sights and sounds, and of the effect it is having upon him.

Paragraph Development.

You have seen that the topic sentence announces, or suggests, the main idea to be discussed. The function of the other sentences is to develop the thought by bringing out clearly the idea expressed in the topic sentence, or the idea as merely kept in the mind of the writer. This, of course, is accomplished by different methods according to the type of paragraph and the subject matter, whether argumentative, expository, narrative, or descriptive.

These methods are many and varied. They may be listed as follows:

1. defining the theme
2. applying the theme
3. explaining the theme
4. amplifying the theme
5. repeating it in other words
6. comparing it with like ideas
7. contrasting it with opposing ideas
8. presenting proofs
9. giving specific details
10. use of illustrations

Every sentence must contribute to one or more of these means of development.

Coherence

This discussion of paragraph development brings us to the second major principle of composition—*Coherence,* for Coherence is that principle which governs the internal structure of the paragraph. A paragraph is coherent when the sentences cohere, that is, when they keep their close relationship to one another and to the subject matter. The various methods of accomplishing this are generally grouped under the three heads of *order, parallel construction,* and *connectives.* You must choose in the specific instance the one best suited to your purpose, the one which will most clearly bring out your meaning.

Order.

The proper sequence of the sentences is usually indicated by the theme itself, or the type of paragraph.

In argument, let your topic sentence constitute the postulate, and the amplifying sentences support the statement by giving proofs, illustrations, and specific details; beginning with the least important points, let the argument increase in strength with each new sentence until it builds up to a climax. The selection I am using as illustration of this is not, as it stands, an isolated paragraph, but since it could very properly be written as such, we shall so consider it. Notice that the author has made more emphatic the important points and brought them out more clearly by numbering them.

> Ohio needs a state board of education to serve as the chief school authority of the state and to give supervision to the state department of education. This need has become more evident than ever during recent years because of the millions of dollars of state aid which have been provided through the School Foundation Program, and because of the many new functions which have been delegated to the state department of education. The state needs such a board for the same reasons that country and local school systems need, and are provided with, boards of education. A state board of education would likely secure the same advantages for Ohio which it has secured in other states; those advantages are:
>
> First, it would be more representative of the interests of all the people than a single individual could be. It would secure different points of view. It would be more democratic.

Second, it would more likely select the state director of education and his assistants on the basis of merit than has been true under gubernatorial appointment. Subject to legislative enactments, it would determine educational policies, would direct the state director of education in executing the policies, and would keep him and his staff in office as long as their services were satisfactory. In brief, it would help to remove the state department of education from the cloud of "politics."

Third, it would have greater prestige with the legislature, the governor, and the school officials than a single individual could have. It would give the public greater confidence in the management of its schools.

Fourth, it would give greater stability and continuity to state educational policies which are now likely to shift with each change of the directorship. School progress throughout the state is best served when policies and programs can be planned with complete confidence that they will not suddenly be cast into the discard by each new director of education. School officials, school employees, and the general public would profit immeasurably from long-term planning thus made possible.*

A similar order may be used in exposition, which often amounts to the same thing as argument since in both you make a statement and then develop the paragraph by building up evidence in support of that statement. Here is an illustration:

A TREASURE HOUSE OF MINERALS

The mountains [of Peru] themselves are a treasure house of minerals of all kinds. The mining industry offers endless potentialities and as it is developed, there might well be a concomitant development of the large supply of hydraulic power inherent in the many streams that tumble down the steep mountain sides. Peru today is the largest producer of vanadium and bismuth in the world. The copper output there has increased over 50 per cent since 1932. Gold production has more than tripled since 1932, the estimated figure for 1938 being 8,000 kilos. Other minerals which are being mined include nickel, zinc, antimony, tungsten, molybdenum, tin and mercury. Besides the petroleum fields and rich beds of coal, large deposits of iron ore and borax are known to exist. Peru's aggregate mineral output grew in value from 129,000,000 soles ($25,000,000) in 1932 to 350,000,000 soles ($70,000,000) in 1937.

---

*Ward G. Reeder: The Amendment for a State Board of Education, *Educational Research Bulletin*, October 11, 1939, College of Education, Ohio State University.

Frequently, in argument or exposition, the reverse method is used. The proof is given first, and the discourse ends with the postulate as in the following:

> Many honest investigators are deceived by the fact that when rainfall is light, dead leaves, moss and tangles of undergrowth in the forest may modify and restrict the flow and absorption of that which is precipitated, and rush to the conclusion that the forests restrain and minimize floods. But the fact is that when the rainfall is heavy and continuous, as it must be to cause noteworthy floods, there is practically no difference in the flow of water in the forest and in the open, for it can be shown that the run-off from a smooth surface and a rough one covered with debris is equal after the rough surface becomes well wetted. As it is only after all surfaces are saturated that flood conditions occur, *the rain that falls before saturation has little or no influence on freshets.**

Sometimes a subject naturally falls into divisions. In such a case, mention these in the topic sentence, then discuss each in its order as in the following:

> Any carefully considered scheme of education will strongly emphasize these three types of child development: the development of the physical, the development of the mental, the development of the social and the spiritual. The proper development of the first can take place only when intelligent attention is given to all those conditions in life which make the child so strong and healthy that he will be able to carry on his daily work with enjoyment and vigor, and a sense of animal well-being. The development of the mental assumes a type of instruction that will, through systematic discipline and regular creative tasks, develop each pupil's intellect to its highest degree of achievement. The development of the social and the spiritual is designed to make of the child a good citizen in his community and at the same time arouse in him those inner concepts and queries that make him conscious of the significance and the mystery of life.

Often the idea of a paragraph may be made clear by contrast, by presenting with it an opposite thought, as in the illustration given below:

> We all know how beautiful and noble modesty is; how we all admire it; it raises a man in our eyes to see him afraid of boasting;

---

* Willis Luther Moore, copyright, 1927, *The American Mercury.*

never showing off; never pushing himself forward.—Whenever, on the other hand, we see in wise and good men any vanity, boasting, pompousness of any kind, we call it a weakness in them, and are sorry to see them lowering themselves by the least want of divine modesty.

—Charles Kingsley, *Country Sermons*

In expositions, if you are explaining a process, you will describe the various steps in their normal sequence. Take as an example this rule for making kipfel:

> For the sweet tooth there are no more gratifying morsels than kipfel, which have the added attraction of being by no means commonplace. Into the making of kipfel go equal quantities of butter, flour and tender cottage cheese, all blended thoroughly and carefully. The usual pinch of salt is added and the mixture set into the icebox. When it has become cold and firm enough to be handled it is rolled out, cut into squares and each square bedecked with an overflowing teaspoonful of rose-red raspberry jam.*

In describing a scene, choose for your point of view the position from which you wish your reader to visualize the objects you are depicting. Let your topic sentence (expressed or implied) suggest the atmosphere or general idea, and then mention the details in logical and realistic order—the order in which the eye would naturally take them in. You may begin with some object in the foreground, and let the eye move along to the horizon; or you may choose as a starting point something in the far distance and from there come back to the things nearest you.

In describing a room, you might imagine yourself standing in the doorway opposite the fireplace; and with the fireplace for the central point, describe the general impression you get of the room—whether homelike, tidy, overcrowded, formal, gloomy, or cheerful. Then mention various objects, letting the eye progress from the remote toward the surroundings nearest you. Do not try to mention every detail, as that leads only to confusion. Just a general description including the most important objects.

In a purely narrative paragraph, the natural order of sentences would be chronological. Of course, in narration, any type of writing may occur, according to the need of the story. A complete story may be

---

*"That Seventh Breakfast," by Kiley Taylor, copyright, 1939, *The New York Times.*

told in an isolated paragraph; but even in so brief a narrative, the element of description, at least, must usually be introduced, to give the setting, and frequently exposition is necessary to make the story satisfactory; but none of this need interfere with the recounting of events in the order in which they would normally occur.

Parallel Construction.

Sometimes you can present your subject most effectively and hold together the thought of a paragraph by the use of balanced sentences —*parallel construction*. The device of repetition of the idea and similarity of sentence structure, keeps the sentences closely related not only in thought, but in form. All sentences of a series may begin with the same word or with similar phrases; or a series of complete sentences may be alike in structure. This method may be applied to an entire paragraph or to only a portion of a paragraph. It is used whenever the writer deems it desirable to give the main idea equal prominence in each sentence.

As a perfect example of *parallel construction*, I have chosen one of the most beautiful passages in literature, the Thirteenth Chapter of First Corinthians. For our purpose, I am taking the liberty of presenting it as a single paragraph.

> Though I speak with the tongues of men and of angels, and have not charity, I am become as sounding brass or a tinkling cymbal. And though I have the gift of prophecy, and understand all mysteries, and all knowledge; and though I have all faith, so that I could remove mountains, and have not charity—I am nothing. And though I bestow all my goods to feed the poor, and though I give my body to be burned, and have not charity, it profiteth me nothing. Charity suffereth long, and is kind; charity envieth not; vaunteth not itself, is not puffed up, doth not behave itself unseemly, seeketh not her own, is not easily provoked, thinketh no evil; rejoiceth not in iniquity, but rejoiceth in the truth; beareth all things, believeth all things, hopeth all things, endureth all things. Charity never faileth: but whether there be prophecies, they shall fail; whether there be tongues they shall cease; whether there be knowledge, it shall vanish away. For we know in part, and we prophesy in part. But when that which is perfect is come, then that which is in part shall be done away. When I was a child, I spoke as a child, I understood as a child, I thought as a child: but when I became a man, I put away childish things. For now we see through a glass darkly; but then face to face: now I know in part; but then shall I know even as also I am known. And now

abideth faith, hope, charity, these three; but the greatest of these is charity.

There are many passages in the Bible written in this style, notably the Lord's Prayer, and the Twenty-third Psalm. You would find it interesting to discover other examples for yourself. In profane literature, excellent illustrations are found in Burke's *Obedience to Instructions*, in his *Speeches*, and in the description of Westminster Hall in Macaulay's essay on Warren Hastings. A portion of the latter will give a good idea of the effectiveness of parallel construction in description.

> The place [Westminster] was worthy of such a trial. It was the great hall of William Rufus, the hall which had resounded with acclamations of the inauguration of thirty kings, the hall which had witnessed the just sentence of Bacon and the just absolution of Somers, the hall where the eloquence of Strafford had for a moment awed and melted a victorious party inflamed with just resentment, the hall where Charles had confronted the High Court of Justice with the placid courage which has half redeemed his fame. Neither military nor civil pomp was wanting. The avenues were lined with grenadiers. The streets were kept clear by cavalry. The peers, robed in gold and ermine, were marshaled by the heralds under Garter King-at-Arms. The judges in their vestments of state attended to give advice on points of law. Near a hundred and seventy lords, three-fourths of the Upper House as the Upper House then was, walked in solemn order from their usual place of assembling to the tribunal. The junior baron present led the way—George Elliot, Lord Heathfield, recently ennobled for his memorable defense of Gibraltar against the fleets and armies of France and Spain. The long procession was closed by the Duke of Norfolk, Earl Marshal of the realm, by the great dignitaries, and by the brothers and sons of the King. Last of all came the Prince of Wales, conspicuous by his fine person and noble bearing. The gray old walls were hung with scarlet. The long galleries were crowded by an audience such as has rarely excited the fears or the emulations of an orator. There were gathered together, from all parts of a great, free, enlightened, and prosperous empire, grace and female loveliness, wit and learning, the representatives of every science and of every art. There were seated round the Queen the fair-haired young daughters of the House of Brunswick. There the ambassadors of great kings and commonwealths gazed with admiration on a spectacle which no other country in the world could present.
> —Thomas Babington Macaulay, *The Trial of Warren Hastings*

Connectives.

Sometimes neither order nor construction of sentences is sufficient to make clear the thought of the paragraph, but there is a third method of securing Coherence to which we may have recourse—the use of *connectives*. Connectives rightly used will bring out the proper relation of ideas and conduct the reader from one point to another throughout the paragraph. It will be well for you to familiarize yourself with the following list of connectives and their respective denotations.

I. *Coordinating Connectives* (those used to connect elements of equal rank) denoting:

1. *addition*	2. *contrast*	3. *conclusion*	4. *alternation*
and	but	consequently	either—or
also	however	hence	neither—nor
besides	nevertheless	so	whether—or
moreover	notwithstanding	therefore	
	still	accordingly	
	than	thus	
	yet		
	while		

II. *Subordinating Connectives* (those used to connect elements of unequal rank) denoting:

1. *concession*	2. *condition*	3. *purpose*	4. *comparison*
though	if	that	as
although	unless	lest	

5. *Adverbial Connectives*, denoting:

a. *cause*	b. *manner*	c. *time*	d. *place*
as	as	when	whence
because	how	whenever	whither
for		now	where
since			

6. *Relative Pronouns*
   who, which, what, that

7. *Interrogative Pronouns*
   who, which, what (when used in direct questions)

III. *Connective Phrases*, such as:

on the other hand	in contradistinction to
in addition to	at the same time
in the first place	at least
for instance	in fact
for example	for that matter
in such cases	not only—but also

Others may occur to you, and still others you will discover in your reading.

Connectives may be used either at the beginning or in the midst of sentences. Most sentences cannot properly begin with "and" or "but"; yet in certain cases they may do so with perfect propriety. For instance, if you make a brief contrasting statement which you do not intend to enlarge upon, place a comma or semicolon after the original assertion and begin the following with "but," as: "There was a picnic yesterday, but we did not go." If, however, the contrasting statement is of special significance, or if you wish to discuss it further, you will give it prominence by putting it in a separate sentence beginning with "but." "There was a picnic yesterday. But we did not go."

Similarly, when you want to add to a statement further details which are of importance, you may emphasize them by putting them in a separate sentence, beginning with *and*. The following paragraph from Macaulay's *Life of Johnson* illustrates both these points:

> Mannerism is pardonable and is sometimes even agreeable, when the manner, though vicious, is natural. Few readers, for example, would be willing to part with the mannerism of Milton or of Burke. *But* a mannerism which does not sit easy on the mannerist, which has been adopted on principle, and which can be sustained only by constant effort, is always offensive. *And* such is the mannerism of Johnson.

For the sake of Coherence and clarity of thought sentences may begin with *for, yet, still, however, nevertheless, moreover,* and other such connectives which ordinarily would not be appropriately placed at the beginning.

The judicious use of connectives gives a smoothness of style which is lacking in unconnected sentences and phrases, however closely related in thought. A style without connectives has an unpleasant jerkiness; it is like jolting along in an old-fashioned wagon on a rough country road. This is especially true if the sentences are very short. For very simple examples, take these two paragraphs:

> There was a circus in town. Jane and Johnny's father would not let them go. They could not stand it! They went out to the garden. They could not play. They cried. Jane was eight. Johnny was six.

That is the way a small child, or a grownup with an immature mind might write the paragraph that is given below:

> A circus had come to town *and* most of the school children were going; *but when* Jane and Johnny had asked their father's permission to go, he had refused. With the feeling that their hearts were breaking they went off hand-in-hand toward the garden; *but* they could not play, *for* they were weighed down with sorrow *and* their eyes were full of tears. Instead of playing they threw themselves down on the grass *and* cried. *For* Jane was only eight *and* Johnny was only six *and* they could not go to the circus!

One method of connecting, or binding together the sentences of a paragraph is by repetition of words and phrases, or of synonyms and synonymous phrases. This is called dovetailing style. The italicized words in the following paragraph from an editorial in the *Boston Herald* illustrate this point.

A TOWER OF SECURITY

> Once more the attention of the *public* has been called to that *vastly* useful and altogether *democratic financial institution*, American *life insurance*. Its *vastness* is indicated by the operations reported for last year. The *amount* of *insurance* in force was more than $110,000,000,000, and the *total* paid out in death claims and to living *policyholders* was $2,600,000,000. The *democracy* of this *great business* is shown by the fact that half the *population* of the United States are *policyholders;* the average amount of *insurance* held by these 64,000,000 *people* is $1730.

A most excellent example of the use of synonyms and synonymous phrases is found in Macaulay's *Essay on Addison:*

> Such were Addison's *talents* for conversation. But his *rare gifts* were not exhibited to *crowds* or *strangers*. As soon as he entered a *large company*, as soon as he saw an *unknown face*, his lips were

sealed, and his manners became constrained. None who met him only in *great assemblies* would have been able to believe that he was the same man who had often kept a few friends listening and laughing *around a table* from the time when the play ended till the clock of St. Paul's in Covent Garden struck four. Yet even at such *a table* he was not seen to the *best advantage*. To enjoy his conversation at the *highest perfection*, it was necessary *to be alone with him*, and to hear him, in his own phrase, think aloud. "There is no such thing," he used to say, "as real conversation, but *between two persons*."

Emphasis

You have seen the importance of Unity and Coherence in paragraph structure. Both are closely allied to the third major principle of composition, *Emphasis*. Frequently, a method which will produce one will produce either of the others. But a paragraph, however unified and coherent, may be lacking in character and significance if it be lacking in Emphasis.

Emphasis governs the external structure of the paragraph, and here, as in Unity, the topic sentence is of value. The most important positions in a paragraph are the beginning and the end, therefore the *most important* ideas must be placed at *the beginning and at the end*. Open with your topic sentence, phrased as in your outline, or in different words, and give special significance to the theme by allowing the summarizing sentence to emphasize forcibly the main idea.

In argument, state your postulate and build up with ever increasing forcefulness to the closing sentence, ending with the most important point, and so clinching the argument. As an illustration of this we may use the same excellent one already used in the discussion of Unity—the paragraph from Horace Mann on page 141 in this chapter.

Proportion.

Another point in securing Emphasis which demands special attention is the law of *Proportion*. To emphasize adequately the important points you must observe strictly the comparative values of principal and subordinate matter. Express subordinate ideas in subordinate forms and place them in subordinate positions, giving the more prominent position and the greater amount of space to the more important ideas. The following will illustrate this point:

> The ordinary citizen, reasonably well educated, feels the need for at least four kinds of reading. In the first place, he usually gives

at least half an hour to the daily newspaper; he wants to keep thoroughly informed concerning local, national, and international affairs; in the second place, he relies upon his trade or professional journal to keep him fully abreast with the important facts pertaining to his vocational life; in the third place, he ordinarily wishes to do a certain amount of magazine reading—magazine reading that is divorced from his practical, everyday occupation and discusses in a thorough manner significant movements in the nation and the world. And, finally, he will naturally devote a good deal of time to the reading of good books, both old and new, that will enlarge his intellectual horizon and deepen his spiritual insight.

In description, atmosphere is the all-important thing. You must leave the reader with a clearly visualized image, and a definite feeling of the significance of the scene. Suggest the dominant tone and then mention only the important points, and end with a sentence or phrase which will emphasize the atmosphere of beauty or ugliness, bleakness or joy, warmth or chill, whatever has been the suggested tone.

In the following paragraph, notice how the impression of cheer and happiness prevails:

> The early sunshine was already pouring its gold upon the mountain tops; and though the valleys were still in shadow, they smiled cheerfully in the promise of the bright day that was hastening onward. The village, completely shut in by hills, which swelled away gently about it, looked as if it had rested peacefully in the hollow of the great hand of Providence. Every dwelling was distinctly visible; the little spires of the two churches pointed upward, and caught a fore-glimmering of brightness from the sun-gilt skies upon their gilded weathercocks. The tavern was astir, and the figure of the old, smoke-dried stage-agent, cigar in mouth, was seen beneath the stoop. Old Graylock was glorified with a golden cloud upon his head. Scattered likewise over the breasts of the surrounding mountains, there were heaps of hoary mist, in fantastic shapes, some of them far down into the valley, others high up toward the summits, and still others, of the same family of mist or cloud, hovering in the gold radiance of the upper atmosphere. Stepping from one to another of the clouds that rested on the hills, and thence to the loftier brotherhood that sailed in air, it seemed almost as if a mortal man might thus ascend into the heavenly regions. Earth was so mingled with sky that it was a day dream to look at it.
>
> —Nathaniel Hawthorne, *Ethan Brand*

Climax.

A narrative paragraph may be effectively emphasized by *climax*. This is excellently illustrated by the following short passage:

> No more firing was heard at Brussels—the pursuit rolled miles away. Darkness came down on the field and city; and Amelia was praying for George, who was lying on his face, dead, with a bullet through his heart.
> —William Makepeace Thackeray, *Vanity Fair*

Related Paragraphs

Once more, let me remind you that the principles of Unity, Coherence, and Emphasis, which apply to the construction of the isolated paragraph, apply also to the *related paragraph*. In general, too, the same methods are used in carrying out these principles and practices—the outline, the topic sentence, the devices of amplifying, defining, illustrating, comparing, contrasting, restricting, repetition, all the various constructions. Indeed, every device that is used in the development of the isolated paragraph may also be used in the related paragraph. The topic sentences, expressed or implied, are suggested by the headings and subheadings of the outline.

But while the isolated paragraph is complete in itself, related paragraphs are more or less dependent on each other. They must do for the essay what the sentence does for the paragraph. As a paragraph is made up of sentences upon which depend its Unity, Coherence, and Emphasis, so is a longer composition made up of paragraphs upon which depend its Unity, Coherence, and Emphasis.

The Introductory Paragraph.

The introductory paragraph performs the same service for the essay that the topic sentence does for the individual paragraph. It might, indeed, be called the *topic paragraph*, for it states, or implies, the subject in hand, and in formal discourse, at least, it expands the theme sufficiently to indicate the way in which it will be developed.

In narrative writing, the introductory paragraph may be treated in almost any way that will give the setting for the story—by describing the scene or the appearance of a character or group of characters, or by explaining past events or situations to make clear the way for the development of the story. Frequently an author ignores the introduction and plunges at once into the story.

Thackeray opens the first chapter of *Vanity Fair* in a manner combining several methods.

> While the present century was in its teens, and on one sunshiny morning in June, there drove up to the great iron gate of Miss Pinkerton's academy for young ladies, on Chiswick Mall, a large family coach, with two fat horses in blazing harness, driven by a fat coachman in a three-cornered hat and wig, at the rate of four miles an hour. A black servant, who reposed on the box beside the fat coachman, uncurled his bandy legs as soon as the equipage drew up opposite Miss Pinkerton's shining brass plate, and as he pulled the bell, at least a score of young heads were seen peering out of the narrow windows of the stately old brick house. Nay, the acute observer might have recognized the little red nose of good-natured Miss Jemima Pinkerton herself, rising over some geranium-pots in the window of that lady's own drawing-room.

Thackeray not only sets the stage and suggests the atmosphere but introduces several characters and gets the story under way.

In *O Pioneers*, Willa Cather begins: "One January day, thirty years ago, the little town of Hanover, anchored on a windy Nebraska tableland, was trying not to be blown away." Then follows a rather long description of the little town, in the midst of the cold and snow, and "the howling wind."

Newspaper articles often combine the functions of the introductory and the concluding paragraphs, and give the gist of the subject and the summary at the beginning, leaving the details to the amplifying paragraphs.

You will find in this set of books numerous examples of introductory paragraphs in exposition.

The Amplifying Paragraph.

After the introduction, follow the amplifying paragraphs. These develop the theme as the sentences following the topic sentence develop the paragraph. There will be one or more of these amplifying paragraphs, according to the number and importance of the headings and subheadings of the subject as you have outlined it.

The Transitional Paragraph.

The transitional paragraph corresponds to the connectives between words, phrases, and sentences. It serves as the connecting link between paragraphs. It makes the transition from one phase of the subject to another, thus preserving Coherence, clarifying the meaning, and avoiding abruptness in style. It is seldom necessary that it should be a long paragraph; the briefer one is usually better. As a rule, it indicates the connection between the main ideas of the composition; a change in time, or place, or conditions. In general, it should first refer to something in the preceding paragraph and then suggest the idea to be discussed in the succeeding one. In argument or exposition it may serve to emphasize some important point by repeating the thought of the immediately preceding paragraph and indicating the thought in the paragraph that follows. In narrative, it may refer briefly to the events related in the preceding paragraph, and then foreshadow the situation to be discovered as the story progresses. Frequently, it merely suggests a change in time, place or weather. One that might take a prize for brevity is this: "Day had come."—from *What Vasile Saw*, by Queen Marie of Roumania. It might have been expanded, making rather a smoother transition, in this way: "After the long, terrifying night, it was a relief to see that day had come." Transitions between two paragraphs may sometimes be made also by beginning them with the same connectives with which sentences may begin—*but, and, yet, still,* and so on.

The Concluding Paragraph.

The concluding paragraph does for the whole what the final sentence does for the isolated paragraph. It must be a summary of all the others, leaving in the reader's mind a clear idea of the subject. In old-fashioned novels this paragraph left the reader with a very definite idea as to the way the story ended—every character well accounted for, everything perfectly satisfactory; but often in modern fiction the concluding paragraph either merely suggests the outcome, leaving it to our imaginations to do the rest, or simply stops in the midst of everything.

In this discussion of paragraphs, I have apparently considered only the written ones; but you may have noticed references not only to the *reader*, but to the *hearer*. This, of course, has indicated to you that paragraphs may be spoken as well as written. They may be indicated in spoken discourse in several ways, which have been discussed in Chapters V and VI of *Your Command of Spoken English*. Another thing which might be mentioned is the fact that the principles of paragraph structure may be applied to the writing of letters—both social and business.

In all these matters common sense is the ruling factor. Naturally a writer or a speaker is concerned not merely with the expression of his own ideas; he is concerned with the communication of these ideas to others. In this communication, paragraphs and the indentations which externally mark them, and the major principles of Unity, Coherence, and Emphasis which internally fuse them, become a guide; they serve the readers as directors and interpreters.

PRACTICES

Those who in their writing are anxious to construct their paragraphs in such a way as to communicate their ideas most effectively should try to carry out all the suggestions here offered.

PRACTICE 1
Paragraphing When Revising Manuscript

In revising your manuscript or in correcting your proof, you frequently wish to change your own paragraph structure. What struck you as the proper and logical division while you wrote now strikes you as improper and illogical. There are naturally two types of changes that suggest themselves. One type suggests a new paragraph—a new indentation. This you indicate by inserting the symbol ¶ at the beginning of the sentence which is to mark the new paragraph. If you are preparing your manuscript for a printer, you may also place this symbol in the margin. The other type suggests a coalescing of two or more of your present paragraphs into one. At the point where you now think there should be no indentation, you write the symbol *No* ¶. You may place this direction also in the margin.

We can illustrate these instructions concretely by proposing certain changes in the foregoing paragraph. As an editor or as an author, you decide that there should be a new paragraph—an indentation—at the beginning of the third sentence. You accordingly place your paragraph symbol ¶ before the word *There*. You decide furthermore, that you would like a new paragraph beginning with the seventh sentence—*The other type suggests*, etc. You accordingly place before the word *The* the symbol ¶.

Reversing this process, you may assume that the material was originally written in three paragraphs.* In revising you feel it should be printed or rewritten as one. Therefore at the two designated places, you insert your symbol *No ¶*.

Study the following extract carefully. Be able to answer these questions:

1. Do you prefer to let this paragraph stand as it is?
2. Are there changes in indentation that should unquestionably be made?
3. Are there changes that might possibly be made?

With regard to sexual matters, the best opinion of our best medical men, the practice of those nations which have proved most vigorous and comely, the evils that have followed this or that, the good that has attended upon the other should be ascertained by men who, being neither moral nor immoral and not caring two straws what the conclusion arrived at might be, should desire only to get hold of the best available information. The result should be written down with some fullness and put before the young of both sexes as soon as they are old enough to understand such matters at all. There should be no mystery or reserve. None but the corrupt will wish to corrupt facts; honest people will accept them eagerly, whatever they may prove to be, and will convey them to others as accurately as they can. On what pretext therefore can it be well that knowledge should be withheld from the universal gaze upon a matter of such universal interest? It cannot be pretended that there is nothing to be known on these matters beyond what unaided boys and girls can be left without risk to find out for themselves. Not one in a hundred who remembers his own boyhood will say this. How, then, are they excusable who have the care of young people and yet leave a matter of such vital importance so almost absolutely to take care of itself, although they well know how common error is, how easy to fall into and how disastrous in its effects both upon the individual and the race? Next to sexual matters there are none upon which there is such complete reserve between parents and children as on those connected with money. The father keeps his affairs as closely as he can to himself and is most jealous of letting his children into a knowledge of how he manages his money. His children are like monks in a monastery as regards money and he

---

*In this instance there are no urgent reasons for preferring the single paragraph to the three paragraphs. Either form is correct. The three paragraphs may draw more particular attention to the two separately designated points. However, a succession of short paragraphs presents on the page a somewhat fragmentary appearance.

calls this training them up with the strictest regard to principle. Nevertheless he thinks himself ill-used if his son, on entering life, falls a victim to designing persons whose knowledge of how money is made and lost is greater than his own.*

—Samuel Butler, *Young People*

Having made your decision concerning the paragraphing of the foregoing, why not write out your own personal comments on the opinions Samuel Butler here expresses? Plan your procedures carefully. Decide in advance the number of paragraphs you will write and the ideas that you will include in each.

PRACTICE 2

Paragraphs of Definite Purpose

Develop a short editorial—a single paragraph from each of these sentences.

1. Everything presages a Republican (Democratic) victory at tomorrow's polls.
2. The community-chest drive deserves your enthusiastic support.
3. Adult learning contrasts strongly with adolescent learning.
4. To know the principles of Unity, Coherence, and Emphasis is to realize their value in the writing of paragraphs.
5. We shall never have any great improvement in our language habits until we have acquired a respect for craftsmanship.
6. There is a vast difference between the *denotation* and the *connotation* of words.

PRACTICE 3

Descriptive Paragraphs

Test your power to write a descriptive paragraph by using one of these sentences as the beginning:

1. From the general appearance of the young woman, I knew that she had been in a serious accident.
2. The house was furnished in perfect taste.
3. The garden spoke immediately of long neglect.
4. I think I have never seen a man whose countenance expressed such despair.
5. The whole house breathed an atmosphere of hospitality.

---

*From *Notebooks of Samuel Butler*, courtesy of Jonathan Cape Limited, London, England.

PRACTICE 4

Topic Sentences

In any of the longer compositions you have written, preferably one of an expository nature, go over your topic sentences. Check them for power, for precision and for economy and vigor of statement. Below are the initial sentences, most of them topic sentences, of the first ten paragraphs of Emerson's "Self-Reliance." Compare your sentences with these.

1. I read the other day some verses written by an eminent painter which were original and not conventional.
2. There is a time in every man's education when he arrives at the conviction that envy is ignorance; that imitation is suicide; that he must take himself for better or worse as his portion; that though the wide universe is full of good, no kernel of nourishing corn can come to him but through his toil bestowed on that plot of ground which is given to him to till.
3. Trust thyself: every heart vibrates to that iron string.
4. What pretty oracles nature yields us on this text in the face and behavior of children, babes, and even brutes.
5. The nonchalance of boys who are sure of a dinner, and would disdain as much as a lord to do or say aught to conciliate one, is the healthy attitude of human nature.
6. These are the voices which we hear in solitude, but they grow faint and inaudible as we enter into the world.
7. Whoso would be a man, must be a nonconformist.
8. Virtues are, in the popular estimate, rather the exception than the rule.
9. What I must do is all that concerns me, not what the people think.
10. The objection to conforming to usages that have become dead to you is that it scatters your force.

PRACTICE 5

Development by Definition

A forceful kind of paragraph is developed by definition: that is, by telling what a thing is or does. In the two selections here given, defining (*a*) the capital letter, and (*b*) a true classic, study the method.

   a. The initial capital letter is all that remains of our originally all-capital alphabet. It survives because it serves a definite purpose, such as introducing a sentence or an enumeration, distinguishing an individual within a class, or indicating preeminence,

respect, or distinction attaching to a certain individual, position, or object. By thus emphasizing words, the capital letter helps the reader to grasp their significance more readily. Purpose, therefore, rather than mere opinion, is the logical criterion in deciding whether a particular word should be capitalized.
—*Style Manual of the Government Printing Office*

b. A true classic ... is an author who has enriched the human mind, increased its treasure, and caused it to advance a step; who has discovered some moral and not equivocal truth, or revealed some eternal passion in that heart where all seemed known and discovered; who has expressed his thought, observation, or invention, in no matter what form, only provided it be broad and great, refined and sensible, sane and beautiful in itself; who has spoken to all in his own peculiar style, a style which is found to be also that of the whole world, a style new without neologism, new and old, easily contemporary with all time.
—Sainte-Beuve, *What Is a Classic?*

Now try the method by definition in developing a paragraph on one or two of these topics:

1. The good life.
2. The bore.
3. The masterpiece.
4. The cultured person.
5. The speech that pleases.
6. The man of character.

PRACTICE 6

Sound and Movement in Paragraphs

Prose pleases by its distinction of thought and phrase; it pleases, as well, by ease of movement and beauty of sound. In writing the paragraphs specified in the preceding Practices, you have been concerned chiefly with thought and expression; now consider sound and movement.

Just how the ease and swiftness of the paragraph below was secured is a complicated and elusive problem. But one thing is clear: alliteration was largely instrumental. The dominantly alliterative letters are italicized here. Change, for instance, some of the *w*'s in the first sentence; and though you may not mar its rhythm, you spoil its sound. Shift the position of the phrases, and see how the movement is affected.

Rip Van *W*inkle, ho*w*ever, *w*as one of those happy mortals, of foolish, *w*ell-oiled dispositions, *w*ho take the *w*orld easy, eat *w*hite bread or brown, *w*hichever can be got *w*ith least thought or trouble, and *w*ould rather starve on a penny than *w*ork for a

PARAGRAPH STRUCTURE

pound. If left to himself, he would have whistled life away in perfect contentment; but his wife kept continually dinning in his ears about his idleness, his carelessness, and the ruin he was bringing on his family. [Do you detect the disappointment the ear suffers here?] Morning, noon and night, her tongue was incessantly going, and everything he said or did was sure to produce a torrent of household eloquence. [This is especially swift.] Rip had but one way of replying to all lectures of the kind, and that, by frequent use, had grown into a habit. [This falls down.] He shrugged his shoulders, shook his head, cast up his eyes, but said nothing. [This picks up.] This, however, always provoked a fresh volley from his wife; so that he was fain to draw off his forces, and take to the outside of the house—the only side which, in truth, belongs to a hen-pecked husband. [Here *t*, *h*, and *f* share honors; *r*, you may have noted, has been prominent throughout the paragraph, though unmarked.]

—Washington Irving, *Rip Van Winkle*

Now examine the paragraphs that you have written in Practice 5. Do they "ride," do they please the ear? If not, make changes: shift phrases, transpose words, repeat like sounds.

PRACTICE 7

Emphasis by Contrast

One of the simplest and most effective ways of bringing out your points in a paragraph is the use of contrast. In this paragraph, for instance, the delights of biography are contrasted with the shortcomings of actually knowing the great. Observe the method.

The delights of biography are those of the highest human intercourse, in almost limitless diversity, which no one could hope to enjoy among the living. Even though you were placed so favorably that you became acquainted with many of the most interesting personages of your own time, were it not for this magic art, which makes the past present and the dead to live, you would still be shut out from all acquaintance with your forerunners. But thanks to biography, you have only to reach out your hand and take down a volume from your shelf in order to converse with Napoleon or Bismarck, Lincoln or Cavour. You need spend no weary hours in antechambers on the chance of snatching a hasty interview. They wait upon your pleasure. No business of state can put you off. They talk and you listen. They disclose to you their inmost secrets. Carlyle may be never so petulant, Luther never so bluff, Swift never so bitter, but they must admit you, and the very defects which might have interposed a screen between each of them living and you are as loopholes through which you look into their hearts. So you may come to know them better than their contemporaries knew them, better than you know your intimates, or, unless you are a master of self-scrutiny, better than you know yourself.

—W. R. Thayer, *Lectures on The Harvard Classics*

Now try your hand at a paragraph on any one of these subjects:

1. The delights of the drama—over actual life.
2. The pleasure of living alone—rather than with others.
3. The life of obscurity—rather than of celebrity.

PRACTICE 8

Specific Detail in the Paragraph

If you analyze these two paragraphs written by the Brontë sisters, you will discern that a good part of the effect is produced by the writers' having chosen specific words rather than general words: *primroses and crocuses* (instead of "spring flowers"), *larks* (instead of "birds"), *soft western or southern gales* (instead of "gentle winds").

> That Friday made the last of our fine days for a month. In the evening the weather broke: the wind shifted from south to north-east, and brought rain first, and then sleet and snow. On the morrow one could hardly imagine that there had been three weeks of summer: the primroses and crocuses were hidden under wintry drifts; the larks were silent, the young leaves of the early trees smitten and blackened. And dreary, and chill, and dismal, that morrow did creep over!
>
> —Emily Brontë, *Wuthering Heights*

> April advanced to May; a bright, serene May it was; days of blue sky, placid sunshine, and soft western or southern gales filled up its duration. And now vegetation matured with vigour; Lowood shook loose its tresses; it became all green, all flowery; its great elm, ash, and oak skeletons were restored to majestic life; woodland plants sprang up profusely in its recesses; unnumbered varieties of moss filled its hollows, and it made a strange ground-sunshine out of the wealth of its wild primrose plants...
>
> —Charlotte Brontë, *Jane Eyre*

Remembering to keep your detail specific, write a paragraph on one of these common, and wondrous, sights:

1. A wintry day. 2. A day in autumn. 3. A June day.

CHAPTER VI

SENTENCE STRUCTURE

JUST A LITTLE while before I commenced writing this chapter, my eye chanced to fall upon a bit of writing that contained this sentence: "Walking along the spray-drenched shore this morning the wild, swift-running waves were more beautiful and more riotous than I had ever before seen them." Now there are some things to admire in that sentence. I am sure that the writer clearly visualized the scene; I am equally sure that he has a certain ability to communicate his experiences and his sense impressions to others; he has a real feeling for word values. But we can all easily see that he needs to develop a more critical attitude toward his sentence patterns; he needs to learn that the phrase *walking along the spray-drenched shore* cannot logically belong to *waves*—as the grammatical form of the sentence implies. It wasn't the *waves* that were *walking;* it was the unexpressed *I*. He should revise the sentence so as to make the logic and grammatical form agree—"Walking along the spray-drenched shore this morning, I watched the wild swift-running waves. They were more beautiful and more riotous than I had ever before seen them."

This faulty construction—*Walking along the shore, the waves*—is an example of a "dangling participle"; it is only one type out of scores of errors that untrained writers make in constructing their sentences. Indeed, this particular fault is one that not infrequently traps even professional authors—authors who chance at the moment to be a bit unwary. And because it is so necessary that he who aspires to proficiency in written English should guard against this and other lapses, we shall endeavor in this section to examine in some detail both the commoner faults and the commoner virtues of sentence structure.

You will recall that this matter of correct sentence structure has already been discussed in *Your English and Your Personality*, but in a less detailed manner than that adopted for this chapter. The subject deserves very special treatment in the present volume, which is dealing with written English, for a sentence once expressed in written or printed form is set in a pattern more firmly fixed, more fully moulded.

It lacks the easy plasticity of one that is orally formed; its faults and its virtues are subjected to more leisurely and more impartial scrutiny. In printed form, especially, it is too obvious and too permanent to escape criticism.

Moreover, the subject of sentence structure is one that can be very definitely taught and very definitely learned. While we admit the possibility of many varied ways in which an individual sentence may be written, we are at the same time able to discover the essential principles that constantly act as practical working guides in both grammar and rhetoric. The entire topic can perhaps best be treated by offering detailed suggestions in a series of postulates numerous enough to cover all the important points.

1. *We grant the value of the simple sentence.*

The *simple* sentence is here to be compared with the *compound* and the *complex*. This first postulate is a simple sentence; it has but one subject—*we*; and one predicate—*grant*. Usually a simple sentence is short, crisp, and direct. It is unencumbered by many modifiers. Used too frequently in a paragraph it produces a choppy, chugging effect. But we need constantly to be reminded of its power to present an idea in a clear, concise fashion. The makers of proverbs have realized this, as is apparent in such examples as these:

a. A penny saved is a penny earned.
b. Mighty strokes fell giant oaks.
c. A boy's will is the wind's will.
d. Whatever is, is right.
e. An honest man is the noblest work of God.
f. Go to the ant, thou sluggard.
g. Misery loves company.
h. Haste makes waste.

As you study the work of writers who reveal a marked predisposition to the simple sentence, you will probably discover that it produces a decisive, clear-cut style of expression that lends vigor and conviction to the utterance. If it be employed too freely, however, these effects will have been secured at some sacrifice; the simple sentence too often produces monotony—and gives a more or less explosive motion to the movement of the prose. An easy flow of language is not secured by simple sentences arranged in a long sequence. Simple sentences often have a special force of their own, but they need to be mingled with the compound and the complex.

2. *The compound sentence allows two or more coordinate ideas to link and express themselves jointly in a single sentence.*

Sometimes two similar ideas are connected by an *and* or an *or:*

I shall go to my office, *and* there I shall soon complete the writing of my report.

Will he now dreamily sleep *or* will he sleepily dream?

And sometimes we shall have a compound sentence that expresses two contrasting notions connected by *but:*

He will begin the study of commercial law, *but* he will never complete it.

By turning to the Book of Proverbs we can discover many examples of the effective use of contrasting ideas expressed in compound sentences. To the following examples, many readers will be able to add others.

Hatred stirreth up strifes: but love covereth all sins. x, 12

He that gathereth in summer is a wise son: but he that sleepeth in harvest is a son that causeth shame. x, 5

He that walketh uprightly walketh surely: but he that perverteth his ways shall be known. x, 9

The mouth of a righteous man is a well of life: but violence covereth the mouth of the wicked. x, 11

The righteous shall never be removed: but the wicked shall not inhabit the earth. x, 30

Even though the forms of the verb give these verses an archaic note, the compound construction is the same as that freely employed in modern prose. Selecting at random from the books within easy reach, I picked up a copy of Percy Boynton's *Literature and American Life.* The volume opened by chance to a paragraph that discusses Sidney Lanier's interest in music. Here is a compound sentence moulded in a matrix similar to the one used in sentences from the Proverbs: "He had reveled in concerts in New York, but in San Antonio he fell in with a group of musicians as a fellow player."

And now, glancing at a paragraph of my own that has just come from the typist, I find that I have written a brief compound sentence similar in structure to the one I have just quoted. The sentence is in a section that discusses the difficulty a person of earth-bound, commonplace, and unimaginative mind experiences in following the lines of a highly fanciful poem: "He may pronounce the words, but he cannot read creatively."

Readers of these sentences will realize that here is a common form which they have frequently used in both conversation and writing. Common sense has probably emphasized the care needed in keeping appropriate the items linked by such conjunctions as *or, and,* and *but.* There should be a certain naturalness and congeniality and propriety between the elements thus conjoined. Unless we wished to be deliberately absurd, we would not, for example, write: "He was a Republican, but he regularly rode home on the six-o'clock train." And certainly we would see the impropriety in this: "He was the father of the tariff bill and brother of the mayor of his home town." Here the nature of the fault is apparent; the word *father* used in a figurative sense is linked with the word *brother* used in a literal sense. Such a linking is almost sure to be ludicrous. The factors that best save us from such minor tragedies are common sense and humor.

But even though the compound sentence encourages the yoking of elements of equal rank, it imposes a limit on the number of the yokings. Here is an example of such over-yoking: "She became recklessly enamored with the social life of Greenwich Village and she went out every evening and she neglected her regular work and she came near losing her position and her repeated disappointments finally brought on a sense of deep depression." It is evident that such piling up of coordinate ideas not only clutters up the sentence with too many details, but also produces an inexcusable monotony. The fault is common among immature writers who have as yet attained no sense of style and no control in the weaving of artistic sentence patterns.

3. *Special care should be given to the proper punctuation of the compound sentence.*

Here, for example, is a common type of error:

I met my mother at the railway station, she had gone there with Cousin Ellen.

This is what we call the "comma blunder" or the "comma splice." Instead of the comma after *station* we should have a semicolon (;). The two principal clauses—"I met my mother at the railway station" and "she had gone there with Cousin Ellen" taken together compose the compound sentence. The break between the two ideas is too marked to be indicated by a comma; good usage favors the semicolon. Some writers are indeed so careless or so untrained as to have no punctuation mark at all after *station*. Such a fault is called the "run-on" sentence.

4. *A complex sentence is of special value in expressing subordinate ideas in subordinate forms.*

The significance of this postulate is obvious to those who will recall the nature of two contrasting kinds of clauses—the *principal* and the *subordinate*. Here are examples:

a. ———Principal clause——— ——Subordinate clause——
 I had more trouble with my English | when I was much younger.

b. ———Subordinate clause——— ———Principal clause———
 Since my vacation comes in August, | we cannot spend it as we had planned.

c. ———Principal clause——— ———Subordinate clause———
 We shall now visit the Tower, | where the Queen was imprisoned.

d. ———Subordinate clause———
 Washington, | who was president for eight years, | declined a third term.

The principal clause here is *Washington declined a third term*.

Writers often reveal a lack of discrimination in their expression of ideas. If a writer has two ideas which he thinks are really coordinate he may then appropriately bring out this equality by using the compound-sentence pattern—as in this instance: "He had worked unusually hard and he had exceeded his last year's sales record." This is a perfectly justifiable form. If the writer desires, however, to make the form of the expression express the causal relationship and place a slightly greater emphasis on the result, he could use the complex form: "Since he had worked unusually hard, he had exceeded his last year's sales record."

The demand for a change from the compound to the complex is more urgent in the following: "I went downtown this morning and I had the most exciting experience of my life." As it is immediately obvious that these two ideas are not of equal rank, we put the less important thought into a subordinate clause: "While I was downtown this morning I had the most exciting experience of my life." This change places the emphasis upon the principal clause; it expresses the lesser idea in a subordinate form.

Again, we may express a truism: Good English is largely a matter of clear thinking and common sense. If ideas are coordinate, put them into a coordinate form — the compound sentence; if one idea is subordinate, put it into a subordinate clause. Or perhaps this phrasing may be more easily remembered: Put principal ideas into principal clauses; put subordinate ideas into subordinate clauses or phrases.

5. *We should learn the proper use of the participial phrase.*

The word *phrases* at the end of the previous discussion under Postulate 4 was added in order to give proper recognition to such typical expressions as those here italicized:

a. *Having long been interested in writing*, he decided to enter upon a literary career.

b. *Being assured of an adequate income from annuities*, he decided that he could afford to put some of his capital into speculative securities.

c. *By mastering each new word that he met in his reading*, he was finally able to express his ideas with rare flexibility and precision.

d. *The arrangements all made*, he now awaited the arrival of the book.

Such participial phrases provide another pattern for the expression of subordinate ideas. They arrange the scene or provide the setting in which the principal action may take place. Ordinarily a subordinate clause could express the same idea as do these participial phrases; but a writer who has control of each of the two forms may, by a diversified interplay of the patterns, easily avoid monotony—one of the arch enemies of an effective style.

6. *The relationship of the parts of sentences must be unmistakable.*

Faults in the structure of compound and complex sentences—and sometimes, indeed, in simple sentences—are almost sure to occur when the exact relationship of the various ideas is not both clearly seen and clearly expressed. The sentences that follow provide illustrations of faulty relationships.

> a. We can readily jot down three points in the narrative skill of the author, because he has given careful attention to the plot, the characters, and the setting.

When you are tempted to use the word *because* in situations analogous to this, pause a moment to study the relationships expressed by the different ideas. As a matter of fact, the causal idea may here be left out of account. The persons comprehended by the *we* may not, as a matter of fact, readily see the narrative skill. The sentence can be revised to read: "We can readily jot down three points in the narrative skill of the novelist: he has given careful attention to the plot, the characters, and the setting." The portion of the sentence following the word *novelist* simply mentions concrete items under the main assertion.

> b. Chess is my favorite recreation, and here is a brief description of the game.

The sentence thus constructed gives undue prominence to the fact that chess is the writer's favorite game. The first element—*chess is my favorite recreation*—should not be made coordinate with the second element—*here is a brief description of the game*. You can establish the correct relationship between the two parts by revising the sentence: "The game of chess, which is my favorite recreation, may be described as follows."

> c. I was greatly interested in watching a flock of sheep gracefully weaving their way among the men and dogs that were being driven to market.

The fault here is due to misplacement of the relative clause—*that were being driven to market*. The relative pronoun *that* is here too far removed from its antecedent, *flock of sheep;* its antecedent seems to be *men* and *dogs*. The sentence may be recast to read: "The flock of sheep on their way to market interested me greatly as I watched them weaving their way among the men and dogs."

Oftentimes you will discover that a sentence contains too many ideas to be expressed as a single unit. Split it in two. In the case of the sentence about the sheep you may prefer such a decided recasting as this: "I was interested in watching a flock of sheep that were being driven to market. The graceful way in which they wove in and out among the men and dogs was particularly impressive." Let common sense and good taste be your dual guides.

7. *Good sentence structure demands proper tense sequence.*

You will recall the items in grammar that tell us that the tense of a verb indicates the time of the action, being, or state. There are six tenses—here illustrated by the forms of the verb *to write*.

Present—I write
Present perfect—I have written
Past—I wrote

Past perfect—I had written
Future—I shall write
Future perfect—I shall have written

Tense sequence implies that the time indicated by verbs used together must be consistent. The incorrect forms below indicate common violations of this principle; the correct forms indicate the proper revisions.

INCORRECT	CORRECT
Mr. and Mrs. Alden regret that they *will be unable* to accept Mrs. Whitney's invitation for Friday evening.	Mr. and Mrs. Alden regret that they *are unable* to accept Mrs. Whitney's invitation for Friday evening.
I imagine Mr. Walker would not have wanted me *to have come*.	I imagine Mr. Walker would not have wanted me *to come*.
The captain *rode* his horse rapidly, *reaching* home before the storm broke.	The captain, *riding* his horse rapidly, *reached* home before the storm broke.
Copernicus taught that the earth *was* round.	Copernicus taught that the earth *is* round.*
If I knew that Mary *intends* to go, I would go, too.	If I knew that Mary *intended* to go, I would go, too.

*We express permanent truths in the present tense.

8. *The mingling of loose and periodic sentences helps to secure variety in sentence structure.*

You will recall the distinction between the loose and the periodic sentence. A loose sentence is grammatically complete at one or more stages of the structure; a periodic sentence is grammatically complete only at the end.

Loose sentence.

I saw what damage had been wrought when I returned from my trip to the country last Sunday morning.

Periodic sentence.

Last Sunday morning, when I returned from my trip to the country, I saw what damage had been wrought.

Some sentences are partly loose and partly periodic. This type is sometimes called the *composite* sentence. Here is an example:
"When the orator spoke of peace, he deliberately lowered his tone; but when he spoke of war, he raised his voice to a high pitch that betrayed his emotion."

We cannot say that one of these forms is regularly to be preferred to the other; we can say, however, that in simple narratives or simple descriptions, as, indeed, in our ordinary informal letter writing or conversation, the loose sentence is more naturally used. Conversely, in discourse that is formal and dignified, the periodic form is more freely used.

It may be noted, furthermore, that the structure of the loose sentence enables the reader to get more immediate grasp of the idea which is being expressed. He does not have to hold in mind so many ideas the full import of which is not apparent until he reaches the end.

But this last characteristic is not important in short sentences or phrases. Such expressions, for example, as *the house beautiful* and *the retort courteous* are periodic in effect. They gain certain emphasized values from the very unexpectedness of the form. There is slight suspense and there is considerable vigor.

The periodic sentence may have a stronger effect upon some readers simply because they experience a sense of gratification that comes when the suspense is ended. The last words come at the termination of a deep breath. The meaning is complete; the curtain falls; the play is ended.

Usually, however, the interplay of forms is dictated by a desire for variety. To join several ideas in a loose sentence may be all right in a single sentence—all right, perhaps, for two or more sentences in sequence. But continued for too long a time, the effect is monotonous and the mind rebels.

It is, of course, evident that in the midst of composition no one stops to question these technical items. Imagine a writer saying, "Shall I make this sentence loose or periodic? Simple, compound, complex?" It would be absurd. We go hastily along, driven by this impulse, driven by that, impelled now to make a bold statement, impelled almost immediately to insert a qualifying parenthesis. And even when our task is finished, these technical distinctions may never be accurately made. When our rereading discloses that our ideas are confused, our sentences slovenly, our general style ponderous and drab—only then do we carefully examine the technical machinery, discover faults, and proceed to make the proper changes. In that procedure, we may discover that this particular sentence is too loose, this other one faultily periodic. A third, which is now compound, will benefit by changing to a complex form. And indeed we may make all these changes without consciously labeling a single one by its technical term. We shall be guided by common sense and our developed concept of craftsmanship.

9. *Your sentences should be euphonious.*

You can, if you prefer, emphasize the same preachment by expressing it as a warning—*Avoid cacophony*. In my first tentative phrasing of Postulate 7, I was guilty of a fault. I wrote: "Good sentence structure demands strict attention to tense sequence." My inner ear immediately telegraphed its protest: "Get rid of the repetitions." I noted the *ten* in *attention* and the *ten* in *tense*; the *ence* sound in *sentence, tense,* and *sequence*. But that was not all. There were too many *t* sounds in that short sentence. A quick revision gave me the altered form—"Good sentence structure demands care in the expression of time sequence." The original idea was fully expressed; the phrasing was not cacophonous.

The offense against euphony here illustrated was due to the repetition of syllables. An even more common one is due to the inartistic repetition of words, as is evident in such a sentence as this: "My *present* intention is to buy a *present* for my wife. We must decide quickly; she will be here *presently*." It can be revised to read: "My present intention is to buy a gift for my wife. We must decide quickly; she will be here soon."

A marked example of euphony in Tennyson's *The Princess* you may have already memorized:

> The moan of doves in immemorial elms
> And murmuring of innumerable bees.

Euphony is a highly desirable quality; an over-indulged tendency is highly undesirable. John Lyly in his *Euphues* shows us how such over-indulgence impresses us with the artifice of expression; we may become more engrossed with the manner than with the matter. Here is one of Lyly's sentences that illustrates both his alliteration and his balanced form.

> Things which cannot be altered are to be borne, not blamed: follies past are sooner remembered than redressed, and time lost may be repented, but never recalled.

It was Lyly's title *Euphues* that is responsible for our word *euphuistic*, applied principally to identify a style of writing that is artificially elegant and high-flown. Sometimes you will catch in such writing the merit of precision, but you will be more impressed by its artifice. Where artifice is obvious it is not effective. Euphony thus purchased is purchased at too dear a price; but this trenchant fact will not lessen the force of a repeated warning against cacophony.

A feeling for euphony can be developed by reading aloud the sentences you write and testing them for the sound effects. Reading good literature will also increase your sensitiveness to the beauty and rhythms of both prose and poetry. As you continue your own writing practices you may become more appreciative of this quality of euphony. Keep in mind these simple suggestions:

a. Avoid unintentional rhymes, as, *a soldier of high rank maneuvered the armored tank.*

b. In writing simple prose do not allow yourself to make extended use of the blank-verse measure—such as is evident is this passage: *He wandered far in plowing ground where Sam and Jane indulged in play and ran their sticks in blackened soil from hour to hour.*

c. Remember that a smooth and flowing style may often be secured through a proper use of vowels and the liquids *l, m, n, r*.

d. Guard against the use of too many long words or too many short words. We need variety in word length as well as sentence length.

e. Learn the value of parallel structure, but do not overwork this method. The Beatitudes offer good examples of parallel structure.

> Blessed are the poor in spirit: for theirs is the kingdom of heaven.
> Blessed are they that mourn: for they shall be comforted.
> Blessed are the meek: for they shall inherit the earth.
> Blessed are the pure in heart: for they shall see God.
> Blessed are the merciful: for they shall obtain mercy.

f. Determine to acquire such a command of vocabulary and patterns of phrasing as will enable you to avoid monotonous repetitions of words and a dreary sameness in sentence structure.

This sentence, clipped from the morning paper is not wholly bad, but a rich vocabulary and a delicate ear might have prevented the repetition revealed by the italicized words.

> *Regardless* of the outcome, however, we must consider it imperative to maintain our present attitude *regarding* the possibility of sending the youth of this nation to sacrifice their lives for principles that cannot approach Americanism.

10. *Good sentences must possess unity.*

Unity in a sentence demands expression of a single complete thought. Coherence demands that all ideas cohere—stick together. Emphasis demands that these ideas be properly proportioned and properly placed.

Only the highly trained should ever allow mere fragments to be dressed out in sentence form. Study the following examples:

Avoid: There are four items to remember in acquiring new words. Exact meaning. Derivation. Spelling. Pronunciation.

Adopt: In acquiring a new word, master these four items: its exact meaning, its derivation, its spelling, and its pronunciation.

Avoid: I don't learn many new words. Not having a dictionary of my own.

Adopt: Not having a dictionary of my own, I do not learn many new words.

Avoid: I am further hampered in my choice of words. Because I do not know how to use a thesaurus.

Adopt: I am further hampered in my choice of words: I do not know how to use a thesaurus.

Avoid: I met him at the show, he was standing near the elephant's tent.

Adopt: a. I met him at the show; he was standing near the elephant's tent.

b. I met him at the show. He was standing near the elephant's tent.

c. When I met him at the show, he was standing near the elephant's tent.

Avoid: I am writing a novel and I am going to Baltimore tomorrow.

Adopt: As I must be sure of an episode that I am introducing into my next novel, I am going to Baltimore to verify certain hazy ideas concerning the scene of this incident.

(The sentence as originally written mentions two items without establishing the relationship which was in the writer's mind.)

Avoid: He has just bought a new book, and which he will read at once.

Adopt: a. He has just bought a new book—one which he will read at once.

b. He has just bought a new book, which he will read at once.

(The *and which*, without a preceding coordinate clause should never be used. This sentence is perfectly proper: "Here is a book which was published this year and which has now gone into the third printing.")

Avoid: The parents were strict with their child; he learned to obey promptly.

Adopt: The parents were strict with their child; they taught him to obey promptly.

(While the sentence as originally written might be accepted, the revision shows how a retention of the same subject secures a firmer unity. The change demands no necessary shift of the mind's direction. In general we may say that when we place coordinate clauses in sequence the idea which is the subject of the first clause should also be the subject of the second clause.)

11. *Good sentences must possess coherence.*

Coherence, you will recall, is that rhetorical principle which demands that the ideas in a sentence be closely related and stick together. It accomplishes its purpose by the proper arrangement of the words, phrases, and clauses. The principle, moreover, may apply not only to the single sentence, but to the sentences that may follow.

Some of you in your childhood may have played with those thin wooden blocks that have teeth at each end. When these blocks were new you could fit them together into a long single strip. If you took hold of one of these strips and held it in a vertical position, the separate blocks would be so well dovetailed that they would hold together; they would *cohere.* Apply that test to your sentence. Do the words and phrases and clauses stick together? Furthermore, apply the test to your paragraphs. Are they so deftly dovetailed that they stick together?

Let us examine a series of sentences that are incoherent and then make the revisions that will make them coherent.

Incoherent: This cider is so pure a child can drink it and so appetizing it will beg for a second glass.

Coherent: The child who drinks this pure, appetizing cider will beg for a second glass.

Incoherent: My father was opposed to novel reading and never allowed them in the house.

Coherent: My father was opposed to novels and never allowed them in the house.

Incoherent: Parking places have been provided at the school for the students.

Coherent: The school has provided parking places for the students' cars.

Incoherent: Look at those men running through the marshes who are robbers!

Coherent: a. Look at those men running through the marshes; they are robbers!

b. Look at those robbers running through the marshes!

Incoherent: Going down Highland Avenue yesterday, a girl called to me from her upper porch.

Coherent: As I was going down Highland Avenue yesterday, a girl called to me from her upper porch.

Incoherent: Trusting that you can accept my invitation, this letter must now be brought to a close.

Coherent: a. I am closing this letter in a trustful mood; I am hoping that you can accept my invitation.

b. Trusting that you can accept my invitation, I am closing this letter in a hopeful mood.

Incoherent: This new scythe can remove the tallest grass that ever grew in five minutes.

Coherent: This new scythe can in five minutes remove the tallest grass that ever grew.

12. *Good sentences must possess emphasis.*

Emphasis in a sentence requires that the words which express important ideas should command important positions. Usually the important positions are the beginning and the end. Remembering that of these two the end is the stronger, we must consistently practice the maxim: "End with words that deserve distinction."

The sentences that follow illustrate how sentences weak from lack of emphasis may by revision be strengthened.

Weak: You just made a remark; please repeat it again.

Strengthened: You just made a remark; please repeat it.

Weak: Isn't it too bad that Johnson and Company failed up?

Strengthened: Isn't it too bad that Johnson and Company failed?

Weak: On their way to New York my uncle and my brother were brutally attacked and murdered—that is, my uncle was murdered but my brother escaped.

Strengthened: On their way to New York both my uncle and my brother were brutally attacked; my brother escaped, but my uncle was murdered.

Weak: A writer must be careful of his words, phrases, clauses, etc.

Strengthened: In constructing his sentences a writer must give careful attention to each word, phrase, and clause.

Weak: He had a bad cold, which condition interfered with his speaking.

Strengthened: His bad cold hampered his speaking.

Weak: The Red Sox lost the final game, due to bad pitching, poor batting, and faulty fielding.

Strengthened: On account of bad pitching, poor batting, and faulty fielding the Red Sox lost the final game.

Weak: The prosecutor charged the prisoner with speeding, murder, and burglary.

Strengthened: The prosecutor charged the prisoner with speeding, burglary, and murder.

Weak: The embargo should be removed, I think

Strengthened: The embargo should be removed.

Weak: In writing his sentences he paid little attention to the principles of unity, coherence, and emphasis, which is difficult to excuse.

Strengthened: In writing his sentences he paid little attention to the principles of unity, coherence, and emphasis—a negligence which is difficult to excuse.

All these varied suggestions for improving your sentence structure may be epitomized in a single mandate: *Be alert, be intelligent, and use your common sense.* The practice of this precept will prevent mistakes in grammar and lapses in rhetoric. Knowing what your more exact thought is, you will discover the more exact expression of that thought. And knowing what your mood is, you will find the sentence pattern that more fully communicates that mood to others. You will never develop an expertness that will inevitably obtain all your desired effects in your first drafts; but you will acquire a growing skill in ferreting out your faults and contriving ways of revision. Genuine effectiveness, moreover, does not lie in a dearth of error; it more splendidly reveals itself in a wealth of power.

PRACTICES

Some mistakes in sentence structure are due to faulty thinking. More frequently, however, they are due to faulty phrasing. Be especially watchful of both thought and expression in these Practices.

PRACTICE 1
Sentence Structure

Make whatever changes you find necessary for the coherence of the following sentences.

1. Walking along the margin of the beach, the ocean looked very calm and blue.
2. Marion just bought a smart new roadster and which I like very much.
3. The baby is beginning to eat herself.
4. He lives a long distance from here which probably accounts for his being late.
5. Continuing to speak after the allotted time was up we became very bored with the speaker.
6. After the instructors had set conference dates for the students they dismissed the classes.
7. She told Marion that it was extremely necessary that she finish the work by Saturday.
8. This poem expresses an idea in a striking way which will be of interest to the readers.
9. The boy dropped the package he was carrying to his mother in the mud.
10. She turned to the old gentleman as he smiled at her and took out her dainty lace handkerchief.

PRACTICE 2
Sentence Structure

Make whatever changes you think will improve the structure of the following sentences.

1. It was a very warm day and not as many people as had been expected went to see the parade.

2. My sister went in town yesterday and bought a coat, which is very pretty and very becoming.
3. The house was white with green shutters, but it was very pretty.
4. The story was about an exciting adventure and which pleased the children very much.
5. I met her in town yesterday, she was shopping for a new hat.
6. It was a beautiful, warm, sunshiny day and I took a long walk.
7. John is a senior in high school, his brother, Bill, is a sophomore.
8. Read the article on page 67, it is the best one in the magazine.
9. I crossed the street and was run over by an automobile.
10. I like my class and the teacher understands all us boys.

PRACTICE 3
Sentence Structure

Read each of the following sentences carefully. Determine and write down whether the sentence is simple, compound, or complex.

1. The man took a great deal of luggage with him on his last trip.
2. Although we have not sold many tickets as yet, we are expecting a large group to attend the dance.
3. We shall be lonesome when he leaves.
4. Please return the book soon.
5. How interesting this book is!
6. Each class had a share in the program, and everyone was pleased with the results.
7. I did not recognize her until she came up and spoke to me.
8. Who took the newspaper from my desk?
9. We have asked Martin Wilson to take over the advertising department of the magazine, because he has had a lot of experience in that line.
10. He will have to hurry or we shall be late.
11. No, they have been unable to get the material yet, but they have not given up.
12. Mary lives next door to me.
13. If we ask him, I am sure he will be very glad to help us.
14. Why don't you take a trip to New York?
15. Mary is backward in her studies, but her brother Bill is at the head of the class.

PRACTICE 4
Sentence Structure

Make whatever changes you feel will improve the effectiveness of the following sentences as to euphony and structure.

1. We decided to take the shore road so that we could enjoy the cool ocean breezes as we rode along.
2. I did not know that such a rule was existent in our school.
3. Each of the personages in the pageant wore a costume representing a different age in history, a different stage in the story of civilization.
4. He did not have enough sense to realize that we could see through his pretense.
5. Hidden in one of the cubbyholes of the desk in the den we found a carton of cigarettes we had been looking for.
6. The action of the play was slow but the lines were clever and so it held our attention anyway.
7. He turned from his book with a look that took me by surprise.
8. I think you have misunderstood Miss Masters.
9. Mary felt badly that the pin was broken because it was a token she had received from a very dear friend.
10. The suspense of the play held the audience tense.

PRACTICE 5
Original Sentence Structure

After reading the excellent paragraph from Robert Malcolm Gay's *Writing Through Reading**, make a series of sentences of your own, but adopt the patterns here illustrated.

> If your sentences are elementary in form—short, simple, disjointed, or loose-jointed—and faulty in rhythm, it is exceedingly hard for your instructor to tell you how to improve them. He can describe them adversely, and direct you to handbooks of rhetoric, or he can give you advice. The advice, however sound in the abstract, is always dangerous as applied to practice, as he well knows. If he tells you to use longer sentences or complex sentences, for example, he may merely cause you to change from one fault to a worse one; and all the rules of the rhetoric books may do little better. The sound and natural way to master the art of framing sentences is to read the sentences of an author who knows how to make them, and to read them over and over, pref-

---
*Copyright, 1920, The Atlantic Monthly Press, Inc.

erably aloud, in their place and context, until their lengths, phrasing, and rhythms have been, so to speak, learned by heart. If to this practice you add the other of trying to make a series of your own, using different thoughts, but following the exact model of those you have read, one of yours for each of the others, you will learn more about the art of framing sentences in an hour than anybody or any book can tell you in many hours. But you must do this, not with parrot-like slavishness, but with alert intelligence, observing how each sentence owes its form solely *to the thought*, its parts and their relations.

PRACTICE 6

The Sliced Paragraph Device

As children we amused ourselves with the reassembling of sliced animals, or solving jigsaw puzzles. The principles that govern the solutions of those puzzles may aid you in making your paragraphs more coherent.

Here are the shuffled sentences of a paragraph that opens a story of a man's experience in a haunted house. These sentences are so formed that originally they clamped together. The end of one fitted into the beginning of the one that followed. Your problem is to discover the sutures and do the dovetailing as in the actual story.

Each sentence is a slice of your paragraph unit. Cut out and separated from its related sentences, it corresponds to a portion of a sliced animal or an irregular jigsaw item. Studying its contour, you decide upon the neighboring item that makes a perfect fit. When all the items are in their proper places you have your complete mosaic. Similarly when the shuffled sentences are reassembled in proper sequence you have your coherent paragraph.

1. But if to the dutiful function of physical protection you wish to add the protecting calm of mental rest and soul contentment, then I must enter a disclaimer, for the shadow of a creeping horror seems mysteriously to reappear whenever a chance reminder brings to me the chilling thoughts of that lonely haunted house.

2. The house that used to disturb my boyish dreams reappears in my vision now as clearly as it did on that somber August afternoon when a sudden and violent shower drove me into its grim shelter.

3. If those villagers could have told me even one or two of the minor happenings, you may be sure that I would not now be setting forth in this personal journal the dramatic details of that

fateful August afternoon—details that for thirty years and more I have never dared relate.

4. This haunted house was, I later learned, notorious in its own neighborhood, but as I was a stranger in that country I had known nothing of the ghastly stories repeated by the neighboring villagers.

5. If shelter means simply protection from sudden wind and rain and pounding hail, the deserted mansion performed its dutiful function.

The next step is to write a paragraph with correspondingly careful dovetailing of the sentences. If for this dovetailing experiment you can get a small group of persons together and have each one compose such a paragraph, each member of the group can later cut his own sentences into separate units, shuffle them thoroughly, and pass them on to his right-hand neighbor for reassembling.

In this reassembling you will discover that accurate and inevitable dovetailing requires most careful phrasing. Practice in the exercise will convince you of the value of establishing and emphasizing this major principle of Coherence in your writing.

PRACTICE 7
Correct Placing of Words, Phrases, and Clauses

In the following sentences you will find certain words, phrases, and clauses that are misplaced. Rearrange the sentences so that the emphasis is correct and forceful; so that the meaning is clear and coherent.

1. The duties of an announcer are to present material concerning the program being broadcast in a pleasing manner.
2. This boy will be very helpful to you, I think.
3. It was too late to consider the proposal however.
4. It was possible by just skimming the book to get the main idea.
5. It was relaxing to just sit and look at the picturesque setting.
6. In my opinion the suggestion is a good one, worthy of serious consideration.
7. He addressed the group on current books in an interesting manner.
8. He watched the feats of the clown with amazement.
9. We peered out of the window to watch them depart standing on tiptoe.

PRACTICE 8
Split Infinitives

The proper position of adverbs is naturally connected with a bit of advice with which you are doubtless familiar—*Never split an infinitive*. This usually means that you must never let an adverb come between an infinitive and its sign *to*. Applied to a specific case it would mean that we should not say, "I wish *to immediately warn* you." Say rather, "I wish *immediately to warn* you." —or "I wish *to warn you immediately*."

Since many good writers and speakers have, in special situations, split their infinitives, it is impossible to say that a split infinitive is always wrong. Here are three phrasings of the same idea:

1. "To thoroughly understand the present situation we should carefully review the events."
2. "Thoroughly to understand the present situation, we should review the events."
3. "To understand the present situation thoroughly, we should review the events."

Considering both logic and euphony, which do you prefer? Any of these may be justified.

Certainly a good argument could be made for the first. The three words easily coalesce into an important concept. The second phrasing may impress some readers as an obvious attempt—a too obvious attempt—to avoid a split infinitive. The third throws rather needless emphasis upon *thoroughly*. All in all, the first phrasing is preferable.

In most cases, however, both logic and euphony plead against splitting the infinitive.

Revise the following—provided each sentence needs revision.

1. I told him to personally warn the workers.
2. It is unwise to in any circumstances disturb them.
3. I desire to immediately discharge that group.
4. Why is it necessary to so persistently delay action?
5. Do you think we ought to again petition the owners?
6. Will they consent to a second time raise our wages?
7. Do you think they expect to again secure a compromise?
8. I think I ought to jocularly answer that note.
9. He pleaded for them to finally acquiesce.
10. She has apparently decided to finally consent to his proposal.

PRACTICE 9
He, She, It, They

Read this editorial from *The Boston Herald* and write a paragraph that expresses your attitude toward the ideas developed.

Even our best writers have trouble with "everybody." Is it singular, dual or plural; masculine, feminine, neuter or epicene? It is a problem for the great Stagyrite himself. "Everybody thinks they can do a better job than the person (not man or woman) who is doing it." Something wrong there; but what are you going to do about it? If you use "he" instead of "they" you get yourself into trouble with the influential race of feminists. And yet—

" 'Tis with our judgments," says Pope, "as our watches, none go just alike, yet each believes his own." Poetic license, no doubt, else how defend such atrocities as a plural verb with "none" and "his" instead of "their" own? And yet there are some who, while disputing Pope's title to high poetic rank, concede to him mastery of style. Such benighted ones even point out that "none" can properly take a plural verb.

Might "his" be defended as both masculine and feminine? Our possessive ending is a contraction of the possessive adjective. "Mary's hat" is short for "Mary his hat." How about it? We have outgrown the age in which woman was hardly believed to have any gender at all (in Germany girls are still neuter). That is all right; but we should do something about the all-important effect on the language.

An eminent writer in an esteemed contemporary says Malory or Poe "creates a universe sufficient for their imaginative purposes." This is an evident slip, for there is no objection to "his" instead of "their"; but that a practised writer should make it is significant of the existing confusion in the use of pronouns.

A kindred problem is as to the number of a verb where there is (or are?) a singular subject and a plural predicate, or the other way around. "The issue is the rights of minorities." "The rights of minorities are the issue." Some of our doctors of philosophy are puzzled with such sentences, and try to recast them. And yet, the rule is plain. The verb agrees with the subject and not with the predicate. Stick to that, and you are all right.*

PRACTICE 10
A Paragraph Expressing Opinion and Criticism

After reading this clipping from the *Cleveland Plain Dealer*, write in a single paragraph your views on the matter treated. If you

---
*Courtesy of *The Boston Herald*.

disagree with the writer, feel free to express your opposing opinion.

A writer in "Better English" thinks that the words oftenest mispronounced nowadays are: Quintuplets, rodeo, clique, address, aviator, data, garage, gratis, leisure, Nazi, often, radiator, route.

I don't believe it. Some of those words are generally mispronounced, but not all of them. Aviator, garage, often and radiator are, according to my own observation, very seldom mispronounced. It has been a long time since I have heard anybody trying pathetically to sound the t in "often" or saying "raddiator" or "avviator" or "garridge." Ninety-nine out of a hundred have learned to pronounce "Nazi." But a lot of people do still say quinTUPlets or quinTOOplets. ADDress, grattis, datta, click, roDAYo and lezher.

I suggest for a filling-in of the list of words most frequently mispronounced, the following: Administrative, adult, amateur, apparatus, automobile, despicable, financier, program, probably. And almost everybody says "pinchers" for pincers. This list could be extended to include hundreds of words: I list only the very commonest.*

PRACTICE 11

The Point of View

Read Edward W. Frentz's *The Point of View*† aloud, with careful attention to expression. Read it silently for paragraphing, variety of sentences, punctuation, choice of words, style. Rewrite from memory.

There was a shriek from the pantry, and, almost simultaneously, a metallic clang; then the cry from Emily: "A mouse! A mouse in the bread box! Come quick and kill him!"

It is a part of my good fortune—the outcome of my equable temperament—to be calm in moments of the greatest stress. I was calm now. My movements were deliberate, and I could detect no acceleration in my pulse. I even had the forethought, as I moved toward the pantry, to provide myself with a lethal weapon in the form of a clothes stick, which stood by the kitchen sink.

The bread box is a large cubical container, of tin, japanned in black, with BREAD in such large gilt letters on the cover that not even a mouse could mistake them. The clothes stick is a billet of wood about three feet long, an inch thick, and two inches wide. Its usual function is to stir the clothes in the boiler on wash days, but now it was to become the weapon of the executioner.

As I approached the bread box I noticed that the lid was closed.

---
*Courtesy of *Cleveland Plain Dealer*.   †Courtesy of Edward W. Frentz.

It is curious how often our subconscious selves act for us when the conscious part of our being is paralyzed by fear. Even in the moment of surprise and the face of imminent peril, Emily had had the presence of mind to slam that cover down!

I lifted the box and listened. Not a sound!

"Are you sure he is in there?" I asked.

"Yes, I know he is."

I brought the box out into the kitchen and set it down in the middle of the floor.

"Oh, not here, not here! He'll be sure to get away! They always do when you try to kill them. Take him outdoors."

So I took the box and the clothes stick and carried them into the back yard and placed the box on the board walk. On my way I tilted the box a little, and as I did so I thought I heard a tiny movement inside—a slight scratching sound.

Out in the yard I raised the lid a trifle and peeped in. I could see nothing but part of a loaf of bread. I shook the box, and a gray shadow flashed across the bottom and essayed to climb one of the sides. I jabbed with the end of the clothes stick and missed. The shadow darted behind the piece of bread. I pushed it aside and jabbed again. Another miss! I raised the lid a little more, to get a better view. The mouse was still there, crouched, wary and watchful, in a corner, his heart beating so hard that it shook his sides. Two or three more vigorous blows failed to touch him, but they made so much noise that Norton and Pettigrew, my neighbors on the north and the west, came out and looked over the fence to see what I was doing.

On a hunting trip after big game some years ago I got into a tight corner with a bear. For some reason the incident came back to me now. The situation was the same, except that the positions were reversed. I began to recall how it had seemed when I was on the receiving end, and to think what sort of story the mouse would tell if he should get away.

"You see," he might say to his attentive and admiring listeners, "I had gone farther away than usual—into a new region—and had hunted for some time without any luck. Then I began to smell things—good things, and all round me, too; but they seemed to be stored in great buildings, ten times as tall as I am, with no openings, and made of something too hard for me to cut my way through.

"But at last I found it—the greatest store of food I ever saw; a mass larger even than the biggest house that any of our family ever built. You wouldn't believe there was so much anywhere in the world.

"It was in an immense building or room, large enough for a dance hall or a meeting place where all of us could get together.

It had straight, smooth walls like the other buildings, without doors or windows; but on this one there seemed to be no roof, so all I had to do was to climb in.

"I had begun to eat, when suddenly there was a tremendous crash. A roof dropped down and everything became dark. In a little while the building began to move and the floor tilted and rocked from side to side, so that I couldn't keep my balance; but by and by it came to rest again, and the roof seemed to rise, so that I could see light.

"I was just going to make a spring for it when a great beam, thicker through than my whole body, crashed down beside me like a flash of lightning. An eighth of an inch more and it would have crushed me flat! I leaped for the top of the wall, where the light still showed, but missed and fell back. Again that great beam came down, and the whole room rang till it nearly deafened me. I dashed for shelter behind an overhanging face of the mass of food, but the giant pushed the whole mass aside as if it had been a mere crumb, and struck again. This time I wasn't quite quick enough, and the beam caught me a glancing blow that maimed this foot.

"I crawled behind a sort of cliff or high bank of the mass of food, but it was hurled aside again, and the timber smashed down right where I had been a moment before.

"But the giant was clumsy—not half so quick as I am. In spite of his strength—and his blows had power enough to move a mountain—he touched me only that once. When I was in one corner of the room the beam would crash against the side, and twice when I slid across the floor it came down in the corner.

"The oftener he missed me, the more furious he seemed to grow. The blows came so hard and fast, and made such a terrible noise, that other giants who live in neighboring castles came out and looked over the battlements and watched; but still, by some miraculous good fortune, not another blow touched me.

"At last, I think, the giant must have grown tired, for he stopped a moment, as if to take breath. It was my chance, and I took it. In a flash I reached the top of the wall, doubled over the side, and dodged into a sort of cave. The giant struck one last tremendous blow, which grazed the side of the building and made a deep ravine in the earth beside it. Then he took up the whole building and walked off with it as easily as I could carry a crumb of bread.

"Strange, isn't it, that a creature with so much food as he has should try to kill me for taking what little I needed?

"I know, of course, that I am lucky to be alive, but I'm afraid I shall never be the same mouse again, on account of this foot."

Norton and Pettigrew were still leaning over the fence, grinning. Without seeming to notice their untimely mirth, I picked up the bread box and the clothes stick and returned to the kitchen.

SENTENCE STRUCTURE

As I looked out of the end window I thought I saw a small, pointed, bewhiskered face peering for a moment with beady eyes from under one edge of the board walk. When I looked again it was gone.

"Did you kill him?" asked Emily.

"Kill him! Didn't you hear me lamming the daylights out of him?"

"Yes, you certainly made noise enough; you always do. I'll bet you let him go."

"Huh! Do you suppose any mouse could stand such a pounding as that? He's out there in the back yard, and you needn't be afraid of his getting into the bread box again—especially if you keep it closed."

I am afraid that Emily's attitude toward life is hopelessly homocentric.

KEYS TO PRACTICES

Key to Practice 1: Sentence Structure

1. The ocean looked very calm and blue, as we were walking along the margin of the beach.
2. Marion just bought a smart new roadster, which I like very much.
3. The baby is beginning to feed herself.
4. The fact that he lives a long distance from here probably accounts for his being late.
5. We became very bored with the speaker when he continued to speak after the allotted time was up.
6. After setting conference dates for the students, the instructors dismissed the classes.
7. She told Marion that it was extremely necessary that the latter finish her work by Saturday.
8. This poem expresses in a striking way an idea which will be of interest to the readers.
9. The boy dropped in the mud the package he was carrying to his mother.
10. As the old gentleman smiled at her she turned to him and took out her dainty lace handkerchief.

Key to Practice 2: Sentence Structure

1. Since it was a very warm day, not so many people as had been expected went to see the parade.
2. When my sister went in town yesterday she bought a coat, which is very pretty and very becoming.

3. The house was white with green shutters, and it was very pretty.
4. The story was about an exciting adventure, which pleased the children very much.
5. I met her in town yesterday; she was shopping for a new hat.
6. Since it was a beautiful, warm, sunshiny day I took a long walk.
7. John is a senior in high school; his brother, Bill, is a sophomore.
8. Read the article on page 67; it is the best one in the magazine.
9. When I crossed the street, I was run over by an automobile.
10. I like my class especially well because we have an understanding teacher.

Key to Practice 3: Sentence Structure

1. Simple
2. Complex
3. Complex
4. Simple
5. Simple
6. Compound
7. Complex
8. Simple
9. Complex
10. Compound
11. Compound
12. Simple
13. Complex
14. Simple
15. Compound

Key to Practice 4: Sentence Structure

1. We decided to take the shore road so that we could enjoy the cool ocean breezes as we drove along.
2. I did not know that we had such a regulation in our school.
3. Each of the characters in the pageant wore a costume representing a different period in history, a different stage in the story of civilization.
4. He did not have enough sense to realize that we could see through his pretext.
5. Concealed in one of the cubbyholes of the desk in the den we found a carton of cigarettes we had been looking for.
6. Although the action of the play was slow, the lines were clever enough to hold our attention.
7. He turned from his novel with an expression that took me by surprise.
8. I think you have wrongly interpreted what Miss Masters said.
9. Mary felt badly that the pin was broken because it was a gift she had received from a very dear friend.
10. The suspense of the play held the audience in rapt attention.

SENTENCE STRUCTURE

Key to Practice 6: Paragraph

The house that used to disturb my boyish dreams reappears in my vision now as clearly as it did on that somber August afternoon when a sudden and violent shower drove me into its grim shelter. If shelter means simply protection from sudden wind and rain and pounding hail, the deserted mansion performed its dutiful function. But if to the dutiful function of physical protection you wish to add the protecting calm of mental rest and soul contentment, then I must enter a disclaimer, for the shadow of a creeping horror seems mysteriously to reappear whenever a chance reminder brings to me the chilling thoughts of that lonely haunted house. This haunted house was, I later learned, notorious in its own neighborhood, but as I was a stranger in that country I had known nothing of the ghastly stories repeated by the neighboring villagers. If those villagers could have told me even one or two of the minor happenings, you may be sure that I would not now be setting forth in this personal journal the dramatic details of that fateful August afternoon—details that for thirty years and more I have never dared relate.

Key to Practice 7: Correct Placing of Words, Phrases, and Clauses

1. The duties of an announcer are to present in a pleasing manner material concerning the program being broadcast.
2. This boy will, I think, be very helpful to you.
3. However, it was too late to consider the proposal.
4. By just skimming the book it was possible to get the main idea.
5. It was relaxing just to sit and look at the picturesque setting.
6. The suggestion is, in my opinion, a good one, worthy of serious consideration.
7. In an interesting manner he addressed the group on current books.
8. With amazement he watched the feats of the clown.
9. Standing on tiptoe we peered out of the window to watch them depart.

Key to Practice 8: Split Infinitives

1. I told him personally to warn the workers.
2. It is unwise in any circumstances to disturb them.
3. I desire to discharge that group immediately.
4. Why is it necessary to delay action so persistently?
5. Do you think we ought to petition the owners again?

6. Will they consent to raise our wages a second time?
7. Do you think they expect again to secure a compromise?
8. I think I ought to answer that note jocularly.
9. He pleaded for them to acquiesce finally.
10. She has apparently decided finally to consent to his proposal.

Key to Practice 10: Pronunciations

FIRST SET OF WORDS	PREFERRED	ALLOWABLE
address	ă drĕs′	ăd′ rĕs (on a letter)
aviator	ā′ vĭ ā′ tēr	
clique	clēk	
data	dā′ tȧ	dä′ tȧ
garage	gȧ räzh′	găr′ äzh găr′ ĭj (British)
gratis	grā′ tis	
leisure	lē′ zhēr	lĕzh′ ēr (British)
Nazi	nä′ tsê	
often	ŏf′ ĕn	ŏf′ tĕn (rare)
quintuplets	kwĭn′ tû plĕts	
radiator	rā′ dĭ ā′ tēr	
rodeo	rō′ dê ō	rô dā′ ō
route	rōōt	route (military and railroad usage) ou as in out

SECOND SET OF WORDS	PREFERRED	ALLOWABLE
administrative	ăd mĭn′ ĭs trā′ tĭv	
adult	ȧ dult′	ăd′ ŭlt
amateur	ăm′ ȧ tûr′	ăm′ ȧ tûr
apparatus	ăp′ ȧ rā′ tŭs	ăp′ ȧ răt′ ŭs
automobile	ô′ tō mō bēl′	ô tō mō′ bĭl or bēl
despicable	dĕs′ pĭ kȧ b′l	
financier	fĭn′ ăn sēr′	fī′ năn sēr′
pincers	pĭn′ sērz	
program	prō′ grăm	
probably	prŏb′ ȧ blĭ	

CHAPTER VII

WORDS

THE OTHER DAY one of my friends, John Walters, reading the morning paper, ran across the sentence: "The infantry lacks the trained cadre." To another friend, Frank Martin, who happened to be near, John turned for specific information. He confessed that here was a word, *cadre*, that to him was entirely new. "I don't know how to pronounce it; I don't know what it means. Can you tell me, Frank?"

Frank's answer was vague. "Well, I'm not sure. It's a military term, I think. It's French, isn't it? Let's see what Webster says."

Yes, it is the French word *cadre*. It is allied to the Italian *quadro*, from the Latin *quadrus*, which means *square*. Carried over to the English it is the equivalent of *frame*, or *framework*. Another meaning is a *skeleton organization*. Most military men will know that it is pronounced kä' dēr. The word designates the framework of a regiment or other unit, usually consisting of the officers around whom newly enlisted men may be formed. This definition of the word makes the newspaper sentence perfectly clear; the writer is simply saying that the infantry lacks a trained staff of commissioned and noncommissioned officers.

To a watchful reader anxious to acquire a larger vocabulary, the experience of meeting new terms or phrases in his reading is likely to be a daily occurrence. Our best modern newspaper reporters are keenly alert to the value of words—new and old, technical and nontechnical, general and specific. No matter how hastily their work is written, it is seldom shabby or drab or monotonous. Though remembering always the limitations of their readers, these writers nevertheless do not hesitate to employ words that are a bit bizarre, provided such words give color, freshness, and perspective to the picture they are painting—or give to their style the precision that a sense for the accurate demands. If *cadre* seems to the individual reporter more appropriate than *official staff*, then it is *cadre* that goes to the copyreader's desk. And John Walters and Frank Martin, and Mrs. Richard Roe, who do not know the word, but who have the intellectual curiosity to master it, all become the immediate beneficiaries. With each newly acquired term, there is just that much enlargement, just that much brightening, of the reader's intellectual horizon.

And now, once again, let us take time to consider in some detail the worth of words; let us discover more particularly how they may aid us in the fields of creative written expression. Pursuing the same method used in the chapter on sentence structure, we shall cast the specific comments and suggestions into a series of easy, concrete postulates.

1. *Make frequent use of vocabulary tests.*

If you have already taken the different vocabulary tests that appear in various sections of *Your Mastery of English*, you have learned something definite concerning your own degree of achievement. Those who have made high scores on these objective tests will naturally feel a glow of suffusing pride; but they will not rest content with present accomplishments. They will, on the contrary, feel the stimulus to new adventures and new conquests. Those who received low scores will not allow themselves to be discouraged; they will gird their mental loins, prepared to make the immediate and the continued efforts necessary to establish a higher personal record. A test taken every thirty days should yield encouraging results—assuming, of course, that the daily opportunities for vocabulary attainments are eagerly grasped and diligently pursued. It is surprising to learn what daily practice finally achieves.

Make an immediate trial with the following:

Ten-Word Vocabulary Test

DIRECTIONS: *Place within the parentheses the number of the word which is the nearest synonym to the italicized word.*

1. The king was *ensconced* in his castle.
    1. murdered 2. crowned 3. fortified 4. established
    5. entertained   (   )
2. She marveled at his *insidious* methods.
    1. honorable 2. objectionable 3. careful
    4. treacherous 5. outmoded   (   )
3. It was *intrinsically* valuable.
    1. slightly 2. essentially 3. exceedingly
    4. historically 5. eminently   (   )

4. That is a *prerogative* of the office.
    1. demand 2. privilege 3. limitation 4. purpose
    5. misuse   (   )
5. The man was arrested during the *sedition*.
    1. session 2. revolt 3. celebration 4. performance
    5. reception   (   )
6. She suffered from many *tribulations*.
    1. misgivings 2. troubles 3. attacks 4. causes
    5. disturbances   (   )
7. She *beguiled* them with many words.
    1. berated 2. complimented 3. deluded 4. guided
    5. blamed   (   )
8. It was certainly *libel*.
    1. approval 2. acclamation 3. license 4. larceny
    5. defamation   (   )
9. The student suffered from *nostalgia*.
    1. homesickness 2. colds 3. boredom 4. daydreaming
    5. fatigue   (   )
10. His *perspicacity* in dealing with the situation was commendable.
    1. deliberateness 2. capability 3. frugality
    4. perseverance 5. discernment   (   )

Key to Ten-Word Vocabulary Test

1. (4)   3. (2)   5. (2)   7. (3)   9. (1)
2. (4)   4. (2)   6. (2)   8. (5)   10. (5)

Many years ago in one of our frontier states the last question on a teachers' examination read: "What means would you employ to enlarge your vocabulary?" Two hopeful neophytes, chancing to leave the examination room together at the end of the period, naturally discussed on their way to the railway station the various items of the test. When one of them asked about the last question, the other one —the more illiterate of the two—made a revealing confession: "Well, I read it over carefully—'What would you do to enlarge your vocabulary?'*—but I didn't know the meaning of *vocabulary*, so I made a brave stab at it and wrote: 'I'd drink eight glasses of water daily and exercise every night with dumbbells fifteen minutes before going to bed. Three months of this program should double the size of my vocabulary.' "

---
*He pronounced it *voc a bu' lary*.

I wish I knew of some system that would in three months—or three years, if you will—double the size of my present vocabulary. Each of us does make a gradual accretion. Indeed, if we read the better newspapers and magazines, and if we in conversation with our associates keep abreast with the major topics significant in the history of our culture and in current thought, we need constantly to augment our store of words and to gain more discrimination in precise shadings and nuances. Or course, no one of us is interested in the mere acquisition of new terms. We are concerned with the scope and the nicety of thought, and these advantages and values we cannot secure without knowing the symbols which express them.

The extent of the vocabulary mastered by the individual—either the passive vocabulary that enables him to comprehend the pages that he reads or the active vocabulary that enables him to express his own thoughts and emotions—this exact numerical mastery we can never know. The vocabulary employed by Shakespeare is said to be 15,000 or 20,000 words, depending upon the method of counting; by Milton, 8,000 or 15,000. But in superior writing of this sort it is easily apparent that there are hundreds of words—common household words, for example—that would not be likely to occur. Investigations have been made of the vocabulary range of school children. While the results are varied and confusing, one of the more careful of these studies has the following summary:

> Age 8— 3,600
> 10— 5,400
> 12— 7,200
> 14— 9,000
> Average adult—10,000
> Superior adult—13,500

I personally made an accurate listing of the vocabulary of my own son from the time he was three until he was six. At the latter age the total number of different words—counting no derivatives—totaled 1,997.

A most elaborate study of the vocabularies of children and adults is the investigation, extending over a period of ten years, made by Dr. Edwin W. Doran and recorded in *The Pedagogical Seminary.** Dr. Doran's method was a tedious one—too involved to explain here. His

---
*Copyright, 1907, The Journal Press.

statement of certain individual adult accomplishments is somewhat startling—and, of course, I cannot myself vouch for the accuracy of the figures.

A young lady 19 years old, who had not quite finished the literary course in a young lady's seminary, tested by the use of the Student's Standard Dictionary, apparently knew 20,537 words. But with one of the large dictionaries the result would have been much higher.

A physician in Little Rock, Ark., 30 years old, who had not taken a college course other than his medical course, tested with the International Dictionary, knew 57,154 words. Some tests have been made on the students of the James Millikin University. While most of the tests were made by classes to determine the effect of sex upon vocabulary, the following five were private tests more extensive than the others. The Standard Dictionary was used.

Miss Alice Finfrock, second-year Academy, 23,100 words.
Miss Augustine Southworth, third-year Academy, 26,600 words.
Mr. Paul S. Welch, fourth-year Academy, 41,895 words.
Mr. E. J. Witzemann, Junior, college, 40,681 words.
Mr. E. A. Meserve, Junior, college, 53,130.

Most of these, perhaps all of them, ranked above the average of the class, as far as I was able to test the members of the class. These all took other tests in class, the results of which are not included in these records. Mr. Welch's record is especially good, as he is still in the academy department. Mr. Meserve, so far, heads the list. Probably few, if any, in the university could surpass him. But Miss Finfrock's record, considering the fact that she is only 14 years old, is remarkably good. These five had nearly the same list of words, some more than the others.

The following are recent individual tests made upon young people in Jackson, Mississipi. The figures given are estimates based upon a list of nearly two thousand words. All had the same words, except that a few missed some of the tests.

Name	Age yr.	m.	Words
Sallie Ligon	14	8	11,340
Emily Harper	11	9	12,516
Mollie Smith	15	8	14,595
Elaine Ward	13	3	18,753
Osborn Young	12	8	22,722
Archie Owen	13	3	26,376
Minter Gant	12	9	28,480

The best vocabulary I have ever found, so far as any extensive test has been made, is that of Miss Rosa Rhee Kevil. She spent some months in Decatur last fall and I had opportunity to make a very full and careful test. The result of the test showed she could define 92,161 words. A careful test was made on three different occasions. While there was considerable variation from page to page as to the number of words defined, yet taking the results of each test separately, the averages were almost the same, varying less than half of one per cent. As in perhaps every test given, the record of the first part of the test was the lowest.

It will not be amiss, I trust, for me to put on record some tests upon my own vocabulary, as several other writers have done. Ten years ago, when I first became interested in the subject, I made a pretty extensive test of my own knowledge of words, using the Century Dictionary. The result of the test showed I could define about 84,000 words. But I feel sure I have outgrown that. I noticed especially in Miss Kevil's test that I could define many words she could not. Hence I feel that I am not immodest in estimating my vocabulary at 100,000 words. Though the test with the dictionary did not show this, it is borne out by the fact that I know thousands of words not found in any one dictionary. For a number of years I have been making a study of the common, or vernacular, names of animals, especially of Vertebrates and Insects. In this study it is necessary to know both the technical and the vernacular names. By a careful consultation of the dictionaries with reference to all these names, I believe I know four or five thousand technical and vernacular names in Zoology alone which are not found in any dictionary. Botany and other sciences add many more to the list.

Woodrow Wilson, whose masterly command of our language is generally acknowledged, is said to have used in seventy-five of his speeches 6,200 different words; in his writings he used at least 60,000. His entire vocabulary was, of course, considerably above this total.

A recent article by Mr. Johnson O'Connor, "Vocabulary and Success," published in the *Atlantic Monthly*, stimulated many readers to write the Harvard Graduate School of Education for further information concerning the Inglis Tests which he mentioned and which the school constructs. From a reading of many of these letters, I found that not a few of these eager correspondents, envisaging a short way to success, had made a wrong inference, which I should like here to point out.

Mr. O'Connor, in testing vocabulary achievement, discovered the apparently remarkable fact that important executives in great business organizations made high scores—higher than those of even college professors, who as a class are generally accredited with an unusual degree of manipulative skill with words. On reflection, it is, however, logically sound, is it not, to expect a man of exceptional mental fibre, whose capabilities and training have won him his business promotion, to have acquired a marked command in thought and expression? He has needed exact knowledge of terms to interpret the general and the special reading which he has done; he has needed an even more exact knowledge in communicating his ideas to others—his associates, his clientele, and his competitors. Both his native ability and the exactions of his position have directed his learning, extended his range, and sharpened his accuracy. His vocabulary achievement has been secured without a direct interest in words as words; his alertness in the realm of ideas is responsible for his acquired mastery over the symbols of these ideas.

And this method of acquisition is exactly counter to the implication in much of the correspondence which seeks information concerning the Inglis Tests. The mere acquisition of many words as a preliminary to ideas which may subsequently float into one's mental vision is a vain and false method of acquisition. What education demands is real knowledge, real power—not a simulacrum of knowledge and power.

It is certainly to be hoped, therefore, that anyone who makes use of vocabulary tests will first and foremost stress ideas and the proper organization of these ideas into significant truths. With the grasp of significant concepts there will come to the majority of educated men a command of words and phrases that will enable them to communicate these concepts to others. A minority, it must be granted, will need special drill and a special artificial stimulus. With them it may be desirable in particular instances to reverse the process and throw emphasis upon the making of the grooves and the matrices into which ideas can be made to flow. But this does not refute our major contention: the main stress in the learning process falls heavily upon the inception and the clarification of substantial ideas.

2. *Distinguish carefully between the denotation and the connotation of words.*

The denotation of a word expresses its bare, actual, objective meaning; the connotation expresses all the various associative values and subtleties that cluster about the term. Take, for illustration, such a word as *home*. You notice one morning in the real estate section of your newspaper an advertisement—"A new home for sale in the Forest Avenue section." And that very afternoon you receive from your sister a letter with this sentence: "Yesterday our childhood home on Tenth Street was sold at public auction." Here is the same four-letter word—h-o-m-e. You read the two fragments; one is cold, impersonal, objectively aloof; the other is warm with the fire which your imagination has relighted; the rooms which you have not seen for years are again repeopled with groups that gave direction to childish trends and quickened the beat of your earliest affections. These and a thousand other remembered and unremembered items assemble to give their rich connotative values to this single-syllabled word!

The contrasts between connotation and denotation as here illustrated by the word *home* are similar in kind, if not in degree, for great multitudes of words in the English language. The difference lays its demonstrating hand upon every passage that we read and upon every passage that we write. Perhaps in this distinction you discover one reason why you may often fail in conveying to others the particular thoughts and the particular emotions that seemed to you to be clearly expressed in your paragraphs. Your own set of connotations as you wrote were so different from the sets which severally built themselves up in the minds of each of the different readers. Something of this difficulty there will always be as long as you are you and he is he and she is she and they are they. It is the price we pay for being individuals.

3. *Develop an interest in the derivation and history of words.*

We are told that everybody needs a hobby. That may or may not be true. In any event, if you are on the search for one, how would you like to consider words—particularly their derivations and their history? You will find the study most fascinating.

Behind nearly every single important word in English there is an interesting history, and while it is impossible to go searchingly into many of these origins and changes, an excursion into even a limited sector will reveal alluring characteristics.

As an illustration of the sort of information a short individual excursion may yield, let us first take the common word *curfew*. In medieval France royal decree demanded that the fires be covered at an early hour each evening. The village bell rang the signal, which, in the French phrase—*couvre feu*—meant "Cover the fire." And soon both the bell and the time it was ringing came to be known as *couvrefeu*, or *cuevrefu*. When William the Conqueror established a similar decree in England the word became *curfew*.

The word *kerchief* also is of French origin. It is formed from the word *chef=head* and *couvre=cover*. The English word *kerchief*, a combination of *chef* and *couvre*, became the name for a cloth used to cover the head. When a similar type of cloth came later to be carried in the hand, the combination of *handkerchief* was easily made. And in modern times, *kerchief* being a bit old-fashioned, a lady who covers her head with a cloth similar to a handkerchief designates it with the roundabout term "head handkerchief," thus unconsciously saying *head hand-head-covering*.

The casual reader of books, newspapers, and magazines is naturally most interested in getting the immediate message of the printed page. He is seldom aware of the picturesque origin of terms and the various changes which time has wrought. Concrete instances when presented to the curious-minded may start many a learner on a pleasant bit of wayfaring.

My chance use of *wayfaring* reveals an instance of easy transition. The first syllable, *way*, is from the Anglo-Saxon *weg;* the second comes from the Anglo-Saxon verb *faren—to go*. The two elements have naturally coalesced into *wayfaring*.

Let us consider a word that most of us recognize as of comparatively recent origin—the word *taxicab;* it offers something more complicated in etymology. "*Taxicab* is an abbreviation of *taximeter-cabriolet*—a vehicle carrying an instrument for automatically registering the fare. Before the days of the automobile, a *cabriolet* was a light, horse-drawn carriage. The name *cabriolet* is the diminutive of the French *cabriole*, 'a leap' like that of a goat, and was applied to this type of carriage because, being light, it bounced on a rough road. French *cabriole* was borrowed from Italian *capriola*, 'a somersault,' from Latin *caper*, 'a he-goat,' *capra*, 'a she-goat.' "* Doubtless all of us, in our past ridings in cabs, knew that we were being heavily *taxed;* we often knew, furthermore, that we were being severely *bounced*. But only in less anxious moments—in the leisurely reading of this present hour, for example—do we pause to contemplate these intricacies of verbal origins.

I discover as I glance at the preceding sentence that I have quite

---

*Picturesque Word Origins, Copyright, 1933, by G. & C. Merriam Company.

undesignedly used the word *contemplate*. Ordinarily we use it without thought of its root significance; *con* is, of course, the common Latin prefix meaning "with"; *templum* means, I discover, "a space marked out"; hence, in particular, in the language of augury, "an open place for observation" marked out by the augur with his staff. It conveys, you see, the notion of openness, extent, with the idea of sanctity predominating. To contemplate the intricacies of verbal origins is really a more Olympian performance than I intended to enact.

Let us turn to the A's and try something simpler. Here is the word *accumulate*. "When, in colloquial speech, a man refers to the accumulating of a fortune as 'making his pile,' he is using exactly the same figurative language as that which first suggested the word *accumulate*. *Cumulus* is Latin for 'a heap or pile,' and *cumulare* means 'to pile up.' With the prefix *ad*, 'to,' we have *accumulare*, 'to heap together,' which is the source of our English word *accumulate*."

Since 1929 most of us have felt the need of a word with just the opposite meaning. *Decimate* won't do; it suggests the loss of a *tenth* only. *Evacuate* seems better—*e* "out," *vacuare* "empty," "to empty out." *Evaporate*, too, is a rival candidate—*evaporare*, "to pass off in vapor." And 1929 suggests the painful word *panic*. It comes from the mythical god Pan, a curious creature, half man, half goat. At certain times when he appeared he had the ability to inspire great terror. When the swift Athenian runner Phidippides was sent to solicit the aid of the Spartans against the Persians, Pan met him on the way and said that if the Athenians would bow to his godship in worship, he would fill the hearts of the Persians with terror. He gave a terrible fright to the Titans in their fight against the gods. Edmund Clarence Stedman makes a calm and placid demigod of this creature piping musically near "Trinity's undaunted steeple"; but the wild actions of the terror-stricken "bears" in October, 1929, gave credence to the ancient significance of the Greek word *panicos* and its English derivative *panic*.

And this word *candidate*. "In Latin *candidus* means 'glittering,' 'white.' In ancient Rome, a man campaigning for office wore a white toga and was consequently called *candidatus*, 'clothed in white.' From this comes our word *candidate* with the meaning 'one campaigning for office'—but without the original significance as to dress. From the same Latin word *candidus* we have our adjective *candid*. This word was first used in English with its literal meaning 'white' but is now applied figuratively to a mental quality unclouded by dissimulation or bias."

"When we speak of the *inauguration* of a president we use a word that carries us back to ancient times when people believed in omens and looked for them on every important occasion. Latin *augur* meant a member of the highest class of official diviners of ancient Rome, whose duty it was to observe and interpret the omens, such as the flight of birds, at the time of any important event. *Inaugurare* meant 'to take omens' before entering upon a critical undertaking, such as the proclamation of an emperor. From the past participle *inauguratus* is derived English *inaugurate*, though the ceremony of *inauguration* today does not call for the observation of omens."

Enthrall presents a case of a word "the original and literal sense of which is cruel, but the modern, figurative use of which is much more pleasant. When we say that we are enthralled by a song, or a book, or something else with captivating charm, it is interesting to remember that the original meaning of the word was 'to enslave.' *Thrall* is Anglo-Saxon for 'slave.' To *enthrall* meant, therefore, 'to enslave,' 'to reduce to the condition of a thrall.' The literal sense of 'enslave,' 'make captive,' easily yields a figurative sense, 'captivate the senses,' 'hold spellbound,' 'charm,' as with a song or a story."

"In modern use *seminary* denotes a place of education such as a preparatory school, or sometimes a special sort of college. It would be appropriate to say 'a place where seeds are planted in the minds of the pupils,' because *seminary* is derived from a word meaning 'seed.' Latin *semen, seminis,* 'seed,' made the noun *seminarium,* 'a nursery' for plants, then a place for raising and training the young. English borrowed this as *seminary*, with the same senses as the Latin."

Pedigree has a curious origin. It comes from the Latin through Old French—*pié de grue* "foot of a crane," the fancied resemblance to the sign used in showing lines of descent in the graphs of genealogical trees or tables.

Common Names from Persons. Many single words, common nouns in current usage, had their origin in the name of the man or character first associated with them—*mackintosh* from James Mackintosh, the inventor; *forsythia* from James Forsyth, who brought the shrub from China; *fuchsia* from Leonard Fuchs, a German botanist; *wistaria* from a certain Caspar Wistar; *martinet* from a French general who was a strict disciplinarian; *malapropism* from Mrs. Malaprop, a character in Sheridan's *The Rivals;* *braggadocio* from a character in Spenser's *Faerie Queene; boycott* from Captain Boycott, the first boycotted landlord in Ireland; *sandwich* from the Earl of Sandwich who was so passionately devoted to gambling that he diverted the time ordinarily spent at meals by having his servant bring him slices of bread with meat in the center; *mesmerism* from F. D. Mesmer, who brought it into notice; *listerine* from Dr. Lister; *robot* (pronounced rō'bŏt or rŏb' ŏt) from Karel Capek's famous play *R.U.R.* In Russia, I am told, sewing machines are called *singers*, for the Singer Sewing Machine Company pre-empted the sales territory. The word *simony* comes from Simon Magus, whom the Apostle Peter rebuked for the sorcerer's attempt to purchase the power of giving the Holy Ghost.

Common Names from Places. Many an article imported from foreign countries seems naturally to take its name from the place whence it originated: *calico, champagne, sauterne, sherry, cambric, gin, china, japan, cashmere, madras, tweed, damask, morocco, landau, berlin, surrey, arras, fez, nainsook, canary.* And this last word warrants a special note. We have the canary bird, canary wine, canary grass, canary color—all associated with the Canary Islands; but the word *canary* came originally from Latin *canis*, "dog," for a certain type of large dog was so distinctive on the islands that the name *canary* seemed especially appropriate. Thus linguistically the dog and the canary are closely related; dietetically we think of a closer connection between the *cat* and the canary.

The root meaning of the word *surprised*, from the Old French *surprendre* is "seized upon"; *astonished* is probably derived from the Old French verb *estoner*, "to shock." The philologist who surreptitiously kissed the pretty parlor maid of the household was suddenly caught in the act. "Why, Dr. Blank," his shocked wife exclaimed. "I am *surprised!*"

"No, my dear," he philologically answered, "you are entirely wrong. *I* am *surprised; you* are *astonished.*"

All foregoing instances are but a fraction of the numberless picturesque origins that come to light in a study of derivation and change in the form and the meaning of words. Such stories, as you see, are often highly revealing in the light they throw upon historical events and older customs. In our actual use of the words, however, we are chiefly concerned with the part they play in their modern everyday service. Unmindful of their etymology, we use them generally to express our present thoughts, our present sensations, our present emotions.

4. In actual everyday practice, never mind whether your words are derived from the Anglo-Saxon or Latin.

Many critics may have set up for you this foolish warning: "Never use a Latin word when you can use an Anglo-Saxon word." Why not, may a challenger ask? And when there is no satisfactory response, you can say to yourself: It isn't etymology—interesting as that study is—that best serves as a guide; it is present usage and the appropriateness of the present choice for the present situation; it is skill in choosing the proper word for the proper occasion.

This matter of appropriateness of the Anglo-Saxon or Latin demands attention to such topics as these: repetition, rhythm, euphony, clearness, flavor, dignity, informality, precision, suggestiveness, fitness—indeed all the qualities of phrasing within the wide-unfolding realm of style. We can take advantage of the generally accepted distinction between Anglo-Saxon and Latin. In most of the homely, domestic, workaday situations Anglo-Saxon words are naturally applicable; in areas military, diplomatic, courtly, scientific, ecclesiastical, and aristocratic, there is a more liberal use of the Latin element. But when it comes to an individual choice of a given word in a given situation, we need not be governed by derivation; we shall be governed, as we have just said, by correct present usage and a sense of appropriateness. And the best way to learn the appropriate—if you did not inherit it—is to read the best prose writers. Emily Post can quickly teach certain external items in social behavior; no one can easily teach a boorish male to be a gentleman, or a tawdry female to be a lady. If you haven't an instinctive feeling for the appropriate expression, spend your reading periods with those who have it. It is indeed remarkable what attitudes and concepts come to us in by-productive ways.

Here are three passages of well-known prose, examined as to percentages of Anglo-Saxon words as contrasted with foreign words.

> Thus they discoursed together till late at night; and after they had committed themselves to their Lord for protection, they betook themselves to rest. The pilgrim they laid in a large upper chamber whose window opened toward the sun rising; the name of the chamber was Peace; where he slept till break of day and then he awoke and sang.
>
> —John Bunyan, *The Pilgrim's Progress*

The percentage of Anglo-Saxon words is 88.2.

> To talk in a manner intentionally above the comprehension of those whom we address is unquestionable pedantry; but surely complaisance requires that no man should, without proof, conclude his company incapable of following him to the highest elevation of his fancy, or to the utmost extent of his knowledge. It is always safer to err in favor of others than of ourselves, and therefore we seldom hazard much by endeavoring to excel.
> —Dr. Samuel Johnson, *The Rambler*

The percentage of Anglo-Saxon words is 71.9.

> Religion, in a large sense, doth signify the whole duty of man, comprehending in it justice, charity, and sobriety; because all these being commanded by God, they become a part of that honor and worship which we are bound to pay to him.
> —Jeremy Taylor, *Holy Living*

The percentage of Anglo-Saxon words is 69.8.

A glance at the foregoing selections proves that not all Latin words are long, and that not all Anglo-Saxon words are short; yet the general distinction is clear. Anglo-Saxon generally names the ideas that are specific, tangible, and simple; Latin generally names the ideas that are general, intangible, and complicated. The distinction does not imply that the one is better than the other; it does imply that the principle which determines choice is the nice adjustment of the word to the idea. Where exactness is the aim, the etymology of the word will sink to its properly subordinate plane.

5. *In most instances, choose the specific rather than the general word.*

"Can't you spend next week with me here in my shack on the cool shores of Winnepesaukee?"

Your eye pauses upon this sentence in Wendell's letter that the postman has just brought in the afternoon mail. It's hot in your apartment—hotter than Sheol. And you could escape it all and spend next week in Wendell's shack. You have never seen it; you don't know much about it, but you immediately catch the odor of fir and hemlock, you hear the soughing of pine trees and the swishing of waters on the shore. Soon your cool, vigorous body is breasting those New Hampshire waters. It's all delightfully refreshing, delightfully careless, delightfully informal. And the alchemy that has wrought the change? Oh, yes, to be sure, the waters of Winnepesaukee are there. And, of course, Wendell is in the background as friend and guide and gracious host. But the active agent among the ingredients that the pestle of your imagination is braying in the mortar, is that word *shack*.

House is the general term for man's shelter, but the scores of specific items subordinate to the idea have each a connotation of their own. Here is a partial list:

cabin	shanty	log house	lodge
hut	dugout	mansion	hermitage
hovel	chalet	villa	manse
flat	log cabin	pension	bungalow
parsonage	apartment	three-decker	duplex
cot	trailer	camp	tent

As *house* is the general name for shelter, *workers* is a general name for those engaged in some occupation. You would find it interesting to take a single occupation, such as *mining*, or *merchandising*, or *publishing*, and see how extensive a list of special terms you could list in a separate category. Here is only a selected enumeration of kinds of workers—alphabetized under A, B, and C.

accountant	baker	captain
actor	banker	cartoonist
admiral	barber	chemist
advertiser	bishop	civil engineer
architect	blacksmith	clergyman
artist	bookkeeper	clerk
astronomer	bootblack	comedian
auctioneer	bricklayer	composer
author	broker	contractor
automobile mechanic	builder	critic

Specific Verbs. If you wish to use a verb that paints a vivid picture of your brother Henry as he left the house just before dinner, you will not be satisfied with just the general statement that Henry *went away;* you will choose something more specific—one of these, perhaps:

He swept past all of us.
He flung himself down the pathway.
He shot suddenly out the hall door.
He sidled out of our midst.
He deftly threaded his way through the crowd.
He stalked grimly through the assembled group.
He strutted proudly from the room.
He strolled aimlessly away.
He sauntered along the walk.
He ambled lazily along.
He drifted away from us.
He cushioned his stealthy footsteps on the grassy path.
He quietly withdrew.
He stepped gingerly along.
He marched out at once.

He glided gracefully out of the room.
He stole quietly away.
He strode angrily from the group.
He stalked angrily away.
He crept out the doorway.
He inched his way out.
He slippered his way through the dust.
He shuffled slowly along.
He skipped out like a young girl.
He stumped along awkwardly.
He slunk guiltily away.
He minced his way along the gravel.
He pirouetted down the driveway.
He blustered his way along the street.
He Charlie Chaplined his way out.

Varied as these expressions are, they will doubtless remind you of others that you would select in certain different situations. As you think of various possibilities, you may decide upon two important warnings: guard against a mere commonplace verb that paints no specific picture even where a picture is demanded; guard against an expression that seems so far-fetched that it convicts the author of a rather too arduous striving after effect. Only in rare instances, indeed, would you allow yourself to say, *He Charlie Chaplined his way out.* We all appreciate the clever sentence of Stephen Leacock which satirizes the phrase-seeking novelist who describes the angry heroine stepping indignantly away from the hero—*Back she iced.*

You will note that the postulate says, "In *most instances*, choose the specific rather than the general." There are, of course, instances where you want the general or the abstract rather than the specific or the concrete. Your common sense will usually be the arbiter.

6. *For vivid and effective description and narration, use words that appeal to the senses—sight, sound, touch, taste, and smell.*

It is a well-established principle that clear writing demands clear thinking. A principle that correlates very closely with this is that clear description or clear narration demands clear *sensing*. If as writers you are to make your senses re-picture their impressions or make your events dramatically re-enact themselves in the minds of your readers, you must select the words that have this re-sensing power. And in saying this I am not thinking principally of what some would call *literary writing;* I am thinking also of the sentences and paragraphs that you write in your practical, everyday affairs. Many times during an ordinary week we find that our writing makes a practical demand for sense appeals and a call to our skill to re-create them. This single slogan from a well-known advertisement provides an immediate illustration—"The skin you love to touch."

How verbs, adjectives, nouns, and adverbs combine in actual writing can be illustrated by almost any good piece of narrative writing that you may chance to select. Some time ago in searching for specific paragraphs that vividly reveal sensory effects, I was fortunate in lighting upon two—one from Maxim Gorky and the other from Jack London. Those extracts and the comments I made are especially pertinent to the present topic. The first quoted passage, a character sketch of an old jailbird, is from Gorky's *Tchelkache*.

> When the 'longshoremen, leaving their work, were dispersed in noisy groups over the wharf, buying food from open-air merchants, and settling themselves on the pavement, in shady corners, to eat, Grichka Tchelkache, an old jail-bird, appeared among them. He was game often hunted by the police, and the entire quay knew him for a hard drinker and a clever, daring thief. He was bareheaded and bare-footed, and wore a worn pair of velvet trousers and a percale blouse torn at the neck, showing his sharp and angular bones, covered with brown skin. His tousled black hair, streaked with gray, and his sharp visage, resembling a bird of prey's, were all rumpled, indicating that he had just awakened. From his mustache hung a straw, another clung to his unshaved cheek, while behind his ear was a fresh linden leaf. Tall, bony, a little bent, he walked slowly over the stones, and turning his hooked nose from side to side, cast piercing glances about him, appearing to be seeking some one among the 'longshoremen. His long, thick, brown mustache trembled like a cat's, and his hands, behind his back, rubbed each other, pressing closely together their twisted and knotty fingers. Even here among hundreds of his own kind, he attracted attention by his resemblance to a sparrow-hawk of the steppes, by his rapacious leanness, his easy stride, outwardly calm but alert and watchful as the flight of the bird he recalled.

Now the general thought presented in this extract is that of a man's personal appearance, but the words are so well chosen that the reader forms a vivid picture of the old jail-bird. His "tousled black hair," his "long, thick, brown mustache," with the single straw hanging to it, his tall, long, slightly bent form, his piercing eyes and hooked nose—all these details, conveyed by a happy selection of adjectives, form a definite picture in the mind of the reader and could easily be transferred by a painter to the canvas. We should have to supply unessential details, but we should not find this task difficult; for all important suggestions are given us—even in matters of dress, such as the worn, velvet trousers and the torn, open shirt. All these details, or counterparts of these, we have seen in just the combination here revealed. The result is, that something original and concrete is produced.

Now that the foregoing description has revealed certain secrets of specific attainment in style and composition, let us see what the following narrative excerpt from Jack London's *The Call of the Wild* will reveal. The reader will recall that the passage describes a scene which occurs after "Black" Burton has picked a quarrel with a tenderfoot, and Thornton has good-naturedly interfered. Burton resists the interference, suddenly strikes Thornton a blow that sends him spinning toward the rail of the bar, and in that hurried movement arouses the fierce ire of the dog, Buck.

> Those who were looking on, heard what was neither bark nor yelp, but a something which is best described as a roar, and they saw Buck's body rise up in the air as he left the floor for Burton's throat. The man saved his life by instinctively throwing out his arm, but was hurled backward to the floor with Buck on top of him. Buck loosed his teeth from the flesh of the arm and drove in again for the throat. This time the man succeeded only in partly blocking, and his throat was torn open. Then the crowd was upon Buck, and he was driven off; but while a surgeon checked the bleeding, Buck prowled up and down, growling furiously, attempting to rush in and being forced back by an army of hostile clubs.*

When we examined the descriptive selection from Gorky, we noted that the intense visualization was largely effected by a happy selection of adjectives; here, in this lively narrative sketch of London's, we see that the energy and the vividness of the scene are largely due to the choice of effective verbs and nouns. Now let us examine the selection

---

*Copyright, 1903, The Macmillan Company.

more carefully, and select some of the words and phrases that London used to reproduce the action which he saw so clearly in his own mind.

The spectators saw Buck's body "rise in the air" toward Burton's throat. Burton "threw out his arm," but Buck "hurled" him "backward." Then Buck "loosed his teeth" from the arm, and immediately "drove in again" for the throat. This action Burton only partially "blocked," and his "throat was torn open." Buck was then "driven off" by the crowd, and a surgeon "checked the bleeding," but Buck continued to "prowl" up and down, "growling" furiously.

The verbs here used, together with the nouns, express the successive actions that make up the incident. The words are so strong and so simple that they make us think of our own experiences. This is an illustration of what psychologists term *Empathy*. We have not seen the identical actions, but we have seen similar actions; and our imagination readily unites the diversified concrete acts into a connected whole. Furthermore, these words appeal to us in varied ways.

Most of these phrases which we have quoted appeal to the eye—to our sense of form, as in "Buck," "throat," "arm," "teeth"; to our sense of color, as in "bleeding." But the words "bark," "yelp," "roar," and "growl" appeal to the ear; and such a phrase as "loosed his teeth from the flesh of the arm," not only recalls visual experiences, but also revives muscular sensation (the sense of feeling).

The general term *sensation* comprehends all impressions that are made on our sense organs—the sensations of sight, hearing, touch, taste, and smell. In order to express vividly the different appeals which the five senses make, we should diligently search for the vivid and specific word. When, in our narrative and descriptive writing or speaking, we are trying to suggest to our friends the images, sensations, and actions which we have in mind, we should try to select words that convey definite, concrete, clear-carved impressions. In this endeavor we shall succeed best by using the specific word, for the idea which this specific word expresses will most readily connect itself with the reader's experience and force a resensing.

7. *In choosing your words, dare at times to get out of the beaten track and be boldly individual in your phrasing.*

I have already told you about the little neighbor boy of five who, vibrantly commenting one evening on the colors of the sunset sky, noted the adjoining areas of light orange and of brilliant blue. As the light softened and the colors faded he announced the various slowly sombering changes. "Now," he said, "the orange is *luke* orange and the blue is *luke* blue." Nobody ever told him that; he just instinctively assumed the privilege of applying the word that expresses a lessened degree of temperature to a lessened degree of color-tone intensity. It was a bit of verbal improvising.

A youth of sixteen recently assumed a similar privilege in his bold characterization of a demure maiden named Elsie. Elsie was a girl whom his mother had suggested for Ralph's party companion at the coming assembly. Ralph refused, and would not be cajoled.

"But why won't you take Elsie?" his mother pleaded.

Reluctantly Ralph blurted his reason, "Oh, she is such a *dim bulb!*"

A little girl of eight awoke one morning recently all aglow with excitement. "Oh, Mother," she exclaimed, as she rushed downstairs, eager to impart her new experience, "I have just had a wonderful two-featured dream! I wish you could have seen it! The whole thing was in technicolor!"

And that was a quick response that the policeman humorously made when the judge, turning to the traffic officer, inquired:

"And, what's the charge against this man, officer?"

"Arson, your honor. Burning up the road!"

A self-satisfied and highly sophisticated and somewhat inscrutable character in a story was recently described by the novelist as a woman who *Mona Lisaed* her placid way among her guests. A reckless and devastating gardener hoeing among the rows of tall lima beans was characterized by his employer as one who *Hitlered* his truculent way among the poles.

A writer, describing one of his characters who was forever showing himself off, who was always on display, revealed the young man's habitual trait by a single sentence: "Harold, throughout his career pushed himself to the front of the parade. Here at the very head of the procession he proudly sought to drum-major his way through life."

Mr. C. V. R. Thompson in his cleverly satiric volume, *I Lost My English Accent,*[*] gives recurrent proof of this ability to give a quick and telling twist to his phrasing of an idea. Here are some of his random shots:

---

[*]Copyright, 1939, G. P. Putnam's Sons.

> Broadway is a lady of the evening. In the sunlight she looks like a suddenly awakened chorus girl who went to bed with her make-up on.
>
> Washington was ... as full of gossip as a ladies' cloakroom.... Scientists would be interested in Washington, because it confounds all their theories. It's the only place where sound travels faster than light.
>
> The first thing a New Yorker does when he finds a home is to look for a way of keeping out of it as much as possible.
>
> American men are very much like parole boards—they simply will not let you finish your sentence.
>
> About the only thing she (the debutante) does away from the lens is to have a bath.

Senator Vandenberg, pleading in Congress for the proviso in a bill forbidding the sale of war munitions to a belligerent nation, expressed his idea aptly when he said that the United States cannot become the arsenal for one nation without becoming at the same time the target for another nation.

Those of you who have read John Steinbeck's *The Grapes of Wrath* may recall the author's effective use of the verb *whispered* in connection with Ma Joad's breakfast cooking: "She put grease in the frying pan, and when it whispered with heat, she spooned the dough into it."

From my files, I have extracted a few modern similes that may stimulate you to invent others.

> As out of date as the rustle of a skirt.
> As disconnected as the dictionary.
> As certain as applause at a professional matinée.
> As useless as a crossword puzzle that has been solved.
> As worthless as a campaign poster the day after election.

Shakespeare is of course full of these ready turns of speech. Seldom is he more felicitous than in the passage in which Hamlet protests that he is not flattering his friend Horatio, who is poor, who has no revenue but good spirits to feed and clothe him:

> Why should the poor be flattered?
> No, let the candied tongue lick absurd pomp,
> And crook the pregnant hinges of the knee
> Where thrift may follow fawning.

Emphasis upon original turns of speech and clever repartee must not so dazzle the writer as to dim his serious purpose. While we shall keep our vision clear for the discovery of unsuspected likenesses that will encourage the simile or metaphor, or the ingenuity of the revealing phrase, we shall remember that the chief use of language is to express the plainer purposes of the everyday. Sincerity and simplicity and naturalness remain constants among the higher virtues of daily expression—as they remain constants among the higher virtues of daily behavior. But even the homely firefly may, I assume, take a satisfied pleasure from its easy disclosure of a phosphorescent glow.

8. *Beware of malapropisms.*

Malapropisms are words which, though quite different in meaning, are so similar in spelling and sound as to be easily confused by the insufficiently informed. Be sure you know the meaning of such words before attempting to use them, lest you commit the linguistical sin of malapropism, by saying "I had *ulsters in my throat*," when you mean *ulcers*, or "The policeman *caressed* (instead of *coerced*) the prisoner." When a very dirty tramp, charged with *vagrancy*, was brought into police court, he replied to the judge's question as to the charge, "I was arrested for *fragrancy*, your honor." Then there is that famous remark of Shakespeare's Dogberry, "Comparisons are *odorous*," by which he meant *odious*.

Malapropism is a word with an easily remembered etymology. It comes from the French phrase *mal à propos* (*mal*—evil + *à propos*—to the purpose); loosely translated, the entire phrase means *to the wrong purpose*. The word *malapropism* gained wide currency after Richard Brinsley Sheridan (1751-1816) created his character *Mrs. Malaprop*, who by her word blunders contributes so liberally to the humor of Sheridan's famous eighteenth-century play, *The Rivals*. Many will recall her frequently quoted rejoinder.

> MRS. MALAPROP. There, sir, an attack upon my language! what do you think of that?—an aspersion upon my parts of speech! was ever such a brute! Sure if I reprehend anything in this world, it is the use of my oracular tongue, and a nice derangement of epitaphs.

Here are some practices by which you may test your ability to avoid making such errors.

PRACTICES

All students of English appreciate the values that accrue from concentration upon details. Careful focusing of attention upon each of the items here presented will gradually increase your command of words. And increased command of words will prove of great service in each phase of your life.

PRACTICE 1

Malapropisms Corrected

In the blank at the right of each sentence write the correct word in place of the malapropism which is italicized.

EXAMPLE: Comparisons are *odorous*.   *odious*

1. James seems to shrink from meeting people. He ought to conquer that *temerity*.
2. The robbers were *arranged* in court.
3. It was very *official* of that stranger to order the rest of us about.
4. The girl said, "My mother made me promise to *insult* her, before I decided to get married."
5. She was very ill with *ammonia* last winter.
6. There were some lambs *gambling* in the meadow.
7. The boy has a very brilliant mind—in fact, he might be called a *progeny*.
8. Their house is *contagious* to ours.
9. She is very *malevolent*. I shall never forget her kindness to me when I was in need.
10. Let me make you a *preposition*.

PRACTICE 2

Malapropisms—Lapsed-Letter Test

In the following test the correct word will be indicated by the lapsed-letter device, and the wrong one will be written above it. Write the correct one on the line at the end of the sentence.

ulsters
EXAMPLE: The girl said she had u - - e - - in her throat.   *ulcers*

interceded
1. The letters were i - - e - - e - - - d.

                 participated
2. The one remark p - - c - - i - - t - - a quarrel. ....

                 comparisoned
3. The knight's horse was richly c - - a - - s - - e -. ....
4. The recent happenings there brought about a real
   antistrophe
   c - - a - - r - - h -. ....

                 ineligible
5. Your writing is almost i - - e - - b - -. ....

                 contemptuous
6. Stealing is a most c - - t - - p - - b - - act. ....

                 indigenous
7. Those people are so i - - i - - n - that they are actually
   starving. ....

                 termagants
8. I found a nest of - - r - - t - - in the yard. I fear they may
   eventually destroy the house. ....
9. The child was a little upstart, and spoke very
   impotently
   i - - u - - n - - y to the old gentleman. ....

                 ingenuous
10. It was a most - - g - - i - - s device. ....

PRACTICE 3

Choice of Words to Avoid Malapropisms

In the following sentences a choice of three words is given—only one of which is correct. Underscore the correct one.

1. The patient is very ill; I have been told that he is now in a ....
   comma
   coma
   comic

2. The girl was in a .... mood, evidently thinking deeply about something.
   pensile
   pentane
   pensive

3. The .... was that the boy had stolen the watch.
   implication
   imprecation
   impletion

4. Don't .... to be innocent.
    portend
    portent
    pretend

5. How can I .... myself from this situation?
    extirpate
    extricate
    execrate

6. She said, "I washed my hair last night, and now I have no .... over it."
    affluence
    influence
    effluence

7. Did you use .... coconut on this cake?
    decimated
    desecrated
    desiccated

8. You will find the law recorded in that volume of ....
    statues
    statutes
    statures

9. The girl sat with her feet comfortably resting on a ....
    cassock
    cossack
    hassock

10. The young man was soliciting .... for magazines.
    prescriptions
    subscriptions
    proscriptions

PRACTICE 4

Malapropisms Corrected

The malapropism is italicized. Write the correct word in the blank at the right.

1. Thomas made no *illusion* to the European situation.
2. The letter was returned marked *diseased*, because the person addressed was dead.
3. I *formally* lived in New York.
4. I remain *respectively* yours.
5. Do you like the color of this *stationary*?
6. He *flouted* his honors in our faces.
7. This is a very *specious* room.
8. The two cars were in *collusion*.
9. I do not believe in teachers whipping the children; *capital* punishment should be prohibited in schools.
10. She is very angry. Do you think you can *modify* her?

PRACTICE 5

Malapropisms Corrected

The malapropism is italicized. Write the correct word in the blank at the right.

1. He has *spatial* fingers. ....
2. The doctor gave me a *subscription* for my headache. ....
3. A few generations ago, all ministers *prescribed* theatre-going. ....
4. My friend is in great trouble. I must go and *condone* with her. ....
5. She was inclined to *condole* her husband's crime. ....
6. I had a *tuition* that that would happen. ....
7. It was a *pretentious* event. ....
8. The girl was in a *purport* of joy. ....
9. That one letter *consists of* your mail for today. ....
10. An artist has *acetic* tastes. ....

PRACTICE 6

Choice of Words in Narration

From the five words given at the right of each sentence or phrase, choose and underscore the word that most exactly corresponds in meaning with the italicized one.

1. A soldier *straggled* by. — labored   wandered   stalked   limped   rushed
2. We *stress* this point. — select   attack   emphasize   criticize   sharpen
3. He fell into a *stupor*. — cellar   fortune   well   mud-hole   daze
4. My statement was *substantiated*. — verified   understood   meaningless   unimportant   impudent
5. It *sullies* your reputation. — increases   diminishes   clears   stains   destroys
6. He *supplanted* his friend. — buried   insulted   took-the-place-of   worked-under   assisted
7. He *survived* his brother. — distrusted   excelled   outlived   followed   disappointed
8. *Synchronous* events. — simultaneous   peculiar   timely   alarming   prophetic
9. A *tantalizing* problem. — serious   teasing   important   mythical   algebraic

WORDS

10. A *temerarious* person.   rash   cowardly   treacherous ambitious   moderate
11. She has a life *tenure*.   sentence   hold   insurance mission   income
12. They managed *thriftily*.   skillfully   imprudently   generously economically   honestly
13. A *titanic* force.   fairy   gigantic   troublesome artistic   naval
14. A *torrid* day.   clear   humid   hot   nasty rainy
15. It *transcends* description.   requires   invites   lacks   belies surpasses
16. *Transports* of joy.   realms   raptures   trances ships   descriptions
17. A *triplicate* copy.   typewritten   threefold   counterfeit genuine   bound
18. He *twiddled* his thumbs.   sprained   broke   sucked twirled   hammered
19. An *unbridled* temper.   uncertain   erratic   even wicked   uncontrolled
20. An *unfailing* friend.   dependable   false   unreliable insolvent   cordial
21. They spoke in *unison*.   favor   anger   concert   peace sequence
22. An *unsophisticated* youth.   ingenuous   wasted   unknown spoiled   college
23. He *uttered* the document.   wrote   read   recited discovered   published
24. A position of *vantage*.   danger   responsibility   honor advantage   disgrace
25. He *vented* his wrath.   restrained   provoked   poured-forth regretted   excused

PRACTICE 7

Choice of Words in Narration

Five words are given at the right of each sentence or phrase. Underscore the word agreeing in meaning with the italicized word.

1. The *quiescent* crowd.   noisy   inactive   angry reverent   shouting
2. The wires *ramify*.   cross   sag   hum   branch-out short-circuit
3. The village was *razed*.   built   rebuilt   plundered leveled-to-the-ground   burned

4. Commendable *rectitude*. — promptness / ambition / righteousness / accuracy / preaching

5. A *refulgent* smile. — repellent / very-bright / mischievous / sour / flattering

6. The argument lacks *relevancy*. — justice / applicability / support / importance / vigor

7. We *repaired* to the parlor. — betook-ourselves / walked-slowly / referred / sent-tools / took-food

8. A *repulsive* sight. — disgusting / exciting / interesting / winsome / immoral

9. He *resolves* to act. — delays / wishes / determines / declines / hesitates

10. He *retracts* his criticism. — repents / expresses / repeats / withdraws / withholds

11. A *revolving* fan. — electric / broken / rotating / waving / feather

12. She has *ruddy* cheeks. — wrinkled / pale / fat / red / freckled

13. *Sacerdotal* rites. — priestly / blasphemous / legal / usual / annual

14. We saw a *samovar*. — open-fire / altar / Indian-holy-man / legal-officer / tea-kettle

15. He has many *schemes*. — interests / difficulties / doubts / wild-ideas / plans

16. *Scrupulous* in all things. — conscientious / miserly / persistent / distrustful / careless

17. The water *seethes*. — boils / tumbles / rushes / cleanses / roars

18. He *severed* the cord. — tied / spliced / selected / cut / twisted

19. He *shuffled* along. — dug / sailed / fought / walked-awkwardly / scampered

20. A *skittish* mare. — sleek / well-trained / dappled / balky / nervous

21. His manner was *solemn*. — haughty / insolent / grave / peculiar / playful

22. A *scurrilous* rogue. — hurrying / frantic / desperate / diseased / abusive

23. A *spiritual* nature. — non-physical / tempestuous / languid / didactic / dreamy

24. His *stature* is noteworthy. — image / height / law / design / position

25. A *stilted* manner. — irresolute / formal / improper / vicious / cordial

WORDS

KEYS TO PRACTICES

Key to Practice 1: Malapropisms Corrected

1. timidity
2. arraigned
3. officious
4. consult
5. pneumonia
6. gambolling
7. prodigy
8. contiguous
9. benevolent
10. proposition

Key to Practice 2: Malapropisms—Lapsed-Letter Test

1. intercepted
2. precipitated
3. caparisoned
4. catastrophe
5. illegible
6. contemptible
7. indigent
8. termites
9. impudently
10. ingenious

Key to Practice 3: Choice of Words to Avoid Malapropisms

1. coma
2. pensive
3. implication
4. pretend
5. extricate
6. influence
7. desiccated
8. statutes
9. hassock
10. subscriptions

Key to Practice 4: Malapropisms Corrected

1. allusion
2. deceased
3. formerly
4. respectfully
5. stationery
6. flaunted
7. spacious
8. collision
9. corporal
10. mollify

Key to Practice 5: Malapropisms Corrected

1. spatulate
2. prescription
3. proscribed
4. condole
5. condone
6. intuition
7. portentous
8. transport
9. constitutes
10. aesthetic

Key to Practice 6: Choice of Words in Narration

1. wandered
2. emphasize
3. daze
4. verified
5. stains
6. took-the-place-of
7. outlived
8. simultaneous
9. teasing
10. rash
11. hold
12. economically
13. gigantic
14. hot
15. surpasses
16. raptures
17. threefold
18. twirled
19. uncontrolled
20. dependable
21. concert
22. ingenuous
23. published
24. advantage
25. poured-forth

Key to Practice 7: Choice of Words in Narration

1. inactive
2. branch-out
3. leveled-to-the-ground
4. righteousness
5. very-bright
6. applicability
7. betook-ourselves
8. disgusting
9. determines
10. withdraws
11. rotating
12. red
13. priestly
14. tea-kettle
15. plans
16. conscientious
17. boils
18. cut
19. walked-awkwardly
20. nervous
21. grave
22. abusive
23. non-physical
24. height
25. formal

CHAPTER VIII
THE FRIENDLY LETTER

EVEN in commercial correspondence, we endeavor to reveal something of the personal spirit that every corporation or every individual business man possesses. With the thousand and one crowding situations this personal emphasis is sometimes difficult. In the hurry of business procedure the office may lose its warmer and more individual tone. Routine demands may result in a series of form letters and stereotyped paragraphs that betray a lowered temperature and a less individualized appeal. But whatever be the final effect upon business correspondence, we shall, if we are faithful to the responsibilities of friendship and intimate association, always infuse our friendly letters with the warmth and cheer of our sincerer and more intimate selves.

For this very reason it is difficult to lay down many hard and fast rules for the writing of intimate or informal letters. The very connotation of the epithets *intimate* and *informal* carries with it a privilege of freedom—the same privilege that perforce exists when friends have been so long acquainted with each other that the use of first names or nicknames is easy and natural. Here in the genial atmosphere of a hospitable, convivial living room the free flow of harmless gossip may be lightly interwoven with whatever matter of more momentous import the serious-minded may choose to interject.

Moreover, among our hosts of friends there are widely varying degrees of intimacy. Of this fact we are vividly aware when, perhaps in a single day, we may chance to write to five or six of our scattered friends. A very powerful but a very mysterious instinct discerningly selects for each a particular tone and mood of address. Just as we are a bit different in the presence of each of our different friends and acquaintances, so we are a bit different toward each of our friendly correspondents. The keen humor of one may stimulate our own sense of humor; the fancy of a second may send us out on our own fanciful adventure; the habitual seriousness of another may keep us rather closely tethered to a similar stake.

But all these natural indulgings in differences do not lessen a demand for our own rigid sincerity. A weather vane is not inaccurate when it veers with the wind; it would indeed be inaccurate if it failed to make its frequent responses. We would indeed be stolid in the style of our letter writing if we were insensitive to the various personal traits and individual qualities of our correspondents.

The difficulty of laying down any hard and fast rules for friendly correspondence is apparent. We can, however, examine some concrete examples of letters that were, we may assume, appropriate to their specific occasions. They may offer suggestions that will prove personally helpful as you, in a different situation, attempt, in altered phrasings and changed mood, to acknowledge a gift, to write a letter of condolence, or meet some other of the many situations that daily life so freely offers each of us.

Letters of Famous People.

Always it is pleasant to discover in persons to whom fame has granted resplendent honors the genial glow that friendly letters of the right sort habitually impart. Here is a letter of James Russell Lowell, alluding retrospectively to a friendship that had lasted for three long decades.

> Elmwood, Feb. 27, 1867
>
> My dear Longfellow,—On looking back, I find that our personal intercourse is now of near thirty years' date. It began on your part, in a note acknowledging my "Class-poem," much more kindly than it deserved. Since then it has ripened into friendship, and there has never been a jar between us. If there had been, it would certainly have been my fault and not yours. Friendship is called the wine of life, and there certainly is a stimulus in it that warms and inspires as we grow older. Ours should have some body to have kept so long.
>
> I planned you a little surprise in the *Advertiser* for your birthday breakfast. I hope my nosegay did not spoil the flavor of your coffee. It is a hard thing to make one that will wholly please, for some flowers will not bear to be handled without wilting, and the kind I have tried to make a pretty bunch of is of that variety. But let me hope the best from your kindness, if not from their color or perfume.
>
> In case they should please you (and because there was one misprint in the *Advertiser*, and two phrases which I have now made more to my mind), I have copied them that you might have them in my own handwriting.

In print, you see, I have omitted the tell-tale ciphers—not that there was anything to regret in them, for we have a proverbial phrase, "like sixty," which implies not only unabated but extraordinary vigor.

Wishing you as many happy returns as a wise man should desire, I remain always

Affectionately yours,
J. R. L.

To this letter I would apply the adjective *simple*. You will, however, recognize a deft use of figurative language and a subtle compliment in the closing lines—"Wishing you as many happy returns as a wise man should desire."

We have already learned that even though the friendly letter is a highly personal message and defies capture by any rule-of-thumb trap, hints may be gleaned from the way other searchers go out after their quarry. Doubtless James Russell Lowell has convinced you of an acquired skill in letter-writing. Here is a letter from Charles Dickens to Washington Irving; it imparts a flavor that delectably lingers on the palate:

My dear Sir,—

There is no man in the world who could have given me the heartfelt pleasure you have, by your kind note of the thirteenth of last month. There is no living writer, and there are very few among the dead, whose approbation I should feel so proud to earn. And with everything you have written upon my shelves, and in my thoughts, and in my heart of hearts, I may honestly and truly say so. If you could know how earnestly I write this, you would be glad to read it—as I hope you will be, faintly guessing at the warmth of the hand I hold out to you over the broad Atlantic.

I wish I could find in your welcome letter some hint of an intention to visit England. I can't. I have held it at arm's length, and taken a bird's-eye view of it, after reading it a great many times, but there is no greater encouragement in it this way than on a microscopic inspection. I should love to go with you— as I have gone, God knows how often—into Little Britain, and Eastcheap, and Green Arbour Court, and Westminster Abbey. I should like to travel with you, outside the last of the coaches down to Bracebridge Hall. It would make my heart glad to compare notes with you about that shabby gentleman in the oilcloth hat and red nose, who sat in the nine-cornered back-parlour of the Masons' Arms; and about Robert Preston and the tallow-chandler's widow, whose sitting-room is second nature to me;

and about all those delightful places and people that I used to walk about and dream of in the daytime, when a very small and not over-particularly-taken-care-of boy. I have a good deal to say, too, about that dashing Alonzo de Ojeda, that you can't help being fonder of than you ought to be; and much to hear concerning Moorish legend, and poor unhappy Boabdil. Diedrich Knickerbocker I have worn to death in my pocket, and yet I should show you his mutilated carcass with a joy past all expression.

I have been so accustomed to associate you with my pleasantest and happiest thoughts, and with my leisure hours, that I rush at once into full confidence with you, and fall, as it were naturally and by the very laws of gravity, into your open arms. Questions come thronging to my pen as to the lips of people who meet after long hoping to do so. I don't know what to say first or what to leave unsaid, and am constantly disposed to break off and tell you again how glad I am this moment has arrived.

My dear Washington Irving, I cannot thank you enough for your cordial and generous praise, or tell you what deep and lasting gratification it has given me. I hope to have many letters from you, and to exchange a frequent correspondence. I send this to say so. After the first two or three I shall settle down into a connected style, and become gradually rational.

You know what the feeling is, after having written a letter, sealed it, and sent it off. I shall picture you reading this, and answering it before it has lain one night in the post-office. Ten to one that before the fastest packet could reach New York I shall be writing again.

Do you suppose the post-office clerks care to receive letters? I have my doubts. They get into a dreadful habit of indifference. A postman, I imagine, is quite callous. Conceive his delivering one to himself, without being startled by a preliminary double knock.

Always your faithful Friend,
Charles Dickens

And here is a letter* that Lafcadio Hearn's publisher has graciously left unsealed. We are thus allowed to share the sentiments which Hearn's intimate friend, Henry Watkin, must have greatly enjoyed.

Yokohama, April 25, 1890

Dear Old Dad:

I was very happy to feel that your dear heart thought about me; I also have often found myself dreaming of you. I arrived

---

*Copyright, 1907, by Albert & Charles Boni, Inc., New York.

here, by way of Canada and Vancouver, after passing some years in the West Indies. I think I shall stay here for some years. I have not been getting rich,—quite the contrary; but I am at least preparing a foundation for ultimate independence,—if I keep my health. It is very good now, but I have many gray hairs, and I shall be next June forty years old.

I trust to make enough in a year or two to realize my dream of a home in the West Indies; if I succeed, I must try to coax you to come along, and dream life away quietly where all is sun and beauty. But no one ever lived who seemed more a creature of circumstances than I; I drift with various forces in the direction of the least resistance—resolve to love nothing, and love always too much for my own peace of mind,—places, things, and persons, and lo! presto! everything is swept away, and becomes a dream,—like life itself.

Perhaps there will be a great awakening; and each will cease to be an Ego, but an All, and will know the divinity of Man by seeing, as the veil falls, himself in each and all.

Here I am in the land of dreams,—surrounded by strange gods. I seem to have known and loved them somewhere before: I burn incense before them. I pass much of my time in the temples, trying to see into the heart of this mysterious people. In order to do so I have to blend with them and become a part of them. It is not easy. But I hope to learn the language; and if I do not, in spite of myself, settle here, you will see me again. If you do not, I shall be under big trees in some old Buddhist cemetery, with six lathes above me, inscribed with prayers in an unknown tongue, and a queerly carved monument typifying those five elements into which we are supposed to melt away. I trust all is well with you, dear old Dad. Write me when it will not pain your eyes. Tell me all you can about yourself. Be sure that I shall always remember you; and that my love goes to you.

Lafcadio Hearn

I could tell you so much to make you laugh if you were here; and to hear you laugh again would make me very happy.

The following letter, you will note, reveals some of the deeper thoughts of the writer and grants us a glimpse of the relationship existing between Gilbert and Manning.

Sharing a Friend's Grief.

Dear Manning:

When I left you on Tuesday how impossible it would have been for either of us to imagine that your father would so soon be the victim of this fatal accident. He looked so firm and so stalwart and so enduring as he stood there on the driveway and bade me an affectionate good-bye. His was the heart of a true host.

Death has that mysterious power of vivifying a personality—of making the lifeless eyes rekindle and allowing the silenced voice to re-echo its friendly vibrant tones and overtones. All this I am vividly experiencing now as I think of you in your new loneliness and realize how difficult it will be for you—or any of us—to understand why these things have to happen.

In the many, many days in which you are readjusting yourself to this tragic loss, be assured that I shall be thinking very affectionately of you and of all the members of your family.

The deeply understanding heart of your mother will know how genuinely tender is my thought of her. She will know my feelings—even if these words of mine somehow seem to lack the warmth that I so eagerly yearn to give them.

Very sympathetically yours,
Gilbert

A Letter of Condolence.

Here is a brief letter which nevertheless expresses most clearly the sympathy the writer feels for his friend.

Dear Raymond,

When our own little daughter died a year ago, you were among the first to send us your message of sympathy. And now you yourself are suffering a similar sorrow. How well I understand your feelings at this hour. Even if I were actually with you, I could do little more than press your hand in affectionate grasp as a silent symbol of our common grief!

Faithfully yours,
Edward

A Letter to a Sick Friend.

What a thoroughly comfortless experience the hospital sojourn would be, did we not have friends like Lucile to divert our minds from our ills!

My dear Cousin Ethel,

So you have eluded your relatives and slipped away to the hospital for a week or two of quiet contemplation and release. Your mother has written that you are not seriously ill; that you are not going to have even a minor operation; that you are just going over there to that quiet retreat to crawl snugly into bed where you will be "resting comfortably"—as the attendant always says when troubled friends telephone their anxious inquiries.

There have been subtle suggestions passed around that you didn't want to see anyone for a few days; but if you discover that you are tired of doctors and nurses and X rays—and of your own rotating thoughts—just send me a hint that when I'm not in one of my philosophical moods, I might perhaps drop around to beguile you with a grist of harmless palavering.

In the meantime, maybe you would like to let your eyes wander aimlessly over this recent collection of short stories that I am mailing you from the quiet bookshop where I've been scratching down this ambling screed.

Yours till then—and always!
Lucile

The Letter Acknowledging a Gift.

The manner of expression exemplified in the letter following may be foreign to your own way of writing; if this be true, keep to your own style. We all realize, however, that the merely drab and commonplace method of acknowledging a gift may give to the sender the same sort of feeling that we receive from a limp and languid handshake. Put some savor and some flavor into your note of thanks.

My dear Eleanor,

How could you have known that I had lost my only fountain pen? You had such a keen understanding of my need that you just graciously decided to crowd this beautiful gold-banded Waterman in among the other packages of my Christmas stocking? You have immediately granted me the means of setting down here in this sprawling screed my deep appreciation of this additional evidence of your unfailing kindness and your mysterious power of always knowing exactly what gift to choose.

And what an attractive maroon case for the pen and its little brotherly pencil! Even the most fastidious of my friends will not object to a penciled note from me when I tell them of the artistry of this pencil's shape and color—and casually add that it was selected by one whose sense of the aesthetic and the appropriate never, never goes astray. My sincerest thanks!

Appreciatively and affectionately yours,
Louise

The giver would surely feel rewarded for the time and pains spent in finding exactly the right gift by some such gracious thank-you as this or the one below it.

Dear Aunt Helen,

You have a real talent for selecting gifts. Whenever a package arrives from Chicago, bearing evidence of having been sent from your apartment, I always know that after the wrappings are cast aside and the box lid is finally sprung, there will emerge something bearing unmistakable evidence of your discriminating skill in selecting a present of genuine worth, of excellent taste, and perfect appropriateness.

This Gladstone bag is simply another proof of your genius; talent is too weak a term. And my thanks are not alone for the bag itself, and its splendid fittings—but, most of all, for the spirit that prompted this gift. I'll have a chance to use it next week when I start on that long-contemplated trip to Bermuda. I'm wondering if you can possibly realize how often my thoughts will be winging their way gratefully to you!

Most affectionately,
Your nephew,
Bradford

Dear Louise,

How did you know of my interest in the opera and my eagerness to get all possible information concerning those masterpieces which the Metropolitan is broadcasting every Saturday? This gift of yours is perfect; Newman's book not only gives the various plots in detail, but it includes so many passages of value to those who are eager to deepen their appreciation of music.

And it wasn't sent as a Christmas gift or a birthday present or as a reminder of any occurrence—it was just the substantial symbol of a generous impulse from your own understanding heart. How deeply I appreciate it!

Can't you come down some Saturday in March? We can have lunch here in my balcony; then later we can listen all afternoon to Wagner—or to some other composer. As you have been such a thorough student of music, you will be able to make just the sort of discriminating comment that will be illuminating to me. Please let me know when you will come. Your word of acceptance will be as gratefully received as was this deeply appreciated gift of yours.

Most sincerely,
Elizabeth

The Congratulatory Letter.

We are all of us too prone to remain silent when we learn that one of our friends has been successful in his campaign for a public office or been given a promotion in his business firm. These four have done in their letters what many persons are prompted to do—and indefinitely postpone doing!

Dear Jane,

My heart tingled rejoicingly when I read in the evening paper of your election as president of the United Real Estate Council. My mind slipped back to our school days and your alert interest in everything connected with business. While the rest of us were talking of frills and furbelows your mind was playing with profits and percentages. You early displayed a genius for handling your weekly allowance. While the rest of us were weeping over our deficits you were rejoicing over a surplus.

I recall that you were only eighteen when your father died, and you almost immediately took over his real-estate business. When you told us that you were planning to take a photograph of every home in our city we thought your little whim was a will-o'-the-wisp that would lead you into the wild marshes. Instead, it served as a magnet for processions of dollars that have been clinking in your till.

And what we all admire is the high ethical standard to which you have so steadfastly adhered. It's been a great adventure for you—and a great satisfaction to us. Tonight I am but one among hundreds of your friends who are crowding around you to warm their hearts under the glow of your bright new halo.

Rejoicingly yours,
Ann

Dear Bertram,

And so you are now a partner in Loring, Greening, and Graves! Please congratulate your older colleagues for their wisdom and good sense. They didn't have to be King Solomons or Benjamin Franklins to know your competence and thus make their fortunate decision. It is, however, a satisfaction to your friends to learn that your merits have been duly recognized. This promotion will give you added incentive for those extra shoves that in crucial times are always necessary to push the pigskin over the goal lines. I shall be eagerly watching for the bulletin board that is to register your mounting score!

Enthusiastically yours,
Winthrop

Dear Neal,

Your father has very thoughtfully written me of the coming changes in your firm—changes that are likely to mean so much in his life, in your life, and in the business life of your community.

It is a bit surprising to learn that your father is retiring from the firm of which he has for thirty-six years been the directing genius; it was less surprising to learn that you have been elected to take the helm. Fortunately, the older captain will be within call when navigation through tumultuous waters proves too perplexing.

I wish to express my entire confidence in your qualifications. You have come into a splendid heritage of property and tradition. You know what standards have been set up; you will know how to maintain them. And you will, moreover, know how to take advantage of new situations and new ideas and to give them the direction that changing conditions demand. As an old friend of the family I shall watch your work with confidence and affection.

Very sincerely yours,
Barrett Carmichael

The following is a letter from a local club secretary to the president-elect of the national organization.

Dear Mrs. Baxter,

It was indeed gratifying to the members of our local club to hear this afternoon that you have been elected to the presidency of the national organization. Even though we had all anticipated this recognition of your qualifications for the office, it was a real satisfaction to learn that your associates at Washington so enthusiastically share our confidence in your ability as an executive.

You will, we hope, graciously allow us to plan some sort of appropriate celebration for the honor that has come to you and to us. Since we know that you would object to anything elaborate, we are keeping the program brief, simple, and dignified— and genuinely sincere! Mayor Trobridge will give the welcoming address; there will be two or three short talks by some of our leading members; and then we are, of course, expecting from you a word in response.

Very sincerely yours,
Martha Russell, Sec'y

There are in everyday life acts, personal or civic, which occasion immediate response. Witness the many letters to the editors of your newspapers. Here is a note of appreciation for a bit of crusading.

Dear Mr. Elwood,

How surprised, how delighted I was the other evening when by mere chance I turned on the radio and heard your voice rolling out in its full-timbred strength and rhythm! It was as clear and natural as if you had been speaking here in our own living room.

And then as soon as I could calm my tingling nerves, I became absorbed in your message—your vibrant plea for immediate slum clearance. I had heard you speak on the same theme before—but never so convincingly. How can anyone resist your logic and your humanity! Our city has suffered long enough from those disgraceful buildings on Spearman Street. Now the flint-souled owners must submit to your argument, to your demands. If you need any help, please call on me—but it's my belief that you have already won the battle.

Faithfully yours,
Margaret Dawson

And then; there are marriages—and the arrival of babies.

Dear Constance,

I can't tell you how sorry I was not to be at your engagement party. A fire, a hurricane, or a flood wouldn't have stopped me, but unfortunately the obligation of earning my daily bread and butter—and the contingencies of time and distance—worked their havoc. Needless to say, I was with you in thought all Wednesday afternoon, sharing in your happiness and contentment.

I know that Emily Post says a girl should *never never* be congratulated upon her engagement; but, dearest Connie, you and I are too good friends to stop for mere formalities. I do most heartily congratulate you—for I think Jack is a splendid young man. Your common interest and your confidence in each other will make your life together one of complete and happy companionship, I know. I feel sure that the fates have had great fun in contriving those paths which led you to each other.

At the very first opportunity I want to see you and talk with you, for, of course, a mere letter can't pretend to discuss all the things that we both have to say. Until then,

Love,
Dorothy

Dear Edith,

Jim and I are exulting with you and Austin over the arrival of your little Nancy. We know that your happiness is now going to be complete and satisfying—as only the presence of a child can make it.

Jim and I have found in our children not only the incentive for working together always, but we have found in them a new hope for our own unrealized ambitions and dreams; and later, I fancy, when we are old—that seems such a long way off, doesn't it?—we shall find in their lives a mirage-like reflection of our own.

Do you remember, Edith, when you and I used to spend the early evening hours in our room at college talking so seriously about our careers? You were to be a famous writer, and I, a famous painter. Somewhere in the picture, I suppose we did conceive of an Austin and a Jim—and probably a little Nancy; but they were all vague, almost irrelevant, and certainly not very important. Then along came Jim for me and Austin for you, and now—Nancy. How shadowy and unreal our fabulous careers now seem! I am old-fashioned enough to believe that our greatest achievement lies in a successful and happy home life.

At the very first opportunity, her already adoring "aunt" will make the trip to see the already adorable Nancy. My dearest love to you and Austin and the baby.

Wilma

The occasion for testimonial letters is, again, not infrequent. In this one the president of the country club voices the club's appreciation of the services of a retiring hostess.

Dear Mrs. Dunwoody,

We are not assuming because you are giving up your position as official hostess of our Country Club that you are permanently withdrawing from the social life of our organization. We are, on the contrary, assuming that you are to remain helpfully near and that on special occasions we may seek your aid and counsel. In any event won't you kindly allow us to crown you now with an appropriate halo? We offer it in appreciative acknowledgment of the gracious manner in which you have for so many years performed this valuable and highly individualized service. Always, we know, your spirit will radiate cordiality and comradeship.

All our members realize that yours has been no ordinary achievement. Your leadership and your welcoming words have repeatedly warmed the hearts of our members and our visiting friends. The strangers who have entered our doorways have instantly felt the charm and the cordiality of your greetings. You have indeed been a true interpreter of the pervading friendliness of our social group. And because you have done these things with simple and unaffected kindness you have made all of us your debtors. You will, we feel sure, recognize the deep sincerity of our tribute.

And you needn't lay aside your halo while you are having this check cashed. It is a great pleasure to present it to you.

Most cordially yours,
John L. Townsend, *President*

The Letter of Invitation.

The written informal invitation offers the correspondent an excellent opportunity to show true individuality. His ingenuity is not shackled by any conventional form that must be paralleled as is the case with the semiformal and formal invitation. In fact the one requisite of a good informal invitation is that it should have a note of individuality—that the letter itself should be infused with the personality of the writer. The most effective way to achieve this is by writing in a conversational manner—writing as if you were speaking to the person. Here is an invitation from William Cowper to Lady Hesketh. Cowper writes spontaneously and with enthusiastic expectancy—as if he were talking to Lady Hesketh. He anticipates her queries and protestations and answers them. Instead of merely telling her that he and his friends will be happy to have her visit them, and anticipate much pleasure in her company, he describes specific things that they will do together and makes the incidents so inviting that it would be impossible to refuse his hospitality.

My dearest Cousin,
I have been impatient to tell you that I am impatient to see you again. Mrs. Unwin partakes with me in all my feelings upon this subject, and longs also to see you. I should have told you so by the last post.... And now, my dear, let me tell you once more that your kindness in promising us a visit has charmed us both. I shall see you again. I shall hear your voice. We shall take walks together. I will show you my prospects, the hovel, the alcove, the Ouse, and its banks, every thing that I have described. I anticipate the pleasure of those days not very far distant, and feel a part of it at this moment. Talk not of an inn! Mention it not for your life! We have never had so many visitors, but we could easily accommodate them all; though we have received Unwin, and his wife, and his sister, and his son all at once. My dear, I will not let you come till the end of May, or beginning of June, because before that time my greenhouse will not be ready to receive us, and it is the only pleasant room belonging to us. When the plants go out, we go in. I line it with mats, and

spread the floor with mats; and there you shall sit with a bed of mignonette at your side, and a hedge of honeysuckles, roses, and jasmine; and I will make you a bouquet of myrtle every day. Sooner than the time I mention the country will not be in complete beauty. And I will tell you what you shall find at your first entrance. Imprimis, as soon as you have entered the vestibule, if you cast a look on either side of you, you shall see on the right hand a box of my making. It is the box in which lodges Puss at present: but he, poor fellow, is worn out with age, and promises to die before you can see him. On the right hand stands a cupboard, the work of the same author; it was once a dovecage, but I transformed it. Opposite to you stands a table, which I also made: but a merciless servant having scrubbed it until it became paralytic, it serves no purpose now but of ornament; and all my clean shoes stand under it. On the left hand, at the further end of this superb vestibule, you will find the door of the parlour, into which I will conduct you, and where I will introduce you to Mrs. Unwin, unless we should meet her before, and where we will be as happy as the day is long. Order yourself, my cousin, to the Swan at Newport, and there you shall find me ready to conduct you to Olney.

My dear, I have told Homer what you say about casks and urns, and have asked him, whether he is sure that it is a cask in which Jupiter keeps his wine. He swears that it is a cask, and that it will never be any thing better than a cask to eternity. So if the god is content with it, we must even wonder at his taste, and be so too.

Adieu! my dearest, dearest cousin.

W. C.

The following invitation carries a more modern but an equally cordial tone.

Dear Bob and Betty,

Hortense and I have just been conspiring against your quiet and seclusion. We are down here on the South Shore planning a blitzkrieg against boredom. Don't you want to hitch up your Buick and drive down for the week-end? The flounders are biting freely and our motor boat is running gloriously. There's a picturesque picnic ground not too far away. On sunny afternoons the light has just the right slant for your new camera, and you can catch enough variants in colors to satisfy all the Orient instincts of the Queen of Sheba.

Send us word that you're surely coming. Let us glory in the adventure of filling our pantry shelves with substantial provender—and our hearts with happy anticipations.

Hortense and Allen

The Letter of Acceptance.

If you are really happy to accept an invitation you should not be satisfied with your letter of acceptance until you feel that you have honestly conveyed your enthusiasm and happiness to your host or hostess. A few trite words of thanks and the usual, "I am looking forward to seeing you all," should not be considered a satisfactory reply to the invitation. Perhaps you have visited this particular person before. Recall some of the good times you had on that occasion. Express your enthusiasm over specific plans that are being made for this visit. Use the conversational tone in your reply. Perhaps this letter which Matthew Arnold wrote to Lady de Rothschild in response to an invitation she had extended to Arnold's children will give you some hints that you can apply in your own correspondence.

> My dear Lady de Rothschild,
> Your kind but imprudent invitation transported the boys with excitement, but in the first place they have engagements here to-morrow and Monday which they must keep; in the second, two youthful schoolboys are, for all but their own parents, a luxury to be enjoyed with moderation and for no unnecessary number of days at a time. Heaven forbid that any of them should be represented as having histrionic talent; on the contrary, they appear, giggle, and look sheepish, according to the most approved fashion of youthful actors. What I said to your daughters was that their musical turn made the songs which generally occur in the pieces they choose for acting, no difficulty for them.
> When is the performance to take place? They might come down on Tuesday (with a maid) if that would give them time to learn parts before the play came off. The two must be Trevenen and Dicky, for little Tom has one of his winter coughs, and is a fixture at home. But I really think you hardly know the avalanche you are attracting, and that you had better leave it. I must go for a few days to Westmoreland, though I can ill spare the time, but my mother is not very well, and it is nearly a year and a half since I saw her.
> I hope your invalid is, at least, no worse. Many, many happy years to you.—I am always, dear Lady de Rothschild, sincerely yours,
> Matthew Arnold

The "Bread and Butter" Letter.

The "bread and butter" letter, too, should have individuality. Trite phrases such as "It was so nice being with you" and "I did so enjoy my stay with you" should be ruled out. Try to express your thanks as sincerely and enthusiastically as Charles Lamb did in the following letter to Samuel Taylor Coleridge.

> I am scarcely yet so reconciled to the loss of you, or so subsided into my wonted uniformity of feeling, as to sit calmly down to think of you and write to you. But I reason myself into the belief that those few and pleasant holidays shall not have been spent in vain. I feel improvement in the recollection of many a casual conversation. The names of Tom Poole, of Wordsworth and his good sister, with thine and Sara's, are become "familiar in my mouth as household words." You would make me very happy, if you think W. has no objection, by transcribing for me that Inscription of his. I have some scattered sentences ever floating on my memory, teasing me that I cannot remember more of it. You may believe I will make no improper use of it. Believe me I can think now of many subjects on which I had planned gaining information from you; but I forgot my "treasure's worth" while I possessed it. Your leg is now become to me a matter of much more importance; and many a little thing, which when I was present with you seemed scarce to *indent* my notice, now presses painfully on my remembrance. Is the Patriot come? Are Wordsworth and his sister gone yet? I was looking out for John Thelwall all the way from Bridgewater; and had I met him, I think it would have moved almost me to tears. You will oblige me, too, by sending me my great-coat, which I left behind in the oblivious state the mind is thrown into at parting. Is it not ridiculous that I sometimes envy that great-coat lingering so cunningly behind! At present I have none: so send it to me by a Stowey wagon, if there be such a thing, directing for C. L., No. 45, Chapel Street, Pentonville, near London. But above all, *that Inscription!* It will recall to me the tones of all your voices, and with them many a remembered kindness to one who could and can repay you all only by the silence of a grateful heart. I could not talk much when I was with you; but my silence was not sullenness, nor I hope from any bad motive; but, in truth, disuse has made me awkward at it. I know I behaved myself, particularly at Tom Poole's, and at Cruikshank's, most like a sulky child; but company and converse are strange to me. It was kind in you all to endure me as you did.
>
> Are you and your dear Sara—to me also very dear, because very kind—agreed yet about the management of little Hartley? And how go on the little rogue's teeth! I will see White tomorrow and he shall send you information on that matter; but as

perhaps I can do it as well, after talking with him, I will keep this letter open.

My love and thanks to you and all of you.

C. L.

Perhaps you will be interested to note that Lamb had not waited for Coleridge to extend him an invitation to make this visit. Indeed Lamb had written the following letter to Coleridge, asking if it would be convenient for him to come. Who could refuse a visitor so sincere in his expression of friendship?

> I discern a possibility of my paying you a visit next week. May I, can I, shall I come so soon? Have you *room* for me, *leisure* for me? and are you pretty well? Tell me all this honestly —immediately. And by what *day* coach could I come soonest and nearest to Stowey? A few months hence may suit you better; certainly me, as well. If so, say so. I long, I yearn, with all the longings of a child do I desire to see you, to come among you— to see the young philosopher, to thank Sara for her last year's invitation in person—to read your tragedy—to read over together our little book—to breathe fresh air.... There is a sort of sacrilege in my letting such ideas slip out of my mind and memory. Still that Richardson remaineth—a thorn in the side of Hope, when she would lean toward Stowey. Here I will leave off, for I dislike to fill this paper (which involves a question so connected with my heart and soul) with meaner matter, or subjects to me less interesting. I can talk, as I can think, nothing else.
>
> C. Lamb

The recipient of this letter, with its quiet tone of compliment, would no doubt feel well repaid for the task of entertaining. And that after all, is the function of such a letter.

> Dear Helen,
>
> Since my return home last evening I have been re-living the pleasant days of my week's visit with you. Always when we meet we so easily take up the strands of our separate lives and weave them into patterns that allow friendly examination and easy comment. I wonder if there are many old friends who can thus re-establish themselves so easily.
>
> You seem to me the perfect hostess. You obviously make no great thing of entertaining; and yet there is always in your hospitality the very best of entertainment—good talk, free companionship, a sense of easy comfort and unhurried joy.
>
> What pleasant memories I have brought back of the hours

we spent reading together! Most people nowadays seem to think they have to be constantly going somewhere. You and I find our greatest pleasure in the quieter ways of living. I liked so much your comments on those selections that we read. And I liked equally well the discussions of the intimate family problems that enter into our separate lives. You seem to have solved most of the major ones; I fear I may have been less successful. But I've caught some valuable hints from you—and for that I am most deeply thankful!

I never liked the phrase *a bread-and-butter letter*. I like the British term better—the English, you know, call it a *roofer*. That isn't wholly satisfactory either. I *did* like your bread and butter; and I liked your roof; but most of all I liked the quiet and the friendliness that you so graciously allowed me to share.

Affectionately yours,
Charlotte

If you cannot accept an invitation and if you really regret that other engagements or circumstances prevent your acceptance, convey this feeling to your host. Let him know that you are really sorry that you cannot enjoy the pleasure of a visit with him.

Indeed whatever type of informal note you are writing—whether it is an invitation, a regret at having to refuse an invitation, or the acceptance of an invitation—make it stand out as individual; be sure that it bears the mark of your own personality.

The Semiformal Invitation—Acceptance—Regrets.

The easy informality that prevails in social circles today and the extensive use of the telephone have, to a great extent, eliminated the use of the semiformal written invitation. There are still, however, certain occasions that call for the use of this type of note. For example, when inviting her husband's business associate and his wife to dinner, a hostess should always extend such a written invitation—unless she knows the couple well enough to telephone.

The semiformal invitation and the note of acceptance or regret which follows are always written by hand on personal stationery. The address should be placed in the lower left-hand corner of the note paper. The name and day of the month should be written out below the address. Although it is permissible to write *November 17th*, *November seventeeth* is in better taste. The year should be omitted.

The actual message of the informal invitation should be brief and cordial. The time and place of the engagement should be very clearly given.

Here is an illustration of an invitation of the semiformal type, and following it are models for the letter of regret and the letter of acceptance.

> Dear Mrs. Weston,
>
> It would be a great pleasure for us if you and Mr. Weston can have dinner with us on Tuesday evening, November twenty-sixth at seven o'clock. Perhaps we can have a game of contract later in the evening.
>
> Cordially yours,
Ann V. Pierce
>
> 14 West Park Drive
> November twentieth

> Dear Mrs. Pierce,
>
> Mr. Weston and I are very sorry that we are unable to accept your kind invitation for Tuesday, November twenty-sixth. Unforunately we have already made an engagement for that evening.
>
> Sincerely yours,
Marion S. Weston
>
> 77 Clayton Street
> November twenty-first

> Dear Mrs. Pierce,
>
> Mr. Weston and I are very happy to accept your kind invitation to dinner on Tuesday, November twenty-sixth. We are looking forward with great pleasure to spending the evening with you and Mr. Pierce. I hope you don't take your contract too seriously.
>
> Sincerely yours,
Marion S. Weston
>
> 77 Clayton Street
> November twenty-first

A Letter of Advice.

Older people, people with years of experience behind them, are often called upon to help the young make decisions. In these troublous times, the problem of a choice of vocation, especially, is uppermost.

My dear Nephew,

You wrote me from College House the other day that after graduation you wished to prepare for a career as a professional writer. After I finished reading your letter, I found myself in a definitely hesitant mood.

You had eagerly asked me for my frankest counsel. Well, counsel to the casual office visitor is a very different commodity from advice to a member of your own family circle. It isn't cumbered with so many conflicting facts and facets. When a tall, young stranger tells me he is twenty-two years old, I grant him his regular allotment of maturity; when you remind me that you are twenty-two, I see a little sprawling boy in knee breeches clambering up his uncle's legs begging for a story freshly fetched from the unreal prairies of the unreal fighting West.

Oh, yes, I know you are a senior sporting a cap and gown and expecting a diploma in June. You have been editor-in-chief of the *College Sentinel* and you have won two or three prizes in English. But, forgetting for the moment all the possible concepts of glamour that enshroud a successful writer, what basic and fundamental ideas have you about your proposed work?

Progress, you know, consists in going from *here* to *there*. What can you write me about the *here?* And what steps would you take to get *there?* Answer crisply. I am being very blunt. And I want you to be blunt—with yourself, first; with me, later.

After you have volunteered your answers to these two questions, take time off and run up to see me for a day. We'll talk it over. In the meantime, get this twenty-dollar check cashed—and spend the money as a senior should.

Yours affectionately,
Uncle Edward

A Letter to Help a Young Friend Secure a Position.

If our connections warrant, we go further than merely giving advice. We write a letter securing our young friend an audience.

Dear Wendell,

It has occurred to me that you may possibly have need at this time of the services of a young man who has a keen desire to learn the tricks of the editorial trade. And who is there so qualified as you to teach the more essential techniques?

Merrill Chase has just graduated from Wabash, where he specialized in English. During both his junior and senior years, he was on the staff of the college magazine. He was, moreover, extremely active in the student forums and the public panels. These interests in social and political questions appropriately supplemented and complemented his studies in English.

The basic training of Merrill Chase had its beginning in a home of culture and refinement; and you and I know that the disciplines of this sort of family life provide an experience that gives color and flavor to all subsequent education. The atmosphere of the Chase home has lent a potency that will be apparent throughout Merrill's whole career.

I trust that what I have written will encourage you to make a further investigation of the qualifications of this promising young friend of mine. Nothing that I could add would prove half so revealing to you as a personal interview with him. May I not act as your liaison correspondent?

Fraternally yours,
Richard

A Letter of Apology.

And then, at times, chance, circumstance, our own sins of omission or commission make a letter of apology imperative.

Dear Mrs. Danforth,
This is a letter of apology. The invitation to your dinner on Thursday did not reach me until my return to my apartment on Sunday. When I immediately called you by telephone, I learned that you had gone to San Francisco.

You must have wondered at my silence, for you knew that I had expected to return a week earlier. Well, in these stirring days, a newspaper man can have no fixed schedule. Times are too uncertain for that. Before my boat landed, I had a radiogram to go at once to the Panama Zone and report conditions there. Possibly—if you ever notice the by-lines—you may have seen my crimson-hued article in *The Daily News*.

Please don't forget me when you plan your next dinner party—though I may, unfortunately, be in Abyssinia or Timbuctoo.

Regretfully yours,
Samuel Trow

Summary

This discussion of the friendly and informal letter has strongly stressed the point that the prime requisite is the personal note; what you individually write must have your touch, your flavor, your sentiment, yourself—but as you have several selves the message you send should bear the image of your best self. Here is your record and it cannot be erased. Once it is in the mail chute power to alter or recall it is gone. It bears a cargo that may bring happiness or distress; it may dull someone into a lethargy—or it may stimulate to valiant adventure; it may bring anxious perplexity—it may lighten someone's weighted burden.

Moreover, the writing of letters may prove to be the most vital of all vital self-educational forces. By your own resolve to be a better craftsman it may force you to be rigidly exacting in your mechanics. Here a mispelling or an ungrammatical form is a social blunder; careless and illegible handwriting is a discourtesy; inappropriate stationery is a bit of *gaucherie*—indeed, any gross disregard of correspondence etiquette is a gross disregard of social etiquette. A determination to avoid all these errors is an essential attitude in true craftsmanship.

But these items are largely mechanical. The more potent educational stimulus rests in resolves to lift your mind from narrow horizons; to cultivate a more alert intelligence; to be increasingly accurate in observing common phenomena and increasingly deft in expressing the richness of more accurate observing. Coincident with all this should come a keener imagination, a developed social consciousness, a conviction that actual living implies the actual assuming of responsibilites for the enlargement of spirit. Letter writing is only one way of encouraging such an educational force as this—but it is an important way.

PRACTICES

Reluctance to write letters is an almost universal failing, due generally to the diffidence which prevents us from making a start. When that is once overcome, the pen can trip along surprisingly. Practice is needed; but capacity is enlarged by enthusiasm in the subject, which communicates itself to the reader. Good letters such as those which follow serve not only as examples, but as a stimulus.

PRACTICE 1

The Informal Letter

1. Here is an informal letter, describing commonplace things in a most interesting and highly entertaining manner. Write a letter to a friend that can compare with this letter in flavor and individuality.

My dear Mrs. Kennedy:
 I was really sad at heart at parting with you and Mary Kennedy at Washington. Indeed, had not your establishment fallen to pieces around me, I hardly know when I should have gotten

away. I could almost have clung to the wreck so long as there was a three-legged stool and a horn spoon to make shift with. You see what danger there is in domesticating me. I am sadly prone to take root where I find myself happy. It was some consolation to me, in parting, that I had Mrs. H. and the gentle Horseshoe for fellow-travellers. Without their company, I should have been completely downhearted. The former was bright, intelligent, and amiable as usual; and as to "John," you know he is a sympathizing soul. He saw I needed soothing, so he cracked some of his best jokes, and I was comforted.

I arrived in New York too late for the Hudson River Railroad cars, so I had to remain in the city until morning. Yesterday I alighted at the station, within ten minutes' walk of home. The walk was along the railroad, in full sight of the house. I saw female forms in the porch, and I knew the spy-glass was in hand. In a moment there was a waving of handkerchiefs, and a hurrying hither and thither. Never did old bachelor come to such a loving home, so gladdened by blessed womankind. In fact, I doubt whether many married men receive such a heartfelt welcome. My friend Horseshoe, and one or two others of my acquaintances, may; but there are not many as well off in domestic life as I. However, let me be humbly thankful, and repress all vain-glory.

. . . I sallied forth to inspect my domains, welcomed home by my prime minister, Robert, and my master of the horse, Thomas, and my keeper of the poultry yard, William. Everything was in good order; all had been faithful in the discharge of their duties. My fields had been manured, my trees trimmed, the fences repaired and painted. I really believe more had been done in my absence than would have been done had I been home. My horses were in good condition. Dandy and Billy, the coach-horses, were as sleek as seals. Gentleman Dick, my saddle-horse, showed manifest pleasure at seeing me; put his cheek against mine, laid his head on my shoulder, and would have nibbled at my ear had I permitted it. One of my Chinese geese was sitting on eggs; the rest were sailing like frigates in the pond, with a whole fleet of white topknot ducks. The hens were vying with each other which could bring out the earliest brood of chickens. Taffy and Tony, two pet dogs of a dandy race, kept more for show than use, received me with well-bred though rather cool civility; while my little terrier slut Ginger bounded about me almost crazy with delight, having five little Gingers toddling at her heels, with which she had enriched me during my absence.

I forbear to say anything about my cows, my Durham heifer, or my pigeons, having gone as far with these rural matters as may be agreeable. Suffice it to say, everything was just as heart could wish; so, having visited every part of my empire, I settled down for the evening, in my elbow-chair, and entertained the family circle with all the wonders I had seen at Washington.

To-day I have dropped back into all my old habits. . . . I have resumed my seat at the table in the study, where I am scribbling this letter, while an unseasonable snow-storm is prevailing out of doors.

This letter will no doubt find you once more at your happy home in Baltimore, all fussing and bustling at an end, with time to nurse yourself, and get rid of that cold which has been hanging about you for so many days.

And now let me express how much I feel obligated to you and Kennedy for drawing me forth out of my little country nest, and setting me once more in circulation. This has grown out of our fortunate meeting and sojourn together at Saratoga last summer, and I count these occurrences as among the most pleasant events of my life. They have brought me into domestic communion with yourselves, your family connections and dearest intimacies, and have opened to me a little world of friendship and kindness, in which I have enjoyed myself with a full heart.

God bless you all, and make you as happy as you delight to make others.

Ever yours, most truly,
Washington Irving

2. There is an art to writing letters that children will really enjoy. Here is a good model.* Use some of the writer's devices in a letter to a young member of your family.

VERY PRIVATE

Dear Gertie,

This letter is an awful secret between you and me. If you tell anybody about it, I will not speak to you all this winter. And this is what it is about. You know Christmas is coming, and I am afraid that I shall not get home by that time, and so I want you to go and get the Christmas presents for the children. The grown people will not get any from me this year. But I do not want the children to go without, so you must find out, in the most secret way, just what Agnes and Toody would most like to have, and get it and put it in their stockings on Christmas Eve. Then you must ask yourself what you want, but without letting yourself know about it, and get it too, and put it in your own stocking, and be very much surprised when you find it there. And then you must sit down and think about Josephine De Wolf and the

---

Letters From Many Pens, edited by Margaret Coult, copyright, 1922, The Macmillan Company, New York.

other baby at Springfield whose name I do not know, and consider what they would like, and have it sent to them in time to reach them on Christmas Eve. Will you do all this for me? You can spend five dollars for each child, and if you show your father this letter, he will give you the money out of some of mine which he has got. That rather breaks the secret, but you will want to consult your father and mother about what to get, especially for the Springfield children; so you may tell them about it, but do not dare to let any of the children know of it until Christmas time. Then you can tell me in your Christmas letter just how you have managed about it all. . . .

This has taken up almost all my letter, and so I cannot tell you much about Vienna. Well, there is not a great deal to tell. It is an immense great city with very splendid houses and beautiful pictures and fine shops and handsome people. But I do not think the Austrians are nearly as nice as the ugly, honest Germans. Do you?

Perhaps you will get this on Thanksgiving Day. If you do, you must shake the turkey's paw for me, and tell him that I am very sorry I could not come this year, but I shall be there next year certain! Give my love to all the children. I had a beautiful letter from Aunt Susan the other day, which I am going to answer as soon as it stops raining. Tell her so, if you see her. Be a good girl, and do not study too hard. and keep our secret.

Your affectionate uncle,
Phillips Brooks

3. Perhaps you have recently been on a trip that you would like to describe to a friend. Here is an interesting account of Florence sent by Thomas Gray to his mother. Use this as a model in writing your account of your experiences.

We spent twelve days at Bologna, chiefly (as most travellers do) in seeing sights; for as we knew no mortal there, and as it is no easy matter to get admission into any Italian house, without very particular recommendations, we could see no company but in public places; and there are none in that city but the churches. We saw, therefore, churches, palaces, and pictures from morning to night; and the 15th of this month set out for Florence, and began to cross the Apennine mountains; we travelled among and upon them all that day, and, as it was but indifferent weather, were commonly in the middle of thick clouds, that utterly deprived us of a sight of their beauties; for this vast chain of hills has its beauties, and all the valleys are cultivated; even the mountains themselves are many of them so within a little of their very tops. They are not so horrid as the Alps, though pretty near as high; and the whole road is admirably well kept, and paved throughout, which is a length of fourscore miles and more. We left the pope's dominions, and lay that night in those of the grand duke at Fiorenzuola, a paltry little town, at the foot of Mount Giogo, which is the highest of them all. Next morning we went up it; the post-house is upon its very top, and usually involved in clouds, or half buried in the snow. Indeed there was none of the last at the time we were there, but it was still a dismal habitation. The descent is most excessively steep, and the turnings very short and frequent; however, we performed it without any danger, and in coming down could dimly discover mists; but enough to convince us, it must be one of the noblest prospects upon earth in summer. That afternoon we got thither; and Mr. Mann, the resident, had sent his servant to meet us at the gates, and conduct us to his house. He is the best and most obliging person in the world. The next night we were introduced at the Prince of Craon's assembly (he has the chief power here in the grand duke's absence). The princess, and he, were extremely civil to the name of Walpole so we were asked to stay for supper, which is as much to say, you may come and sup here whenever you please; for after the first invitation this is always understood. We have also been at the Countess Saurez's, a favorite of the late duke, and one that gives the first movement to everything gay that is going forward here.... In the meantime it is impossible to want entertainment; the famous gallery, alone, is an amusement for months; we commonly pass two or three hours every morning in it, and one has perfect leisure to consider all its beauties. You know it contains many hundred antique statues, as the whole world cannot match, besides the vast collection of paintings, medals, and precious stones, such as no other prince was ever master of; in short, all that the rich and powerful house of Medicis has in so many years got together. And besides this city abounds with so many palaces and churches, that you can hardly place yourself anywhere without having some fine one in view, or at least some statue or fountain, magnificently adorned; these undoubtedly are far more numerous than Genoa can pretend to; yet, in its general appearance, I cannot think that Florence equals it in beauty. Mr. Walpole is just come from being presented to the electress palatine dowager; she is a sister of the late great duke's; a stately old lady, that never goes out but to church, and then she has guards, and eight horses to her coach. She received him with much ceremony, standing under a huge black canopy, and, after a few minutes talking, she assured him of her good will, and dismissed him. She never sees anybody but thus in form; and so she passes her life, poor woman! . . .

Thomas Gray

PRACTICE 2
The Letter With a Purpose

(a) Imagining yourself to have found that your education has not fitted you for any line of work that is open, write a letter to some important administrator or employment agency, describing your situation and ask for specific advice concerning an immediate program.

Reversing the point of view and imagining yourself this administrator or agency, write a letter filled with practical and very specific advice.

(b) You have an immediate duty. You are in one of the following situations; each of which calls for a letter of some kind. Select your situation and write the appropriate response.

1. You have returned home after a week's visit with a friend in San Francisco.
2. You are planning a house party and are about to send a letter of invitation to a friend in Omaha.
3. You have received a personally autographed book—*Among the Air Forces*—which an intimate friend has just written.
4. Your friend is in the hospital, convalescing from an automobile accident.
5. You have spent your last dollar and are "dead broke." You dislike asking a friend for a loan, but you are in dire need.
6. You are to acknowledge a confidential letter revealing an important bit of personal news.
7. You are about to enter a political campaign and are to ask advice from an acquaintance in Chicago.
8. You are ambitious to enter the advertising business and want some personal advice.
9. A magazine editor has opened his columns to persons under thirty and you are invited to contribute.
10. You are conscious of some physical weakness and wish a physician's advice.
11. A young married friend of yours has asked your advice concerning a personal domestic problem.
12. You are asked, in the light of your own experience, to advise a friend concerning his choice of a college.
13. Your son or younger brother is just entering business and has asked your advice concerning a specific problem.

14. You are anxious to become identified with the television industry.
15. As secretary of an organization you are inviting someone to address a public meeting which your association is sponsoring.
16. You are accepting the invitation just extended by this organization.
17. A friend has asked your advice concerning a method to improve his speaking voice.
18. You are in a strange land short of funds, and you are about to write to the American Consul concerning your situation.
19. You have received an expensive gift which you cannot accept.
20. You are balancing in your own mind two alternatives—buying a cheap house in the country or renting an apartment in the city. You think your father will advise you wisely.
21. You are bothered about a specific point in English and you think a friend can solve the problem.
22. You are greatly concerned about some phase of your future and you think of someone whose advice you would value.
23. You have wronged someone and you are planning a letter of apology.
24. Your neighborhood needs a library. You are writing a letter to the editor of your local paper.

PRACTICE 3

Creative Writing Skill and Letter Writing

All persons interested in developing additional skill in written expression should practice diligently the art of letter writing. Welcome the art of letter writing. Welcome most cordially each opportunity to write. In every case let your ambition set up a high standard of achievement. This advice is coupled with the warning to be natural; be your own natural self but guard against a self-granted consent to allow your tone to sink below the level which your higher insight wills.

You, of course, know your own personal situation and the demands and desires of your own family and your own friends. You are, therefore, able to set your own letter-writing assignments. The following list may, however, stimulate a resolve to get a specific letter immediately into the mails.

THE FRIENDLY LETTER

SUGGESTIONS FOR LETTERS

1. A friend of long standing has, through unfortunate circumstances, been charged with a serious crime. The daily press has given much space to the affair. You believe in his innocence. Write him, and assure him of your loyalty.

2. In a moment of anger you have spoken to an associate in a manner you now regret. Write a note of apology—but keep the tone dignified rather than abject.

3. You have, while on a visit in a distant state, met with a rather serious accident. As you are able the next day to use your typewriter, send a full account to your family. Tell the truth. It is serious—yes. Assure them that they will receive a daily message that will neither exaggerate nor minimize; it will be frank and accurate.

4. As an imaginary member of the family who receives the foregoing message, write an appropriate answer. Be sensibly sympathetic; be cordial in your promise to do everything that will prevent the patient's worrying.

5. Your most intimate friend has published a book that has quickly won great popularity. Write an appreciative letter—but guard against fulsome praise.

6. You have just had an article printed in one of the leading magazines. Send a copy of the issue and write a brief note. If this friend is of the right sort, he will not think this a display of vanity; he will appreciate your thought of him.

7. One Sunday you attended a church service in a distant city. The minister in his sermon touched upon a theme that at the time concerned you very deeply. The sermon cleared up most of your perplexity. Write him a full account of the way he had unwittingly been of great personal help to you.

8. Let your imagination phrase for you the letter which this minister wrote in response.

9. Imagine yourself an editor of a magazine. You have a general admiration for a story which an unknown contributor has sent in. Write to this contributor and ask him (or her) about possible revisions. Be concrete.

10. You are deeply concerned about a specific situation—local, or national, or international. Write a letter to one of your local papers—or to some cosmopolitan paper, if you prefer.

11. You have just learned that an old school friend is planning to move to your city. Write him (her) expressing your interest and your pleasure. Don't promise too much—just enough!

12. Your son (or some member of your family) has a perplexing problem that one of your old friends may possibly aid the son in solving. Write fully, earnestly, seriously, but keep the tone from being too beseeching.

13. You have been on a long journey. Write to an intimate friend and describe two or three scenes that deeply impressed you. Lift your descriptions far above the level of drabness.

14. Instead of concentrating upon the scenes suggested in No. 13, write of two or three impressive incidents. Go into details. Appeal to the five senses—and give your sense of humor a liberal rein!

15. Two of your friends—perhaps husband and wife—have had serious differences. You know the inherently fine nature of these persons. Write to each of them a letter designed to effect a reconciliation. You realize how tragic a final break would be. Go into details. Make definite suggestions.

CHAPTER IX

THE BUSINESS LETTER

By Peter T. Ward

Instructor in Business English, Columbia University

IN the daily intercourse between the retail shopkeeper and the housekeeper the business letter does not play an important role because almost every transaction is on a face-to-face basis. Sales are made directly; collections are made personally; claims and adjustments are made over the counter. Every one of us has made purchases at Woolworth's or Kresge's, at the A. & P., at Walgreen's, at Whelan's, or at some similar retail shop. It is seldom that a letter enters into such a transaction. There are 1,500,000 retail stores in the country, and the housewife, it has been estimated, does more than eighty per cent of the family buying. Many a person might be inclined to conclude that the letter plays only a minor part in business affairs.

There is, however, another side to this whole process of buying and selling, which we call business. Not all business is transacted over the counter of a retail store. Most of it is done through offices. Those large shipments that are seen passing along on ten-ton motor trucks or on 100-car freight trains, or being loaded on ocean liners and inland steamers, are not, at the moment, all of a retail character. Ultimately some may be. All the merchandise passing through a retail store was at one time or another part of a wholesale quantity, but the major part of the goods bought and sold never passes through a retail store. Airplanes, locomotives, dynamos, bricks, road-building machinery, steel beams, and merchandise sold wholesale are only a few examples. In the exchange of these commodities for money the business letter plays a dominant part. Such transactions originate in the business office. The office of the buyer may be a thousand miles removed from the office of the seller. Even in these days of quick communication by telegraph, telephone, and the radio, the letter still remains the most widely used medium in such negotiations.

The process of buying and selling involves the writing of letters of many types. Let us look for a moment at the several steps. There are sales letters attempting to interest prospects in the goods. Perhaps a letter of inquiry will result, to which, in turn, an answer will be sent. If the inquiry is intelligently answered, an order will be returned by letter, which naturally ought to be acknowledged by another letter. It is quite probable that the transaction will be on a credit, not on a cash, basis. Thus credit letters will come into play; and should the buyer be dilatory in making his payments, one or several collection letters will be required. Then, of course, complaints and claims will arise, and these will require adjustment letters in reply.

Quite obviously anyone engaged in business should have a knowledge of business letters and an understanding of the underlying principles applicable to the writing of each type of letter. Some people in business offices may go through their whole business careers without ever writing a single letter for an employer, but such people are few and far between. Anyone worthy of his salt cherishes the ambition to advance, and just as surely as night follows day, so will the necessity for writing effective letters accompany one as he advances in the business world. The more responsible the position, the greater its demand upon the one who holds it to exercise all his skill and knowledge and experience in writing letters, because to men and women in the higher positions is assigned the task of handling the more difficult letters. The business man who cannot write clearly, concisely, correctly, and persuasively is laboring under a handicap which may be an obstacle throughout his entire business career. Employers nowadays do not have to tolerate the mediocre ability of an indifferent correspondent, because they can readily secure the services of employees skilled in the art of expression. It is altogether within the power of a correspondent to decide to which class he will eventually belong.

The Receiver of the Letter

Many a writer of business letters goes through a cut-and-dried ritual, as it were, in his dictation. He summons the stenographer, squirms uneasily in his chair, fidgets with the batch of letters lying before him, nervously clears his throat, and he is off to an inglorious start. The first words out of his mouth are probably a stereotyped, participial beginning such as "Acknowledging receipt of your kind favor of recent date..." Then he rambles through a series of incoherent, long, involved sentences and concludes with another stereotyped, participial phrase such as "Trusting to receive your favorable response, we beg to remain." The various people to whom he has just dictated letters are just so many names, such as he might find in a telephone book. His mind's eye sees no farther than the mouthpiece of the dictaphone or the pothooks of the stenographer. To him dictation is the dullest part of a day's work—something to be rid of hurriedly and carelessly. That type of correspondent will never write well, for he is lacking in an essential prerequisite. He is unable or unwilling to envisage the "other fellow." He has not employed what is commonly known among business men as the *you* attitude. The able correspondent always looks at the situation from the other person's viewpoint. He must put himself in the recipient's position. It is only natural for a person to write about himself, his products, his prices, his house policy, but the person who persists in writing only about himself and things of interest to him alone is nothing but a common bore. Consider the "other fellow." Suppose you were in his place, how would the letter strike you? Does your letter radiate a spirit of understanding, of cooperation, of helpfulness? Does it reflect his viewpoint? Unless it does—and does so fully—it will never be a resultful letter. The *you* attitude also demands that the writer do not consider all people like so many peas in a pod. No two people are identical in their likes and dislikes, professions, politics, and religion. Identical styles of writing should not be employed in writing to a clergyman and a farmer; to a lawyer and a truck driver; to a physician and a janitor. A real estate agent managing property may have on his lists tenants paying $3000 a year, and others paying $30 a month. Entirely different styles and tones must be adapted to each. One's method of approach must be adjusted to the receiver's position in life, to the likes and dislikes peculiar to people in different sections of the country, and to the whims and caprices existing at the moment.

The absence of the *you* attitude is the outstanding shortcoming of business letters. Too many sales letters are written from the viewpoint of the writer. Too many letters of application are all "I" and omit entirely any reference to how the applicant will be of assistance to his prospective employer. Far too frequently a tone of impatience and irritation penetrates the whole adjustment letter. The collection letter usually tells the debtor why the creditor wants the money rather than why it is to the debtor's advantage to pay. Here is an example of the lack of the *you* attitude in an adjustment letter:

> The explanation of the operation of our kitchen ventilator is given on the card of instructions which accompanied the machines. These instructions are perfectly plain.

The statement implies that the customer is stupid because he cannot understand plain language.

Or consider the following from a credit letter:

> Replying to your letter of April 6th, we cannot allow you credit.

Or this sentence from a letter from a commercial bank to a customer:

> If you cannot maintain an average balance of $400, we ask that you withdraw your account.

Or this from an adjustment letter:

> We were surprised at the contents of your letter of November 12th.

The inference that the customer will draw is that the seller thinks his claim unreasonable; otherwise why the surprise? Remember, then, that it is imperative for anyone who aspires to success in letter writing, to cultivate a lively imagination in order to be able to put himself in the other person's place. Consideration of the customer creates and increases good will, and good will is the life blood of any business enterprise. The correspondent who does not cultivate good will is losing business for his firm; he is a liability rather than an asset.

The Writer

A native wit and intelligence, a kindly disposition, a philosophy of good-fellowship, an insatiable desire to know all about the business, its products, its manufacturing processes, its policy, a liking for and an ability to get along with people—all these are desirable traits in a correspondent. One lacking in any of them should assiduously strive to cultivate the qualities in which he is deficient. A book such as Scott and Howard's *Influencing Men in Business* will be helpful.

He who has taken seriously his English courses in high school or in college, or who has read widely and well, will do a more commendable job in his dictation than he who has had inadequate training in his mother tongue. It is never too late to learn. One whose training in English has been deficient should diligently study all the material in *Your Mastery of English*. Whoever tries to dictate clearly and correctly expressed letters when he suffers from an inadequate grasp of the language is like an automobile running with dirty gas and a clogged carburetor. If you are unfamiliar with the technical rules of expression, learn them by studying, not only *Your Mastery of English*, but also one of the many worth-while handbooks of composition, such as: *College Handbook of Composition* by Woolley and Scott; *Century Collegiate Handbook* by Greever and Jones; *Handbook of Effective Writing* by Smart; *Effective English* by Wann; *Manual of Good English* by MacCracken and Sandison; *College Handbook of Writing* by Woods; *Constructive English* by Ball.

Keep abreast of the language of business by reading regularly such periodicals as *Printer's Ink* (both the weekly and the monthly), *The Reporter*, and *Better Letters in Business*.

Be alert in the office. Learn all you can about the business. Know its why's and wherefore's. Develop in yourself an enthusiasm for your house, its products, and its policy. Enthusiasm is contagious; even cold-blooded customers are susceptible to the contagion.

With a background such as has been outlined above, you can then approach any letter situation, no matter how difficult it may be and no matter what the problem, with the confidence that you are master of the situation.

Each situation presents its own difficulties. Each type of letter must be specially approached and handled. To solve the situation successfully, the writer must give mature thought, not merely to the letter, but to the transaction behind the letter, to the business situation that animates the letter. A business letter without a background is like a landscape painting without perspective. Procure all the data pertaining to the situation at hand. If you are writing an adjustment letter, unearth all the facts that have any bearing whatever on the customer's grievance. If it is a sales letter, fully acquaint yourself with all information bearing on both your product and your prospective customer. In proportion as thought has been given to the business situation behind the letter, in that proportion will the letter be successful.

The Letter

So many rules, theories, and principles have been expounded in books on letter writing that the fundamental function of writing is likely to be lost from sight. The writer of a business letter is not writing for his own information. He has ideas; he wants to transfer those ideas to the minds of other people. Language—either written or spoken—is the medium whereby the ideas are carried across space. The conveyance of ideas is the fundamental function of every business letter.

Unlike other forms of writing, which aim to entertain or amuse, the purpose of every business letter is to secure action—favorable action—from the recipient. The sales letter seeks to secure an order; the collection letter, a check; the letter of application, an invitation to call upon the prospective employer; the claim letter, a satisfactory adjustment of the customer's grievance; the adjustment letter, the return of the customer's business. That the writer may secure favorable action from the reader, his letter should be expressed in language that is accurate, simple, and vigorous.

Accuracy of Diction.

Because many writers do not recognize the real function of the language in a business letter, they write "in the clouds." Pompous language, tortuous sentence structure, weak words, and a generally artificial tone permeate the entire letter. By no stretch of imagination would a writer say to a customer the highfalutin, meaningless abstractions and stereotyped expressions which he sometimes puts into a letter.

Be careful to use words accurately. When a correspondent says to his stenographer, "Miss Jones, kindly take a letter," he probably does not mean "kindly," for in that case he is asking that Miss Jones take the letter in a gracious or cheerful manner. What he is doing is giving a polite command. The word should be "please." A customer writes, "We are forwarding with this letter our check for $21." What the dictator probably means is that he is "mailing," "enclosing," or "sending" a check. He is not forwarding it unless he is relaying a check which he has received from another. Another lazy use of the word "forward" occurs in the expression, "Your shipment is going forward today by Railway Express Agency." Of course, the customer is glad to know that his order is going forward rather than backward, but why use the term at all. It is the same sort of antiquated letter diction as "under the date of" and "over the signature of." With some correspondents everything happens and all letters are written "under the date of—"; and all letters are written "over the signature of—" somebody or other.

One business firm wrote, "The balance of your order will be sent direct from our Baltimore warehouse." The word "balance" was inaccurately used. What the firm meant to write was "rest" or "remainder."

A plant foreman sent to his superior a report, one sentence of which read, "Over three days' time was lost by each riveter because of rainy weather." He meant to write or should have written, "More than three days' time. . . ."

One office memorandum read, "Despite the diligent efforts of our salesman, this prospect still remains disinterested in our product." The dictator should have said "uninterested."

If you are writing a letter selling life insurance, it is better to say "When you die, the Company will pay . . ." rather than "If you die, the Company will pay . . ." Obviously there are no *if's* about death.

Simplicity of Diction.

By far the greatest number of business letters are written to plain everyday folks. The safe rule, then, is to write in the simple language of the common man and woman. Every one understands simple language. Do not put on frills and airs and affectation. Pompous language seldom impresses and may defeat the real purpose of the message in that it may not be easily understood. The word "communication" is a perfectly good word, but it is not so readily understood as the word "letter." Instead of writing a bombastic expression such as "with promptitude," why not be yourself and write "promptly"? Here is an example from a sales letter: "This kitchen gadget has a myriad of uses." Why "myriad"? Would not the word "many" be better? "We thank you for the interest you have manifested in our goods." The word "manifested" is correctly used, but "shown" is preferable unless the letter is addressed to a person known to the writer to be better than average in education or intelligence. "Our portable typewriter can be utilized in the home the year round." A better word for the average person would be "used."

Vigor of Statement.

One valuable aid in imparting vigor to your statements is to eliminate from your message idle or weak words. Use strong, virile words. Do not be content with the first word that comes into your mind. Diligently and patiently search for a stronger one. In the expression, "We sincerely appreciate," the word "sincerely" is an idle word. It adds nothing to the message. By its very definition appreciation cannot be insincere. One frequent business expression is, "This is an unusual proposition." The word "proposition" is so general a word and has been so frequently used that it means almost anything. And, of course, each seller's offer is "unusual"—in his opinion. Why not avoid the word that is lifeless, that does not bear its fair share of the burden of transmitting the message?

You may write "Your order will have our immediate attention." "Immediate attention" is not specific enough. It gives some assurance to the customer, but only negative assurance. Would it not be better to write, "This afternoon we are shipping to you by parcel post..."?

Similarly, do not write to a customer or to a prospect that your product is "best." Everybody says his product is best. If you insist, tell him that your product is best, but also give the convincing details or facts that make it best. In other words, tell why it is best.

Notice that you may often omit the word "very" without serious damage to your thought and quite possibly with advantage. Such expressions as "we think" and "we believe" also may well be omitted in many instances. Words resemble people. Some are weak, spineless, anemic; others are virile, lusty, robust.

Remember, then, that in addition to your words being simple and accurate, they should also be robust.

People who know what they are talking about write convincingly. They know the facts, and they know how to present them. Reading this book or a dozen similar books will not of itself impart a convincing tone to your writing. Facts about your business and its products constitute the material out of which you carve your message. To be poorly supplied with the facts results in a feebleness of expression that will create doubt and uncertainty in the mind of the reader. If you have not faith in yourself, in your firm, and in your product, how can you expect the customer or the prospect to have faith? As an aid to vigorous expression procure all the facts.

When you dictate, are you yourself or only a poor imitation, a mere shadow of someone else? The business world is loaded down with letter writers who are just so many automatons. Heaven endowed each of us with an individual character as it has endowed each with individual fingerprints. The mystery is that so many business men stifle their character when they begin to dictate. Socially they are interesting and delightful. In face-to-face conversation with customers they are likewise pleasant, convincing, persuasive. They are themselves. Once put to the task of dictating a letter, however, these same men mentally congeal. They dictate hollow echoes of the pompous, wordy, and stereotyped letters of two or three generations ago.

Cordial simplicity of real friendship should exist in a letter as it usually does in conversation between two business men. If you wish to give your letter reality, to make it a real living thing, a good practice to follow is to imagine that the person whom you are addressing is sitting directly across from you at the other side of your desk. Suppose he were sitting right there in front of you, what would you say to him, and how would you say it? You would not be shy or rigid or aloof. Why suddenly change your entire mental attitude because you are writing to him? Your letter will breathe a spirit of genuineness and reality only when you adopt a man-to-man attitude toward the recipient. When you dictate, be yourself. Relax that mental tension under which so many labor as they approach the task of dictating. Make your letter a pulsating, living reality, not a dead, artificial abstraction.

Arrangement of Detail.

Planning is essential to the writing of effective letters just as it is to taking an automobile trip, building a house, or winning a football game. Too many letters are written haphazardly. The writer of such letters is pictured earlier in this chapter under the heading *The Receiver of the Letter*. When such a correspondent begins his verbal outburst with the salutation "Dear Sir" or "Gentlemen," only Divine Providence knows when or how he will ever reach the "Yours very truly." The correspondent certainly does not know. He desperately hopes that he will reach the end. His letters resemble Topsy in *Uncle Tom's Cabin*, who just "growed." Consideration of the reader, the selection of the right word, the order of presentation of ideas, the use of imagination—all demand mature thought.

The beginning of the letter belongs to the reader. As you learned in school, put in the same paragraph only sentences pertaining to one phase of the subject. Let your treatment of the subject proceed in a smooth, easy flowing, logical fashion. If you are answering a letter, one good plan is to underscore lightly in pencil the significant points to be discussed in your reply. An alternative method is to draw short vertical lines along either margin. A formal outline is not necessary, but by all means have some sort of outline or plan. With practice the outline may be made mentally. An outline eliminates scatterbrain thinking and wordiness, results in shorter letters and clearer expression, and secures the conviction and cooperation of the reader because it saves his time and effort.

A minute or two spent in planning will be more than made up in the time saved in dictation, in the clarity, coherence, directness, and terseness of the letter, and in the reduction in the number of letters that have to be rewritten because of badly constructed and improperly placed sentences and paragraphs. Sounds too good to be true, doesn't it? Here's an example in point. Not so long ago a firm was sending out a poorly arranged sales letter which was securing only fair results. In sentence after sentence the words were arranged without any great forethought. Sentences likewise were haphazardly placed within the paragraphs. Finally the order of the paragraphs was not logical. One thought did not naturally, smoothly, and logically follow its predecessor. The entire presentation of ideas violated the four steps in sales letter writing, about which you will read a little farther on. A conference was called in an endeavor to determine the reason for the mediocre results. One man, somewhat better trained than the others in the science of arranging ideas in proper sequence, perceived the source of the trouble and volunteered to rewrite the letter. He rearranged the sentences and paragraphs. Not a single word was added or removed. Amazing as it may seem, the results were almost doubled.

The Fault of Wordiness.

A common and costly fault in business letters is wordiness. It is easy for a person dictating to ramble on, piling paragraph upon paragraph. Nowadays letters are not written by hand but are dictated, and "dictated letters" means "talked" letters. Talk is cheap—at least, so it seems. When, however, the personally dictated letter costs upward of fifty cents, and a correspondent employs 200 words to do the work that 150 can do, he is increasing letter cost by about one-third. The extra cost may be a paltry fifteen or twenty cents a letter. If, however, he dictates on the average ten letters every business day during the year, his talk may not be so cheap as it first appeared to be. Planning, which has just been discussed, is one aid to conciseness. Thinking each sentence out in advance just before dictating it, is another excellent means for reducing excess verbiage. "When you have something to say, say it; don't take half a day."

The Form and Appearance of the Letter

When the recipient of a business letter draws it from the envelope, the first thing that strikes his eye is the physical make-up of the letter. It is by the form and appearance of the letter that a firm often is judged. If the letter is the only link between the house and the customer—as so frequently happens—it is the only means that the customer has of appraising the house.

Paper of substantial quality, a neatly printed letterhead (usually in black ink), and a tastefully arranged letter well balanced on the sheet and attractively framed with a margin of white all around—all these play their parts in creating a favorable impression in the mind of the recipient. Better quality in the paper and printing entails only a modest extra outlay of a fraction of a cent in the total cost of the letter. The attractive arrangement of the letter itself requires only the persevering daily attention of the stenographer or of the correspondence supervisor. The extra impression value will always justify the slight extra cost and effort.

Business letters have six physical parts: the heading, the address, the salutation, the body, the complimentary close, and the signature.

Part of the heading is incorporated in the printed letterhead. Only the date needs to be inserted, in the upper right-hand part. It should appear below the printed material and should end about an inch from the right-hand edge of the paper, or, as nearly as possible, where you expect the right-hand margin to begin. The heading for one's own personal business letter (which will probably be written on a plain sheet measuring 8½″ x 11″) should include the street address, the town and the state, and the date. These items should appear in that order. If the street address and the city and state require considerable space, they should occupy two lines, and the date should appear on a third line. If they are short, street address and city and state may be placed on a single line. Occasionally in small communities where street numbers are unnecessary, the city and state and the date may appear on the same line.

The address is composed of the name of the addressee on the first line, the street address (if the addressee is in a large community) on the second line, and the city and state on the third line. The address begins at the left-hand margin. The distance at which it is placed below the printed letterhead and the width of the left-hand margin are determined by the length of the letter. Short letters should be given plenty of margin. Long letters do not permit margins much wider than an inch.

A corporation requires no title. The title "Mr." precedes a man's name. The title "Miss" precedes a single woman's name. The title "Mrs." precedes a married woman's name. Names of partnerships composed of men require the title "Messrs." A firm composed of women takes the title "Mmes." People in public office are accorded the title "Honorable" before their names. A lawyer may have the abbreviation "Esq." after his name, if "Mr." is omitted. Do not use two titles meaning the same thing. For instance, Dr. H. H. Rowland, M.D. is incorrect. Dr. and M.D. are the same.

A salutation is necessary in every business letter. It appears two spaces below the last line of the address. "Dear Sir" is used for a man; "Dear Madam" for a woman; "Gentlemen" for a partnership of men or of men and women and for corporations; and "Mesdames" or "Ladies" for a partnership of women and for women's organizations.

The following are a few illustrations of appropriate headings, addresses, and salutations for business letters: (1) and (2) are arranged in the block style with open punctuation; (3) and (4) are in the block style with closed punctuation; (5) and (6) are shown in the old-fashioned diagonal arrangement with open punctuation; (7) and (8) are in the old-fashioned diagonal style with closed punctuation.

(1)

            476 Thomas Street
            St. Paul, Minnesota
            April 16, 19—

Alumnae Association
Vassar College
Poughkeepsie, N. Y.

Mesdames:

          Yours very truly

(2)

        33 Montana Street
        Boise, Idaho
        September 24, 19—

Miss Willa Cather
3 Bank Street
New York, N. Y.

Dear Madam:

      Yours very truly

---

(3)

        18 Millbrook Avenue,
        Camden, South Carolina.
        September 30, 19—.

Messrs. Hornblower and Weeks,
42 Broadway,
New York, N. Y.

Gentlemen:

      Yours very truly,

---

(4)

        14 High Street,
        Portland, Maine,
        October 1, 19—.

Carl Zeiss, Incorporated,
728 South Hill Street,
Los Angeles, California.

Gentlemen:

      Yours very truly,

(5)

Montauk Arms Hotel
Battersea, Montana
November 1, 19—

Mrs. Marion T. Vanderbeek
  270 Park Avenue
    New York, N. Y.

Dear Madam:

Yours very truly

---

(6)

5 Lafayette Terrace
Middletown, Missouri
November 15, 19—

The Tailored Woman
  742 Fifth Avenue
    New York City

Gentlemen:

Yours very truly

---

(7)

P. O. Box 18,
Bellaire, Ohio,
December 5, 19—.

Mr. Henry Ford,
  Dearborn,
    Michigan.

Dear Sir:

Yours very truly,

(8)

R. F. D. 6,
Woolsey, Indiana,
March 4, 19—.

Mr. and Mrs. Arthur M. Foster,
   322 State Street,
       Boston, Massachusetts.

Dear Sir and Madam:

                    Yours very truly,

What you have to say to the other person appears in that part of the letter called the body. That is the part of the letter that will demand your constant attention and study, including a study of our language, a study of human behavior, and a study of your own business in its relationship to the customers. It is not a subject that is to be studied indifferently for four years in high school or for a year or two in college. It is not a subject that is to be studied intensively for three months or six months in the hope that in that brief span of time one can master the entire subject. For the alert business man it is a lifelong study to be engaged in even during his leisure moments. It is an interesting, a fascinating, and, withal, a rewarding subject.

    Let us pass to the last two parts of the business letter. The fifth part is the complimentary close. When you have said your say, stop; don't clumsily back out of the picture with some such idle participial and stereotyped expression as "Hoping to receive your valued order," "Assuring you of our appreciation of your inquiry," etc., etc. The complimentary close is composed of some brief closing such as "Yours truly," "Yours very truly," "Very truly yours." If the situation warrants, "sincerely" may be substituted for "truly."

    In letters to people holding public office or positions of esteem, such as a clergyman or the president of a university, "Respectfully yours" or "Yours respectfully" is the customary complimentary closing.

    The last part of a business letter is the signature. Remember that a signature is to be read, not to be puzzled over. A man's signature should not increase in complexity and illegibility as he advances to more responsible positions, or, as many times happens, as he pretends to advance. The first signature at the foot of the Declaration of Independence is an outstanding example of how to write one's signature. So also are the signatures of Lincoln, Wilson, and Theodore Roosevelt.

In letters to large firms time is saved and business is expedited by the addition of the notation "Attention of Mr. ...." This notation appears on the same line and to the right of the salutation. It sometimes appears a bit higher than the salutation, and sometimes it is even sandwiched in between the address and the salutation. It is desirable to underscore the notation and to remember that the letter is still addressed to the corporation; therefore the salutation remains "Gentlemen." The notation does not mean that the letter is addressed to the individual.

The Sales Letter

Business concerns are engaged in selling either goods or service. Sales may be made over the counter, by traveling salesmen, or through the sales letter. In over-the-counter sales an already existing need, aided and abetted by a clever and alluring window or counter display, reduces to a minimum or eliminates entirely the necessity of salesmanship. There is much in common between the traveling salesman and the writer of the sales letter. The traveling salesman interviews one prospect at a time and speaks his message. Sales letters are salesmanship on paper. A salesman's talk can always be put in letter form. The salesman has the decided advantage of facing the prospect, of personally studying him and his whims, of changing his sales tactics as the exigency of the particular situation demands. He certainly can close a greater number of sales per hundred calls than can the sales letter. He can, however, call on only one customer or prospect at a time, and many times is limited to a half dozen calls a day. On the other hand, the sales letter can call on a thousand or a hundred thousand customers or prospects on the same morning. The cost of each call by mail is seldom more than a dime.

The products that have been successfully sold by mail are innumerable: sets of books like this that you are reading; life insurance; building lots; financial aid for charitable institutions; support for political candidates; fishing flies; electric refrigerators; pianos; baby chicks; fish; artificial eyes; summer cruises; personal loans. For instance some years ago a single sales letter sold over $2,000,000 worth of raincoats by mail; and one chicken hatchery at Petaluma, California, sells by mail 35,000 chicks daily. It is therefore amusing to hear some people, many times with an ax to grind, condemn the sales letter as an impractical means of selling. It is quite true that many letters are ineffective, and it is small wonder. At least four sales letters out of every five are doomed to failure before they are mailed because of some fatal shortcoming. The writer is unskilled in writing English and especially in writing sales letters. The list may not be suitable; or the appeal may not be effective. If the product is right, if the price is right, if the letter is sent to the right prospect, and if the sales appeal is properly formulated, sales will result.

Years ago the psychologist, the salesman, and the skilled writer of English pooled their efforts. The psychologist contributed as his part of the successful letter the four psychological steps. These four steps really do not lie so much in the field of English as in the realm of psychology—the science that tells us how human beings react to certain stimuli, impressions, or appeals. The skilled sales letter writer must lead his prospect by means of these four steps or stages along the path to the signed order.

The first step is to secure the favorable attention of the writer. Notice that it is not merely *attention*, but *favorable attention*. Even a moron can secure some sort of attention of a reader—probably unfavorable—by a fantastic or absurd statement. Years of observation and tabulation by letter experts indicate that favorable attention can usually be secured in one of five ways.

1. Begin your letter with a statement of a significant fact. A fact significant to the reader will jolt him right out of his mental lethargy.

EXAMPLE: Here is an opportunity for you to save $20 on next winter's coal bill.

2. Ask the prospect a point-blank question that pertains in some way to him or to his interests. Questions, of course, can be answered "yes" or "no." Frame your question in such a way that practically all your prospects will answer in precisely the way you want.

EXAMPLE: Would you like to retire at age 65 with an income of $200 a month? (Worded to elicit a "Yes.")

EXAMPLE: Would you make a thief out of your own son? (Worded to elicit a "No.")

3. A conditional type of beginning is effective. The sentence usually begins with *If*. What follows puts the prospect in a predicament

or dilemma. The remainder of the sales letter offers him a solution to the difficulty.

EXAMPLE: If all your account books were destroyed by fire tonight, it would be serious. (Selling fire-proof filing equipment.)

4. Sometimes a modification or a combination of the foregoing three typical beginnings is used. An introductory clause occupies a line of its own. The concluding part of the sentence follows in a separate paragraph just below.

EXAMPLE: If we could guarantee to reduce your shipping cost by at least 25 percent—

Would you be interested?

5. People are interested in news. Thus a brief news item, if it is relevant to the prospect's interests, is a good means of securing his attention.

EXAMPLE: Yesterday the United·States Navy signed a contract for the purchase of 113 of our generators—the largest order in naval history.

Now that you have secured the favorable attention of the prospect the second step is to create desire. This part of the letter corresponds to the display of the merchandise before a prospective buyer in a retail store. Seeing is believing. It is an essential element in creating the desire of the see-er to own the product. Let a child wander around a toy shop, or a woman around a hat or dress department of a department store, or a man around an automobile showroom. Many will be unable to buy because of an inadequate supply of cash, but they will linger there and long to buy; and some actually will buy. The second step in the sales letter attempts to imitate this process. In this second step the writer describes to the prospect the nature of the product, what it looks like, how it will help him, what it will do for him. Before you describe what the product looks like, be sure that you see it in its every detail. Emphasize important details. Use crisp, incisive, concrete words. The task is difficult. It makes exacting demands on the talents of even the most skilled writers. Usually a person is less interested in the physical appearance of a product than he is in what it will do for him. Will it make life easier for the prospect or improve his lot? Will it make the women prospects better looking, younger looking, more attractive? Will it, by chance, help Mr. and Mrs. Upstart to keep up with the Joneses? Will it enable Mr.

Businessman to make larger profits, have his work done more efficiently? Find in every situation that appeal which will prove most effective.

The third step is to convince the reader that your product or service is really good, and that he needs it. There are seven ways by which you can convince the prospect.

1. Although it is not always possible, one good way is to send a sample of your product. This in miniature corresponds to showing the merchandise in a shop. To some extent it may make amends for mediocre description. It is common for a tailor shop to send two or three swatches of cloth with the sales letter. A department store will send to its customers four samples in different colors of the broadcloth in shirts which it is selling by mail. Small samples of sail and awning cloth are sent to members of boat clubs. Four-inch strips of metal strapping for packing cases are sent with sales letters to manufacturers. Sometimes the prospect is required to write for the sample. This strategy of putting a person to the inconvenience of writing a request deters promiscuous samplers.

2. A testimonial of a satisfied user may be incorporated in the body of a letter. The testimonial should not be more than a short paragraph in length and should be by one prominent in the particular field of endeavor and of unquestionable integrity. It is usually difficult to procure such testimonials because people are reluctant to have their statements broadcast for sales purposes.

3. The product may be guaranteed unconditionally or for a certain length of time against the need for repairs or defective workmanship. Merely to say "We guarantee this product" is insufficient because it is not definite enough. It would be better to say, "If for any reason whatever you are dissatisfied with this product, we will refund your money." Such a guarantee is broadly stated; it is specific, convincing.

4. Another means of convincing takes the form of a list of satisfied users. Nothing succeeds like success. A list of six or eight reputable firms or individuals who are satisfied users, serves to convince the doubting Thomas. The prospect's reaction is, "If the product satisfies them, it ought to be good enough for me."

5. Sometimes the prospect is invited to make a test. If the test is to be made on a sample enclosed, two types of evidence are combined: the sample and the test. Usually, however, the offer is made to send the product to the prospect for the purpose of making a test. For

instance, the prospect is invited to take a ride in the latest model of the Blank motor car to test out its easy riding quality, its power, its acceleration, its effective brakes, its hill-climbing ability.

6. A trial offer is sometimes made. The trial offer may take the form of a small quantity of the commodity to be billed at a nominal price. This type of trial offer is used in connection with commodities on which there are frequent repeat orders. At other times, the product is sent for trial use for ten, fifteen or thirty days. This type of offer is made when the product being sold is a single unit to be ordered at long intervals. The sale to a householder of a vacuum cleaner, a washing machine, or an electric refrigerator would be an example.

7. The last type is a statement of substantiated facts. The facts may be statistics from the government records or certified to by an impartial body. They may be the collected data on a series of experiments. It may be a summary of experiences with the product by a number of different users. The facts must be clearly set forth. They should be attested to by a source that has no selfish purpose to serve.

The fourth step in the successful sales letter is to secure action. Of course, every sales letter aims ultimately at securing an order. Oddly enough, this part of the letter is often omitted by inexpert sales letter writers. At the opportune moment toward the end of a sales talk, the skilled salesman guides the prospect toward the order blank. The last paragraph in a sales letter must perform a similar function. The action getter does not necessarily seek the signed order. In most instances, asking for an order would be demanding too much from an astute prospect, and consequently it would be placing too heavy a burden on the sales letter itself. There may be an easier intermediate step, such as inviting the prospect to send for an illustrated booklet, a catalogue, a representative, further information, or a demonstration. It is usually better sales strategy to aim for that intermediate step.

For instance, it would be folly to expect a person to buy an automobile or a washing machine or an air-conditioning system on the strength of a letter alone. When making rather large outlays of money, people first want to see what the product is like or see it in operation. Take the easier path to the sale. Offer a demonstration or a free trial, because it will not cost the prospect anything. He feels he has nothing to lose. The seller is assuming the risk. Or the prospect may be invited to send for a representative or for an interesting booklet giving additional details. The proposed visit of a salesman should be discreetly handled; otherwise prospects will have visions of a high-pressure salesman, who in the eyes of many, is considered as Public Enemy No. 1.

Another device that aims to push the prospect across the line of indecision is to make the action easy. For instance, if the prospect is asked to sit down and write a letter, he may be busy at the moment. The prospect will shove the letter aside for attention "tomorrow." Procrastination is the thief, not only of time, but also of sales. The moment the sales letter is laid aside for attention "tomorrow" the chances of securing the order are greatly diminished. Give the prospect no excuse or pretext for postponing action. To write the letter involves time and effort. A better strategy is to enclose a return reply card. It is even desirable to save the prospect the trouble of looking around for a postage stamp. Secure a government permit for reply cards and pay the postage upon those received. The reply cards should be expressed in simple language, free of all legal technicalities.

The following excerpt illustrates these four steps in a successful sales letter sent to amateur musicians in public schools and elsewhere. The letter produced 11.8 per cent inquiries and 7 per cent sales.

> Now that you have a good start in music, you no doubt would like to be a real musician—an artist.
>
> You have musical talent or you wouldn't be playing now. But you have no idea how well you could play if you had one of the latest, improved Conns.
>
> No musician, no matter how much natural, inborn talent he may have, can rise above his instrument. There are many school musicians of unusual musical talent who are struggling along under the handicap of a poor instrument. So long as they continue on the inferior instrument, they will remain mediocre. It will take a new model Conn, with its amazing beauty of tone, ease of blowing, and accurate scale, to bring out all their natural talent.
>
> Conns are known all over the world as "Choice of the Artists." If you want to be a REAL artist on your instrument you should do as the great artists have done—you should choose a Conn without delay.
>
> We'd like to tell you about some of the latest developments in Conn instruments. We'd like to send you one of the booklets pictured in the enclosed circular. There is no obligation—it is a pleasure for us to send it.
>
> For your convenience we've enclosed a postage-free return card. You owe it to yourself and your musical future to fill in and mail this card right now. No obligation whatsoever. Mail the card!

Here is a successful informal letter* sent out by a quality bakery to housewives residing in a fashionable suburban community. The letter was a reproduction of an actual hand-written letter and printed in blue ink. The recipient's name was written in the salutation in the same handwriting and in the same color. An envelope such as is generally used for personal correspondence was employed, and first-class postage was used. The letter was intended to pave the way for the visit of the route delivery man who followed up the letter. Naturally no action getter was necessary in this type of situation.

> My dear Mrs. ....
>
> You have problems, like anyone else who has to plan a daily menu. It may be the problem of a wholesome lunch for the children, a specially swank dessert to give the unexpected guests on Friday night. Wouldn't a suggestion now and then help?
> Peter Pan's suggestions will come to your door. All sorts of delicious things to eat fresh from our baking kitchens. There will be homemade bread for the children's sandwiches; a spicy layer cake to follow the evening meal; a specially good butter cream coffee cake to serve with the coffee after an evening of bridge with the Smiths.
> Once you have seen them, we won't need to tell you that they are made from just such ingredients as you keep in your own ice box—table butter, fresh milk, eggs, heavy cream.
> And you'll know, too, that the mixing and baking were carefully supervised by women whose standards compare with your own. We think you will be proud to serve anything baked by Peter Pan.
> We'd be pleased to have you come and see our kitchens in Orange. Baking under such modern and sanitary conditions on such a scale is a fascinating process to watch. And then, of course, you will see that we are just as fussy about little things as you would be yourself.
> Meanwhile, Peter Pan's courteous salesmen will bring you tempting specialties as well as delicious breads and rolls to add variety to your menus.
> We hope you will use and enjoy them; we hope they will make the problem of planning and serving food an easy one to solve.
>
> Very truly yours

When a sales letter goes out singly, in most instances it is sent to a customer or to one sending in an inquiry. In either case it does not

---

*From *Postage and The Mailbag*, courtesy of James H. Wright.

have to adhere so rigidly to the four steps described above. Little effort need be made to secure the attention of the other person because there is an established bond of interest between the house and the customer or the inquirer; the recipient is looking forward to the reply. The style is more informal, more friendly. It is well, however, that the part of the letter creating desire be just as vigorous and vital and concrete in its description as the corresponding part in sales letters sent out in quantities.

Letters to customers do not have to adhere so rigidly to the principles employed in establishing conviction because customers usually have faith in the firm, its statements and products. So far as the inquirer is concerned, however, it is just as essential to convince him as to convince the great mass to whom letters are mailed in quantity. He, too, may be a "doubting Thomas."

In every instance action should be made easy. Everyone, whether he be a prospect, an inquirer, or a customer, should have his task of ordering simplified. Send along order blanks, self-addressed envelopes, or postage paid cards. How ordering can be made easy for the prospect has just been outlined.

Follow-up Letters

Follow-up letters are necessary, first, because there is so much to say about the merits of a product that a single letter cannot adequately develop the sales appeal unless the letter runs into several pages. The mere appearance of a lengthy letter is enough at the very outset to stifle the interest of the prospect. The procedure, then, is to split the entire sales talk into several short, convenient divisions that can be easily read. A second reason is that a sales letter endeavors to exchange a product for the prospect's money. People part with their money with some reluctance. One letter seldom breaks down the sales resistance. Fortunate is the salesman who is so persuasive and dynamic that he can sign up most of his prospects on the first call. Seasoned salesmen know that several calls have to be made, in most instances, before the prospect signs on the dotted line. So, too, several letters are usually required before the signed order is returned.

Follow-up letters to prospects are usually of two types. Even a cursory study of follow-up letters used in present-day business will disclose that the average letter writer is not acquainted with the distinction between the two types of follow-up letters. He is sending out "just a series," and as a result of his indifferent and unintelligent handling and his confusion about the two types, he never injects into his series the greatest degree of sales power. The two types are known as "campaign" and the "wear out." As the name indicates, time is an important factor in the *campaign series*. This series is used in selling a commodity or service that is seasonal in character, or when there is urgent need to dispose of certain products. Easter cruises for teachers, summer camps for children, hotel accommodations in Florida during the winter months, and the rental of summer homes are types of seasonal commodities or services in which the campaign series is employed. The campaign series is really a single, long sales letter cut into convenient lengths. The letters are mailed at short intervals because each letter, as has just been indicated, is closely related to its predecessor, and because time is pressing. They cannot be mailed at intervals of a month or more. The entire series is written in advance because the letters constitute an integrated whole, and because time does not permit of their preparation one at a time.

The probable number of letters in the series is also determined in advance. The skilled writer does not arbitrarily decide on some favorite number for his series. He is largely governed by such factors as (a) what the selling price is, (b) what profit he makes on each sale, (c) what type of person he is writing to, and (d) what the nature of the product is. A person does not spend $300 so readily as he does $15. There is greater sales resistance. A longer series is required. Then, too, the amount of profit on a sale must be considered. If a person is selling by mail a book on which his profit is but $2 he cannot send out a lengthy follow-up series. He is limited to a single letter. On the other hand, if the profit on each sale is several hundred dollars, as in the case of works of art, road-building machinery, or house insulation, he is justified in spending money on a long series. He will make enough on a single sale to justify the extra outlay. The type of prospect must also be considered in determining the number of letters in the series. A list composed of names taken from the city directory or a voters' list is not nearly so promising as a list of people who have sent in a coupon appearing in a magazine. This latter list, in turn, is not nearly so productive of orders as a list compiled of people who have sent in coupons from magazines, but with the addition of 10¢ or 25¢ in cash to cover the cost of a booklet. Finally, a product that is well known does not require the same degree of advertising as does a pioneer product. Electric refrigerators do not meet with the same degree of resistance today as they did twenty years ago. House insulation is now meeting the resistance which electric refrigerators then met. Well-known products require a shorter series than does a type of product or service just being introduced to prospects.

Now let us look for a moment at the *wear-out series*. The letters go out at much longer intervals than do the campaign letters. Why? Instead of a link being established between letters, the opposite is true. A letter in the wear-out series is not mailed until the predecessor has exhausted its sales-getting power. A reasonable length of time elapses to permit as many orders or inquiries as possible to be developed by the earlier letter. Then, and not until then, is the next letter dispatched. A second point of difference is that each letter in the series is a complete sales appeal beginning with the attention-getter and ending with the action-getter. The series continues as long as each successive letter shows a profit. When the letters begin to show a loss, it is then felt that the list has been exhausted of its order-getting possibilities.

The following series of five letters was successfully used by the Remington Arms Company, Inc., to persuade outstanding trapshooters to use a new type of shell. That the letters were successful is indicated by the fact that most competitors in the "Grand American" used the new shells.

I

Dear Fellow Trapshooter:

Ever see a target sail away unbroken when you knew you held right?

Ever lose a championship or wreck a long straight run because of "unaccountable" lost targets, when your form was perfect?

Then read and heed the story of "NO MORE BLOWN PATTERNS" attached here. It tells of the greatest improvement in shotshell performance since choke boring seventy-five years ago. This new shell is a miracle of modern research and manufacturing achievement for *your* benefit.

Now you can see why "unaccountable" lost targets sailed away unbroken . . . and why from five to eight blown patterns out of every 100 shots with ordinary trap loads made "Lady Luck" the mythical champion of many a hard fought race from the smallest club to the grandest "Grand."

But, for the shooter who would break the shackles of habit, precedence, or preference, blown patterns are "bogies" of the past. Relegated to the archives of progress are ordinary trap loads, for with Remington Shur Shot trap loads having New Remington Crimp, there are no more blown patterns.

We invite you to a new experience in trapshooting. New because never before have you had shells that eliminate blown patterns, add five to ten yards to your effective range, help boost your handicap average, and improve your double scores.

Try in your own gun Shur Shot trap loads with the New Remington Crimp, over your own traps, for a feeling of shooting confidence you have never known before.

Very truly yours

II

Dear Fellow Trapshooter:

Until last month only three shooters had broken 100 straight from the twenty-five-yard line, throughout the history of trapshooting.

Last month, a shooter accomplished this feat *twice*. John Rigg broke 100 straight from the twenty-five-yard line at the New Jersey State Shoot on June 10. He repeated the performance a week later at the Pennsylvania State Shoot.

Mr. Rigg shot Remington Shur Shot shells with the New R e m i n g t o n Crimp. Therefore, it was accurate gun pointing, and not luck, that enabled him to make these record-breaking scores.

Before the New Remington Crimp came on the market, luck played an important role. That is why, until last month, there were only three twenty-five-yard 100 straights ever recorded.

Any shells having the old style top wad give blown patterns about five to eight times in 100 shots. When shooting from the twenty-five-yard line, the distance from gun to target is about forty to forty-five yards. A blown pattern will have large open spaces at this range, frequently permitting a target to pass through unbroken.

The New Remington Crimp eliminates blown patterns; eliminates large open spaces. When shooting Shur Shot shells with the New Crimp, you will break your targets . . . whether sixteen yard, handicap, or doubles . . . if you point your gun right.

May we urge you to give the new Shur Shot loads a thorough trial, if you are not already using them?

Very truly yours

III

Dear Fellow Trapshooter:

What is it? . . . How does it work? . . . Why don't you leave it off? . . . What holds it on? . . .

These and many other questions have been fired at us lately about that red disc on Shur Shot trap loads with the New Remington Crimp. In our enthusiasm over the amazing performance of these new shells, we forgot to tell you the interesting story behind the red disc.

1. The red disc improves wetproofing by completely eliminating contact of moisture with the end of the shell body.
2. It is made of special paper of carefully controlled tensile strength so that...
3. It ruptures with ideal pressure build-ups and thus...
4. It assures the most effective burning of modern smokeless powder to deliver uniform ballistic performance.
5. It is mechanically strong so that it can be roughly handled and battered in the magazine or pocket without injury to the crimp... but when the paper disc ruptures...
6. It adheres tightly to the shell body, thus keeping sealing material out of contact with the chamber and bore of the gun.
7. It gives load and shot size information where you expect to find it... on the end of the shell.

You'll agree that's a lot for a little red disc to do, but Shur Shot trap loads with the New Remington Crimp are like that... precision built shells that eliminate blown patterns and give you an extra edge.

Very truly yours

IV

Dear Fellow Trapshooter:

Here is good news! If you attend the Grand American, you will shoot at Blue Rock targets thrown from Remington-Leggett traps. Remington equipment is to be used exclusively at the 1939 "Grand."

Very truly yours

V

Dear Fellow Trapshooter:

Call for N-E-W R-E-M-I-N-G-T-O-N C-R-I-M-P... Call for N-E-W R-E-M-I-N-G-T-O-N C-R-I-M-P.

And what a well justified call it has been! For Championship after Championship at practically every State Trap Shoot from coast to coast has been won by shooters using Remington Shur Shot shells with the New Remington Crimp.

Thirty-seven State shoots have been held to date, and...

...Twice as many combined singles, handicap, and doubles

championships were won with Shur Shot shells with the New Remington Crimp as with any other brand.

... In handicap events alone, three times as many championships were won with these loads as with any other.

... At many State shoots, every important championship was won with Remington New Crimp loads.

Shur Shot shells with the New Remington Crimp give top performance. They eliminate blown patterns, and make higher scores possible.

They give uniform ballistic performance, are wetproof, and are mechanically strong to withstand rough handling or dropping without injury. They are quality shells throughout, from brass base to red disc.

Give yourself the break you deserve at the Grand American. Shoot the shells the winners are shooting, the shells that will help YOU win. Shoot Remington Shur Shot shells with the New Remington Crimp. Very truly yours

Credit and Collection Letters

Because these two types of letters are closely related, they will be considered together. Unless a customer pays cash for the order, credit letters are written when the order is received. Collection letters appear after sale of the article on credit. The seller is unlikely to ship a product without receiving the cash—unless he has some detailed information about the customer's reliability. Thus it is that before the merchandise is sent, a *credit letter*, accompanied by a questionnaire or an information form, is sent to the customer. If the customer's credit standing proves satisfactory, a second letter is sent accepting him as a credit customer. If the customer's record is found unsatisfactory, a letter is sent declining the order, except on a cash basis. The person unfamiliar with business practice may resent a credit man's penetrating questions as insolent. They are much like the elderly lady unaccustomed to traveling who asked the ticket agent for "a ticket." When he inquired of her "Where to?" she replied "That is my business." Business people know that the information requested is essential for the protection of the seller. The task of the letter writer is to be tactful with all, and extremely tactful with those who easily take offense.

The way in which this situation can be diplomatically handled is shown to a nicety by the writer of this letter:

Gentlemen:

We are thankful that you wrote us as frankly as you did in your letter of February 13 because it enables us to explain to you our credit policy. You requested us to ship your order immediately. Because we did not want to delay the shipment in order to make the usual routine credit inquiries, we sent your order on C. O. D. basis. Please do not think, even for a moment, that we thereby intended the slightest reflection on your credit standing. We shipped the goods on this basis solely to get them to you as quickly as possible.

This initial order of yours indicates that you are a customer whom we should very much like to have. It is for that very reason that we are asking you to fill out and return the property statement. Your credit rating will then be established and all such routine annoyances will in the future be obviated.

From your own experience of thirteen years in business, you will readily agree that such a procedure is neither unnecessary nor severe. You—like ourselves—probably make similar requests of all your new customers. It is the only reasonable way to be sure that credit will be extended to the right people.

Those from whom we buy invariably ask that we give them a property statement at the close of each fiscal year. We are happy to comply, for you will admit that sound credit can exist on no other basis.

So that we may come to a better understanding and thus extend to you the fullest degree of service, we are asking that you fill out the property statement which we are enclosing. The addressed stamped envelope is for your convenience in returning the statement.   Yours very truly

There is a cheerful, persuasive, firm, matter-of-fact style of writing in credit letters. If credit is to be granted, the letter extending the privilege should express a genuine welcome to the customer, an appreciation of his order, and an optimistic expectation of many years of pleasant business relations. Write not only from the head but from the heart.

The business-like little note below, which was sent by a department store to a new credit customer, is appropriate to the occasion:

Dear Mrs. Smith:

Thank you for opening a charge account with us.

We are doing our best to render a friendly, helpful, and courteous service, and we consider no transaction satisfactory to us unless it is satisfactory to you. If, for any reason, you ever have cause for complaint, I would consider it a favor if you would write to me personally.

I hope you will visit us often.

                              Very truly yours

The letter that is a severe strain on the credit letter writer's capacity for adroit expression is the letter refusing credit. It is never easy to say "no," but it can be said, and said without its being an abrasive on the sensitive feelings of the customer. The "no" should be said with a smile. There is still much business to be had from among those customers to whom credit cannot be granted. Properly approached, they can be sold on a cash basis. Remember, too, that today's poor credit risk may be tomorrow's gilt-edged risk. Is it not worth while, then, to refuse credit in such a genial manner as to maintain the good will of the customer? Why not, if possible, incorporate in the letter a bit of the *you* attitude discussed in the earlier part of this chapter. The task is difficult; the results, rewarding.

Dear Sir:

Thank you for the order which you gave to our salesman, Mr. Curtis, when he called on you on Tuesday. We also appreciate your attaching to the order form the names of the three references.

Your references speak very well of you personally and leave no doubt in our mind about your personal ability and integrity. Inquiries which we have made through the usual credit channels, however, indicate that it would be unwise for us to extend credit at this time. What would be an unwise credit for us to extend naturally would be an unwise credit for you to accept. After all, we are more interested in the continued success of your business than in securing an unduly large order, for we are looking forward to having you as a customer for many years to come.

Quite frankly, our credit policy is a decidedly conservative one. It does have the advantage, however, of our selling to you merchandise at much lower prices than if we had too liberal a credit policy. In the long run you benefit by our lower prices.

Although we are unable to extend credit to you at the present time, we are quite certain we shall be able to do so in the future.

We shall be glad to fill your order for your current needs on a cash basis. The assortment which you have ordered is numbered among our best-selling items. Our low prices, the unsurpassed quality of our merchandise, and the up-to-the-minute fashions assure you of quick turn-overs.

You may send us a check to be credited to your account, or, if you wish, tell us to send the order on a C.O.D. basis. May we have the pleasure of filling this initial order of yours?

            Very truly yours

Even more difficult for the correspondent is the writing of *collection letters*. Debtors resolve themselves into two groups: The great majority who will pay their bills; the very small minority who will not pay their bills. Any kind of letter will be ineffective with the second group. The strong arm of the law may exact payment, and even then there is a great big "maybe."

It is with the large first group that the correspondent should concern himself. This group, in turn, may be divided into many types. Each collection correspondent should make a classification appropriate to the debtors in his own business. Then, of course, there is the business itself. The character of people in one type of business may be of high caliber; in another the general character level may be mediocre, or even border on the shrewd and crafty. Then again the commodity in one industry may be slow-moving, as in the lumber business, or it may move rapidly as in the chain-store business. These are considerations that enter into the interval between the letters in the series and the exact tone to be employed in each letter. In a more individual sense, the customers of any one firm may differ widely. One customer may have been too lenient with his own customers. He may be dowdy in his business habits. He may have suffered some family tragedy, which will have a temporary influence on his ability to pay.

The fundamental purpose of a collection letter is twofold: first, it must collect the debt; second, it must maintain the good will of the debtor. Any incompetent can do the one at the sacrifice of the other. The able correspondent must accomplish both. Many a correspondent reveals in his letters his lack of self-control and of the mental poise necessary to perform the task properly. Because they fear to give offense, or because they are unable to be both firm and inoffensive, some correspondents are unduly meek to the point of being servile. Others are fearful lest their mildness be interpreted as weakness. They, therefore, resort to a verbal blitzkrieg that ruffles the customer's sweet disposition and sometimes is instrumental in causing the customer to have his name removed from the company's ledger.

There is no need to be subservient in asking for what is rightly one's own. Advancing explanations for the debtor's failure to pay is out of order, as is an apology for asking for the money. Brusque, nagging, tactless letters may bring in the check at the loss of the customer's good will and quite possibly of his business.

Of course, as the collection series progresses towards a climax, the request for payment increases in insistence. Even the patience of a collection letter writer may ultimately be exhausted, but it should be exhausted only when all hope of payment by peaceful persuasion likewise has been exhausted. At this point, however, the situation is rapidly passing out of the realm of letter writing and into the sphere of compulsion in the form of collection agencies, reports to credit associations, and attorney's services.

The four collection letters appearing below were sent to delinquent customers of Geo. G. McKiernan & Co. They were successful in collecting the money in all but three or four unusually difficult cases.

I

Mostly always honesty is the best policy—highwaymen, racketeers and astrologists notwithstanding.

So I am going to be perfectly honest with you. We need cash, and are making an honest appeal to you to help us with your check for $77.50, a balance long overdue.

We feel confident you will help us by using the stamped reply envelope to mail us your check.

II

Likely you are as hard pressed for cash as we are. Otherwise, we are sure you would have answered our letter of May 11 with your check for $77.50.

Under the circumstances, we only ask in the friendliest, most neighborly spirit:

1. Can you spare $38.75—half of the balance due us?
2. If not, please tell us when you will be in a position to remit partially or in full.

The stamped envelope is for your reply. Your check for $38.75 answers No. 1. A few words answers No. 2. And thanks—one way or the other.

III

There must be a reason for everything. Consequently, there must be a reason why you don't answer our courteous letters—written in an honest endeavor to cooperate with you in the payment of an overdue account.

First, we asked you without rancor nor raving to send us your check for $77.50, the amount due us. No answer. Then we asked you, gently, if you could spare us just half the amount due—or tell us when you could conveniently make payment. No answer.

These letters were friendly, and our reason for writing them clearly stated. Everything considered, don't we deserve a reply from you, at least?

Conditions may be responsible for delay in paying bills. We understand that. But we cannot understand why you completely ignore our straightforward request. Such disregard is not like you.

So won't you send us today part of the $77.50 balance you owe —or drop us a note telling us you can't or won't—and why? The familiar stamped reply envelope is enclosed for your convenience.

IV

Suppose Bill had owed you $5 for a long time, and you met him on the street one day and said, "Hello, Bill—how about that five?"

If Bill were the right kind, he'd reach down in his pocket and hand you your money or say, "Sorry, old top, I'm short—but I'll surely square up next Saturday"—and he would.

But what would you think of Bill if he turned his back on you and walked away without a word?

Figuratively, that is just what you are doing to us. We have asked you courteously to pay your debt—and you've turned your back on us without a word. One—two—three times you've done it.

We cannot believe you are that kind. Won't you, therefore, square up or accord us the courtesy of an explanation as to why your check is withheld so long?

We want to be fair—and we want you to be fair, too.

The amount you owe us is $77.50. Please use the enclosed, stamped reply envelope to carry your check or a note of explanation back to us today.

Claim and Adjustment Letters

In the manifold business relations between buyer and seller, friction is bound to develop. Late deliveries, damaged shipments, shortage, defective merchandise, failure to keep promises, misrepresentation—real or imagined—on the part of salesmen, and many similar grievances are the points where friction may arise. The one who has the grievance, the customer, is the one who initiates the exchange of letters. Through the *claim letter* or letter of complaint, the customer writes just what is on his mind, and usually his mind is heavily burdened. Most people are quick to magnify the shortcomings of the other person. Customers are no exception. And how they like to "rub it in." Many seem to consider it a stroke of genius to have Uncle Sam's couriers carry a diatribe for the seller's information and discomfort. Unfortunately, however, such a letter is not a mark of genius but one of bad breeding. No one in his letters—not even a customer—is excused from the exercise of the same consideration which he himself expects. The very same quality of consideration discussed in this chapter is one of the requisites of a good letter. Even an aggrieved customer should retain the attributes of a gentleman. And good breeding is one of them.

Although the following letter may have relieved the feelings of the customer, it is a discourteous letter, lacking in good taste and in consideration of the recipient.

> Gentlemen:
> Your latest letter to me—your fourth—is just about the limit! I cannot quite comprehend why there should be such stupidity and delay in a concern of the size and reputation of Blank and Company.
> On March 28 I returned to you in your own original carton or box the three madras shirts and requested that you return to me three broadcloth shirts of the same color. I do hope that you are not pretending that the shirts are not yours. Your label appears on each shirt and on the box. I have not been in Los Angeles in several years, but I have already told you that they were sent to me as a gift by Mr. Kelley. This explanation would appear to put the quietus on the shop-lifting theory under which you people are laboring.
> Naturally, as I live a considerable distance from Los Angeles, I do not have a charge account with you. And, on second thought, I don't think I should want to, in view of the way in which you treat customers and handle exchanges.
> Now, let us get down to brass tacks: Please send me my three broadcloth shirts or refund the credit amounting to $7.50. I can readily see that this is a rather large assignment for you people to handle. Quite frankly, it seems incredible that there should be so much difficulty, confusion, and explanation over a mere matter of $7.50.
> At the very outset I wrote you people that what I wanted was a simple exchange of three madras shirts for three broadcloth shirts. You have already expended on correspondence pretty nearly the cost of the shirts.
> Exchange for Homer J. Millard three broadcloth shirts for the three madras shirts sent to him by Blank and Company by Mr. Farrar Kelley of Los Angeles. Is this last letter clear? And please give this simple request your immediate attention!

Of foremost importance, therefore, in a letter of complaint is courtesy. State your claim; state it clearly so that the nature of your grievance will be fully understood; state it in detail so that a satisfactory and complete adjustment may be made; state it with forbearance so that you will secure the greatest degree of cooperation; state what you expect by way of an adjustment so that the seller may have some notion of how to approach the situation.

Because of its clear outline of the facts and temperate language, the letter below, written by a retail druggist, will enlist the ready cooperation of the seller in arriving at a satisfactory adjustment.

> Gentlemen:
>
> The shipment of peroxide and of face powder which I ordered on December 8 arrived this morning in a damaged condition.
>
> Upon opening the carton, which, by the way, showed no signs of damage from the outside, I found that two of the bottles had been broken. As a result, the entire two dozen gift boxes of face powder were badly spoiled.
>
> I am holding the material here for your delivery man to pick up. As I should like to have the merchandise for my Christmas trade, will you please see that I receive immediately a replacement delivery of these goods?
>
> Yours very truly

It is easier by far to placate an old customer than it is to go out and procure new ones. The logic of this statement is self-evident; yet a comparison of the sales efforts of many firms with their efforts to regain the good will of estranged customers forms a striking and dismal contrast. Prospects will be besieged by salesmen, by radio broadcasts, by advertisements in newspapers and periodicals, and by sales letters. Money, thought, and energy are expended unsparingly to convert prospects into customers. But let a misunderstanding or even an error of the seller creep in, and as likely as not the seller will assume a curt and arrogant attitude. The very idea of anyone's impugning his business methods! It is startling when one sees the indifferent, insulting, the you-are-all-wrong type of letter. Dozens of them fill the mail daily. Why correspondents think such letters promote good will, and why men in key positions do not occasionally look over the carbon copies of the adjustment letters of their subordinates, is beyond human understanding. A generation or more ago either Marshall Field or John Wanamaker coined the laudable motto: "The Customer Is Always Right." The motto is just as desirable and practical today as it was then because it promotes both good will and good business. It is probably an adaptation of Abraham Lincoln's slogan, "You can catch more flies with molasses than you can with vinegar." Although the customer is not always right, the approach is preferable by far to the assumption that the customer is a crafty wretch who is trying to "put something over" on the firm.

There are five types of *adjustment letters*.

1. When the seller has been guilty of some fault in which a refund, a credit, or a reduction in price can be made, the forthright and honorable business procedure is to admit the fault and to make good.

How to handle such a situation by mail is illustrated below.

> Dear Madam:
>
> We were sorry to hear of your inconvenience in getting the shades you ordered some time ago. Despite the constant and diligent supervision we give to the 25,000 miscellaneous orders received from our customers each month, it seems that once in a very great while an unfortunate experience similar to yours comes up.
>
> Upon receipt of your letter, a complete investigation was made, and the circumstances found are so unusual that perhaps you will be interested in knowing exactly what happened. At the time your order came in, another order for a similar quantity of shades was received from a Mrs. Schaefer in Buffalo. Somehow one order became attached to the other, and you received the shades which should have been sent to the other customer.
>
> Your order is now being filled correctly, and the proper shades will be sent by Special Delivery to you tomorrow afternoon. We should appreciate the return of the first set, at your convenience. Simply send them collect, and we will pay the charges.
>
> In the future if for any reason you are not entirely satisfied, please do not hesitate to ask for our manager. We should like to accept the responsibility for the charges of the telephone call you made; and a credit slip for $2.25, which may be applied in payment for any merchandise listed in our catalogue, is enclosed for your use.
>
> We welcome you as one of our customers, and hope that, in spite of this unusual experience, you will give us the opportunity to prove the general advantages of doing business with us by mail.*
>
> Very truly yours

2. When the fault is the customer's, the claim is sometimes granted. The customer's fault may lie in his use of ambiguous English in order-

---

*From *Teacher's Manual*, Babenroth and Ward, copyright, 1933, Prentice-Hall, Inc., New York.

ing, in ill-treatment of the product, or in an exaggerated notion of what the product will do. For the sake of good will, it is usually better to make a prompt adjustment than to quibble over a dollar or two. The liberal adjustment will be like "bread upon the waters." Retail customers are usually accorded this treatment. The righteousness of the seller's cause cannot be established by documentary proof because the transaction is usually made over the counter or by telephone. The customer's word is just as good as the salesclerk's. It is in this particular field of retail merchandising that the slogan, "The Customer Is Always Right," is particularly applicable. It will be noted that Marshall Field and John Wanamaker were retail merchants.

3. In the third type of adjustment situation the claim is refused when the customer is in the wrong. In transactions between two big concerns there is usually proof in the way of signed orders, contracts, and bills of lading, to establish who is in the wrong. Doubt seldom enters into the situation. The blame can be fixed. The average business enterprise does not expect an adjustment to which it is not entitled. It is in the handling of this type of adjustment that the adjustment letter writer bungles matters. He fusses and frets and fumes at what to him is an obviously wrong claim made in bad faith. Instead of being a master of persuasive writing and of clear and convincing explanation, he loses his temper. The resultant letter cuts the buyer to the quick, and another customer has been lost. It is quite easy to say, "Yes." For that reason the first two types of adjustment letters are not difficult to write. The third type is the clarion call to the expert correspondent to bring every bit of letter strategy to his aid. Many a correspondent writes with an air of condescension which certainly is not balm to the already injured feelings of the customer. Customers seldom go to the trouble of writing claim letters unless they think they are in the right. To each of us, thinking that we are right makes it so. Therefore, every complaint, no matter how trivial or how ridiculous it may appear in the eyes of the adjustment letter writer, deserves the utmost consideration and respect. Only thus can be written the letter that breeds good will; and good will in turn breeds business.

The letter below illustrates a seller's tactful refusal of a claim.

Gentlemen:

Thank you for your letter of October 21 concerning the shipment of bridge tables which we sent to you on October 9. We are glad that you wrote to us in this frank manner because it gives us an opportunity to explain why we do not quote prices F.O.B. the town of the buyer.

It is true that some of our competitors follow a different practice. A word of explanation is, therefore, due you. We quote our merchandise F.O.B. Chicago, the home of our factory, because we can sell you our merchandise at the lowest possible figure. Those firms selling F.O.B. the town of the buyer include in their prices an allowance for freight. Since the prices quoted (including the freight) are identical for all customers, each pays the same amount of freight, even though one customer is only one hundred miles away, and the other is one thousand miles distant.

It is unfair to make our customers divide the total freight charges equally because some are only a few miles away and others are in Maine or California.

We endeavor to bring you the high quality of Biltmore furniture at the lowest possible price. You will find that tables recently delivered to you will meet the approval of even your most exacting customers. We are looking forward to many years of pleasant and mutually profitable business relations.

Yours very truly

4. The fourth type of adjustment letter is the one in which the carrier is at fault. The fault may be that of the Post Office Department, the railroad, the steamship line, or the motor truck company. Of course, the buyer many times imagines the difficulty has been caused by the seller. Even in those instances in which the buyer knows the fault is the carrier's, he feels that the seller should stand behind the carrier. As a matter of legal principle, he is usually wrong. The carrier will make good, but in those rare situations when it does not, a delicate situation develops. How far the seller wishes to go in making an adjustment depends altogether on house policy.

5. The last type of adjustment presents an opportunity for additional business frequently overlooked by many business men. Customers just drift away. Investigation has disclosed that most customers wander off to competitors for no good reason at all. A gracious letter may bring them back into the active customer's list. Some business men are so busy chasing the "will-o'-the-wisp" of prospective orders that they overlook the "acres of diamonds" in their own backyard. Frequent periodic inspections should be made to assemble the names of customers who have not made purchases within the last six or eight months—or whatever the period may be which is considerably beyond

the usual intervals between orders. A suitably worded letter will frequently be the means of retrieving the customer and of procuring gratifying orders. The principle of the follow-up letter can be adopted to this type of situation. If the first letter sent meets with no response, send a second, and even a third. The writing of the letter requires but little time and energy. It is not a difficult letter to write. On occasions without number the letter has been resultful. However, to be resultful, the letter must be written properly.

A silverware company sent out the following letter and received response from 60 per cent of the customers to whom the letter was addressed. More recently a similar letter sent out in the hardware field pulled almost 50 per cent returns.

> I suppose I am what an efficiency expert would call an "old-fashioned president." I like to review the mail when it comes to the office in the morning—seeing the salesmen's orders, the mail orders, the checks, the letters from customers, and the complaints. I really become acquainted with our customers that way, and get to know them as old friends.
>
> I come to expect certain orders when our salesmen are working certain towns—and sometimes I am disappointed. In fact, I am a little disappointed right now. I have been missing your orders, so I asked Miss Chappell, our bookkeeper, to tell me how your purchases from us compare with those of a year and two years ago. Frankly, her answer was disconcerting.
>
> So I am taking this means of asking you "How come, Mr. Barnum?" Our company has made tremendous strides in the last two years in remaking our line so that our customers may be helped in meeting today's difficult conditions. The success of our efforts can best be told in the fact that our customers bought from us nearly 40 per cent more this year than they did last year.
>
> This makes me all the more puzzled that your business with us has dropped off.
>
> Maybe we are at fault here.
>
> If you will drop me a line on the enclosed memo card, telling me your side of the story and enclose it in the stamped, personally addressed envelope enclosed, I shall deem it a favor of the highest kind.
>
> Very truly yours

The Leon Godchaux Clothing Company, Ltd., of New Orleans, sent this letter to 3,172 of its customers. The total cost of the mailing was $120. The letter pulled replies from 1,051 people, a return of 33.1 per cent, and these people purchased $31,413.65 worth of merchandise, an average sale of $29.88.

> Suppose for a moment that some one moved into your neighborhood and became a friend of yours. Suppose, again, that he visited your home from time to time and then suddenly stopped coming to see you—without giving you any reason for staying away.
> You would like to know why, wouldn't you?
> Well, that is just what has happened between you and Godchaux's.
> You came to see us rather often, opened a charge account with us, and then stopped coming to see us altogether. Naturally we would like to have you back with us.
> We would like you to know that we appreciate your patronage. It is through the continued friendship of Orleanians that we have remained in business for over ninety-six years.
> Our merchandise is still of the same high quality that first caused you to open a charge account. Your account is still open. Won't you let us know why you haven't used it?

Letters of Inquiry

Letters of inquiry are not difficult to write. Explain clearly and precisely what you want to know, and why you seek the information. Inquiries are of two types. The first type directly pertains to business. As a result of some form of advertising, the prospect may write to inquire about prices, specifications, terms, and delivery. The advertisement has made the prospect conscious of the need. In many other instances advertising has little to do with stimulating the inquiry. The need arises, and the prospect writes to one or a number of firms manufacturing or selling the particular commodity which he needs. The letter below illustrates a suitably worded inquiry of this type.

> Gentlemen:
>
> Some time ago I bought from you several union suits made of rayon and buttoned at the shoulder with two buttons. Do you still sell this type of suit? If you do, does it come in size 42, and what is the price?
>
> Yours truly

The second type of inquiry is one unrelated to the placing of an order. Business firms are frequently approached for information on some phase of their own business, but the information sought does not have any bearing on the placing of an order. Inquiries of this type are also frequently addressed to governmental bodies, quasi-public committees, boards, foundations, and organizations.

The letter below is an example of a letter addressed to a state Department of Agriculture.

> Dear Sir:
>
> I recently noticed an unusual powdery formation on the beams in the cellar of my farm house. These beams are hewed timbers. The formation is of a light yellowish or brownish color. I have also noticed grooves or tracks in the wood as if made by some sort of insect. There are also a number of small holes starting at the surface and penetrating the beams for several inches. These holes are so narrow in diameter that a match stick is really too thick to enter the hole. I am alarmed at the possibility that these several things may be evidence of the presence of termites.
>
> From the description I have given, do you think it is termites?
>
> If you wish a sample, I could scrape some of the powdery formation from one of the beams and send it to you.
>
> If termites are present, could you give me any advice for ridding the house of the pests?
>
> Yours very truly

Most of us are of an inquiring type of mind. We like to know what makes the wheels go round. Many a business enterprise, aware of this human tendency and quick to sense its relationship to the building of good will, conducts tours through its plants to familiarize interested people with the manufacturing process and company procedure. Far removed from a company's plant, an isolated person of inquiring mind is likely to write for the information he seeks.

All inquiries, regardless of type, should be specific, brief, and courteous. There is no necessity for long-winded, preliminary explanation. Apologies are equally out of order.

Answers to Inquiries

Good business dictates that inquiries about merchandise should be intelligently and promptly answered. Sounds like a truism, doesn't it? Yet many inquiries are not skillfully handled. Here is an example in point: A housewife had been "sold" on a nationally known make of gas range. She wrote to the manufacturer for the name and address of the local dealer. Instead of receiving a direct answer to her inquiry, she received an interesting and well-expressed form letter enclosing a book of recipes. The prospect, however, had asked for the name and address of a dealer, not for a recipe book. The name of the dealer was not given! In these days, or in any day for that matter, a prospect sufficiently interested to write an inquiry is deserving of the same degree of pampering as an only child. Tell him what he wants to know. Answer him clearly, fully, helpfully.

Moreover, the inquiry should be answered promptly. Repeated surveys indicate that many firms are dilatory. Some of them keep the person waiting three or four weeks! One recent survey showed that the average time taken for an inquirer to receive a reply is eleven days. If one house is apparently reluctant to render service or to accept an order, the inquirer can very readily turn to another house that will be delighted at the prospect of an order and quite happy to answer one question or a thousand. There are actually some national advertisers who do not trouble to answer inquiries at all. A recent survey made by *Printers' Ink* showed that 3.18 per cent of advertisers did not respond to inquiries produced by national advertising. Why manufacturers should spend thousands of dollars annually to secure inquiries and then ignore them, is hard to comprehend. Here is a skillful answer to an inquiry:

> Dear Mr. Jones:
>
> Enclosed is a clipping featuring our two-button Union Suits that are made of combed cotton. This style cannot be furnished in rayon. These suits are priced at three for $1.29, or six for $2.58. We know you will be more than pleased with this purchase, and you can rest assured that your order for size 42 will be filled as soon as it reaches us.
>
> Whenever you have any questions about our merchandise always feel free to write us. It's a pleasure to hear from you at any time and to know that we can help you in any way, if it is at all possible. It's the wise shopper who knows that regular and consistent shopping from our catalogue will enable him to count his savings in energy and substantial cash!
>
> Enclosed is an order blank; we'll be looking forward to filling this and many other orders for you.
>
> Yours truly

A word of counsel is in place concerning those inquiries not directly connected with the giving of an order. Even at the sacrifice of some time and trouble, it is good business to answer nonbusiness inquiries. Every opportunity for creating good will should be cultivated. Recently the story has been going the rounds of the boyhood experience of a present-day business executive. As a youngster he had written in a scrawly hand to two automobile manufacturers of natural prominence at that time. He sought information of special interest to him. One firm ignored the inquiry. It was probably assumed—and rightly so—that no order was in the offing. Why answer? Why waste time? The other concern took pains to answer the youngster's inquiry. What has happened in the interval of a quarter of a century? That youngster, today's big business man, has steadfastly refrained from buying the first make of car. As a matter of fact, in the last few years it would have been impossible for him to do so, for the company has gone out of business. On the other hand, he has regularly patronized the other manufacturer. An extreme case, true enough, but quite apposite.

Here is another example! Two men were discussing the comparative area of window space in two models manufactured by the same automobile company. One of the men wrote a letter of inquiry to the headquarters of the company. That inquiry was never answered. He was persistent enough to write a follow-up a month later. He was referred to the nearest local dealer, despite the fact that the blueprints of the two models were readily accessible in the drafting room or engineering department of the main office of the company, that the local dealer would know less about the matter than the maker, and that the inquirer would put himself in a ridiculous light if he strutted with folding ruler in his hand to measure the two cars in the local showroom. Even if the information is unavailable, or it would be indiscreet to disclose it, the inquiry should be promptly answered and the reason why the information cannot be given should be persuasively and tactfully given.

Governmental agencies compare favorably with business houses in the completeness and dispatch with which they answer inquiries. The letter below, received by the inquirer within forty-eight hours after he mailed his letter, shows how the inquiry on page 297 was answered.

Dear Sir:
I am enclosing information on termites, which may answer your question without the necessity of sending samples. Beams in the cellar may be affected with various rot fungi, particularly a dry rot fungi, and they may also be attacked by a number of insects, such as powder post borers and the like. Many people are

much more alarmed over termite damage than is necessary, and although termite damage can be real it is not common and there is sometimes a tendency of some advertisers to scare people into treatment. If the beam is sound, it is quite unlikely that it is termite injury.

Should you wish to send a sample of termite injury, it would be best to cut out a small sample rather than to scrape the beam and to send only the powder scrapings. Samples of insect injury of this character may be sent to Dr. R. D. Glasgow, State Entomologist, Albany; or, if you care to, you can send them to this office.

Very truly yours

Purchasing Letters

Purchasing letters range from the informal note of the housewife written to a department store, to the formal, legalistic and lengthy letter giving a large-sized order by a big business enterprise. The large business has its procedure so systematized that a correspondent need only follow the conventional form approved by his employer. Whether the order letter be brief and informal or lengthy and formal, a few significant points should be borne in mind.

1. Full details of each item should be given. Set forth the quantity desired, the name of the article, the size, color, style, model number, catalogue number, price per unit or per dozen, and the total cost for the one item.

2. Specify the method and time of delivery.

3. Discuss methods of payment. Is the remittance being enclosed, is the purchase on a C.O.D. basis, or is the order to be charged? If the order is to be charged, have credit terms been arranged?

4. Give such special information as may be necessary. If the article is to be used for a special purpose, specify the purpose in order to secure the protection of the Uniform Sales Act, which is the law in almost all states of the Union.

5. Even if only one item is ordered, place the item on a line by itself. If the order consists of several items, they should be arranged in tabular form. At the bottom of the tabulation, the total amount of the several items should be given. This arrangement makes for greater clarity and is an aid both to the bookkeeper and to the shipping clerk of the seller. Should there be a discrepancy or disagreement in price, or a miscalculation, the source of the difficulty can be directly found.

Gentlemen:

Please send to me by parcel post the following articles and charge them to my account.

10 yards of silk ribbon, 3″ wide, light blue (like the sample enclosed) at 49¢ a yard	$4.90
6 bath towels, white, 24″ x 46″ at 79¢ each	4.74
1—6 ft. ironing-board cover at	.79
1 du Pont table cloth, red and white checkered, size 56″ x 56″	2.75
4 Venetian blinds, cedar, 32″ x 64″, automatic stop, painted cream color with light green straps and tapes at $2.99 each	11.96
	$25.14

Please notice that this order is to be sent to me here at Blissville, where I am spending the summer.

Very truly yours

Response to Purchasing Letters

Orders make the wheels of business go round. It is both common courtesy and good business to acknowledge receipt of every order on the day on which it arrives. Unless the situation demands a personally dictated letter, printed forms with the blanks filled in may be used. It is well at the outset to show appreciation of the order by thanking the customer. To avoid possible misunderstanding and to enable the customer to verify the items on his order, it is often desirable to repeat in tabular form the several items in his order.

Give the customer the assurance that he will receive the order without undue delay by letting him know how you are handling the order, when you are shipping it, and when he may expect delivery. Conclude with a persuasive paragraph of sales talk which will inspire confidence in the merchandise he has ordered.

When an order is defective in some essential respect, the correspondent has the task of eliciting the information from the customer without in any way directly charging or even implying that the customer is lacking either in intelligence or care. Expressions such as "You failed to . . ." or "You neglected to . . ." should be avoided.

The following is an appropriate acknowledgment of the order appearing above.

Dear Madam:

Thank you for your order of October 30 as follows:

10 yards of silk ribbon, 3″ wide, light blue at 49¢ a yard	$4.90
6 bath towels, white, 24″ x 46″ at 79¢ each	4.74
1—6 ft. ironing-board cover at	.79
1 du Pont table cloth, red and white checkered size 56″ x 56″	2.75
4 Venetian blinds, cedar, 32″ x 64″, automatic stop, painted cream color with light green straps and tapes at $2.99 each	11.96
	$25.14

We do not have in stock the shade of light blue ribbon exactly matching the sample you sent. We are enclosing samples of the two nearest shades which we have. Please indicate on the enclosed postage paid reply card, which, if either, of these two shades you wish.

The Venetian blinds are, of course, made to order and will require ten-days' time for delivery. These blinds are well made and attractive, and at the recently advertised price of $2.99 offer a substantial saving.

The bath towels, ironing-board cover, and du Pont table cloth are being packed and will be mailed late this afternoon. You should receive them within a day after this letter.

You will especially like the thick, soft texture of the bath towels. The generous number of terry loops in each towel make for rapid absorption and long wear. They, too, are on special sale for this week only.

Very truly yours

In the case of new customers or of credit customers of long standing who are placing unusually large orders in excess of their credit limit, personally dictated letters are required. Such letters really have to do with credit and therefore belong to the credit letter group already discussed. Unusually large orders from cash customers deserve special recognition in the form of acknowledgment preferably signed by some executive in the business. Such letters take only a few minutes of time for attention and pay lasting dividends in continued and increased good will.

CHAPTER X

TELEGRAMS, CABLEGRAMS, AND RADIOGRAMS

AS THE world progresses and a more and a more complex and high-speed age develops, a steady growth results in the volume and importance of our daily use of rapid communication services which annihilate time and command immediate attention. Keeping pace with the age, the telegraph and cable industry has instituted many improvements in methods and services within a few years. The major part of the material on telegrams and cablegrams that follows was specially prepared for *Your Mastery of English* by Mr. George P. Oslin of the Western Union Telegraph Company.

Wide Use of Telegraph and Cable

Hundreds of millions of telegrams and cablegrams are sent each year by American firms for the greatest variety of purposes in the realm of business activity. Telegrams are used with increasing frequency in social correspondence. Thus a clear knowledge of the proper use of telegraph messages and services becomes a matter of general importance. This knowledge is, indeed, one of the factors on which the success of an individual or a business may depend. Incompetent use of telegrams and cablegrams may be a sinkhole of waste and loss.

When to Use Telegrams

The use of telegrams is indicated whenever it is important to avoid delays due to separation by distance, or when it is desired to gain the advantages of terseness, of emphasis, of impressiveness, or of the peculiar attention-compelling properties inherent in a telegram.

Rules for Preparing Telegrams

In this section we present a condensed review of the rules for preparing telegrams, followed by a summary of the telegraph and cable services designed to meet varying needs.

To minimize errors and facilitate handling, all telegrams should be clearly and legibly written or typed. Typing should be double-spaced. If a message is communicated to the telegraph office by telephone, the

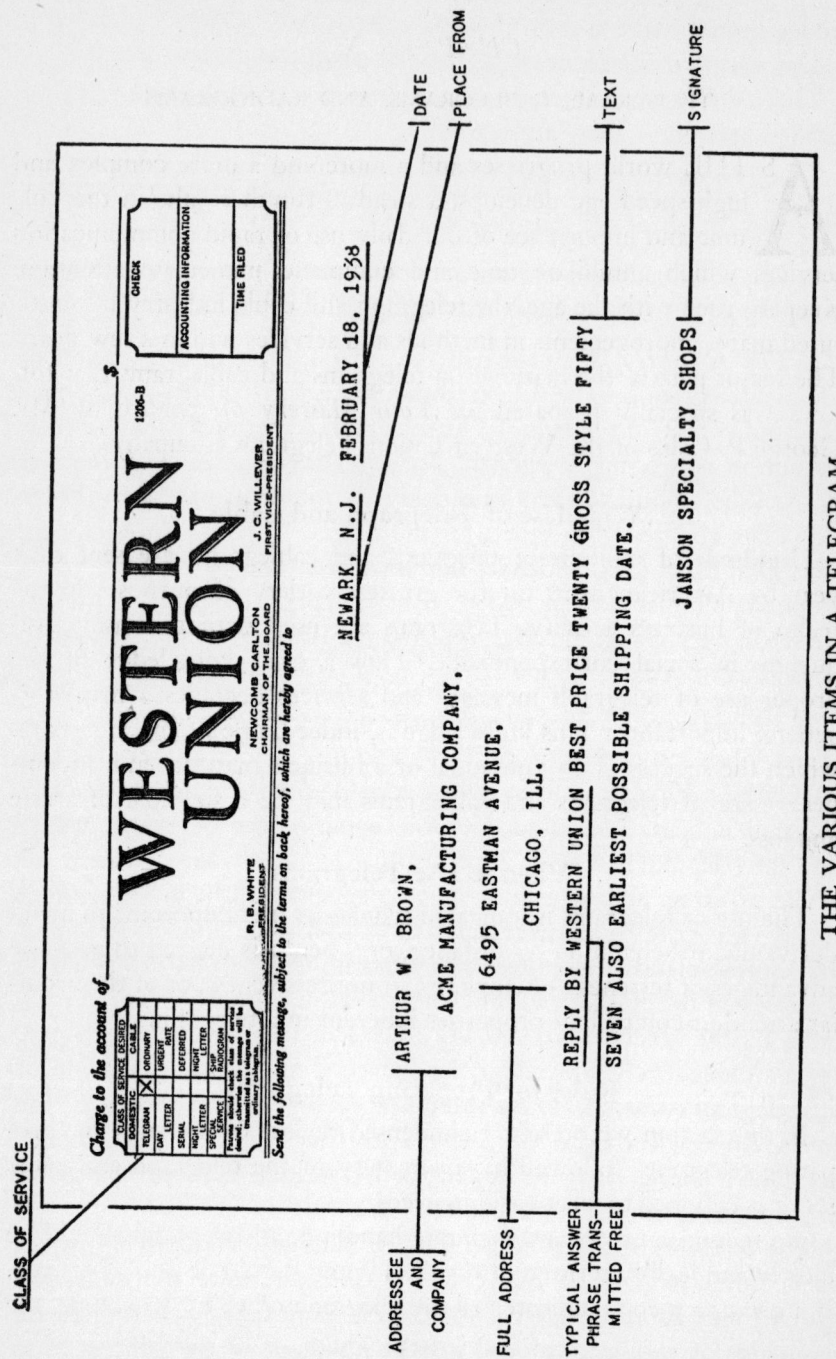

THE VARIOUS ITEMS IN A TELEGRAM

TELEGRAMS, CABLEGRAMS, RADIOGRAMS 305

sender should make certain that the telegraph employee receiving it and repeating it for accuracy has every word right.

There are eight main elements, or parts, to be remembered in preparing a telegram. They are as follows:

1. *The class of service.* This should be marked in a box at the upper left-hand corner of the telegraph blank.

2. *The point of origin and the date.* These two items should be written at the upper right-hand corner of the face of the blank.

3. *The addressee.* The name of the person, firm or corporation to whom a telegram is to be delivered should be written below the upper left-hand corner of the blank. The telegraph companies permit a wide latitude in addressing telegrams, because they want all information that will be helpful to them in quickly locating the addressee. There is no extra charge, for instance, for the address "George P. Oslin, care John Doe Mfg. Co., 7 Meade Terrace, Glen Ridge, N. J." Even a telephone number may be added without charge. The title of the addressee in a company, or "Mr. and Mrs. Joe Roe and family," also may be used without extra charge.

4. *The address.* Code addresses may not be used in domestic telegrams. The most complete address should be given, if known, because it facilitates delivery, and no charge is made for the extra words. If a transient is being addressed, give the name of the person in whose care the telegram is sent. In replying to telegrams from transients for whom no street address can be given, delivery will be aided without cost if you write "an answer date" or "an answer" after the name of the addressee and address the telegram only to the city from which the original telegram was sent. An originating branch office is indicated by the office call, consisting of one or two letters, which may appear immediately preceding the "place from" in the date line of the telegram received. These should be included. For example: "Joe Jones, An Answer Date MS, New York City." The words "Phone" or "Don't phone" may be added to the address without charge, as instructions to the destination office.

The omission of a firm name, a room number, or a part of a street name, often will delay delivery. For example, note the addresses: "John Jones, Empire State Building, New York City," when there are thousands of people employed in that building; or the address "600

Forty-second Street, New York City," which may necessitate attempted delivery at two points far apart, on *East* or *West* Forty-second Street.

If, however, the telegram is addressed to a well-known national or local figure, or a nationally known business or bank, it may be a waste of time to give the room number, building, and street addresses. It would not be helpful, for example, to address a telegram in this manner:

>Honorable Jonathan A. Stout,
>Member of the House of Representatives from Illinois,
>Room oooo, House Office Building, 10 Blank Street,
>Washington, D. C.

This would be adequate and correct:

>Hon. J. A. Stout,
>Member Congress,
>Washington, D. C.

The telegraph companies make no charge for long addresses except in unusual cases. For instance, in a telegram addressed to "John Doe or Richard Roe," the words "or Richard Roe" would be charged for. When the telegram is sent to two persons at different addresses, both telegrams are charged for. If the sender wishes to indicate to each addressee that he is sending the message to the other also, he should say so in the text of the telegram.

In addressing a telegram to a passenger on a train, airplane, or bus, give full details. For example: "John Jones, en route Chicago, care Conductor (or, if Pullman reservation is known, 'Lower 6, Car 92'), N. Y. C. Train Three, due 10:35 P. M. Cleveland, Ohio."

5. *The signature of the sender.* Only one signature will be carried free, but titles, names of departments, and names of firms may be added to let the addressee know just who the sender is, and these are considered a part of the free signature. For example, "George J. Wilson, First Vice President, Standard Can Co.," is all carried free. In family signatures, such as "George and Louise" or Mr. and Mrs. J. A. Jones and Family, no extra words are charged for. Do not add the name of the city from which you are sending a message to your signa-

ture. That is shown in the checkline of the telegram, and to duplicate it would be a waste of money.

6. *Is the telegram sent "Paid" or "Collect"?* This information should be indicated by writing one of these words in the lower left-hand corner of the blank. When the telegram is to be charged to an account, the name of the account should be placed in the space provided for that purpose.

7. *Report on delivery.* If a report on delivery is desired, the words "Report Delivery" should be written conspicuously at the top of the telegraph blank. These words, which are charged for, are then wired to the destination, and a report is wired back, "Charges Collect," stating to whom and when the telegram was delivered.

Occasionally people wish to have important telegrams repeated back at each stage as a guard against inaccuracies. When this is done, an extra charge equal to fifty per cent of the regular tolls is made, in addition to the cost of the two extra words, "Repeat Back," in the original telegram. Few people now observe this practice.

8. *The text of the telegram.* The keynote of the well-worded telegram is conciseness. The message must be stated clearly and, at the same time, briefly (for the sake of economy). In a truly concise telegram every word is necessary to the meaning of the message; no word is used that could be omitted without making doubtful the meaning of the telegram.

Brevity is most desirable, but it should not be carried to the point where the meaning is obscured or where the valuable time of the sender is wasted needlessly in re-writing and re-writing, with no purpose except the saving of a small sum in tolls. The art of telegram writing may be acquired through study and practice. Write several telegrams; see how many words you can omit from each without any loss to your messages—then re-write the telegrams. Start by eliminating the words *the, and, we, I, that,* and *a* where it is possible to do so.

Because of the low word-cost of domestic telegrams, the difference made by a few extra words is slight. For that reason, code language, which is used principally for condensing purposes, is not usually employed in domestic telegrams. The saving is not commensurate with the labor involved in coding and de-coding messages. However, the use of code is permitted in all classes of domestic telegrams. Nouns and verbs convey ideas and meanings more concisely than do other parts of speech. In phrasing a telegram, therefore, nouns and verbs are used more freely than adjectives and adverbs. This usage is modified, however, by the sense it is intended to convey in the message.

It is well, in typing telegrams, to avoid dividing a word at the end of a line.

Be careful to avoid ambiguous phrases. Here is a common error to avoid:

> Arrive on 2 P. M. train. Please meet me.

This message leaves the recipient in doubt as to whether the train leaves the sender's starting point at 2 P. M. or will arrive at its destination at that time. The following wording is clear:

> Arrive 2 P. M. Saturday. Please meet train.

How to Save in Wording Telegrams

You may reduce the cost of your telegrams by making use of the information in the paragraphs that follow:

1. *Punctuation is free.* The word *stop*, which became as familiar in telegrams as the word *love*, is no longer necessary. Most punctuation marks are now free when they are used in the text of a telegram to be sent to a point within the United States.

Free punctuation marks include the comma, the period, the semicolon, the dash or hyphen, quotation marks, parentheses, the question mark and the apostrophe. The *words* "comma," "period," etc., will be charged for, however, if they are written out.

2. *Paragraphs in telegrams.* Telegrams written in paragraphs will be transmitted and delivered in paragraphs, without any extra charge. Use paragraphs whenever they should normally be used in correspondence.

3. *Word-count rules.* It is permissible in telegrams to use any dictionary words from the English, German, French, Italian, Dutch, Portuguese, Spanish, and Latin languages, and such words are counted as one word each. Any word in a language other than these, or any group of letters not forming a dictionary word, is counted as one word for each five letters or fraction of five letters.

Names of cities, states, or counties which are made up of two or more words, such as *East St. Louis, New Jersey,* or *United States,* are charged as one word. Common abbreviations and trade terms, such as O. K., A. M., P. M., F. O. B., and C. O. D., also are charged each as one word.

Combinations of two dictionary words or mutilated words, such as *firstclass, billading, havyu,* and *allright,* are charged as two words each, so there is no reason for writing them in any except their proper form. Telegrams are counted in the way that words would be used in normal correspondence, so the name of a product which is compounded of two words is counted as one word. Initials are counted as separate words, but family names, such as Van der Water, are checked as one word. It is usually safer to spell out the names of companies. B&O counts as three words, just as *Baltimore and Ohio* does. Such designations as *USS* or *SS* should be used, however, because they count as one word. Abbreviations of weights and measures also count as one word each.

4. *Figures in Telegrams.* Former methods of using figures in telegrams must be completely discarded now, and a new manner of using them adopted in order to obtain the substantial saving that is offered. In messages to points in the United States and Mexico, figures and ordinal numbers are counted at one word for every five figures, or fraction of five figures. Decimal points, commas, fraction marks or dashes used with groups of figures are counted as a figure. Other marks are counted as a word each, *e.g.,* the dollar sign, the pound sign, the "and" sign, and the like. In groups of letters and figures, each unbroken sequence of letters and figures of five or fewer units is counted as one word. For example, the following items are each counted as one word: *24th, 12345, 12 1/2,* and *34.25.* On the other hand, *$1.25, 123&, AB123* and *10,000,000* are each counted as two words. Formerly, the practice was to charge for figures at the rate of one word for each figure, so that the figure *100* was charged as three words and usually was written out as *one hundred* to save the charge on one word. The symbols ¢, @ and ° cannot be transmitted, and should be written out as *cents, at* and *degrees.*

In messages to any point in North America outside the United States, other than Mexico, each figure is counted as one word; in groups consisting of letters and figures, each is counted as one word, and each group of letters within the combination at the rate of one word for every five letters or less. For example: A3CDE in a telegram to Canada is three words.

5. *Request for replies.* No charge is made by the telegraph companies for the use in telegrams of such expressions as: Answer Western Union, Reply by Western Union, Wire Answer via Western Union, Advise by Western Union, Quote via Western Union or Order via Western Union. The word *Collect* also may be added to these phrases without charge. In preparing the text of a telegram, it is, therefore, more economical to use these free phrases rather than to use the phrase, *Reply collect at once,* which would cost the tolls for four words.

How to "File" Telegrams

In telegraph jargon, to "file" a telegram means to place it in the hands of the telegraph company for transmission and delivery. The filing of the message may be accomplished in several ways. It may be handed across the counter of a telegraph office to the salesclerk, who will send it on its way. It may be sent from a home or office telephone, by calling the telegraph company and dictating the telegram to a recording operator, who writes it on her typewriter. The toll charges then appear on the sender's telephone bill. In dictating a telegram from a coin box telephone, payment is made by dropping the tolls into the coin slots. To avoid phonetic errors, it is well to pronounce each letter of difficult words. For example, if the word *Sioux* is being sent, it is well to say, "S as in sugar, I as in Ida, O as in ocean, U as in union, and X as in X-ray."

Call boxes, which may be operated by turning a small handle, are installed without charge in business offices. To file a telegram from such an office, it is only necessary to turn the call box handle, and hand the telegram to the telegraph messenger who responds. No charge is made for such messenger service.

Tie lines are direct wires provided without charge by the telegraph company when the volume of business justifies them. These provide instantaneous communication between the business concern and the telegraph company's office, and thus expedite the filing and delivery of telegrams. The operation of such tie lines in the patrons' offices is by employees of the patrons. Most such tie lines are operated by teleprinter, which is a telegraph instrument with a keyboard similar to that of the typewriter. When a key is struck on the teleprinter in a patron's office, the letter so selected is printed on the tape of a corresponding machine in the telegraph company's operating room. When the telegraph company wishes to deliver a telegram to the patron, the procedure is reversed. The tape on which telegrams are typed by teleprinters is gummed on the under side so that, when moistened, it may be affixed to telegraph blanks. The use of similar tape between telegraph offices accounts for the familiar appearance of telegrams with messages on strips on the faces of the blanks.

The original copy of each telegram filed by telephone, and carbon copies of all other telegrams filed, should be retained in the sender's office files for quick reference when needed and also for use in checking the monthly telegraph bill, if the messages were charged. Of course, each business house should standardize its procedure in sending telegrams and cablegrams, as to the number of copies to be made and their disposition. Many companies make two carbons, one for the files and another for the accounting department.

Major Uses of the Telegram in Business

The following are some of the major purposes for which the telegram is largely used in business:

1. *Asking for prices.* Canvassing the market by telegraph for prices enables business houses to buy advantageously.

2. *Quoting prices or making offers.* Prospective buyers may be reached with quotations by telegraph, ahead of competitors.

3. *Accepting offers and acknowledging orders.* Offers involving price concessions are frequently made to close out material quickly. Orders in such cases should be acknowledged by telegraph.

4. *Acknowledging first orders.* Telegraphic acknowledgment of a first order builds prestige and may give a decided advantage over a rival.

5. *Wiring for credit information.* When credit information is obtained by telegraph, it permits prompt acceptance or a suitable limitation of the customer's credits, and the information is available for future reference.

6. *Paving the way for salesmen.* Telegraphic announcements of the

impending arrivals of traveling salesmen tend to elevate salesmen's calls from the category of order-taking to that of important interviews.

7. *Encouraging salesmen.* If a salesman's reports are acknowledged by approving telegrams and constructive suggestions he is stimulated in his efforts.

8. *Telegrams to customers between salesmen's calls.* Telegrams between salesmen's calls prevent fill-in orders, and sometimes accounts, from going to a competitor. The firm might offer to pay the wire charges.

9. *Advices to branches and salesmen.* Branch managers and traveling representatives need to be kept informed of actual and probable market changes and of changes in personnel and policies of their own and competitive organizations.

10. *Salesmen's orders by telegraph.* Telegraphing of rush orders by salesmen makes prompt shipments possible, and customers are impressed.

11. *Financing salesmen.* Telegraphic money orders permit smaller advance accounts, reduce the risk involved in carrying large sums, and spare salesmen the embarrassment of having to cash checks.

12. *Daily sales reports.* Daily or frequent telegraphic reports from the field show headquarters the trend of demand, the changing status of customer credit.

13. *Telegraph blanks prepared as order forms.* Inclusion of telegraph blanks, overprinted with the firm's address and an outline of an order, in catalogues or with sales letters and other advertising material, encourages the prompt placing of orders.

14. *Supplementing advertising and announcing special sales.* Many retailers planning an announcement of new merchandise, or a special sale, send telegrams to selected customers.

15. *Encouraging additional purchases.* Fill-in and other orders present a valuable opportunity to wire an offer of additional items, which can be sent at no increase in shipping cost.

16. *Extending invitations to buyers.* Invitations to buyers vary from

simple announcements of special lines to elaborate invitations to attend special showings.

17. *Reviving inactive accounts.* Telegrams are effective in probing and reviving inactive accounts.

18. *Meeting competition.* Changes in sales tactics, a new advertising policy, improvements in products, can, by means of telegrams, be brought speedily to the attention of those concerned.

19. *Price changes.* Customers, if informed by telegraph of price changes, often will respond with immediate orders. Many manufacturers wire their traveling salesmen regarding price changes. Merchandise brokers, particularly those dealing in perishable commodities, find the telegraph indispensable in keeping up with the rapid fluctuations in their line.

20. *Style changes.* Substantially the same considerations apply to style changes as to price changes.

21. *Tracing orders or shipments.* Telegrams are often effective in speeding shipments and obtaining quick deliveries, also in locating missing merchandise, untangling traffic snarls, and starting on their way goods held up in transit.

22. *Wiring shipping dates.* Telegraphic advices of shipment are particularly valuable to a consignee who has to arrange for removal from a railroad terminal.

23. *Expediting shipments.* Telegraphic orders get first attention and an expedited handling. Where contracts must be fulfilled, delays to materials are apt to be fraught with serious consequences.

24. *Answering inquiries.* A telegraphic reply to an inquiry suggests prompt handling of any order that may be placed.

25. *Acknowledging complaints.* Prompt acknowledgment of a complaint by telegram tends to impress the customer and relieve tension.

26. *Urging replies to unanswered letters.* The telegram may be used to secure overdue replies.

27. *Daily production reports.* Frequent telegraphic production reports from scattered plants enable sales departments to coordinate their activities with the probable supply.

28. *Replenishment of stocks.* Unanticipated developments frequently create such a demand for certain merchandise that dealers are caught with inadequate stocks. Telegraphic orders in such cases bring the quick replenishments needed to serve patrons and prevent them from going elsewhere.

29. *Collecting delinquent accounts.* The telegram is an effective method of speeding up collections, whether as a routine reminder or as an initial message urging prompt payment.

Classes of Telegraph Service

Substantial savings may be made by selecting carefully the class of service to be used. In sending a telegram the location of the addressee and the time of day are factors which should not be wastefully ignored. For instance, persons in states along the Atlantic Coast often forget that when the business day closes in their offices, it still has an hour to go in Chicago, St. Louis or Dallas, two hours in Denver or Albuquerque, and three hours in Reno, Seattle or Los Angeles. Thus there may still be time to send a fast telegram and close a deal that is pending rather than to send an Overnight Telegram and delay the transaction until another day.

Full-Rate Telegrams.

Full-rate telegrams give the fastest service. They may be filed for immediate handling at any hour of the day or night. Unless some other class of service is indicated, all messages are considered to be full-rate telegrams and are handled as such. The minimum charge is for ten words, and words in excess of ten are charged for at a low extra-word rate. The cost of a ten-word telegram ranges from twenty cents for a local telegram to $1.20 between the most distant points in the United States.

Day Letters.

Day-Letter service is suitable for messages of eighteen words or more which can be subordinated in transmission to full-rate traffic on hand and still serve the purpose of the senders. The charge for a fifty-word Day Letter is one and a half times that of a ten-word full-rate telegram. The minimum charge is for fifty words, and one-fifth of the initial fifty-word rate is charged for each additional ten words or less.

Generally the cost of a Day Letter is the same as that of a seventeen-word full-rate telegram, so no message of less than eighteen or twenty words should be sent as a Day Letter. When what might normally be a Day Letter is to be sent to a business house so late in the afternoon that with due regard for time-zone differences its delivery during business hours would be doubtful, full-rate service should be used to insure immediate delivery if the communication is of an urgent character.

Overnight Telegrams (Night Letters).

Overnight Telegrams represent a night service corresponding to the Day Letter service for day communications. Overnight Telegrams may be filed at any hour of the day or night up to 2 A.M. for delivery the following morning in the case of social messages, and on the morning of the next ensuing business day in the case of business messages. The charge for the first twenty-five words or less is substantially lower than the charge for a ten-word full-rate message. The maximum charge for a twenty-five-word Overnight Telegram is fifty cents, even for the greatest distances in the United States. The charge for each additional group of five words or less ranges from one cent to nine cents. The rates decrease progressively as the length of the message increases, so that, for example, five words in excess of 200 cost only three and a half cents. A 200-word letter can now be put on the wire to nearby places for fifty-nine cents and to the most distant correspondent for less than a cent and a half a word, and will be delivered at the opening of business the following morning.

Quantity discounts are allowed on local Overnight Telegrams of identical text, sent by the same sender simultaneously to a number of addressees within the same city in which they are filed, as follows:

NUMBER	DISCOUNT
25–50	10%
51–100	15%
101–250	20%
251–500	25%
501–1000	32½%
1001–2000	40%
Over 2000	50%

Serials.

Serial Service should be used when there is intermittent correspondence with any given addressee during the course of a day. Serials are messages filed in installments. A minimum of 15 text words per installment is counted and a minimum aggregate of fifty words in the course of a day is charged for. Aggregate serial rates are twenty per cent higher than those for Day Letters of corresponding length, so any installment of more than forty words should be sent as a Day Letter, or as a Timed Wire (charged on a time basis) where Timed Wire Service is available.

To be classed as part of a Serial each installment must be marked *Ser*. If an initial message is filed marked as a Serial in the anticipation that there will be other installments going to the same addressee the same day and, contrary to expectation, no further installment is sent, the first installment is charged for either as a Full-Rate Telegram or as a Day Letter, whichever is the cheaper for the number of words involved.

Timed Wire Service.

Timed Wire service should be used for communications of some length as it involves placing the telegraph company's facilities at the customer's disposal on a time basis. The messages are transmitted by a teleprinter operated by an employee of the sender. The charge is based on the time consumed in transmitting the communication and on the distance to the point of destination. The minimum charge is for a period of three minutes and is in most cases the amount charged for a 50-word Day Letter between the same points. The charge for each additional minute or fraction of a minute in excess of three is one-third of the charge for the initial three-minute period.

Telemeter Service.

Telemeter provides a fast and flexible service for business houses or individuals having occasion for the exchange of a considerable volume of communication with each other. The service is charged for according to the number of words exchanged. The minimum monthly charge is for 25,000 words, the rate for words in excess of 25,000 decreasing progressively.

COMPARISON OF SERVICES

Class of Service	Basic Rate	Additional Charge	When Accepted	When Delivered
Full-rate message or "Telegram"	First 10 words 20c to $1.20 according to distance	Each additional word 1c to 8½c	Any time day or night	Immediately —a matter of minutes
Day Letter	First 50 words 30c to $1.80	Each additional 10-word group 6c to 36c	Any time	Subordinated to full-rate telegrams
Overnight Telegram (Night Letter)	First 25 words 20c to 50c	Each additional 5-word group 1c to 9c	Any time up to 2 a.m. of day of delivery	Next morning. Morning of next business day in case of business messages
Serials	A telegram sent in installments. No installment rated at less than 15 words. For a total of 50 words or less, 35c to $2.15	When total words exceed 50, for each additional 10-word group 7c to 43c	Any time. All sections must be filed the same day	
Timed Wire Service	3 minutes' use of printer tie-line facility 30c to $1.80	Each additional minute or less 10c to 60c	Any time	Immediately

Holiday and Social Telegrams

Specially decorated telegram blanks are provided for Christmas, Easter, Mother's Day, Father's Day, St. Valentine's Day, Thanksgiving, Jewish New Year, and for various other social messages, such as Birthday, Birth, Bon Voyage, Commencement, Congratulation, Thank You, Wedding, Condolence, as well as for other social needs. For these uses, the telegraph companies issue lists of suggested texts of messages which may be sent to any point served by the telegraph company in the United States, for twenty-five cents, or for thirty-five cents for the first fifteen words if the sender composes his own message.

Social telegrams have become generally popular, for such uses as informal invitations, acknowledgments, and regrets. Arbiters of social etiquette use social telegrams themselves and permit their use on many occasions of importance in private or public life.

The Tourate Telegram is very popular with travelers who wish to keep their families, friends or business associates posted on the progress of their trips. The Tourate Telegram may be sent to any telegraph point in the United States at a cost of only thirty-five cents for the first fifteen words. The following subjects are permissible: Time of arrival, health of sender or party, state of weather, characterization of trip, time of departure, next destination or destinations, time of arrival at destination.

Other Telegraph Services

Telegraphic Money Orders.

Money may be telegraphed quickly and safely from one point to another. The rates are those of a regular telegram of fifteen words plus a small money-order fee, graduated according to the amount sent. A message may be sent with the order for a small additional charge. For Overnight Money Orders, Overnight Telegram rates apply to the telegraph charges. Money Orders may be sent to almost any point in the world.

Gift Orders.

Gift Orders, sent by telegraph, provide for the purchase of a gift of the recipient's own selection, or they may be cashed if preferred. The order is accompanied by a free message suited to the occasion.

Telegraphic Shopping Orders.

A telegraphic Shopping Order may be sent to any distant telegraph office to cover the purchase by the telegraph company, and delivery of any gift so ordered, with the donor's name on a card, and accompanied if desired by a free greeting selected from the telegraph company's published lists.

Messenger Errand and Distribution Service.

This service is used by business to deliver packages, envelopes, samples, circulars, advertising matter and small articles of all kinds. People use messenger service also to secure articles left at home, deliver

TELEGRAMS, CABLEGRAMS, RADIOGRAMS

invitations, pilot strangers, escort children, get prescriptions filled, obtain tickets and licenses, deliver rush material, and perform other errands and services too numerous to mention.

Air Reservations.

A reservation for an air journey may be made through use of the telegraph money order service. An order for the ticket will be delivered by messenger. The charge for this service is paid by the air lines.

Express Packages.

Messengers of the telegraph companies will pick up packages weighing less than twenty pounds for shipment by rail or air express through the Railway Express Agency, the charge for the service being absorbed by the Agency.

Time Differences for International Communications

In sending international messages by cable, radio or wireless, it is important to have in mind the differences in time between the sender and receiver localities. The charts on the following pages, reprinted by courtesy of RCA Communications, Inc., show these time differences and are to be used as follows:

The time difference between any two points is one-half the difference of the Time Zone numbers given on the Time Chart.

If the zone number of the distant point is greater than that of the local point, their time is ahead of local time. For example:

Greenwich Mean Time (London) .... Zone 25
Eastern Standard Time (New York) .... Zone 15
    Difference 10
    Half Difference 5

Greenwich Mean Time is therefore 5 hours ahead of New York. In other words, when it is noon in New York it is 5 P.M. in London.

If the zone number of the distant point is less than that of the local point, their time is behind (or earlier than) local time. For example:

Eastern Standard Time .... Zone 15
Hawaiian Time .... Zone 4
    Difference 11
    Half Difference 5½

Hawaiian Time is therefore 5½ hours behind (or earlier than) Eastern Standard Time.

In other words, when it is noon in New York, it is 6:30 A.M. in Hawaii.

INTERNATIONAL TIME CHART

FOR POINTS OR COUNTRIES NOT SHOWN ON HERE SEE ALPHABETICAL INDEX ON OPPOSITE PAGE SHOWING THE RESPECTIVE TIME ZONES IN WHICH THEY BELONG

[International time chart table with 40 numbered time zones listing territories including British Samoa, American Samoa, Hawaiian Islands, Society Islands—Alaska (Central), Roca Partida, Alaska—Juneau, Pitcairn Island, Pacific Time—San Francisco, Easter Islands, Mountain Time—Denver (Col.), Galapagos Islands, Central Time—Chicago, Galveston, Ecuador (+16 Mins.), Eastern Standard Time—New York, Montreal, Venezuela (+2 Min's.), Atlantic Time—Halifax, Argentine, Uruguay, Brazil, South Georgia, Cape Verde Islands, Sandwich Islands, Madeira, Iceland, Senegal, Greenwich Mean Time—Gt. Britain, Holland (-10 Min's.), Middle European Time—Germany, Italy, Spain, Svalbard, Eastern European Time—Egypt, Kenya (+15 Min's.), Arabia, Baku, Teheran (-4 Min's.), Seychelle Islands, Afghanistan, Kashgar (China), Calcutta, Tibet, Burmah, Singapore (+20 Min's.), Java, Shanghai, Manila, Vladivostok (-17 Min's.), Japan, Adelaide, Guam, Sydney, Melbourne, Solomon Islands, New Caledonia, New Zealand, International Date Line—Fiji Islands, with corresponding A.M. and P.M. times across columns]

ALL TIMES SHOWN ARE COMMERCIAL TIMES ONLY

EXAMPLE: When it is 9.00 P.M. in New York, it is 11.00 A.M. the next day in Tokio.
When it is 5.00 A.M in Tokio, it is 8.00 P.M. the previous day in London.

NOTE:
WHEN CROSSING THIS LINE IN THE DOWNWARD DIRECTION YOU PASS INTO THE FOLLOWING DAY. WHEN CROSSING IN THE UPWARD DIRECTION YOU PASS INTO THE PREVIOUS DAY.

ALPHABETICAL INDEX

C.	Zone	G.	Zone	L. (Cont'd)	Zone	P. (Cont'd)	Zone	S. (Cont'd)	Zone
A.		Cairo	44	Galapagos Islands	29	Liberia	12	Panama Canal Zone	25	Sofia	29
Adelaide	46	Calcutta	36	Galveston (Texas)	25	Libya	27	Panama City	25	Solomon Islands	46
Aden	13	Calgary (Alberta)	34	Gambia	11	Lisbon	27	Paramaribo (+11 Min's)	29	Somaliland	31
Afghanistan	34	Callao	25	Gambier Islands	15	Liverpool	27	Paraguay (−7 Min's)	25	Soochow	37
Alaska (Central)	5	Cameroons (+9 Min's)	26	Georgia	27	Lithuania	27	Paris (−9 Min's)	25	South Georgia	20
Alaska (Juneau)	7	Canary Islands	25	Germany	29	Little Rock (Arkansas)	25	Peiping	41	Spain	27
Albania (−12 Min's)	28	Capetown	29	Gibraltar	31	London	27	Pernambuco	13	Spanish Guinea	26
Albuquerque (Mexico)	11	Cape Verde Islands	21	Gilbert Islands (−10 Min's)	40	Louisville (Kentucky)	25	Persia (−4 Min's)	32	Stamboul	29
Alexandria	29	Caracas (+2 Min's)	16	Glasgow	27	Luxemburg	29	Perth	31	St. Helena Island	24
Algeria (+2 Min's)	25	Caroline Islands	43	Greece	29			Peru	25	St. John, New Brunswick	17
American Samoa	3	Celebes	41	Greenland	41	M.		Philippine Islands	41	St. Louis, Missouri	13
Amsterdam (−10 Min's)	27	Ceylon	36	Grenada	17	Madagascar	25	Phoenix (Arizona)	5	St. Lucia	17
Angola	26	Charleston (S. Carolina)	15	Guadeloupe	17	Madeira Island	15	Pitcairn Island	8	Stockholm	27
Antwerp	27	Charleston (W. Virginia)	15	Guam	44	Madrid	13	Poland	27	Straits Settlements	27
Antofagasta	31	Cheyenne (Wyoming)	11	Guatemala	13	Makatea Islands	5	Port Arthur	43	Sumatra (Southern)	39
Arabia	17	Chicago (Ill.)	13			Malay States	39	Portland (Maine)	5	Surinam (−11 Min's)	17
Argentine	32	Chihuahua (Mexico)	17	H.		Malta	29	Portland (Oregon)	39	Suva	19
Armenia	32	Chile	43	Hague (−10 Min's)	26	Manaus	14	Portuguese East Africa	29	Svalbard	28
Asuncion (−7 Min's)	5	Christmas Islands	4	Haiti	15	Manila	41	Portuguese Guinea	25	Sweden	27
Athens	29	Cleveland (Ohio)	15	Halifax	17	Maracaibo (+2 Min's)	27	Portuguese Timor	16	Switzerland	27
Atlanta (Georgia)	15	Colombo	48	Hamburg	27	Mariana Islands	41	Prague	45	Sydney	45
Auckland	32	Colon	25	Hankau	39	Marquesas Islands	5	Puerto Rico	17	Syria and Liban	29
Azerbaijan (+4 Min's)	21	Copenhagen	27	Havana	15	Martinique	15				
Azores Islands		Costa Rica	13	Hawaiian Islands	4	Mauritius Islands	33	Q.		T.	
		Cuba	15	Hedjaz	29	Mazatlan	45	Quebec	17	Tahiti	5
B.		Curaçao (−6 Min's)	16	Helsingfors	27	Melbourne	15			Taiwan	43
Bagdad	31	Cyrenaica	27	Holland (−10 Min's)	27	Menat	26	R.		Tampico, Mexico	13
Bahama Islands	19	Czechoslovakia	27	Honduras	13	Memphis (Tennessee)	15	Rangoon	36	Tanganyika	31
Bahia	13			Hongkong	27	Merida	13	Regina (Saskatchewan)	11	Tashkent	34
Bahia Blanca	31	D.		Honolulu	41	Milwaukee (Wisconsin)	13	Reno (Nevada)	15	Tasmania	45
Baku (−4 Min's)	32	Danzig	27	Hungary	27	Minneapolis (Minnesota)	13	Republic of Colombia	27	Teheran (−4 Min's)	32
Bangkok	39	Dawson (Yukon)	7			Monrovia	8	Republic of Panama	25	Tibet	37
Barbados	17	Delhi	36	I.		Monterey	27	Reval	18	Tiflis	31
Barcelona	25	Denmark	27	Iceland	23	Montevideo	17	Reykjavik	23	Tobago	17
Barranquilla	17	Denver (Colorado)	40	India	15	Montgomery (Alabama)	15	Rhodesia	15	Tokio	34
Batavia	25	Detroit (Michigan)	15	Indo-China	43	Montreal (Quebec)	13	Richmond (Virginia)	15	Tonga Island (−10 Min's)	2
Bathurst	25	Dominican Republic	27	Iraq	15	Morocco	31	Riga	29	Toronto (Ontario)	15
Belfast	15	Dublin	25	Ireland	18	Moscow	32	Rio de Janeiro	43	Trinidad	15
Belgium	25	Dutch Guiana (−11 Min's)	18	Irkutsk	43	Mozambique	39	Rio de Oro	29	Tripoli	27
Belgrade	27	Dutch New Guinea	25	Istamboul	25	Mukden		Rome	27	Tunis	27
Berlin	27			Italian East Africa	43			Roumania	29	Turkey	29
Bermuda (+11 Min's)		E.		Italy	25	N.					
Bern	15	Easter Islands	10			New Caledonia	47	S.		U.	
Bogota	18	Ecuador (+16 Min's)	14	J.		Newfoundland (−1 Min)	13	Saar Territory	27	Uganda	30
Boise (Idaho)	16	Egypt	29	Jackonsville (Florida)	15	New Hebrides Islands	45	Saigon	39	Union of South Africa	15
Bolivia	36	England	27	Jamaica	14	New Ireland	45	Salt Lake City (Utah)	13	Uruguay	18
Bombay (−9 Min's)	11	Estonia	29	Japan	29	New Orleans (Louisiana)	15	Salvador	48		
Bordeaux (−4 Min's)	45			Java	40	New York	14	San Diego (Cal.)	9	V.	
Boston (Mass.)	25	F.		Jerusalem	29	New Zealand	29	Sandwich Islands	27	Valparaiso	17
Brazil	15	Falkland Islands	17	Johannesburg	27	Nicaragua	13	San Francisco	17	Vancouver (Br. Columbia)	9
Brisbane	45	Fanning Islands (−10 Min's)	4	Jugoslavia		Nigeria	25	Santiago, Chile		Venezuela (+3 Min's)	16
Br. Guiana (+15 Min's)	17	Faroe Islands	25			Norway	27	Santos	19	Vera Cruz	13
Br. Honduras	13	Fiji Islands	41	K.		Nova Scotia	17	Seattle, Washington		Vienna	27
Br. New Guinea	45	Finland	29	Kabul	34			Senegal	31	Vladivostok (+17 Min's)	42
Br. North Borneo	41	Formosa (Taiwan)	43	Karachi	36	O.		Seychelles Islands	25
Br. Samoa Africa	29	France (−9 Min's)	43	Kashgar	35	Odessa	31	Shanghai	41	W.	
Brunei	25	Frankfort, Main	25	Kenya (+15 Min's)	29	Oklahoma City	13	Siam	39	Warsaw	27
Brussels	17	Fr. Equatorial Africa	25	Kiel	27	Omaha (Nebraska)	13	Sierra Leone	15	Washington, D.C.	15
Budapest	25	Fr. Guiana	25	Kingston	15	Osaka	43	Singapore (+20 Min's)	48	Wellington (N. Carolina)	15
Buenos Aires	17	Fr. Guinea	25	Kyoto	27	Oslo	27	Sinkiang	39	Winnipeg (Manitoba)	13
Bukharest	25	Fr. Indo China	39			Ottawa (Ontario)	15	Sitka Islands	7		
Bulgaria	38	Fr. Sudan	25	L.				Society Islands	5	Z.	
Burma	5	French Sudan	11	La Paz	18	P.		Soerabaya (−10 Min's)	40	Zanzibar (+7 Min's)	30
Butte (Montana)				Latvia	29	Padang	29				
				Leningrad	25	Palestine	31				

Classes of Cable Service

Ordinary or Full-Rate Cablegrams.

The "ordinary" or full-rate cablegram is the standard plain-language or cipher cable service. The rates charged for it constitute the base from which all other cable rates are derived.

CDE or Code Cablegrams.

Code words are restricted to five letters in length, and are charged for at 60 per cent of the "ordinary" rate. Code words may be either artificial words or real words used in a preconcerted manner. They cannot contain the accented letter *E*. Plain language words interspersed with code in CDE messages are counted and charged for at the rate of five letters or less to the word. A minimum of five words is charged in all CDE messages.

Urgents.

The urgent service is designed for communications of extreme urgency requiring the utmost speed in transmission and delivery. They are given priority over all other messages except Government messages. The word "Urgent" identifying the service is placed immediately before the address and is counted and charged for. Urgent messages are charged at double the rate charged for "ordinary" or full-rate messages.

CDE Urgents.

CDE Urgents represent messages of the code class taken at double the CDE rate for the preferential handling. The necessary prefix "Urgent" written immediately before the address is a chargeable word.

Deferreds.

Deferred Cablegrams are subordinated in transmission to all other messages except Night Letters. They may be written in any language that can be expressed in Roman letters. Although code is not admissible in the text, registered (code) addresses may be used in these as in other cable messages. Deferreds are designated by the prefix *LC*, which is placed before the address and is counted and charged for as one word. The rate for Deferreds is one-half the ordinary rate, with a minimum charge for five words.

Cable Night Letters.

Cable Night Letter service is an inexpensive overnight service designed primarily for plain-language business and social communications of some length which are not of sufficient urgency to be transmitted in other classifications. The necessary prefix for this service is *NLT*, which is placed before the address and is counted and charged for as one word. Code is not permitted in the text of Cable Night Letters but registered (code) addresses may be used. The NLT rate is one-third the ordinary rate, with a minimum charge for 25 words.

Preparation of Cablegrams

Cablegrams are constructed similarly to domestic telegrams, except that registered (abbreviated code) addresses are customarily employed to save tolls, and code language is largely used. In cablegrams each word in the address, text and signature is counted and charged for.

Plain-Language Messages.

Plain language is that which presents an intelligible meaning in any language that can be expressed in Roman letters, each word and each expression having the meaning normally assigned to it. In Plain-Language Messages each word not exceeding 15 letters is counted as a single word.

Code Words and Messages.

A code word, whether real or artificial, must not contain more than five letters of the alphabet. They may be formed without condition or restriction. Code Messages are identified by the symbol *CDE*, which is inserted before the message but is not a chargeable word. Plain language may be interspersed with code language in CDE messages and will be counted at the rate of five letters to the word. Figure groups are permissible in CDE messages, but if such groups (counted at five figures to the word) exceed one-half of the number of chargeable words in the text and signature, they are considered as cipher language and subject the entire message to full rates.

All groups of figures of whatever length, except groups appearing in CDE messages in conformity with the conditions specified in the preceding paragraph, and all groups of letters not constituting plain language words, containing more than five letters, are classified as cipher and are counted at the rate of five figures or letters or fraction thereof to the word. Any cipher word appearing in a message subjects the entire message to full rates. Plain language words in a cipher message are counted as one each up to a maximum of 15 letters.

Marks and Terms Identifying Merchandise.

Commercial marks identifying merchandise, or trade terms, such as f.o.b. and c.i.f., in plain language messages do not affect the count of plain language words in the same message, but the presence of code words in an otherwise plain language cablegram subjects all the words in the message to the five-letter CDE count.

Marks Connected With Figures.

A shilling mark or stroke in a group of figures counts as a figure and not as a separate word. The same is true of fraction bars, periods, commas, and other decimal points grouped with figures. Punctuation marks, hyphens and apostrophes are not transmitted, except when expressly requested, when they are charged for as one word each. A dollar sign or a pound sterling mark each counts as a separate word.

Addresses.

The name of the country of destination is seldom necessary. Unregistered addresses must not be unduly shortened, since Government lines abroad hold senders responsible for incorrect or insufficient addresses and will accept corrections or amplifications only by paid service message at the full rate. While the name of the place of destination and of the country, state, or county, is counted as one word each, irrespective of how composed, the names of streets and of persons in addresses are counted at fifteen letters or fraction thereof to a word.

Registered Code Addresses.

Registered code addresses should be used by any firm that sends many cablegrams, because they save the expense incurred in using full addresses. The fee is $2.50 a year.

Acknowledgments of Receipt.

Advices of the date and time of delivery of cablegrams by telegraph or mail, may be arranged by writing the indication *PC* for telegraphic report, or *PCP* for postal card report, immediately before the address and by paying for such indication as one word. The charge

TELEGRAMS, CABLEGRAMS, RADIOGRAMS

for the telegraph report itself is equal to the tolls on six words at full rates between the same points.

Prepaid Replies.

The sender of a cablegram may prepay a reply. The indication *RP* (meaning reply paid), followed by the amount prepaid, must be inserted immediately before the address, such indication being counted and charged for as one word.

The Radiogram in Communication

Messages transmitted by wireless between two points are subject to almost the same classifications as cable messages, that is, *Urgent, CDE Urgent, Full Rate, CDE,* and *Deferred,* and in general similar methods of counting and charging are employed. However, it is well to understand the exact conditions of acceptance under which this type of message is sent, before attempting to use it for business purposes.

Ordinary Radiograms (Full Rate and CDE).

1. The text of an ordinary radiogram may be written in plain language or in secret (code or cipher) language.
2. In radiograms written entirely in plain language, words in the text are counted at the rate of 15 letters to the word. Commercial marks are counted at the rate of 5 characters to the word.
3. In the text of radiograms containing cipher language, each group of figures or of letters, including words in plain language, is counted at the rate of 5 characters to the word.
4. Radiograms in plain language and/or cipher language are chargeable at the full rate.
5. In the text of code radiograms, the words with a secret meaning must not contain more than 5 characters. There is no restriction concerning the formation of the word, but accented letters must not be used.
6. In radiograms containing both code and passages in plain language, the plain language words in the text are counted at the rate of 5 letters to the word.
7. Figures and groups of figures should not exceed one-half of the total number of chargeable words in the text and signature. They are counted at the rate of five figures to the word.
8. The sender of a code radiogram should write the instruction "CDE" before the address. This indicator is not charged for.

9. Code radiograms are chargeable at special CDE rates, subject to a minimum charge for 5 words.
10. Radiograms containing figures in excess of half of the total chargeable number of words and signature are considered as radiograms in cipher language and will be charged at the full rates.
11. Bank and similar radiograms expressed in plain language and containing a check word or check number placed at the beginning of the text are not considered as code radiograms, but the length of the check word or number must not exceed five letters or figures.

Urgent Radiograms.

Priority of transmission and of delivery may be obtained to places where the urgent service is available by writing before the address the paid service instruction "Urgent" or —D— which is counted as one word, and by paying twice the full ordinary or CDE rate.

Deferred Radiograms.

Deferred Radiograms are accepted on the express condition that they may be subordinated in transmission and delivery to all messages that pay a higher rate. The following rules then apply:

1. The sender should insert the paid indicator —LC— before the address; otherwise, it will be assumed that Full Rate service is desired.
2. The text of the Deferred Rate radiogram must be written wholly in plain language having a clear and connected meaning, and only one language is permissible in any one message.
3. Numbers written in figures, commercial marks and abbreviated commercial expressions should be limited to one-third of the chargeable word text and signature.
4. There is a minimum charge for five words.

Radioletters.

Radioletters are subject to the same conditions as Deferred Radiograms. There are, however, two types of Radioletters: (1) the NLT, which are for delivery not earlier than the morning of the first day after filing; and (2) the DLT, which will be delivered not earlier than the morning of the second day after filing. The class of Radioletter service is generally indicated according to countries. The sender must insert the paid indicator NLT or DLT before the address; otherwise,

TELEGRAMS, CABLEGRAMS, RADIOGRAMS

Postal Telegraph
Mackay Radio — All America Cables
Commercial Cables — Canadian Pacific Telegraphs

Send the following message, subject to the Company's rules, regulations and rates set forth in its tariffs and on file with regulatory authorities.

```
ROBERT COLLINS
     SS EXCALIBER
          HONOLULU HAWAII STATION

ARTHUR KENT MEET YOU SINGAPORE

               TOWNSEND
```

RCA RADIOGRAM
R.C.A. COMMUNICATIONS, INC.
A RADIO CORPORATION OF AMERICA SERVICE
TO ALL THE WORLD — BETWEEN IMPORTANT U.S. CITIES — TO SHIPS AT SEA

Send the following Radiogram *Via RCA* subject to terms on back hereof, which are hereby agreed to

OCTOBER 18 1940

```
URGENT
    HERBERT STRUTHERS
         LONDON EXCHANGE LONDON

DARROW OFFERS ONE MILLION PITTSBURGH PLANT SHALL I ACCEPT

                    ROGERS
```

Main Office: 66 Broad Street, New York, N. Y. (Always Open)   Phone: HAnover 2-1811
FULL-RATE MESSAGE UNLESS MARKED OTHERWISE
Sender's Name and Address
(Not to be transmitted)

TYPES OF RADIOGRAM MESSAGES

it will be assumed the full rate service is desired. Generally, Radioletters must have a minimum of 25 words.

Prepaid Replies.

The sender of a radiogram may prepay a reply by depositing a suitable specified amount at the time of filing the original radiogram. He should observe these practices:

1. The indicator "RP" and the amount prepaid should be written as the first word of the address. This indicator is charged for as one word.
2. A reply-paid voucher is then issued to the addressee to forward a message through any office of the issuing administration or company. The voucher is issued by the office of destination and is only up to the value of the addressor's payments. If the receiver does not use the voucher, it should be returned by him to the office from which it was issued, in order that a refund to the sender may be arranged.

Radiograms to Follow Addressee.

The sender may provide for his message to follow the addressee in the event that the latter has left the place to which his message is addressed. The indicator "FS" which is counted and charged for as one word should then be written before the address. This service may be arranged in the following manner:

1. The sender may provide either a single address, or he may furnish a series of addresses. If one address is provided, it is assumed that the addressee will leave a forwarding address at each place he leaves. If the sender furnishes a series of addresses, the message is forwarded to the first address and from there to each subsequent address until it reaches the addressee.
2. The sender pays the charges to the first destination only. The charges for redirecting the message are collected from the addressee. The sender, however, must guarantee to pay all reforwarding charges in the event that the addressee refuses to do so.

Radiograms to Ships at Sea.

Radiomarine service is used for messages from shore to ships or from ships to shore. It is available through all Western Union or Postal Union offices in association with the Radiomarine Corporation of America and the Tropical Radio Telegraph Company, and certain

TELEGRAMS, CABLEGRAMS, RADIOGRAMS

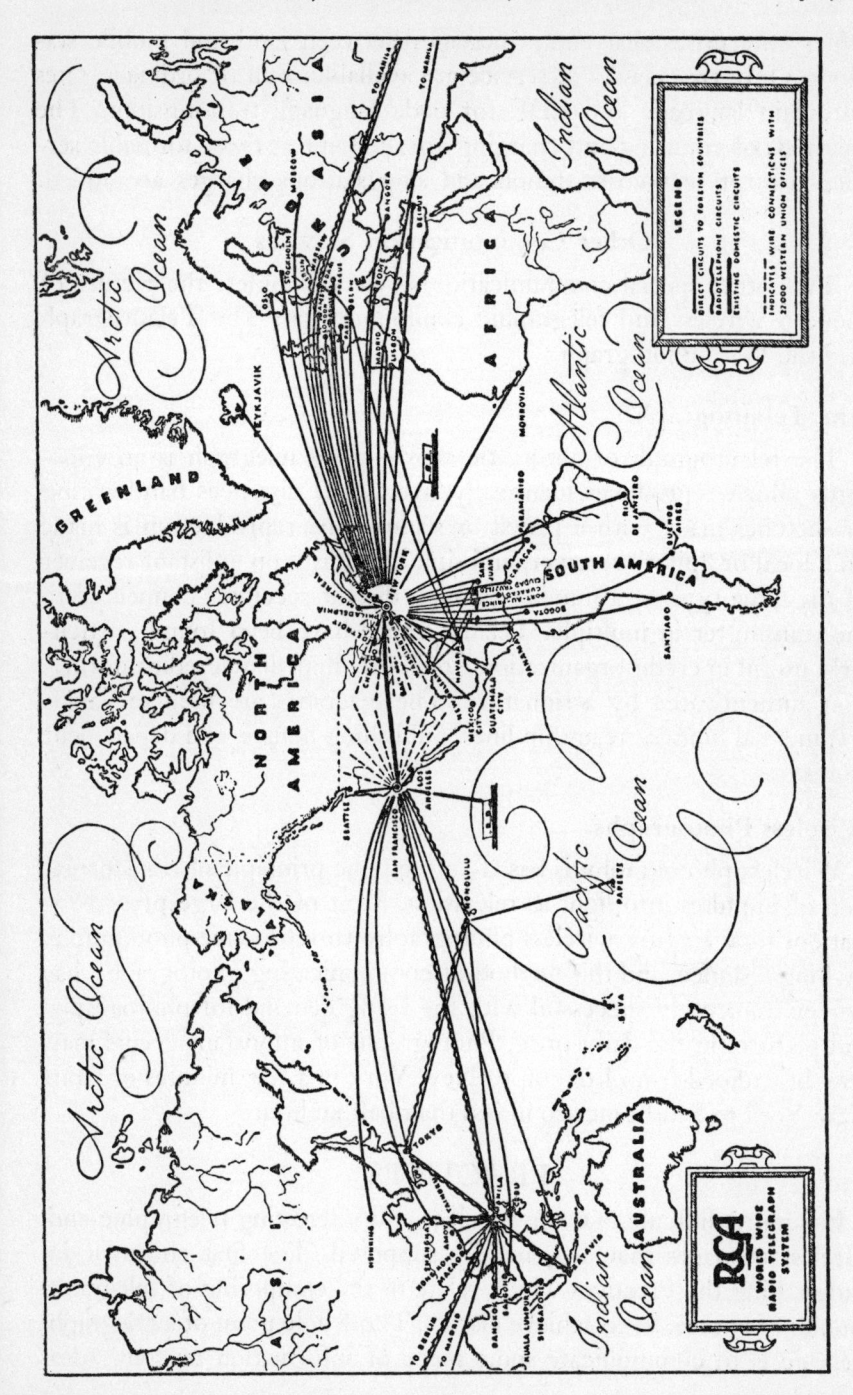

other enterprises that carry messages between land and mobile stations. Only two classes of service are available: Full or ordinary rates for plain language and CDE for code language transmissions. The methods of counting and charging are the same as those for cable services except that coast station and ship stations charges are added.

Other Communication Services

Two other special communication services complete the picture of modern wireless and telegraphic communication: The Telautograph and the Wire Photograph.

The Telautograph.

The telautograph or automatic reproducing telegraph is an apparatus which reproduces identically over great distances handwriting or sketches made with a pencil or stylus. The reproduction is made on a local or "pilot" receiver, and simultaneously on a distant receiver of the same type or a number of such distant receivers connected to the transmitter in multiple. Telautographs have been found particularly useful in credit organizations to secure immediate credit information authenticated by a signature. The machines are used in banks, commercial houses, steamship lines, publishing houses, and department stores.

Wireless Photographs.

Wireless photography is based on the same principle of transformation of impulses into light as television. Most of the large press associations now employ wireless photography to reproduce photographs by long distance, and this method of communicating photography has proven immensely successful with the rising demand for photographs and pictures in the daily press. Photographs of important events may now be radioed from London to New York in a few minutes or from New York to San Francisco in less than half an hour.

PRACTICES

It is more difficult to compose clear and interesting telegraphic and wireless messages than is generally supposed. The first endeavor in undertaking the Practices which relate to the composing of telegrams should, of course, be to achieve clarity. The whole point of a telegraph message is to communicate some piece of information or some idea to another person. However, in social telegrams, it is also desirable to inject into the few bare words which generally compose such messages as much of the writer's personality as possible, and to impart as much flavor and pungency as you can. This is, of course, doubly difficult. It is hard to be gracious in ten or twenty words, and, while brevity may be the essence of wit, it is still difficult to achieve both wit and relevance in a telegram. In the Practices given below which relate to the composing of telegram messages, we urge the reader, first of all, of course, to be clear; secondly, if possible, to impart a flavor to the style; and finally to attempt new and unusual ways of phrasing the ideas.

PRACTICE 1

Interpretations of Telegraphic Symbols

Identify the following telegraphic symbols:

CDE	RP	FS
—D—	LC	Unmarked
NLT	DLT	

PRACTICE 2

Composing Telegraphic Messages Within the Limits of the Ten-Word Charge

This Practice tests the abilities of the reader to convey the following messages by telegraph to their various destinations *within the limits of the ten-word charge.*

1. A friend of yours is to participate in a football game on Saturday. You wish to send him a telegram telling him you will be there to see the game and that you wish him luck.

2. You suddenly remember that one of your friends is to be married within the hour in a distant western city. You wish to send him a message of congratulations and greetings.

3. You desire to inform an associate that you are arriving in Boston from New York on the train that leaves New York at 10:25 on Monday morning and that you hope he can meet you at the South Station in Boston. You would further like him to reply telling you whether he can do this.

4. A girl in whom you are interested but whom you do not know well invites you to a college dance. You telegraph your acceptance, employing the proper degree of familiarity.

5. Your fiancée, Joan, is visiting you on Wednesday. You telegraph your father asking him for ten dollars, in order that you may entertain her properly.

6. A reporter wires his newspaper that the airliner *Alton* has crashed, that twelve persons were killed and twenty injured, and that he will send a detailed report to the editor later.

KEYS TO PRACTICES

Key to Practice 1: Interpretation of Telegraphic Symbols

    CDE means CODE
    —D— means URGENT RADIOGRAM
    NLT means CABLE NIGHT LETTER or
            RADIO NIGHT LETTER
    RP means REPLY PAID
    LC means DEFERRED
    DLT means RADIO DAY LETTER
    FS means FOLLOW ADDRESSEE

UNMARKED means that the telegram or wireless
            is ORDINARY or FULL RATE

Key to Practice 2: Composing Telegram Messages Within the Limits of the Ten-Word Charge

(The numbers of these suggested messages correspond to the numbers of the Practices.)

1. WE WILL BE UP THERE SATURDAY CHEERING. BEST OF LUCK.

2. MY THOUGHTS WITH YOU THIS GREAT AND HAPPY DAY. CONGRATULATIONS.

3. WILL LEAVE NEW YORK 10:25 MONDAY MORNING. MEET ME SOUTH STATION. REPLY BY WESTERN UNION.

4. DELIGHTED TO COME. SAVE SOME DANCES FOR ME. AS EVER.

5. JOAN ARRIVES HERE WEDNESDAY. SEND TEN DOLLARS. FAMILY HONOR IMPERILED.

6. AIRLINER ALTON CRASHED. TWELVE KILLED. TWENTY INJURED. DETAILS FOLLOW.

Supplement · CONVENTIONS IN SOCIAL
AND POLITICAL CORRESPONDENCE
PARLIAMENTARY PRACTICE

CONVENTIONS IN SOCIAL AND OFFICIAL CORRESPONDENCE

The Correct Forms to Be Used in Addresses, Salutations, and Closings of Letters

Most persons at different times in life are likely to face the necessity or desirability of addressing a letter to some high official in church or state—perhaps a Governor, a member of the Supreme Court, the President of the United States, a United States Senator, a Representative, a Bishop, an Archbishop, or a Cardinal. While in democratic America a large grant of individual liberty is allowed, convention has nevertheless set up certain forms that should be rather carefully observed. These forms are important in the great realm of etiquette; the boor and the genius may ignore them and establish trails of their own devising, but the great moving mass of men find it a bit easier to make their direct way along the well-marked pathways that convention has established. For this group the following information has been prepared.

Ambassadors.

AMERICAN AMBASSADOR

Address: His Excellency
　　The American Ambassador
　　　London
　　　　England
　　　or
　　The Honorable .... (full name)
　　　American Ambassador
　　　　London
　　　　　England

Salutation: My dear Mr. Ambassador:
　　　or
　　Your Excellency:
　　　or
　　Sir:

333

Closing: I have the honor to be, Sir,
Your obedient servant,
(old form)
or
Respectfully yours,
or
Very truly yours,

BRITISH AMBASSADOR

Address: His Excellency
The British Ambassador
Washington, D. C.

Salutation: Excellency:
or
Sir:

Closing: I have the honor to be,
With the highest consideration,
Your Excellency's most obedient servant,
or
Yours respectfully,

OTHER FOREIGN AMBASSADORS

Address: His Excellency
The Ambassador of .... (name of embassy)
Washington, D. C.

Salutation: Excellency:
or
Your Excellency:
or
Sir:

Closing: Accept, Excellency, the renewed assurance of my highest consideration,
or
Yours respectfully,

OFFICIAL TITLES OF ADDRESS FOR FOREIGN AMBASSADORS IN THE UNITED STATES

Ambassador of the Argentine Republic	Ambassador of Chile
Belgian Ambassador	Chinese Ambassador
Ambassador of Brazil	Ambassador of Cuba
British Ambassador	Ambassador of the French Republic

SOCIAL AND OFFICIAL CORRESPONDENCE 335

   Ambassador of Spain Royal Italian
   Ambassador of Turkey   Ambassador
   Ambassador of the Japanese Ambassador
    Union of Soviet Ambassador of Mexico
    Socialist Republics Ambassador of Peru
   German Ambassador Ambassador of Poland
    See also **Ministers, Diplomatic.**

    WIVES OF FOREIGN AMBASSADORS

Address: Wives of foreign ambassadors are addressed as Mrs. ....; Madam ....; or by personal titles, if they possess them, as Lady .... The form below is used for an invitation in which both the foreign ambassador and his wife are included:
    T. E.* the Ambassador of .... (name of embassy)
     and
    Madam .... (last name)
     or
    Lady .... (last name)

Archbishop, Anglican.

Address: The Most Reverend His Grace
    The Lord Archbishop of ....
     or
    The Most Reverend .... (first name and last name), D.D.

Salutation: My Lord Archbishop:
     or
    My dear Archbishop:

Closing: Yours respectfully,

Archbishop, Roman Catholic.

Address: His Excellency, the Archbishop of ....
     or
    The Most Reverend Archbishop of ....

Salutation: Your Excellency:
     or
    Most Reverend Archbishop:

Closing: I have the honor to remain,
     Respectfully yours,
     or
    Sincerely yours,

---
*Their Excellencies.

Army Officers.

Address: In correspondence, use the title and last name for all officers of the Army except Lieutenants.
General .... (last name)
Major General .... (last name)

Salutation: In the salutation to Army officers, the title *General* only is used, whether the rank be that of *General* or *Major General*. Likewise the title *Colonel* only is used, not *Lieutenant Colonel*.
If the rank of the addressee is below that of Captain, his title is used only on the envelope address; the salutation in the letter is Dear Mr. ....:

Assembly Member.

Address: The Honorable .... (full name)
Member of Assembly
................, ... (city and state)
or
Assemblyman .... (last name)
The State Capitol
................, ... (city and state)

Salutation: Dear Sir:
or
My dear Mr. ....: (last name)
(informal)

Closing: Very truly yours,

Assistant Professor.

See Professor.

Assistant Secretary of War.

Address: The Assistant Secretary of the War Department
Washington, D. C.
or
The Honorable .... (full name)
Assistant Secretary of the War Department
Washington, D. C.

Salutation: Sir:
or
My dear Mr. ....: (last name)
(informal)

Closing: Very truly yours,

Associate Professor.
See Professor.

Associate Justice of the Supreme Court.
Address: Mr. Justice .... (last name)
Washington, D. C.
Salutation: My dear Mr. Justice:
or
My dear Justice ....: (last name) (informal)
Closing: Very truly yours,
Invitations to an Associate Justice and his wife should be addressed as follows:
Mr. Justice and Mrs. ....: (last name)

Attorney General.
Address: The Honorable
The Attorney General of the United States
Washington, D. C.
or
The Honorable .... (full name)
Attorney General of the United States
Washington, D. C.
Salutation: Sir:
or
Dear Sir:
or
My dear Mr. Attorney General:
Closing: Very truly yours,

Bishop, Methodist Episcopal.
Address: The Reverend Bishop .... (full name)
Salutation: My dear Bishop ....: (last name)
or
Dear Bishop ....: (last name)
Closing: Respectfully yours,
or
Sincerely yours,

Bishop, Protestant Episcopal.
Address: The Right Reverend .... (full name)
Bishop of .... (diocese)
Salutation: My dear Bishop ....: (last name)
Dear Bishop ....: (last name)
Closing: Respectfully yours,
or
Sincerely yours,

Bishop, Roman Catholic.

Address: His Excellency, Bishop of ....
               The Right Reverend ...., D.D.
                  (full name)
                  or
              The Most Reverend Bishop of ....

Salutation: Your Excellency: (formal)
                  or
              Dear Bishop ....: (informal)

Closing: Respectfully yours,
                  or
              Sincerely yours,

British Ambassador.

              See **Ambassadors.**

Brotherhood, Religious.

              See **Member of a Religious Brotherhood; Superior of a Religious Brotherhood.**

Cabinet Officers.

              In general all Cabinet officers should be addressed by the title *Honorable*. The usual form is given below:

Address: The Honorable
                   The Secretary of Agriculture
                   Washington, D. C.
                  or
              The Honorable .... (full name)
                  Secretary of Agriculture
                  Washington, D. C.

Salutation: Sir:
                  or
              My dear Sir:
                  or
              My dear Mr. Secretary:

Closing: Very truly yours,

              See also **Assistant Secretary of War; Attorney General; Secretary of State; Undersecretary of State.**

SOCIAL AND OFFICIAL CORRESPONDENCE 339

Cardinal.

    Address: His Eminence Cardinal ....
                       or
                       His Eminence .... (first name)
                       Cardinal .... (last name)
    Salutation: Your Eminence:
    Closing: I have the honor to remain,
                          Your humble servant,
                       or
                       Respectfully yours,
                       or
                       Sincerely yours,

Chief Justice of the Supreme Court.

    Address: The Chief Justice of the United States
                          The Supreme Court
                            Washington, D. C.
                       or
                       The Honorable .... (full name)
                          Chief Justice of the Supreme Court
                            of the United States
                            Washington, D. C.
    Salutation: Sir:
                       or
                       My dear Mr. Chief Justice:
    Closing: Very truly yours,
    Referred to as: Your Honor.

Consul.

    Address: John Smith, Esq.
                       or
                       The American Consul at ....
                       or
                       John Smith, Esq.
                            American Consul at ....
    Salutation: Dear Mr. Smith:
                       or
                       Dear Sir:
    Closing: Very truly yours,

Countess.

                       See Earl.

Dean of a Cathedral.

Address: Dean .... (full name)
or
The Very Reverend Dean .... (last name)

Salutation: Very Reverend Sir:
(formal)
Dear Dean ....: (last name)
(informal)

Closing: Respectfully yours,
or
Sincerely yours,
or
Cordially yours,

Dean of a College or University.

Address: The mode of address suggested below is appropriate for a man or woman. Outside academic usage a woman may prefer the personal title *Miss* or *Mrs.*
The Dean of .... College
or
Dean .... (full name)
.... (college)

Salutation: My dear Dean ....: (last name)
Dear Doctor ....: (last name)
Dear Miss ....: (last name)
(informal)

Degrees, Academic.

Such titles as LL.D., Litt.D., L.H.D. are often conferred as honorary degrees for distinguished work, but they are not generally used in formal or informal correspondence. The titles *Mr., Mrs.,* or *Miss* are preferred. No academic degrees below a doctorate are used in correspondence. See also **Doctor**.

District Judge.

Address: The Honorable .... (full name)
United States District Judge
Southern District of New York
New York, N. Y.

Salutation: Dear Sir:
or
My dear Judge ....: (last name)

Closing: Very truly yours,

Divorcée.

        See Mrs.

Doctor.

Address: A doctor of medicine is addressed by his title in abbreviated form (Dr.) except in formal invitations, when he is addressed as Doctor ....

The title *Dr.* is sufficient without the degree Ph.D. or M.D. It is correct to say

    Dr. John Wood
      not
    Dr. John Wood, M.D.

It is correct to say John Wood, Ph.D., without the title *Dr.*

A person (man or woman) who is both a doctor and a professor is addressed in academic circles and in social correspondence as *Dr.* unless he has some personal preference.

    Dr. Charles Swift
    Dr. Mary Crane

Duchess.

Address: The Most Noble the Duchess of .... (formal)
or
Her Grace the Duchess of ....
or
The Duchess of ....

Salutation: Madam: (formal)
or
Your Grace:
or
Dear Duchess of ...., (informal)
or
Dear Duchess,

Closing: I remain, Madam,
    Your Grace's most obedient servant, (formal)
or
Believe me, dear Duchess,
    Very sincerely (*or* faithfully) yours, (informal)

Referred to as: Your Grace (not *you*)
Your Grace's (not *your*)

Duke.

Address: His Grace the Duke of ....
or
The Duke of ....

Salutation: My Lord Duke: (formal)
or
Your Grace:
or
Dear Duke of ...., (informal)

Closing: I remain,
Your Grace's most obedient servant, (formal)
or
Believe me, dear Duke,
Very faithfully (*or* sincerely) yours, (informal)

Referred to as: Your Grace (not *you*)
Your Grace's (not *your*)

Earl and Countess.

Address: The Right Honorable the Earl of ....
and
The Right Honorable the Countess of ....

Salutation: My Lord (*or* Madam):
Dear Lord (*or* Lady) ...., (informal)

Closing: I have the honor to be, my Lord (*or* my Lady),
Your Lordship's (*or* Your Ladyship's) obedient and humble servant,

Episcopal Bishop.

See **Bishop, Protestant Episcopal.**

Esquire.

Address: Esquire (*Esq.*) is sometimes used in this country. The term is much more often used in England, for men who have no other title. When used in this country, it is usually written in abbreviated form, *Esq.* It should follow the name of the person and be separated from it by a comma. *Mr.* and *Esq.* are not used together.

The title *Esquire* (*Esq.*) is correctly used with the name of the following officials: Chief Clerks and Chiefs of Bureaus of the Executive Department, Commissioners of the District of Columbia, Mayors of cities, American diplomatic officers below the rank of ministers, American consular officers, clients of the Supreme Court of the United States.

Ex-President.

Address: The Honorable .... (full name)
Salutation: My dear Mr. ....: (last name)
Closing: Yours respectfully,

Fathers, Community of.

Address: The Franciscan Fathers
Salutation: Reverend and dear Fathers:
Closing: I have the honor to be, Reverend and dear Fathers,
Your obedient servant,

Foreign Ambassador.

See **Ambassadors.**

General Manager.

General Manager may follow a name as a title of designation. It does not affect the prefixed title, whatever it may be, as,
Mr. Horace A. Reid, General Manager

Government Officials.

See under separate titles.

Governor.

Address:
The Honorable
  The Governor of .... (state)
    or
The Honorable .... (full name)
  Governor of .... (state)
    or
His Excellency the Governor
  Governor of .... (state)

Salutation: Sir: (formal)
  or
  My dear Governor: (informal)

Closing: I have the honor to be, Sir,
  Your obedient servant, (formal)
    or
  Sincerely yours, (informal)

Justice.

See **Chief Justice of the Supreme Court;**
Associate Justice of the Supreme Court.

King (British).

Address: To His Majesty the King
                or
    The King's Most Excellent Majesty

Salutation: Sir:
                or
    May it please Your Majesty:
                or
    Sire:

Closing: I have the honor to remain
      Your Majesty's most obedient servant,

Referred to as: Your Majesty.

Lady.

Address: *Lady*, the most common of all the English titles, is held by all peeresses under the rank of duchess, by all the daughters of the three highest ranks of the peerage, duke, marquis, earl, and by the wives of baronets and knights. *The* before the title *Lady* designates a lady of the peerage.
    Lady .... (last name)

Salutation: Madam: (formal)
    My dear Lady ...., (informal)

Closing: I have the honor to remain, Madam,
      Your Ladyship's obedient servant, (formal)
              or
    I am, my dear Lady ....,
      Sincerely yours, (informal)

Lecturer.

Address: A lecturer has no other title than his personal title, unless, of course, he has a professional or academic title. such as *Dr.* or *Professor.*

Lieutenant.

    See Army Officers.

Lieutenant Governor.

Address: The Honorable .... (full name)
      Lieutenant Governor of .... (state)

Salutation: Dear Governor ....: (last name)
                or
    Sir:
                or
    Dear Sir:

Closing: Very truly yours,

Mayor.

Address: His Honor the Mayor of .... (name of city)
                    or
                    The Honorable .... (full name)
                        Mayor of .... (city)
                    or
                    Mayor .... (full name)

Salutation: My dear Mayor:
                    or
                    My dear Mayor ....: (last name)
                    or
                    Sir:

Closing: Yours respectfully,
                    or
                    Very truly yours,

Mayor (Woman).

Address: Her Honor the Mayor of .... (city)
                    or
                    Mayor .... (full name)
                    or
                    The Honorable .... (full name)
                    Mayor of .... (city)

Salutation: My dear Madam Mayor:
                    or
                    Dear Mayor ....: (last name)

Member of Assembly.

                    See **Assembly Member.**

Member of a Religious Brotherhood.

Address: Brother .... (name in religion). Followed, if desired, by the initials of his Order)

Salutation: Dear Brother ....: (name in religion)

Closing: Sincerely yours,

Member of a Religious Order of Men.

Address: Use full name, followed by the initials of the Order, and academic degrees if known.
                    Rev. ...., S. J., S.T.D.
                    or
                    Rev. ...., O.F.M.

Salutation: Dear Father ....: (last name)

Closing: Sincerely yours,
                    or
                    Respectfully yours,

Member of a Religious Sisterhood.

Address: Sister Mary Catherine (followed, if desired, by the initials of her Order)

Salutation: My dear Sister Mary Catherine: (formal)
or
Dear Sister Mary Catherine:
or
Dear Sister: (informal)
or
My dear Sister:

Closing: Sincerely yours,

See also Superior of a Sisterhood.

Member of the House of Representatives.

See Representative; also Speaker of the House of Representatives.

Ministers, Diplomatic.

UNITED STATES MINISTERS IN FOREIGN COUNTRIES

Address: The Honorable .... (full name)
   American Minister
   ...., ... (city, country)

Salutation: Dear Sir: (formal)
or
My dear Mr. Minister: (informal)

Closing: Yours respectfully,
or
Very truly yours,

FOREIGN MINISTERS IN THE UNITED STATES

Address: The Honorable .... (full name)
   Minister of .... (legation)
or
Envoy Extraordinary and Minister Plenipotentiary from .... (legation)
or
Mr. .... (followed by official title)

Salutation: Sir:
or
My dear Mr. Minister:

Closing: Accept, Sir, the renewed assurances of my highest consideration,
or
Yours respectfully,

Miss.

Address: Miss is the title by which an unmarried woman is addressed in social correspondence.
Miss Margaret Shephard

Salutation: Dear Miss Shephard: (informal)
My dear Miss Shephard: (formal)

Signature: Her signature will be simply Margaret Shephard. If she should wish, however, to indicate her personal title, as may be necessary in a business letter, she signs herself thus:

(Miss) Margaret Shephard

Notice that *Miss* has no period following it.
Even though an unmarried woman may have the right to use a professional or academic title, such as *Professor* or *Doctor* she may prefer not to use it in social correspondence, but to be addressed as *Miss*.

Monsignor.

Address: The Right Reverend Monsignor .... (last name)

Salutation: My dear Monsignor: (formal)
or
Dear Monsignor: (informal)

Closing: Respectfully yours,
or
Sincerely yours,

Mr.

Mr. is used in the United States in all types of social correspondence for men who have no other title. *Mr.* is used sometimes in preference to a higher title. See also **Esquire**.

Address: Mr. John Jones

Salutation: Dear Mr. Jones: (informal)
or
My dear Mr. Jones: (formal)

Mrs.

Mrs. is the title of a married woman. Although she is addressed as

Mrs. Robert S. Tarbell

in correspondence her correct signature is

Marion Tarbell

If she wishes to indicate her title she may write
>Marion R. Tarbell
>(Mrs. Robert S. Tarbell)

A widow is addressed by her husband's full name:
>Mrs. *Charles* S. Woodrow
>(not Mrs. *Elaine* Woodrow)

A divorcée may not keep her husband's full name. She may use his last name with her first name, as
>Mrs. Emma Dalton

or she may use her maiden name,
>Miss Emma Bolter

or she may, as is customary in society, use her family name and her husband's last name:
>Mrs. Bolter Dalton

A woman who wishes to keep her maiden name after marriage, for professional or other reasons, may do so, according to the privilege granted by the Lucy Stone Act. In correspondence she may be addressed in whatever way seems fitting, according to whether the letter is professional or social.

Even though a married woman may have a right to use a professional or academic title, she may prefer to be addressed as *Mrs*.

Navy Officers.

Address: The officers of the Navy have the following titles:

Ensign	Captain
Lieutenant, Junior Grade	Rear Admiral
Lieutenant	Vice Admiral
Lieutenant Commander	Admiral
Commander	

In correspondence use only the title and last name for all officers of the Navy except Ensigns, Lieutenants, and Commanders.

>Captain ....
>Rear Admiral ....
>Vice Admiral ....

In addressing a naval officer below the rank of *Captain*, use the title and last name only on the envelope, *not* in the salutation.

Salutation: Use *Admiral* only in the salutation rather than *Rear Admiral* or *Vice Admiral*.

Ph.D.

  See **Doctor**; also **Professor**.

Pope.

 Address: His Holiness, Pope Pius XII
       or
       His Holiness, the Pope
 Salutation: Your Holiness:
       or
       Most Holy Father:
 Closing: Your dutiful son, (*or* daughter,)
       or
       Respectfully yours,

President of a College.

 Address: Social notes may be addressed to
       The President of .... (college or university)
       or
       President .... (full name)
      The President of a Theological Seminary would be addressed as:
       The Reverend President .... (full name)
      Invitations to a college president and his wife are often addressed as follows:
       The President of .... (college or university)
       and Mrs. ....
      The title *President* should not be abbreviated in social notes.
 Salutation: My dear President ....: (last name)
 Closing: Respectfully yours,
       or
       Very truly yours,

President of the United States.

 Address: The President
       The White House
        Washington, D. C.
       or
       The President
        Washington, D. C.
      Invitations including the President and his wife should be addressed as follows:
       The President and Mrs. .... (last name)

Salutation: Sir:
  or
  To the President:
Closing: Respectfully submitted,
  or
  Respectfully, (formal)
  or
  Faithfully yours, (informal)
  See also **Wife of the President.**

President of the United States Senate.

Address: The Honorable
    The President of the United States Senate
  or
  The Honorable .... (full name)
    President of the United States Senate
Salutation: Sir:
Closing: Respectfully yours,
  See also **Vice President.**

Priest.

Address: The Reverend .... (full name)
  or
  The Reverend Father .... (last name)
Salutation: Dear Father ....: (last name)
  or
  Dear Father:
Closing: Respectfully yours,
  or
  Sincerely yours,
  See also **Reverend.**

Prince.

See **Royal Prince.**

Principal of a School.

Address: It is incorrect to address the principal of a secondary school as Professor, a title reserved for college and university teachers.
  Mr. Austin Cole, Principal,
Salutation: My dear Mr. Cole:
Closing: Respectfully yours,
  or
  Sincerely yours,

Professor.

Address: In academic circles the title *Professor* may be used unless the person or academic community prefers the title *Mr.* In social correspondence the title *Mr.* is often preferred.

Whatever degree of professorship a man may hold, he is always addressed in writing as *Professor*, not as *Assistant Professor* or *Associate Professor*.

If a person (man or woman) is both a doctor and a professor, he (or she) is addressed in social notes as *Professor* rather than *Doctor*.

In this country degrees do not usually follow the title *Professor*.

    Professor John Howe *or* John Howe, Ph.D.
        not
    Professor John Howe, Ph.D.

The title *Professor* should not be abbreviated in social notes.

The professor in a Theological Seminary would be correctly addressed as

    The Reverend Professor .... (full name)

Queen.

Address: The Queen's Most Excellent Majesty
Salutation: Madam:
    or
May it please Your Majesty:
Closing: I have the honor to remain
    Your Majesty's most obedient servant,

Rabbi.

Address: Rabbi .... (full name)
    or
The Rev. .... (full name)
Salutation: My dear Dr. ....: (last name)
    or
Dear Rabbi ....: (last name)
Conclusion: Respectfully yours,
    or
Sincerely yours,

Representative.

Address: Hon. *or* The Honorable .... (full name)
Invitations including a Representative and his wife are addressed:

The Honorable and Mrs. ....
(full name)

Salutation: My dear Mr. .... (last name)

See also **Speaker of the House of Representatives.**

Reverend.

Address: *Reverend* or *Rev.* should be used with the full name or with initials and the last name. It should not be used with the last name alone.

The Reverend Henry L. Holt *or* Rev. H. L. Holt
not
Rev. Holt

The titles *Reverend* and *Doctor* are usually abbreviated, but for formal usage they are spelled out. Academic titles may accompany the title *Rev.* unless the academic title is the equivalent of *Rev.*, as:

The Rev. John Smith, D.D.
The Rev. Dr. John Smith
The Rev. Professor John Smith
The Rt. Rev. John Smith
The Most Rev. John Smith (Archbishop)
The Very Rev. John Smith (Monsignor)

Salutation: Dear Mr. ....: (last name)
or
Dear Father ....: (Catholic priest)
not
Dear Rev. ....

If the person has some other title besides *Rev.* that title may be used, of course, in the salutation.

Dear Dr. ....: (last name)

Roman Catholic Church Officials.

See each official under separate title.

Royal Duke and Royal Duchess.

Address: His (Her) Royal Highness
The Duke (Duchess) of Kent

Salutation: Sir (Madam);
or
May it please Your Royal Highness:

Closing: I have the honor to be, My Lord Duke,
Your Grace's most obedient and humble servant,
or
I am, Madam, Your Grace's most obedient servant,

SOCIAL AND OFFICIAL CORRESPONDENCE

Royal Prince and Royal Princess.

    Address: His (Her) Royal Highness
                           Prince (Princess) ....

    Salutation: Sir (*or* Madam):
                           or
                           May it please Your Royal Highness:

    Closing: I remain, Sir (Madam), with the greatest respect,
                           Your Royal Highness's most dutiful and obedient servant,

Royalty.

                           See under separate titles.

Secretary of State.

    Address: The Honorable
                           The Secretary of State
                              Washington, D. C.
                           or
                         The Honorable .... (full name)
                           Secretary of State
                              Washington, D. C.

    Salutation: Sir:
                           or
                         Dear Sir:
                         or
                         My dear Mr. Secretary:

    Closing: Very truly yours,

Senator.

    Address: The Honorable .... (full name)
                           United States Senate,
                              Washington, D. C.
                         or
                         The State Senate
                           ...., ... (city and state)
                         or
                         Senator .... (last name)
                            Washington, D. C.
                         or
                         State Capitol
                             .... (city and state)

Salutation: Sir:
　　　　　　　　or
　　　　　　Dear Sir:
　　　　　　　　or
　　　　　　My dear Senator ....: (last name)
Closing: Very truly yours,

Sisters (Community of).
Address: The Sisters of .... (name of Order)
　　　　　　　　or
　　　　　　Mesdames of .... (name of Order)
Salutation: Reverend and dear Sisters (*or* Mesdames):
Closing: I have the honor to be, Reverend and dear Sisters, (Mesdames,)
　　　　　　Your obedient servant,

See also **Superior of a Sisterhood** and **Member of a Sisterhood.**

Speaker of the House of Representatives.
Address: The Honorable .... (full name)
　　　　　　　Speaker of the House of Representatives
　　　　　　　　or
　　　　　　The Honorable
　　　　　　　The Speaker of the House of Representatives
　　　　　　　　Washington, D. C.
Salutation: Sir:
　　　　　　　　or
　　　　　　My dear Mr. Speaker:
Closing: Very truly yours,

Superintendent of Schools.
Address: Mr. .... (full name)
　　　　　　　Superintendent of Schools
Salutation: My dear Mr. ....: (last name)
Closing: Very truly yours,

Superior of a Brotherhood.
Address: The Rev. Brother .... (name in religion: as Thomas, Leo, followed by the initials of the Order, if desired)
Salutation: My dear Reverend Brother ....: (name)
　　　　　　　　or
　　　　　　Dear Brother ....: (name in religion)
Closing: Respectfully yours,
　　　　　　　　or
　　　　　　Sincerely yours,

Superior of a Sisterhood.

Address: Reverend Mother .... (name, followed by the initials of the Order if desired)

or

Reverend Mother Superior (without initials of Order)

Salutation: My dear Reverend Mother: (name may be added if desired)

or

Dear Reverend Mother:

Closing: Respectfully yours,

or

Sincerely yours,

Supreme Court Justices.

See **Associate Justice; Chief Justice.**

Teacher.

Address: A teacher normally has no other title than *Mr., Mrs.,* or *Miss.*

Trustees of an Institution.

Address: The Board of Trustees of .... College
Salutation: Gentlemen:
Closing: Very truly yours,

Undersecretary of State.

Address: The Undersecretary of State
Washington, D. C.

or

The Honorable .... (full name)
Undersecretary of State
Washington, D. C.

Salutation: Sir:

or

Dear Sir:

or

My dear Mr. Undersecretary:

or

Dear Mr. ....: (last name) (informal)

Closing: Very truly yours,

Vice President.

Address: The Vice President
    The United States Senate
        or
    The Honorable
        The Vice President of the United States
            Washington, D. C.

  If the Vice President and his wife are included in an invitation:
    The Vice President and Mrs. .... (last name)

Salutation: My dear Mr. Vice President:
        or
    Sir:

Closing: Respectfully yours,
        or
    Very truly yours,

  See also **President of the United States Senate.**

Wife of the President of the United States.

Address: Mrs. .... (last name)
    The White House

Salutation: My dear Mrs. ....: (last name)

Closing: Very truly yours,
        or
    Sincerely yours,

PARLIAMENTARY PRACTICE

Parliamentary Practice is the sum of those rules by which a group of persons agree to abide for the mutual furtherance of their collective aims. When two or three people gather together to discuss any subject, they generally observe the dictates of courtesy in the social world in which they move. In large gatherings, however, it is important that some sort of order and procedure be followed, so that the gathering may not degenerate into a melee or fall into an uproar. The rules governing such large assemblies have been evolved, through long periods of time, in the deliberative assemblies of civilized peoples, finally crystallizing into the formulas which we present below. These rules now generally prevail in all types of gatherings, from the formal convocation of the United States Congress to the small informal social or study club.

Principles of Parliamentary Procedure

The principles of parliamentary law are the same for all assemblies and should be kept in mind by the man whose business may bring him into contact with large groups of persons or whose social life may impose on him the duties of a club member. There are five fundamental principles:

1. Every member of an assembly has parliamentary rights equal to those of every other member.
2. The will of the majority prevails and must be carried out.
3. Only one subject should claim the attention of the assembly at one time.
4. Each proposal presented should receive full and free consideration and debate under the parliamentary rules.
5. The parliamentary rights of the minority must always be upheld.

If these fundamental rules are remembered, the specific rules and the precedence of each rule may be more readily understood, since the whole structure of parliamentary law is built upon these principles. It should be pointed out here that no assembly, however informal or social, can afford to disregard these principles themselves, even if the group may, for some reason, dispense with much of the specific ritual.

The Constitution.

Persons who wish to come together repeatedly for a specific purpose, as in clubs, political gatherings, town councils, literary societies, or business organizations, must so organize themselves that they can carry out their purposes with the greatest dispatch and efficiency. The fundamental instrument of their organization is the constitution. The constitution generally contains that body of important laws on which the club or assembly founds its existence and through which it proceeds on its business. We shall now present a model constitution for a club, and from this model may be derived the essential elements of any constitution of almost any type:

MODEL CONSTITUTION
ARTICLE I
Name

This Club shall be called ....

ARTICLE II
Membership; Dues

Section 1. The membership shall consist of not more than ....

Section 2. Names of candidates for membership, having been nominated and seconded at a regular meeting, shall be submitted to the Membership Committee and, upon a favorable report, shall be submitted at the next regular meeting and elected upon receiving a majority of votes of the members present.

Section 3. Any member who has been absent from three consecutive meetings, without excuse, may be dropped from the roll upon a vote of the majority present at a regular meeting.

Section 4. The dues shall be one dollar a year, payable in advance at the first regular meeting in the autumn. Any member whose dues remain unpaid for six months may be dropped from the roll upon a vote of the majority present at a regular meeting.

ARTICLE III
Meetings

Section 1. The club shall meet regularly on the afternoon of the second Tuesday of each month from September to June inclusive, at places designated by the Place Committee.

Section 2. The May meeting shall be the annual meeting for hearing reports from all officers and Standing Committees and for electing the same.

Section 3. Any regular meeting may be postponed by the President, with the concurrence of the Vice-President and the Secretary.

Section 4. Special meetings may be called at any time by the President, with the concurrence of the Vice-President and the Secretary.

ARTICLE IV

Officers

Section 1. The officers shall be a President, Vice-President, Secretary, and Treasurer, whose duties shall be such as are customary for these officers.

Section 2. The officers shall be elected by ballot at the May meeting each year, a majority vote of those present being necessary for election.

ARTICLE V

Committees

Section 1. The Standing Committees of five members each shall be elected annually by ballot at the May meeting. They shall be as follows: Membership, Program, Place, Hospitality.

Section 2. The Membership Committee shall consider all names nominated for membership and report to the Club.

Section 3. The Program Committee shall have charge of the arrangement of the program of each regular meeting and also of a yearbook to be issued to the members at the June meeting.

Section 4. The Place Committee shall arrange the location of the meetings of the Club and make announcements at least one meeting in advance.

Section 5. The Hospitality Committee shall attend to the social life of the Club.

Section 6. The Nominating Committee shall be appointed by the President at the April meeting to report nominations of officers and committees at the May meeting.

ARTICLE VI

Order of Business

The order of business at the regular meetings shall be: Call to order, Secretary's Report, Reports of the Committees, Business, Program.

ARTICLE VII

Amendments

The Constitution may be amended at any meeting of the Club by a two-thirds vote of the members present, notice of amendments proposed having been given at the preceding meeting of the Club.

This model constitution presents a fundamental framework upon which any organization may be erected. It does not, of course, provide the details necessary for the most complicated types of assemblies, but these details will vary with the purpose and character of the organization involved. Unquestionably, the most notable of governmental constitutions is the *Constitution of the United States*, which might well serve in many ways as a model for extremely vast and complicated political organizations.

The Quorum.

The quorum is the number of persons who must be present in order that any business may be carried out. A quorum is generally, but not necessarily, a majority of the members of any assembly. However, the number of persons and the kind of persons who shall constitute a quorum may be specifically designated in the Constitution of the assembly.

The Majority.

The majority is simply the greater number of any body of persons in question. The majority decision of a quorum generally prevails. Thus, in a club of twenty members, if eleven members have been designated as a quorum, then, at any meeting of eleven members, six members would constitute the majority and their vote would bind the entire membership. It can thus be seen that the quorum is extremely important and the majority is the key force which binds all rules.

The Motion.

The motion is the lever which sets all club machinery in action. It is the strategic procedure by which a member of an assembly may present any proposal for the consideration or action of that assembly. The motion is accomplished in eight steps:

1. The member rises and addresses the presiding officer.
2. The member is recognized by the presiding officer, who calls him by name.
3. The member makes his proposal.
4. The proposal is seconded by a second member present who without rising merely calls out, "I second the motion."
5. The presiding officer then states the proposal to the assembly.
6. The proposal is then fully discussed and debated, and, if the rules permit, amended or left intact.
7. The presiding officer then takes a vote on the proposal.
8. The presiding officer then announces the result of the vote.

This constitutes the basic outline of every motion, whether it be a resolution, a petition, or a proposal made by one of the assembly present. This procedure is so important that, in its outline as given above, it would be of great advantage to any club man to memorize it. It is the very foundation of all parliamentary procedure.

Types of Motions.

It is obvious that all the proposals or motions presented through this very efficient and powerful machinery are not of the same kind or of equal importance, and furthermore cannot claim the same attention from an assembly as certain other motions or proposals. It was therefore necessary to evolve a system of grouping proposals or motions according to type, and according to importance or precedence, and to establish rules which would keep these motions or proposals in their proper relation to their importance. At the end of this dissertation, we shall present a chart which makes clear the types of motions, their relative importance and precedence, and the rules which govern their presentation. First of all, however, we shall discuss the types of motions.

The four general types of motions in order of precedence are: (1) the Privileged Motion, (2) the Subsidiary Motion, (3) the Main Motion, and (4) the Incidental Motion.

The *main motions* are those general proposals which most persons usually mean when they use the term "motion." All the other types of motions are devoted in one fashion or another to the machinery of the assembly, which in turn is concerned with carrying on the business brought up by the main motions or proposals. Thus all roads lead to the main motion or proposal, while the other privileged, subsidiary or incidental motions are concerned with the preserving and the functioning of the assembly.

A *privileged motion* is one which, because of its very nature, demands immediate consideration. Such a motion would be the motion to adjourn, which must be put to a vote without debate and immediately, since its very nature makes it undebatable and of pressing import. Other privileged motions are: motions to fix the time at which to adjourn; to take a recess; to rise to a question of privilege; and to call for the orders of the day.

A *subsidiary motion* is one which by its very nature has an immediate effect upon the business being proposed and therefore should receive immediate attention. An example of a subsidiary motion would be a motion to limit debate on any subject. Other subsidiary motions would be: to lay on or take from the table, to call for the previous question, to postpone definitely, to refer to a committee, to amend, or to postpone indefinitely.

Incidental motions are motions which arise out of the proposal of any other motions, and, while they have no specific order of precedence among themselves, they are always of immediate importance and must be disposed of immediately except in the case of privileged motions. An example of an incidental motion is one to appeal from the decision of the chair. This, in all cases except in connection with privileged motions, must be put to a limited debate and vote before going on to the main business, since it is obvious that if the Chairman is not making his decisions correctly or is showing prejudice, a member should have the right to appeal such a matter before the assembly is asked to consider a main proposal. Other incidental motions are: to withdraw a motion; to suspend rules; to read papers; to object to consideration; to rise to a point of order; to rise to a parliamentary inquiry; to call for a division of a question; and to call for a division of the house.

Precedence of Motions.

The Presiding Officer should generally not take part in the debates of an assembly, unless one of his decisions is appealed, when he has the privilege of explaining his decision before it is voted on. Secondly, every assembly should base its procedure upon some well-known authority, and in its constitution make provision for the use of the dictates of this authority exclusively, so that there can be no conflict of authorities in matters of parliamentary procedures. We shall refer at the end of this section to two well-known works on Parliamentary Practice which may be used as authorities in such circumstances.

CHART OF PRECEDENCE OF MOTIONS AND RULES GOVERNING SUCH PRECEDENCE

Key to Abbreviations of Rules

In.—May interrupt a speaker
NS.—Does not require a second
Un.—Undebatable
L.—Limited as to debate
⅔—Requires a ⅔ vote for adoption

A.—May be amended
NR.—Not renewable (that is, the motion may not be made again in the same form at the same meeting)

Privileged Motions — Rules
1. To Fix Time at which to Adjourn............L., A., NR.
2. To Adjourn ....Un.
3. To Take a Recess................................L., A.
4. To Rise to a Question of Privilege..........In., NS., Un.
5. To Call for the Orders of the Day..........In., NS., Un.

Subsidiary Motions
6. To Lay on, or Take from, the Table.................Un.
7. To Call for the Previous Question..............Un., ⅔.
8. To Limit, or Extend Limits, of Debate........L., ⅔, A.
9. To Postpone Definitely............................L., A.
10. To Refer to a Committee........................L., A.
11. To Amend ....NR., A.
12. To Postpone Indefinitely ....

Main Motions
13. (a) General Main Motion ....NR.
　　(b) Specific Main Motion ....NR.
　　　　To Take from the Table ....Un.
　　　　To Reconsider ....In., NR.
　　　　To Reconsider and Have Entered on the
　　　　　　Minutes ....In., Un., NR.
　　　　To Rescind ....⅔, NR.
　　　　To Expunge ....⅔, NR.
　　　　To Adopt a Report ....NR.
　　　　To Adjourn (with qualifications)..................
　　　　To Create Special Orders of the Day............⅔.
　　　　To Amend (Constitution, etc.)..................⅔.

Incidental Motions

To Appeal from the Decision of the Chair	In., L., NR.
To Withdraw a Motion	NS., Un.
To Read Papers	Un., NR.
To Suspend Rules	Un., ⅔, NR.
To Object to Consideration	In., NS., Un., ⅔, NR.
To Rise to a Point of Order	In., NS., Un., NR.
To Rise to a Parliamentary Inquiry	In., NS., Un., NR.
To Call for a Division of a Question	Un., A.
To Call for a Division of the House	In., NS., Un., NR.

Explanation of Terms.

While it will be necessary for anyone who desires a complete and detailed knowledge of parliamentary terms to study one of the authorities on Parliamentary Practice, it may be advantageous nevertheless to list a few of the more important terms here. The "Question of Privilege," which ranks fourth as a privileged motion, is a term worth discussing. The purpose of the Question of Privilege is to enable a member to secure immediate action on any motion which he believes affects the rights, privileges, comfort or convenience of the assembly itself. If the Chairman decides that the member's motion is not, however, a question of privilege, he states: "The Chair does not grant the privilege."

Another term "To call for the orders of the day," which ranks fifth as a privileged motion, deserves some explanation. Orders of the day are subjects whose consideration has been assigned to a definite time, and at the time to which they were assigned any member is privileged to call for them in case the Chairman neglects to do so.

In the Chart of Precedence, it will be noted that the motions are numbered from 1 to 13, while none of the Incidental Motions are numbered. This is because Incidental Motions have no special precedence, but arise from the exigencies of the moment and may be proposed at any time. They take precedence over all *except privileged motions*.

Duties of the Chairman.

The burden and responsibility of conducting the assembly with effectiveness and dispatch rests principally on the shoulders of the Chairman or Presiding Officer. His duties are many and varied, and they involve a sure and accurate grasp of all the principles and most of the important rules of parliamentary practice. Specifically, the Chairman has the following important responsibilities:

1. He opens the sitting by taking the chair and calling the members to order.
2. He announces the business before the assembly in the order in which it must be acted upon.
3. He submits and receives in the proper manner all motions presented by the members.
4. He puts all proper questions and motions to vote and he announces the results.
5. He enforces the rules of parliamentary procedure on members engaged in debate.
6. He enforces the observance of order and decorum.
7. He receives all messages and communications and announces them to the assembly.
8. He inscribes his signature, for purposes of authentication, on all acts, orders, and necessary proceedings of the assembly.
9. He informs the assembly, when necessary or called upon, in points of order or practice.
10. He generally names members who are to serve on committees.
11. He represents the assembly and is charged with obeying and carrying out its commands.

The Session.

In parliamentary practice, the session is a meeting of an assembly, which, although it may last for days, weeks, or months, nevertheless constitutes a single meeting in concept. The session has the connotation of unity. It may be broken up by recesses for periods of days, weeks, or months, but until it is ended by the adjournment *sine die*, it represents a single convening of the assembly. Thus, a distinction exists between a meeting and a session. Sessions are generally provided for in the constitution, which usually states: "The Club (or other organization) will meet once a week on Tuesdays..." In this case, each Tuesday meeting is one session, and it may last, unless terminated by adjournment to the next session which begins under the laws of that particular constitution on the next Tuesday.

This raises two problems which should be mentioned here: (1) The assembly cannot enact any permanent standing rule which will materially interfere with the rights of future sessions, since by doing so, it would tend to destroy itself. Thus, each session must have the same parliamentary rights as every other session, although this is not necessarily true of each meeting. (2) The second peculiarity of a session is that it cannot extend the consideration of any question to such a time that the next session would be passed over, since this would have the effect of denying to the next session the right to consider any question it desires to consider. Thus under a constitution which established meetings every Tuesday, one Tuesday session could not postpone consideration of a question for two weeks later, because the next Tuesday session would then have been deprived of its right to consider that question.

Committees.

In large assemblies, and often even in small ones, committees do the greater proportion of the productive labor of the convention. A committee is, therefore, of pressing importance to the smooth functioning of the gathering. A committee may be defined as a body of one or more persons appointed or elected by an assembly to take some definite action on any business which that assembly designates to it. Committees fall generally into five classes:

(1) permanent committees; (2) representative committees; (3) standing committees; (4) special committees; (5) committee of the whole and quasi committee (as if in a committee of the whole).

Permanent committees are those committees which have been provided for in the constitution, such as a Membership Committee and a Nominating Committee. These bodies are generally key committees without which the assembly could not function effectively.

Representative committees are committees composed principally of directors or officers of the assembly itself, such as the Chairman, the Secretary, the Treasurer and others, who are to represent the whole assembly, when the whole assembly does not meet very often. With assemblies which meet only annually or semi-annually, it is often necessary to form a committee of this sort and to endow this committee with virtually all the assembly's authority to be exercised between the assembly's meetings. Thus Boards of Managers and Directors, Boards of Trustees and other similar representative committees loom large in many business and financial organizations, which have stockholders or which are owned by large numbers of persons.

Standing committees are simply committees that are appointed for a definite time as for a year or for a session.

Special committees are committees appointed for a special purpose. They usually remain in existence until that purpose is accomplished.

The committee of the whole is made up of the entire assembly, which, by a special procedure, may form itself into a committee with all the freedom of a committee, in order to discuss a subject of general or pressing importance to itself. A member rises and makes the motion to commit thus: "I move that this assembly resolve itself into a committee of the whole to consider this question." If the motion is adopted, the assembly then becomes a committee of the whole and the presiding officer immediately calls another member to the chair and takes his place as a member of the committee. When the committee of the whole has thoroughly discussed its business in which only the motions to amend and to adopt are at that time in order, it can then make the final motion "to rise and report" which, when taken, converts it once more into the whole assembly. No committee of the whole can adjourn or order the "yeas and nays," because this would be usurping the powers of the whole assembly. It can only convert itself back into the whole assembly by the simple procedure of adopting the motion to "rise and report."

A variation of the committee of the whole is often used in small gatherings. This is simply to adopt a motion *to consider the question informally*. This motion has the same effect as one to convert the assembly into the committee of the whole. A second variation, used in the United States Senate, is to make the motion: "I move that the resolution or question be considered *as if in a committee of the whole.*" This motion also throws the subject open to debate and amendment with all the freedom of the committee of the whole, but with two added advantages: (1) the presiding officer retains his chair, and (2) the adoption of any motion, except an amendment, puts an end to this condition of assembly.

Committees are, of course, merely miniature assemblies and proceed in the same way in which the whole assembly proceeds. The committee cannot transact business without a quorum, and it adopts or takes action on its particular business by majority vote just as does the main assembly. It also has the power to subdivide itself into so-called *subcommittees*, which must always be composed of members of its own body, except when the committee has been given the power to use all possible means to accomplish its business. Such a committee is called a *committee with power*, and it may secure experts that are not in its own body for its subcommittees on investigation. A committee derives its powers solely from the whole assembly, and it cannot indulge in business or make use of authorities that have not been specifically designated to it.

Writing of Minutes.

The Minutes are the records of the assembly's meetings, and of any actions taken in these meetings. Since these records constitute the only permanent file of an organization's actions, they should be carefully kept and accurately transcribed. They are used constantly (1) in confirmation of an action of the assembly (2) as a source of information and (3) as historical records. Minutes are generally modified in accordance with the type of assembly for which they are written. They should always be concise, however, and they should always be accurate. The degree of formality to be observed in these records will depend to some extent upon whether they are to be published, in which case they should be carefully scrutinized by the president or presiding officer and the secretary of the organization. The contents and essentials of the Minutes, or the Record, or the Journal, as these records are variously called, are as follows:

1. The type of meeting, whether regular or special.
2. The name of the assembly or organization.
3. Date, including the hour, and the number of the meeting.
4. Location of meeting.
5. The names of the president and the secretary and of those members present and absent (in very formal assemblies).
6. The fact of the reading and approval of the previous Minutes, or, if the reading was dispensed with, a note to that effect.
7. Unfinished business and reports of committees of investigation or information.
8. All main motions, except those withdrawn, and all other motions except those withdrawn.
9. Informal discussion.
10. Date and place of next meeting.
11. Adjournment, time of adjournment, and signatures of executive officers.

The above essentials are for a large or formal assembly or organization. In informal or smaller assemblies and clubs, the Minutes are generally much simpler. The debates may be dispensed with, and only what is actually "done" during a meeting recorded. We give below a sample record to show one of the common forms:

MINUTES OF THE FALLANBEE SOCIETY

At a special meeting of the Fallanbee Society, held December 3, 1940, at 4 P.M. in their Club House, the president in the chair and Mr. R acting as secretary, the reading of the minutes of the previous regular meeting was dispensed with. The Committee on Membership reported the name of Mr. L as an applicant for membership and on motion of Mr. R, Mr. L was admitted as a member. The Committee on .... reported through Mr. Z the resolution on .... which, when thoroughly discussed and amended, was finally adopted as follows:

Resolved, That ....

On motion of Mr. X the Society adjourned at 6 P.M.

Signed: Y.................... President
R.......................... Acting Secretary

Framing of Resolutions.

Resolutions are the formal expressions of the opinion or will or desires of an organization. They are generally couched in formal language, although the practice of expressing a resolution without the complicated use of *Whereas* and *Therefore be it resolved*, has gained favor in more informal and smaller assemblies. The formal statement has the following form:

"*Whereas* there is pressing need for a new library in the Town of D.......................... and

Whereas in the opinion of the members of this Assembly the projected library will constitute a vital asset to this Town, increasing the enjoyment, the knowledge and the cultural resources which will accrue to the Town's inhabitants; be it therefore

Resolved, That the Assemblymen of the Town of D....................... do hereby express that body's deep appreciation of the benefaction of the late Oliver H. Merrill, and be it

Resolved further, That the proposed Library be named in honor of the late Oliver H. Merrill, namely, *The Oliver H. Merrill Library*.

John Cummins, Chairman
Arthur Roe, Secretary"

There are countless other forms of resolutions of the informal type. The general informal resolution, however, is simply a direct statement, enclosed in a letter, published in the records, or read before the assembly. One form of this type of resolution may be as follows:

"The Assembly of the Town of D............................, in its official capacity as the Town Council, wishes to express its deep appreciation of the signal generosity of our beloved townsman, the late Oliver H. Merrill, in securing to the Town the means of building a library.

"The Assemblymen of the Town of D............................ wish it further to be known that this body feels it only fitting and proper, as a small token of the Town's gratitude, that this projected library be named after our beloved benefactor, the late Oliver H. Merrill, namely, *The Oliver H. Merrill Library*."

Resolutions are framed for a great variety of purposes, the most common of which are:
1. To honor one who has achieved distinction.
2. To acknowledge benefactions of all types.
3. To indicate action taken by an assembly.
4. To present a program to be carried out by an organization.
5. To express regret at the resignation of an assembly's official.
6. To celebrate an important occasion.
7. To recognize the loss by death of a prominent or beloved citizen and to extend sympathy to his family.

In conclusion, there are a great number of good, authoritative works on all phases of parliamentary law which may be used as standard authorities in any assembly. Among those widely used are *Rules of Order*, by H. M. Robert and *Manual of Parliamentary Practice*, by L. S. Cushing.